A·N·N·U·A·L E·D·I·T·I

SO-AKE-200

Human Development

03/04

Thirty-First Edition

EDITOR

Karen L. Freiberg

University of Maryland, Baltimore County

Dr. Karen Freiberg has an interdisciplinary educational and employment background in nursing, education, and developmental psychology. She received her B.S. from the State University of New York at Plattsburgh, her M.S. from Cornell University, and her Ph.D. from Syracuse University. Dr. Freiberg has worked as a school nurse, a pediatric nurse, a public health nurse for the Navajo Indians, an associate project director for a child development clinic, a researcher in several areas of child development, and a university professor. She is the author of an award-winning textbook, *Human Development: A Life-Span Approach*, which is now in its fourth edition. Dr. Freiberg is currently on the faculty at the University of Maryland, Baltimore County.

McGraw-Hill/Dushkin

530 Old Whitfield Street, Guilford, Connecticut 06437

Visit us on the Internet
http://www.dushkin.com

Credits

1. **Genetic and Prenatal Influences on Development**
   Unit photo—WHO photo.
2. **Development During Infancy and Early Childhood**
   Unit photo—Courtesy of Louis P. Raucci.
3. **Development During Childhood: Cognition and Schooling**
   Unit photo—© 2003 by Cleo Freelance Photography.
4. **Development During Childhood: Family and Culture**
   Unit photo—© 2003 by Cleo Freelance Photography.
5. **Development During Adolescence and Young Adulthood**
   Unit photo—Courtesy of Louis P. Raucci.
6. **Development During Middle and Late Adulthood**
   Unit photo—Courtesy of Cheryl Greenleaf.

Copyright

Cataloging in Publication Data
Main entry under title: Annual Editions: Human Development. 2003/2004.
1. Human Development—Periodicals. I. Freiberg, Karen L., *comp*. II. Title: Human Development.
ISBN 0–07–254819–3   658'.05   ISSN 0278–4661

© 2003 by McGraw-Hill/Dushkin, Guilford, CT 06437, A Division of The McGraw-Hill Companies.

Copyright law prohibits the reproduction, storage, or transmission in any form by any means of any portion of this publication without the express written permission of McGraw-Hill/Dushkin, and of the copyright holder (if different) of the part of the publication to be reproduced. The Guidelines for Classroom Copying endorsed by Congress explicitly state that unauthorized copying may not be used to create, to replace, or to substitute for anthologies, compilations, or collective works.

Annual Editions® is a Registered Trademark of McGraw-Hill/Dushkin, A Division of The McGraw-Hill Companies.

Thirty-First Edition

Cover image © 2003 PhotoDisc, Inc.
Printed in the United States of America   1234567890BAHBAH543   Printed on Recycled Paper

Editors/Advisory Board

Members of the Advisory Board are instrumental in the final selection of articles for each edition of ANNUAL EDITIONS. Their review of articles for content, level, currentness, and appropriateness provides critical direction to the editor and staff. We think that you will find their careful consideration well reflected in this volume.

EDITOR

Karen L. Freiberg
University of Maryland, Baltimore County

ADVISORY BOARD

Tyrone R. Burkett
Pennsylvania State University - Abington

Stephen S. Coccia
Orange County Community College

Gregory F. Harper
SUNY at Fredonia

Alice S. Honig
Syracuse University

Steven J. Kirsh
SUNY at Geneseo

David S. McKell
Northern Arizona University

Carroll Mitchell
Cecil Community College

Martin D. Murphy
University of Akron

Thomas R. Scheira
D'Youville College

Gary M. Schumacher
Ohio University

Barbara Smith
Johns Hopkins University

William H. Strader
Mitchell College

Harold R. Strang
University of Virginia

Adrian Tomer
Shippensburg University

James R. Wallace
St. Lawrence University

Gloria Wellman
Santa Rosa Junior College

Karen M. Zabrucky
Georgia State University

Staff

EDITORIAL STAFF

Ian A. Nielsen, Publisher
Roberta Monaco, Senior Developmental Editor
Dorothy Fink, Associate Developmental Editor
Iain Martin, Associate Developmental Editor
Addie Raucci, Senior Administrative Editor
Robin Zarnetske, Permissions Editor
Marie Lazauskas, Permissions Assistant
Diane Barker, Proofreader
Lisa Holmes-Doebrick, Senior Program Coordinator

TECHNOLOGY STAFF

Richard Tietjen, Senior Publishing Technologist
Jonathan Stowe, Executive Director of eContent
Marcuss Oslander, Sponsoring Editor of eContent
Christopher Santos, Senior eContent Developer
Janice Ward, Software Support Analyst
Angela Mule, eContent Developer
Michael McConnell, eContent Developer
Ciro Parente, Editorial Assistant
Joe Offredi, Technology Developmental Editor

PRODUCTION STAFF

Brenda S. Filley, Director of Production
Charles Vitelli, Designer
Mike Campell, Production Coordinator
Laura Levine, Graphics
Tom Goddard, Graphics
Eldis Lima, Graphics
Nancy Norton, Graphics
Juliana Arbo, Typesetting Supervisor
Karen Roberts, Typesetter
Jocelyn Proto, Typesetter
Cynthia Powers, Typesetter
Cathy Kuziel, Typesetter
Larry Killian, Copier Coordinator

To the Reader

In publishing ANNUAL EDITIONS we recognize the enormous role played by the magazines, newspapers, and journals of the public press in providing current, first-rate educational information in a broad spectrum of interest areas. Many of these articles are appropriate for students, researchers, and professionals seeking accurate, current material to help bridge the gap between principles and theories and the real world. These articles, however, become more useful for study when those of lasting value are carefully collected, organized, indexed, and reproduced in a low-cost format, which provides easy and permanent access when the material is needed. That is the role played by ANNUAL EDITIONS.

In the United States and Canada 2002 was a year of debating what to do after the September 11, 2001, terrorist attacks. What might hold terror at bay? What could keep terror from taking root again? Is our democracy safe for human development? Is reform needed in our American way of life, or just in the Arab world? Is the value of human life great in a country with high rates of homicide and suicide? What can we do to make the world safer for human beings?

An anthology on human development that looks chronologically at development from birth through death could choose to start with birth. But, does human life begin at birth, at conception, or somewhere in between? Is a cloned organism new or recycled? Cloning and stem cell research are to scientific debate what the war on terrorism is to political debate. George W. Bush's administration, with its strong pro-life stance, has infuriated many scientists by suggesting that a stem cell (a fertilized egg a few days old) is already a human life. If a stem cell is a human life, can it be transformed from a future baby into some type of replacement tissue to cure diabetes, Parkinson's, Alzheimer's, or heart disease? Even some opponents of abortion are arguing that an embryo on a Petri dish is not a human life, while the same embryo attached to a woman's uterine lining is a life. This thorniest of human ethical dilemmas is yet to be resolved. This question speaks as much to the value of human life as does terrorism.

The Human Genome Project's completion in 2000 allowed us to decode the human genome. This means that we have knowledge of the sequencing of CATG (cytosine, adenine, thymine, guanine), the chemicals that form DNA. It means that we can replace strands of DNA (genes) with altered CATG sequences. It means that we can alter human development!

Should twenty-first-century scientists be allowed to alter genes? Who will pay for resequencing of CATG to bring about new behaviors? Will human cloning be allowed for exceptional individuals? These and other questions are likely to lead to contentious debates for many years to come.

Annual Editions: Human Development 03/04 has been developed to look at genes and environment/free-will issues. Selected articles look at other important questions about growth and change as well: shared versus unique, non-shared events, and continuity versus discontinuity in human development.

As you explore this anthology, you will discover that many articles ask questions that have no answers. As a student, I felt frustrated by such writing. I wanted answers, right answers, right away. Lessons that are necessary to achieve maturity include accepting relativity and acknowledging extenuating circumstances. Life frequently has no right or wrong answers, but rather various alternatives with multiple consequences. Instead of right versus wrong, a more helpful consideration is "What will bring about the greater good for the greater number?" Controversies, whether about terrorism or stem cells, promote healthy discussion. Different viewpoints should be weighed against societal standards. Different philosophies should be celebrated for what they offer in creativity and adaptability to changing circumstances.

The selections for *Annual Editions: Human Development 03/04* have attempted to reflect an ecological view. Some articles deal with microsystems such as family, school, and employment. Some deal with exosystems such as gender roles and community. Some discuss macrosystems such as economics and culture. Most of the articles deal with mesosystems, those that link systems such as health, nutrition, and stress. The unique individual's contribution to every system and every system's linkage are always paramount.

We hope you will be energized and enriched by the readings in this compendium. Please complete and return the postage-paid *article rating form* on the last page to express your opinions. We value your input and will heed it in future revisions of *Annual Editions: Human Development*.

Karen Freiberg

Karen Freiberg, Ph.D.
Editor

Contents

UNIT 1
Genetic and Prenatal Influences on Development

Five selections discuss genetic influences on development and the role of lifestyle, including the effects of substance abuse, on prenatal development.

Part A.   Genetic Influences

Part B.   Prenatal Influences

The concepts in bold italics are developed in the article. For further expansion, please refer to the Topic Guide and the Index.

UNIT 2
Development During Infancy and Early Childhood

Six selections profile the impressive abilities of infants and young children, examine the ways in which children learn, and discuss the development of ethics and morality in early childhood.

The concepts in bold italics are developed in the article. For further expansion, please refer to the Topic Guide and the Index.

UNIT 3
Development During Childhood: Cognition and Schooling

Seven selections examine human development during childhood, paying specific attention to social and emotional development, cognitive and language development, and development problems.

The concepts in bold italics are developed in the article. For further expansion, please refer to the Topic Guide and the Index.

UNIT 4
Development During Childhood: Family and Culture

Five selections discuss the impact of home and culture on child rearing and child development. The topics include parenting styles, family structure, violence, and cultural influences.

The concepts in bold italics are developed in the article. For further expansion, please refer to the Topic Guide and the Index.

UNIT 5
Development During Adolescence and Young Adulthood

Six selections explore a wide range of issues and topics concerning adolescence and early adulthood.

The concepts in bold italics are developed in the article. For further expansion, please refer to the Topic Guide and the Index.

UNIT 6
Development During Middle and Late Adulthood

Eight selections review a variety of biological and psychological aspects of aging, questioning the concepts of set life stages.

The concepts in bold italics are developed in the article. For further expansion, please refer to the Topic Guide and the Index.

The concepts in bold italics are developed in the article. For further expansion, please refer to the Topic Guide and the Index.

Topic Guide

This topic guide suggests how the selections in this book relate to the subjects covered in your course. You may want to use the topics listed on these pages to search the Web more easily.

On the following pages a number of Web sites have been gathered specifically for this book. They are arranged to reflect the units of this *Annual Edition.* You can link to these sites by going to the DUSHKIN ONLINE support site at *http://www.dushkin.com/online/*.

ALL THE ARTICLES THAT RELATE TO EACH TOPIC ARE LISTED BELOW THE BOLD-FACED TERM.

Adolescence
24. Meet the Gamma Girls
25. Why the Young Kill
26. Generation 9-11

Adulthood, late
34. The New Unretirement
35. The Disappearing Mind
36. The Nun Study: Alzheimer's
37. Start the Conversation

Adulthood, middle
30. Man Power
31. Sorting Through the Confusion Over Estrogen
32. An American Epidemic: Diabetes
33. 12 Things You Must Know to Survive and Thrive in America

Adulthood, young
26. Generation 9-11
27. The Feminization of American Culture
28. The Happy Divorce: How to Break Up and Make Up
29. The Coming Job Boom

Aggression
11. Raising a Moral Child
18. The Trauma of Terrorism: Helping Children Cope
19. Raising Happy Achieving Children in the New Millennium
22. Are Boys the Weaker Sex?
23. Effects of Maltreatment and Ways to Promote Children's Resiliency
24. Meet the Gamma Girls
25. Why the Young Kill
26. Generation 9-11
30. Man Power

Aging
30. Man Power
31. Sorting Through the Confusion Over Estrogen
37. Start the Conversation

Anxiety
30. Man Power
31. Sorting Through the Confusion Over Estrogen

Attachment
6. Four Things You Need to Know About Raising Baby
9. Wired for Thought
24. Meet the Gamma Girls

Brain development
7. The World of the Senses
9. Wired for Thought
12. Intelligence: The Surprising Truth
25. Why the Young Kill

Career
33. 12 Things You Must Know to Survive and Thrive in America

Child abuse
23. Effects of Maltreatment and Ways to Promote Children's Resiliency
25. Why the Young Kill

Children
6. Four Things You Need to Know About Raising Baby
13. Child Psychologist: Jean Piaget
25. Why the Young Kill

Cognition
5. The Mystery of Fetal Life: Secrets of the Womb
6. Four Things You Need to Know About Raising Baby
7. The World of the Senses
9. Wired for Thought
10. Psychosexual Development in Infants and Young Children
12. Intelligence: The Surprising Truth
13. Child Psychologist: Jean Piaget
14. Metacognitive Development
16. The Future of Computer Technology in K–12 Education
19. Raising Happy Achieving Children in the New Millennium
23. Effects of Maltreatment and Ways to Promote Children's Resiliency
30. Man Power
31. Sorting Through the Confusion Over Estrogen
34. The New Unretirement
35. The Disappearing Mind

Cognitive maturation
12. Intelligence: The Surprising Truth
17. Choosing to Learn

Creativity
13. Child Psychologist: Jean Piaget
15. "High Stakes Are for Tomatoes"
16. The Future of Computer Technology in K–12 Education
17. Choosing to Learn
19. Raising Happy Achieving Children in the New Millennium
29. The Coming Job Boom
34. The New Unretirement

Culture
11. Raising a Moral Child
15. "High Stakes Are for Tomatoes"
16. The Future of Computer Technology in K–12 Education
18. The Trauma of Terrorism: Helping Children Cope
19. Raising Happy Achieving Children in the New Millennium
22. Are Boys the Weaker Sex?
23. Effects of Maltreatment and Ways to Promote Children's Resiliency
24. Meet the Gamma Girls
26. Generation 9-11
27. The Feminization of American Culture
29. The Coming Job Boom
33. 12 Things You Must Know to Survive and Thrive in America
34. The New Unretirement

Death
37. Start the Conversation

World Wide Web Sites

The following World Wide Web sites have been carefully researched and selected to support the articles found in this reader. The easiest way to access these selected sites is to go to our DUSHKIN ONLINE support site at *http://www.dushkin.com/online/*.

AE: Human Development 03/04

The following sites were available at the time of publication. Visit our Web site—we update DUSHKIN ONLINE regularly to reflect any changes.

General Sources

Association for Moral Education
http://www.wittenberg.edu/ame/index.html
This association is dedicated to fostering communication, cooperation, training, curriculum development, and research that links moral theory to educational practices.

Behavior Analysis Resources
http://www.coedu.usf.edu/behavior/bares.htm
Dedicated to promoting the experimental, theoretical, and applied analysis of behavior, this site encompasses contemporary scientific and social issues, theoretical advances, and the dissemination of professional and public information.

Healthfinder
http://www.healthfinder.gov
Healthfinder is a consumer health site that contains the latest health news, prevention and care choices, and information about every phase of human development.

Social Influence
http://www.workingpsychology.com/intro.html
Persuasion, compliance, and propaganda are the main focus of this site. It includes practical examples and applications.

UNIT 1: Genetic and Prenatal Influences on Development

American Academy of Pediatrics (AAP)
http://www.aap.org
AAP provides data for optimal physical, mental, and social health for all children. The site links to professional educational sources and current research.

Basic Neural Processes
http://psych.hanover.edu/Krantz/neurotut.html
An extensive tutorial on brain structures is provided here.

Evolutionary Psychology: A Primer
http://www.psych.ucsb.edu/research/cep/
A link to an evolutionary psychology primer is available on this site. Extensive background information is included.

Genetics Education Center
http://www.kumc.edu/gec/
The University of Kansas Medical Center provides information on human genetics and the human genome project at this site. Included are a number of links to research areas.

Serendip
http://serendip.brynmawr.edu/serendip/
Organized into five subject areas (brain and behavior, complex systems, genes and behavior, science and culture, and science education), this site contains interactive exhibits, articles, links to other resources, and a forum.

UNIT 2: Development During Infancy and Early Childhood

Aggression and Cooperation: Helping Young Children Develop Constructive Strategies
http://ericps.crc.uiuc.edu/eece/pubs/digests/1992/jewett92.html
This ERIC Digest report is on helping children deal effectively with aggression. Developing prosocial attitudes and behaviors is its goal.

Children's Nutrition Research Center (CNRC)
http://www.bcm.tmc.edu/cnrc/
CNRC is dedicated to defining the nutrient needs of healthy children, from conception through adolescence, and of pregnant and nursing mothers.

Early Childhood Care and Development
http://www.ecdgroup.com
Child development theory, programming and parenting data, and research can be found on this site of the Consultative Group. It is dedicated to the improvement of conditions of young children at risk.

Zero to Three: National Center for Infants, Toddlers, and Families
http://www.zerotothree.org
Zero to Three is dedicated solely to infants, toddlers, and their families. Organized by recognized experts in the field, it provides technical assistance to communities, states, and the federal government.

UNIT 3: Development During Childhood: Cognition and Schooling

Children Now
http://www.childrennow.org
Children Now focuses on improving conditions for children who are poor or at risk. Articles include information on education, the influence of media, health, and security.

Council for Exceptional Children
http://www.cec.sped.org
This is the home page of the Council for Exceptional Children, which is dedicated to improving education for exceptional children and the gifted child.

Educational Resources Information Center (ERIC)
http://www.ed.gov/pubs/pubdb.html
Sponsored by the U.S. Department of Education, this site will lead to numerous documents related to elementary and early childhood education.

Federation of Behavioral, Psychological, and Cognitive Science
http://federation.apa.org
The Federation's mission is fulfilled through legislative and regulatory advocacy, education, and information dissemination to the scientific community. Hotlink to the National Institutes of Health's Project on the Decade of the Brain.

The National Association for the Education of Young Children (NAEYC)
http://www.naeyc.org

NAEYC is the nation's largest organization of early childhood professionals. It is devoted to improving the quality of early childhood education programs for children from birth through the age of eight.

Project Zero
http://pzweb.harvard.edu

Following 30 years of research on the development of learning processes in children and adults, Project Zero is now helping to create communities of reflective, independent learners; to enhance deep understanding within disciplines; and to promote critical and creative thinking.

UNIT 4: Development During Childhood: Family and Culture

Childhood Injury Prevention Interventions
http://depts.washington.edu/hiprc/

Systematic reviews of childhood injury prevention interventions on such diverse subjects as adolescent suicide, child abuse, accidental injuries, and youth violence are offered on this site.

Families and Work Institute
http://www.familiesandworkinst.org

The Families and Work Institute conducts policy research on issues related to the changing workforce, and it operates a national clearinghouse on work and family life.

The National Parent Information Network (NPIN)
http://ericps.crc.uiuc.edu/npin

NPIN's site contains resources related to many of the controversial issues faced by parents raising children in contemporary society. Discussion groups are also available.

Parentsplace.com: Single Parenting
http://www.parentsplace.com/

This resource focuses on issues concerning single parents and their children. The articles range from parenting children from infancy through adolescence.

UNIT 5: Development During Adolescence and Young Adulthood

Adolescence: Change and Continuity
http://www.personal.psu.edu/nxd10/adolesce.htm

This site offers a discussion of puberty, sexuality, biological changes, cross-cultural differences, and nutrition for adolescents, including a look at obesity.

AMA—Adolescent Health On-Line
http://www.ama-assn.org/ama/pub/category/1947.html

This AMA adolescent health initiative describes clinical preventive services that primary care physicians and other health professionals can provide to young people.

American Academy of Child and Adolescent Psychiatry
http://www.aacap.org/web/aacap/

Up-to-date data on a host of topics that include facts for families, public health, and clinical practice may be found here.

Ask NOAH About: Mental Health
http://www.noah-health.org/english/illness/mentalhealth/mental.html

NOAH's Web site contains information about child and adolescent family problems, mental conditions and disorders, suicide prevention, and much more.

UNIT 6: Development During Middle and Late Adulthood

The Alzheimer Page
http://www.biostat.wustl.edu/ALZHEIMER/

Links to a wide range of sites devoted to Alzheimer's disease and dementia can be found here.

American Psychological Association's Division 20, Adult Development and Aging
http://www.aging.ufl.edu/apadiv20/apadiv20.htm

Dedicated to studying the psychology of adult development and aging, this division provides links to research guides, laboratories, instructional resources, and other related areas.

Grief Net
http://rivendell.org

Produced by a nonprofit group, Rivendell Resources, this site provides many links to the Web on the bereavement process, resources for grievers, and support groups.

National Aging Information Center (NAIC)
http://www.aoa.dhhs.gov/naic/

This service by the Administration on Aging is a central source of data on demographic, health, economic, and social status of older Americans.

Rose.Net's "For Seniors Only"
http://www.rose.net/seniors.htm

Several sites are listed here that could be of interest to members of the senior community.

We highly recommend that you review our Web site for expanded information and our other product lines. We are continually updating and adding links to our Web site in order to offer you the most usable and useful information that will support and expand the value of your Annual Editions. You can reach us at: *http://www.dushkin.com/annualeditions/*.

UNIT 1

Genetic and Prenatal Influences on Development

Unit Selections

1. **Brave New World**, James Trefil
2. **The First Human Cloned Embryo**, Jose B. Cibelli, Robert P. Lanza, Michael D. West, and Carol Ezzell
3. **A State of the Art Pregnancy**, Karen Springen
4. **Shaped by Life in the Womb**, Sharon Begley
5. **The Mystery of Fetal Life: Secrets of the Womb**, John Pekkanen

Key Points to Consider

• Will knowledge of the human genome and embryonic stem cell research lead to an operating and repair manual for the human body? Why do some people oppose stem cell research?

• What is cloning? What is therapeutic cloning? What is parthenogenesis? What ethical considerations are involved in these new technologies?

• How will technology change the course of pregnancy in the future? Will state-of-the-art gestation include medical care of the fetus?

• What are the long-term effects of pregnancy on adult health?

• Describe the long-term effects of health status during pregnancy on the development of mental abilities in infants and children.

 **Links: www.dushkin.com/online/**
These sites are annotated in the World Wide Web pages.

American Academy of Pediatrics (AAP)
http://www.aap.org
Basic Neural Processes
http://psych.hanover.edu/Krantz/neurotut.html
Evolutionary Psychology: A Primer
http://www.psych.ucsb.edu/research/cep/
Genetics Education Center
http://www.kumc.edu/gec/
Serendip
http://serendip.brynmawr.edu/serendip/

June 26, 2000, will be remembered historically as the day that the combined teams of scientists from the Human Genome Project (international, public) and Celera Genomics (U.S., private) announced "Human DNA is deciphered!" With this knowledge of the human genome it became possible to document where DNA sequences code certain human structures, functions, behaviors, and traits.

The use of stem cells (undifferentiated embryonic cells) in animal research has documented the possibility of morphing stem cells into any kind of human structure. Stem cells will turn into desired tissue cells when the gene sequence (CATG) of the wanted tissues are expressed. Scientists can eventually use their knowledge of the human genome, plus embryonic stem cells, to treat or cure diseases. Should they be allowed to? Are stem cells human life or property to be used for research purposes? Within this unit you will find answers to some of the questions about how the decoding of the human genome will change your lives in the new millennium.

Genetic precursors of human development and the use of stem cells, morphing, and cloning will be hot topics of the next decade as genetic manipulation becomes feasible. As DNA sequences associated with particular human traits (genetic markers) are uncovered, pressure will appear to alter these traits, not just cure diseases. How far will scientists go in altering human behaviors?

Human embryology (the study of the first through seventh weeks after conception) and human fetology (the study of the eighth week of pregnancy through birth) have given verification to the idea that behavior precedes birth. The genetic hardwiring of CATG directs much of this behavior. However, the developing embryo/fetus reacts to the internal and external environments provided by the mother as well. Substances diffuse through the placental barrier from the mother's body. The embryo reacts to toxins (viruses, antigens) that pass through the umbilical cord. The fetus reacts to an enormous number of other stimuli, such as the sounds from the mother's body (digestive rumblings, heartbeat) and the mother's movements, moods, and medicines. How the embryo/fetus reacts (weakly to strongly, positively to negatively) depends, in large part, on his or her genetic preprogramming. Genes and environment are so inextricably intertwined that the effect of each cannot be studied separately. Prenatal development always has strong environmental influences and vice versa.

The two articles in the genetic influences section of this unit are state-of-the-science expositions on how decoding of the human genome will affect our future views about human development. The information in them is central to many ongoing discussions of human development. The potentialities for altering structures and behaviors, by altering the CATG messages of DNA on chromosomes within cells or by cloning humans, are massive. We all need to understand what is happening. We need to make knowledgeable and well-thought-out choices for our futures.

The first article, "Brave New World," is introduced as "everything you wanted to know about stem cells, cloning, and genetic engineering but were afraid to ask." James Trefil describes

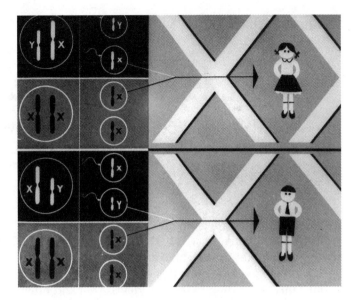

genes and DNA, gene therapy, altering DNA to "engineer" characteristics, cloning, and stem cell research today. He discusses the arguments pro and con of the public funding of human embryonic stem cell use, the need for regulation, and the future possibilities of the new technology.

The second article, "The First Human Cloned Embryo," describes the process of parthenogenesis, cloned human embryos in early stages, generated only from eggs. The authors are acknowledged experts. Jose Cibelli created the first cloned genetically modified calves in 1998. Robert Lanza is the vice president of medical and scientific development of Advanced Cell Technology, a leading biotechnology company. Michael West is the chief executive officer of Advanced Cell Technology. Together these professionals explain what has been accomplished, why, and the strict ethical principles that have been followed.

The first article in the prenatal section of this unit discusses high-technology prenatal tests that can detect abnormal development during pregnancy. Skilled doctors may soon be able to treat many problems of fetuses in the uterus in order to change the birth outcome and, potentially, alter the health of the future human being.

The second article, "Shaped by Life in the Womb," is an update on discoveries about environmental influences on embryonic and fetal development. It is no longer accepted that behavior is only a consequence of nature (genes) or nurture (caregiving after birth). Many human diseases may have their roots in uterine conditions before birth.

The third article, "The Mystery of Fetal Life: Secrets of the Womb," answers questions on fetal psychological development. Human behaviors such as intelligence and personality may also be profoundly influenced by the environment of the mother's uterus. Nurture occurs before and after birth. Mr. Pekkanen addresses issues such as over-the-counter drugs, caffeine, infections, pets, and environmental pollutants. He reviews what is known about fetal memory, including the much misunderstood "Mozart effect."

BRAVE NEW WORLD

EVERYTHING YOU WANTED TO KNOW ABOUT STEM CELLS, CLONING AND GENETIC ENGINEERING BUT WERE AFRAID TO ASK

BY JAMES TREFIL

IT WAS NOT BY CHANCE THAT PRESIDENT BUSH'S FIRST TELE-vised address, last August, was about stem cell research, coming as it did at the height of a summer swirling with heated debate over the issue ("one of the most profound of our time," according to the President). That and other recent debates have raised questions not only about changes in science and medicine but about such profound issues as the nature and value of human life, and whether humans have the moral right to tamper with genetic material, on the one hand, or the obligation to develop technologies that would alleviate the suffering of millions, on the other. Such questions are important, but only by understanding the science involved can we begin to address the ethical conundrums coming our way.

With nearly every advance in medicine, from the smallpox vaccine to organ transplants, there has been controversy over how much we should be altering nature. When Louise Brown, the world's first test-tube baby (now a healthy 23-year-old), was born in England in 1978, some people called conception outside the body immoral and tried to have the technique banned.

Back in the 1970s, science made advances in two areas that seemed, on the surface, unrelated—but which have veered ever closer to each other. One was a growing understanding of, and ability to manipulate, deoxyribonucleic acid (DNA), the molecule that provides our genetic code. The other involved the advent of in vitro fertilization (IVF), the technology responsible for Louise Brown and nearly a million babies since.

IVF is a process by which eggs are removed surgically from a woman's ovaries and fertilized with sperm in a laboratory. After undergoing a few cell divisions, several of the resulting embryos are inserted into a woman's uterus where, with luck, at least one will develop into a full-term fetus. In any one trial of IVF, as many as 10 to 20 eggs may be extracted and fertilized, and the majority of the resulting embryos are often frozen at an early stage of development, in case they will be needed for later attempts at implantation in the uterus.

Though IVF offered new hope to many who could not otherwise conceive, it also opened up a slew of ethical questions, beginning with the status of those embryos that remain unused in the lab. Then there is the fact that the woman who donates the egg need not be the one who carries the embryo or who raises the child. It is, in fact, possible to have as many as five adults who could claim parenthood in an IVF scenario: the sperm donor, the egg donor, the woman who carries the fetus and a couple responsible for its upbringing.

Still, for all the potential issues it raises, IVF was in many ways just the beginning, a relatively simple manipulation of the natural order. The closer science has gotten to deciphering our genetic makeup, the more complicated the landscape has grown.

GENES AND DNA

BY THE MIDDLE OF THE 20TH CENTURY, SCIENTISTS HAD BE-gun to realize that "genes"—the name given to whatever it was that passed down inherited traits—were made of DNA and that they were located on chromosomes, threadlike structures found in cell nuclei of almost all living things.

For molecular biologists, the second half of the 20th century was devoted to divining the structure of the DNA molecule (the double helix, discovered in 1953) and then figuring out how the molecule's fundamental components—called nucleotides—combined to form genes, how genes provided the instructions for making the molecules that allow living things to function, which genes did what, and where they were located. Just last year, scientists announced that they'd sequenced the human genome. Though they are far from figuring out what all of our genes do, they now know the order and location on our chromosomes of all of the nucleotides and have identified about half of our genes.

Much of the research on human DNA has focused on diseases that are prevalent in families or in certain ethnic groups—starting with such single-gene disorders as cystic fibrosis, Tay-Sachs disease and sickle-cell anemia—because medical histories of affected families were available and the fruits of such research might save, or at least improve, countless lives.

In laboratories around the world, scientists bank and analyze DNA from families with genetic diseases.

As our understanding of our genes has increased, so have our choices dealing with birth and conception. For several decades, couples with family histories of particular diseases have sought the advice of genetic counselors about whether to have children. With amniocentesis—a procedure in which amniotic fluid is extracted from the womb and examined—expectant mothers have long been able to determine if a developing fetus has certain chromosomal disorders. But more recent advances have brought the potential for couples to be advised not only on the basis of family history but on the presence of genetic markers of hereditary disease in the DNA. And with IVF technology came the ability to screen embryos for chromosomal anomalies—and for specific genetic traits, including genetic diseases.

Along with advances in screening in recent decades, there has been a surge of research on ways to treat existing genetic disorders. That research was based largely on two great truths that had been revealed about DNA. The first is that the sole function of most genes is to give cells encoded instructions for churning out particular proteins, the building blocks of life. There are tens of thousands of different proteins in the human body—from collagen and hemoglobin to various hormones and enzymes—and each is encoded by a particular order of nucleotides in a gene. (Many diseases are caused by defective genes that don't produce their protein correctly—and treatments that introduce missing proteins have long been used for such disorders as diabetes and hemophilia.)

The second insight is that all living things use the same basic genetic code. Just as all the books in a great library can be written in a single language, so, too, are all living things the result of different messages "written" in the same exact DNA language—and "read" by our cells. This means that if a stretch of DNA is taken from a donor and inserted into the DNA of a host's cells, those cells will read the new message, regardless of its source.

Though there are endless possible applications for this phenomenon (and at least as many complicating factors), doctors found particularly promising the idea of fixing broken genes by manipulating DNA through a process known as gene therapy, a form of genetic engineering.

GENE THERAPY

IN SOME WAYS, MANIPULATING DNA IS A COMPLETELY NATURAL phenomenon. Certain kinds of viruses—including HIV and others—infect us by inserting their genetic information into our cells, which then haplessly reproduce the invading virus. In some forms of gene therapy, this kind of virus itself is engineered so that the viral gene that causes the disease and allows the virus to reproduce is removed and replaced with a healthy version of the human gene that needs "fixing." Then this therapeutic, engineered virus is sent off to do its work on the patient's cells. There are hundreds of procedures using such "viral vectors" in clinical trials today, targeting diseases that range from rheumatoid arthritis to cancer. So far there have been few, if any, real successes—and the field received a serious setback in 1999 when a patient died while undergoing gene therapy trials for liver disease.

But even if this form of gene therapy, or one like it, can be made to be safe and effective, it still represents a relatively short-term approach to genetic disease—compared with what is theoretically possible. After all, even if individuals can be successfully treated, their descendants would likely still inherit the gene or genes that caused their ailments. The form of gene therapy we've been discussing affects so-called somatic cells, which make up the vast majority of cells in our body. But it is not somatic cells but germ cells—our eggs and sperm—that pass our genes to our offspring.

GENETIC ENGINEERING

WHEN TALKING ABOUT CHANGING THE DNA IN HUMAN germ cells, scientists use the term "germ line therapy." But in plants or animals, it's what we commonly think of as "genetic engineering." Either way, it means altering the DNA of an organism in a way that increases the likelihood (or, in some cases, ensures) that all of its offspring will have the same, engineered, characteristics.

Once genes that cause diseases are identified, individuals—even embryos—can be screened for them.

So far, this form of genetic engineering has not been attempted on humans (as far as we know), but it is used on nearly every other life-form—from bacteria to plants to livestock. Virtually all insulin used to treat diabetes comes from bacteria whose DNA has been modified by the addition of the human gene for insulin, which the bacteria then produce. Plants are routinely engineered so that they will be resistant to certain pests or diseases, withstand particular herbicides or grow in previously unusable soils. One area of intense debate concerns the extent to which such genetically modified organisms should be used in agriculture. In the United States, about half of the soybeans and a quarter of the corn grown on farms have been genetically modified. While the industry and many experts argue that products that are easier to grow or contain more nutrients (or even produce pharmaceuticals) could help prevent worldwide hunger and disease, critics question the possible side effects—particularly to the environment—of introducing new genes into agricultural products.

The truth is, there is still an inestimable amount that we don't know about the functions of particular genes or how they work in tandem. Much of the concern about genetic engineering—in plants or in people—rests on this fact. Yet with the promise of tomatoes that prevent cancer, salmon many times the size of those produced in nature, even pets engineered to be nonallergenic, many people hope that similar enhancements can be made to human genes as well. After all, such techniques as genetic screening of embryos, gene therapy and genetic engineering have the potential not only to prevent disease but to increase the likelihood of desired traits—from eye color to intelligence and other attributes. (Though we're very far from custom-designing our offspring, there are already cases of genetic screening of embryos for desired traits—including parents seeking bone-marrow matches for older, ill children.)

CLONING

THERE ARE ALSO THOSE WHO SEE GREAT PROMISE IN ANOTHER form of custom-designed offspring: cloning. Though most scientists oppose human cloning, three researchers caused quite a stir earlier this year when they each, independently, announced that they were working to create human clones.

The modern age of cloning can be said to have begun in 1996, when Ian Wilmut of Roslin Institute in Scotland oversaw the birth of Dolly, the first mammal known to have been produced by cloning from an adult cell. Worldwide "Hello, Dolly" headlines announced the breakthrough, and subsequently, scientists working with goats, pigs, mice and cows followed in Wilmut's path.

In animal cloning—which has often resulted in serious birth defects— the first step is emptying an egg of its genetic material.

To "create" Dolly, Wilmut and his colleagues took an unfertilized egg from a ewe and removed its chromosomal material, replacing it with a somatic cell (replete with DNA) from another ewe. In normal fertilization, when sperm and egg merge, the resulting cell—containing all the genetic information necessary—immediately starts dividing. In cloning Dolly, the somatic cell and the egg were fused with an electric current, which somehow prompted the package to act as though it were a newly fertilized egg. The resulting embryo was inserted into the uterus of a third ewe, using the techniques that had seen such success in in vitro fertilization.

In some respects, cloning can be likened to a construction project. The egg is like a crew of workers ready to build according to the specifications on a blueprint (DNA) once the plan is finalized and the whistle blows (fertilization). Whatever the crew sees on the blueprint, it will build. In the cloning process, scientists insert an already-completed blueprint and—in the form of an electric current or some other prompt—blow the whistle.

But just as independent builders using the same blueprint can build slightly different structures, so cloning does not create absolute replicas. Though a newborn clone will have chromosomal DNA identical to that of the adult donor and in that way would be the adult's genetic twin, it would also be a twin developed as a fetus in a different womb, flooded with a different bath of chemicals at different points in its development, born decades later and raised in a different environment. The clone could also differ from the donor due to trace DNA in the donor's egg—in structures called mitochondria, for instance—that could affect the clone's development. (In fact, there have been recent reports of human babies who have genetic material from three adults, due to a technique that uses healthy mitochondria from a donor's egg to enhance fertility.) So, though Dolly resembled her DNA donor, other sheep that Wilmut and his colleagues have cloned vary in appearance and temperament from their DNA donors as well as from other clones developed from the same DNA.

It is also important to note that Dolly was born only after more than 200 other clones were spontaneously aborted or stillborn. Attempts to clone animals since have often resulted in severe birth defects—from dramatically increased birth size to enlarged organs to immune deficiencies. Going back to the blueprint analogy, Cornell professor and cloning expert Jonathan Hill adds, "It seems the cloned DNA is not only a 'used' blueprint but one that may have certain pages stuck together, making some of the details particularly hard to read."

As a result of these and other factors, many scientists—and politicians—believe there should be a ban on human cloning. Others are wary that such a ban might be too restrictive, since some techniques used in cloning are also used in other promising areas of science—including applications of IVF technology and stem cell research.

STEM CELL RESEARCH

CLONING AND STEM CELL RESEARCH ARE CONNECTED IN AT least one important way. Every one of the trillions of cells in our bodies (including our eggs and sperm, which have but one set instead of two) contain the same DNA. The cells in your skin, for example, contain the same gene for producing insulin as those in certain regions of your pancreas, but only the latter actually make the protein. Most of the genes in our cells are inactive, leaving only the relevant ones to do their work. Though we know little about how this occurs, we do know that there is a period early in development when the cells have yet to begin the processes of determination and differentiation into blood, muscle or any other kind of cell, and all cells can still develop into any cell in the adult. In humans, this property—called pluripotency—is lost by the end of the second week after fertilization.

There are those who want to use only adult stem cells in research rather than cells from embryos left over from IVF.

Part of what made Wilmut's success with Dolly so extraordinary was that he seems to have been able to revert an adult sheep cell back to its pluripotent state (though with all of the unexplained complications we've already detailed). Other techniques are being pursued for isolating adult stem cells—cells that are only partially differentiated—and reverting them to a pluripotent state, or nudging them to develop in particular directions. In the meantime, there is another source of pluripotent cells: the embryo itself. Pluripotent cells from human embryos are the embryonic stem cells at the center of last summer's debate.

Much of that continuing debate centers on the fact that human embryonic stem cells are obtained, almost exclusively, from embryos left over from IVF. Though proponents of research on them point out that they would be destroyed anyway, many opponents believe that these embryos, though composed of just a few dozen cells, are human lives, and so should be saved.

The other reason that stem cells have burst into the news has to do with their exceptional promise. Scientists have learned to culture human embryonic stem cells and allow them to divide and multiply, while preventing them from switching on or off any of their genes. By exposing these stem cells to different molecular compounds, they are trying to understand how that switching process works so that they can direct this cell to become a neuron, say, or that one to become a blood cell. (These two examples, in fact, are feats at which they have already had some measure of success.)

Eventually, some believe, we may be able to control the development of these pluripotent cells so that we can replace tissues damaged by disease or accident. Nerve cells damaged by Parkinson's or spinal cord injury, for example, or heart tissue of cardiac patients, might ultimately be replaced by tissue grown from stem cells.

Some scientists see even the potential to create custom-made tissue by using stem cells that are exact matches to a particular person, thus obviating the greatest problem in transplant surgery—rejection of the implant by the host's immune system. "Therapeutic cloning," as this procedure has been called, would involve inserting a patient's own DNA into an egg and then prompting the cell and egg to fuse and start dividing, as was done in creating Dolly. Each cell in the resulting embryo, and thus its stem cells, would have exactly the same DNA as the patient, and tissues derived from these cells would match exactly the patient's own tissues.

Along the wide spectrum of debate, there are those for whom embryonic stem cell research is acceptable as long as embryos are used with the consent of the egg and/or sperm donors (or, in the case of therapeutic cloning, the sole DNA donor); there are those who believe it is acceptable as long as it is done with embryos that would be destroyed anyway; and there are those for whom destroying even these "extra" embryos is abhorrent, and creating embryos for research or therapy all the more so.

Louise Brown was the world's first IVF birth, following more than 80 failed IVF attempts.

President Bush, in his August address, announced that the federal government would fund research with human embryonic stem cells but only that which uses those "lines" (cells developed from the original stem cells of a single embryo) already in existence. The scientific community has argued (and the administration has conceded) that there are fewer lines developed for research than the "more than 60" the President mentioned in his speech. Those that do exist, they say, may be inappropriate for use in human therapies, because they have been cultivated in mouse-cell cultures and represent a very limited gene pool. Other critics of the President's position point out that—as in many areas of research—curbing public funding does not mean that the research won't go on, just that it will go on, unregulated, under private sponsorship. Still others feel that the President was wrong to let any such research continue, let alone with public funding. Clearly, the debate isn't ending any time soon.

We are often reminded that just because we can do something—such as exploit the latest technology—does not mean that we should. Ian Wilmut—a vocal opponent of human cloning despite (or perhaps because of) his work with animals—offers a complementary observation: "What is 'natural,'" he points out, "is not necessarily right, and what is 'unnatural' is not necessarily wrong."

It is always risky navigating uncharted territory. President Bush stated it adroitly, in August, when he said: "As we go forward, I hope we will always be guided by... both our capabilities and our conscience."

James Trefil, a professor of physics at George Mason University, is a frequent contributor.

From *Smithsonian*, December 2001, pp. 38-46. © 2001 by James Trefil, a Clarence J. Robinson Professor of Physics at George Mason University. Reprinted by permission.

The First Human Cloned Embryo

Cloned early-stage human embryos—and human embryos generated only from eggs, in a process called parthenogenesis—now put therapeutic cloning within reach

By Jose B. Cibelli, Robert P. Lanza and Michael D. West, with Carol Ezzell

THEY WERE SUCH TINY DOTS, YET THEY HELD SUCH immense promise. After months of trying, on October 13, 2001, we came into our laboratory at Advanced Cell Technology to see under the microscope what we'd been striving for—little balls of dividing cells not even visible to the naked eye. Insignificant as they appeared, the specks were precious because they were, to our knowledge, the first human embryos produced using the technique of nuclear transplantation, otherwise known as cloning.

With a little luck, we hoped to coax the early embryos to divide into hollow spheres of 100 or so cells called blastocysts. We intended to isolate human stem cells from the blastocysts to serve as the starter stock for growing replacement nerve, muscle and other tissues that might one day be used to treat patients with a variety of diseases. Unfortunately, only one of the embryos progressed to the six-cell stage, at which point it stopped dividing. In a similar experiment, however, we succeeded in prompting human eggs—on their own, with no sperm to fertilize them—to develop parthenogenetically into blastocysts. We believe that together these achievements, the details of which we reported November 25 in the online journal *e-biomed: The Journal of Regenerative Medicine,* represent the dawn of a new age in medicine by demonstrating that the goal of therapeutic cloning is within reach.

Therapeutic cloning—which seeks, for example, to use the genetic material from patients' own cells to generate pancreatic islets to treat diabetes or nerve cells to repair damaged spinal cords—is distinct from reproductive cloning, which aims to implant a cloned embryo into a woman's uterus leading to the birth of a cloned baby. We believe that reproductive cloning has potential risks to both mother and fetus that make it unwarranted at this time, and we support a restriction on cloning for reproductive purposes until the safety and ethical issues surrounding it are resolved.

Disturbingly, the proponents of reproductive cloning are trying to co-opt the term "therapeutic cloning" by claiming that employing cloning techniques to create a child for a couple who cannot conceive through any other means treats the disorder of infertility. We object to this usage and feel that calling such a procedure "therapeutic" yields only confusion.

What We Did

WE LAUNCHED OUR ATTEMPT to create a cloned human embryo in early 2001. We began by consulting our ethics advisory board, a panel of independent ethicists, lawyers, fertility specialists and counselors that we had assembled in 1999 to guide the company's research efforts on an ongoing basis. Under the chairmanship of Ronald M. Green, director of the Ethics Institute at Dartmouth College, the board considered five key issues [*see box* "The Ethical Considerations"] before recommending that we go ahead.

The next step was to recruit women willing to contribute eggs to be used in the cloning procedure and also collect cells from individuals to be cloned (the donors). The cloning process appears simple, but success depends on many small factors, some of which we do not yet understand. In the basic nuclear transfer technique, scientists use an extremely fine needle to suck the genetic material from a mature egg. They then inject the nucleus of the donor cell (or sometimes a whole cell) into the unucleated egg and incubate it under special conditions that prompt it to divide and grow [*see illustration*].

We found women willing to contribute eggs on an anonymous basis for use in our research by placing advertisements in publications in the Boston area. We accepted women only between the ages of 24 and 32 who had at least one child. Interestingly, our proposal ap-

Therapeutic Cloning:
How It's Done

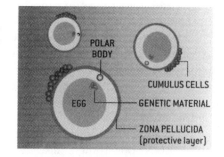

POLAR BODY
CUMULUS CELLS
GENETIC MATERIAL
EGG
ZONA PELLUCIDA
(protective layer)

1 Eggs are coaxed to mature in a culture dish. Each has a remnant egg cell called the polar body and cumulus cells from the ovary clinging to it.

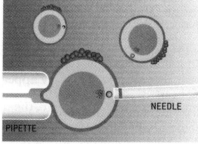

NEEDLE
PIPETTE

2 While an egg is held still with a pipette, a needle is used to drill through the zona pellucida, removing a plug.

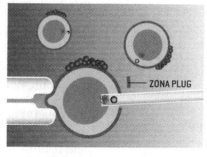

ZONA PLUG

3 After ejecting the zona plug, the needle is inserted back in the egg through the hole to withdraw and discard the polar body and the egg's genetic material.

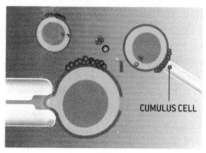

CUMULUS CELL

4 A cumulus cell from another egg is taken up into the needle. Cells called fibroblasts (or their nuclei) can also be used in this step.

5 The cumulus cell is injected deep into the egg that has been stripped of its genetic material.

6 The injected egg is exposed to a mixture of chemicals and growth factors designed to activate it to divide.

7 After roughly 24 hours, the activated egg begins dividing. The cells contain genetic material only from the injected cumulus cell.

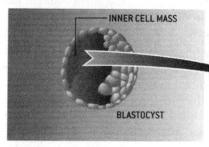

INNER CELL MASS
BLASTOCYST

8 By the fourth or fifth day, a hollow ball of roughly 100 cells has formed. It holds a clump of cells called the inner cell mass that contains stem cells.

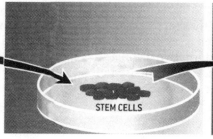

STEM CELLS

9 The blastocyst is broken open, and the inner cell mass is grown in a culture dish to yield stem cells.

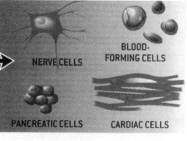

NERVE CELLS
BLOOD-FORMING CELLS
PANCREATIC CELLS
CARDIAC CELLS

10 The stem cells, in turn, can be coaxed to grow into a variety of cells that might one day be injected into patients.

JANA BRENNING

7

pealed to a different subset of women than those who might otherwise contribute eggs to infertile couples for use in in vitro fertilization. The women who responded to our ads were motivated to give their eggs for research, but many would not have been interested in having their eggs used to generate a child they would never see. (The donors were recruited and the eggs were collected by a team led by Ann A. Kiessling-Cooper of Duncan Holly Biomedical in Somerville, Mass. Kiessling was also part of the deliberations concerning ethical issues related to the egg contributors.)

We asked potential egg contributors to submit to psychological and physical tests, including screening for infectious diseases, to ensure that the women were healthy and that contributing eggs would not adversely affect them. We ended up with 12 women who were good candidates to contribute eggs. In the meantime, we took skin biopsies from several other anonymous individuals to isolate cells called fibroblasts for use in the cloning procedure. Our group of fibroblast donors includes people of varying ages who are generally healthy or who have a disorder such as diabetes or spinal cord injury—the kinds of people likely to benefit from therapeutic cloning.

On the Web/*Human Cloning*

- For updates on this breaking story, visit a special report on human cloning and stem cells at our Web site, **www.sciam.com/explorations/2001/112401ezzell/**

- The site includes previous *Scientific American* articles on the subject as well as reports on adult stem cells and the current status of reproductive cloning projects.

Our first cloning attempt occurred last July. The timing of each attempt depended on the menstrual cycles of the women who contributed eggs; the donors had to take hormone injections for several days so that they would ovulate 10 or so eggs at once instead of the normal one or two.

We had a glimmer of success in the third cycle of attempts when the nucleus of an injected fibroblast appeared to divide, but it never cleaved to form two distinct cells. So in the next cycle we decided to take the tack used by Teruhiko Wakayama and his colleagues, the scientists who created the first cloned mice in 1998. (Wakayama was then at the University of Hawaii and is now at Advanced Cell Technology.) Although we injected some of the eggs with nuclei from skin fibroblasts as usual, we injected others with ovarian cells called cumulus cells that usually nurture developing eggs in the ovary and that can be found still clinging to eggs after ovulation. Cumulus cells are so small they can be injected whole. In the end, it took a total of 71 eggs from seven volunteers before we could generate our first cloned early embryo. Of the eight eggs we injected with cumulus cells, two divided to form early embryos of four cells—and one progressed to at least six cells—before growth stopped.

Parthenogenesis

WE ALSO SOUGHT TO DETERMINE whether we could induce human eggs to divide into early embryos without being fertilized by a sperm or being enucleated and injected with a donor cell. Although mature eggs and sperm normally have only half the genetic material of a typical body cell, to prevent an embryo from having a double set of genes following conception, eggs halve their genetic complement relatively late in their maturation cycle. If activated before that stage, they still retain a full set of genes.

Stem cells derived from such parthenogenetically activated cells would be unlikely to be rejected after transplantation because they would be very similar to a patient's own cells and would not produce many molecules that would be unfamiliar to the person's immune system. (They would not be identical to the individual's cells because of the gene shuffling that always occurs during the formation of eggs and sperm.) Such cells might also raise fewer moral dilemmas for some people than would stem cells derived from cloned early embryos.

Under one scenario, a woman with heart disease might have her own egg collected and activated in the laboratory to yield blastocysts. Scientists could then use combinations of growth factors to coax stem cells isolated from the blastocysts to become cardiac muscle cells growing in laboratory dishes that could be implanted back into the woman to patch a diseased area of the heart. Using a similar technique, called androgenesis, to create stem cells to treat a man would be trickier. But it might involve transferring two nuclei from the man's sperm into a contributed egg that had been stripped of its nucleus.

Researchers have previously reported prompting eggs from mice and rabbits to divide into embryos by exposing them to different chemicals or physical stimuli such as an electrical shock. As early as 1983, Elizabeth J. Robertson, who is now at Harvard University, demonstrated that stem cells isolated from parthenogenetic mouse embryos could form a variety of tissues, including nerve and muscle.

In our parthenogenesis experiments, we exposed 22 eggs to chemicals that changed the concentration of charged atoms called ions inside the cells. After five days of growing in culture dishes, six eggs had developed into what appeared to be blastocysts, but none clearly contained the so-called inner cell mass that yields stem cells.

Why We Did It

WE ARE EAGER FOR THE DAY when we will be able to offer therapeutic cloning or cell therapy arising from parthenogenesis to sick patients. Currently our efforts are fo-

The Ethical Considerations

Advanced Cell Technology assembled a board of outside ethicists to weigh the moral implications of therapeutic cloning research, which aims to generate replacement tissues to treat a range of diseases. Here are the five major questions the board considered before the company went forward with cloning the first human embryo.

By Ronald M. Green

What is the moral status of the organisms created by cloning?

If a cloned organism were implanted into a womb, as was done in the case of Dolly the sheep, it could possibly go on to full development and birth. Because of this potential, some would argue that the organism produced in human therapeutic cloning experiments is the equivalent of any ordinary human embryo and merits the same degree of respect and protection.

Most members of our advisory board did not agree. We pointed out that, unlike an embryo, a cloned organism is not the result of fertilization of an egg by a sperm. It is a new type of biological entity never before seen in nature. Although it possesses some potential for developing into a full human being, this capacity is very limited. At the blastocyst stage, when the organism is typically disaggregated to create an embryonic stem cell line, it is a ball of cells no bigger than the period at the end of this sentence. (Embryos normally do not attach to the wall of the uterus and begin development until after the blastocyst stage.) It has no organs, it cannot possibly think or feel, and it has none of the attributes thought of as human. Although board members understood that some people would liken this organism to an embryo, we preferred the term "activated egg," and we concluded that its characteristics did not preclude its use in work that might save the lives of children and adults.

A cloned organism is a NEW TYPE OF BIOLOGICAL ENTITY never before seen in nature.

Is it permissible to create such a developing human entity only to destroy it?

Those who believe that human life begins at conception—and who also regard activated eggs as morally equivalent to human embryos—cannot ethically approve therapeutic cloning research. For them, such research is equivalent to killing a living child in order to harvest its organs for the benefit of others. Some of those who think this way, however, might nonetheless find acceptable research on human stem cells derived from embryos left over from in vitro fertilization [IVF] procedures. They reason, rightly or wrongly, that these embryos are certain to be destroyed and that at least some good might result from using the cells. But therapeutic cloning remains totally unacceptable to such people because it involves the deliberate creation of what they deem to be a human being in order to destroy it.

Many who do not accord moral status to the entities produced by therapeutic cloning disagree with that view. Like our board members, they argue that the benefits of this research and the possible therapies it could produce far outweigh the claims of the activated eggs. Remarkably, some who share this moral view nonetheless oppose the research on symbolic grounds. They maintain that it is unseemly to create human life in any form only to destroy it. They worry that it might start society down a slippery slope that could lead to the scavenging of organs from adults without their consent.

These symbolic and "slippery slope" arguments often have powerful emotional force, but they are hard to assess. Is it really true that using activated eggs for lifesaving therapies will lead to these imagined abuses? On the contrary, if medical science can increase people's chances of healthy survival, might not this research even enhance respect for human life? Members of the board took note of the fact that the U.K., until very recently, has legally permitted the deliberate creation and destruction of human embryos in research since the early 1990s [*see box* "Cloning and the Law"]. There has been no apparent ill effect of this permission on British society. In the end, the symbolic and slippery slope arguments did not persuade board members that the therapeutic cloning research should not go forward.

Is it right to seek human eggs for scientific research?

The need to obtain a supply of human eggs leads to one of the most sensitive ethical issues in therapeutic cloning research. In each of her monthly cycles, a woman usually produces only one or two mature eggs. To increase that to a number that can be used in research, she must be given stimulatory medications such as those used in reproductive IVF procedures. In rare cases, these drugs can provoke a so-called hyperstimulation syndrome that can lead to liver damage, kidney failure or stroke. According to some studies, ovulation-stimulating drugs have also been associated with a heightened risk for ovarian cancer. The surgery to retrieve the eggs also carries risks, such as the dangers of general anesthesia and bleeding. Is it ethical to subject a woman to these risks for research purposes? If women are offered payment to undergo these risk, might that cause human reproductive material to become viewed as a commodity that can be commercialized? We do not permit the sale of human organs or babies. Are eggs any different?

In responding to these concerns, members of the board took note of two facts. First, a substantial market in human eggs for reproductive purposes already exists. Young women are being paid substantial sums to provide eggs that can help single women or couples have children. If women can undergo risks for this purpose, we asked, why should they not be allowed to undertake the same risks to further medical research that could save human lives? And if they can be paid for the time and discomfort that egg donation for reproductive purposes involves, why can't they receive reasonable payment for ovulation induction for research purposes?

Second, we noted that research volunteers often accept significant risks to advance medical knowledge. If a person can agree to undergo a dangerous malaria vaccine study to help cure disease, why should they be prevented from donating eggs for similar lifesaving research?

(continued)

9

(The Ethical Considerations *continued*)

In the end, we concluded that it would be unduly paternalistic to prohibit women from donating eggs for this research. At the same time, we established a rigorous informed-consent procedure so that egg donors would be made fully aware of the possible dangers. We insisted that ovulation-stimulating medications be administered at safe dosages. And we set payment for participation at a modest level: $4,000 [about $40 an hour], which is roughly the average paid in New England for egg donation for reproductive purposes. We wanted to prevent payment from becoming an undue influence that could blind women to the risks.

What are the ethical issues relating to the person whose cells are being cloned?

It may seem that individuals who provide the cells [usually skin fibroblasts] that are fused with enucleated eggs in therapeutic cloning research face no risk apart from the remote possibility of an infection at the site of the skin biopsy. But cloning is a controversial issue that exposes all research participants to novel risks. Cell donors, for example, might find themselves at the center of a media storm if they are identified as having allowed themselves to be cloned. To prevent this, the ethics advisory board insisted on procedures ensuring strict confidentiality for both egg and cell donors [unless they choose to come forward].

Cell donors might find themselves at the CENTER OF A MEDIA STORM if they are identified as having allowed themselves to be cloned.

One question that occupied much of our time was whether children could donate cells for this research. We concluded that in general this is not advisable, because on reaching maturity the child may feel morally compromised by having been made to contribute to a cloning procedure. We made an exception, however, in the case of an infant with a fatal genetic disease. We knew that a stem cell line based on the child's DNA might be a powerful tool in research aimed at curing the disease. Although the child would probably not survive long enough to benefit from this research, we concluded that the parents had a right to make this decision on the child's behalf. This child's cells have not yet been used in a cloning procedure.

Will therapeutic cloning facilitate reproductive cloning, the birth of a cloned body?

A final major question raised by this research is whether it will hasten the day when people undertake human reproductive cloning. This concern presumes that reproductive cloning is and always will be ethically wrong. Many who hold this view cite the incidence of deaths and birth defects in cloned animals. Others worry about more remote dangers. They point to possible psychological risks to children produced in families in which a parent may also be a child's genetic twin. They fear

that cloned children may face unrealistic expectations to live up to the achievements of their genetic predecessor. And they worry about possible social risks of cloning if societies decide to replicate a limited number of desired genomes on a large scale for military or other purposes. In opposition to this, some people hail the prospect of cloning. They see it as a new way to provide biologically related offspring for some infertile couples or as a means of reducing the risks of some inherited genetic diseases.

Whatever one thinks about the ethics of reproductive cloning, placing a ban on therapeutic cloning will not make reproductive cloning less likely. Although therapeutic cloning could help scientists perfect techniques for reproductive cloning, it could also make much clearer the dangers of trying to produce a human being in this way. There is already evidence that some cloned animals can experience improper gene expression and disruptions in imprinting, the normal pattern of silencing genes not needed in particular tissues. Such problems could discourage prospective parents for using this technology to have a baby. Thus, therapeutic cloning research could actually reduce the likelihood that cloning would be seen as a viable reproductive option.

A ban on therapeutic cloning also would not prevent unsupervised researchers from going ahead with reproductive cloning efforts on their own. Groups such as the Raëlians, a religious cult, or renegade scientists such as Richard G. Seed, a physicist based in Riverside, Ill., who has also been involved in embryology, have announced their intent to clone a human being and presumably will try to do so regardless of whether therapeutic cloning research is banned. A ban on therapeutic cloning will block useful research while allowing less responsible people to try reproductive cloning wherever they can find a permissive legal environment. By shutting down responsible research on the cell biology of human cloning, such a ban would also guarantee that the first efforts at cloning a human being would be based on scanty scientific information.

Our ethics board has had to wrestle with new and challenging questions, but we believe we have managed to give Advanced Cell Technology a firm ethical base for its therapeutic cloning research program. After researchers derive stem cells from cloned human activated eggs, ethicists will need to determine at what point it will be safe to try to transplant such cells back into volunteer donors. The tasks ahead for ethics boards like ours are demanding. The reward is assisting at the cutting edge of medical knowledge.

RONALD M. GREEN is director of the Ethics Institute at Dartmouth College and chair of the ethics advisory board of Advanced Cell Technology in Worcester, Mass.

Other current board members are Judith Bernstein of Boston University; Susan Crockin, a health care lawyer in private practice in Newton, Mass.; Kenneth Goodman, director of the Forum for Bioethics at the University of Miami; Robert Kaufmann of the Southeastern Fertility Center in Mount Pleasant, S.C.; Susan R. Levin, a counselor in private practice in West Roxbury, Mass.; Susan L. Moss of San Diego State University; and Carol Tauer of the Minnesota Center for Health Care Ethics. Michael D. West, president and CEO of Advanced Cell Technology, is an ex officio member of the ethics advisory board.

Cloning and the Law

Will therapeutic cloning end up being against the law?

Legislative activities threaten to stand in the way of the medical benefits that therapeutic cloning could provide. On July 31, 2001, the House of Representatives voted for a broad ban on human cloning that would not only prohibit the use of cloning for reproduction but would also prohibit cloning for research purposes, such as to derive stem cells that could be used in therapies. The legislation, which was sponsored by Representative David Weldon (R-Fla.) and Bart Stupak (D-Mich.), would carry penalties of up to 10 years in prison and fines of $1 million for anyone who generates cloned human embryos. An amendment introduced by Representative Jim Greenwood (R-Pa.) that would have allowed therapeutic cloning failed. (Greenwood has his own pending bill on the subject that would outlaw only reproductive cloning.) Such laws would affect all scientists in the U.S., not only those working with government funding.

The Weldon/Stupak bill has now been referred to the Senate, which is expected to take up the issue in early 2002. Senator Sam Brownback (R-Kan.), who has also introduced a bill, opposes human cloning for any purpose. He tried to add amendments banning human cloning to the fiscal 2002 spending bill for the Department of Health and Human Services

last November. Such measures face an uphill battle, however, in the Democrat-controlled Senate. The Bush administration supports a total cloning ban and has endorsed the Weldon/Stupak bill.

The matter of human cloning is also being taken up once again by the U.K. Parliament. In 2000 the U.K. altered its Human Fertilization and Embryology Act of 1990 to specifically allow human therapeutic cloning. But last November antiabortion activists succeeded in having the provision struck down on the grounds that cloning does not involve an embryo created by the union of an egg and a sperm and therefore cannot be included under the act.

In a related issue, last August President George Bush barred the use of federal funds for research involving stem cells derived from embryos, including those generated using cloning. The bar permits federally funded scientists to experiment only with stem cell cultures, or lines, created before the August announcement. But many scientists have criticized the quality and availability of these stem cell lines. Others claim that without cloning, stem cells have no promise, because they would probably be rejected as foreign by a patient's immune system.

Legislative attempts by Senator Arlen Specter (R-Pa.) in November that would have allowed scientists to use government money to make new stem cell lines were squelched when Brownback threatened to counter with a total ban on human stem cell research.

—*Carol Ezzell*

cused on diseases of the nervous and cardiovascular systems and on diabetes, autoimmune disorders, and diseases involving the blood and bone marrow.

Once we are able to derive nerve cells from cloned embryos, we hope not only to heal damaged spinal cords but to treat brain disorders such as Parkinson's disease, in which the death of brain cells that make a substance called dopamine leads to uncontrollable tremors and paralysis. Alzheimer's disease, stroke and epilepsy might also yield to such an approach.

Besides insulin-producing pancreatic islet cells for treating diabetes, stem cells from cloned embryos could also be nudged to become heart muscle cells as therapies for congestive heart failure, arrhythmias and cardiac tissue scarred by heart attacks.

A potentially even more interesting application could involve prompting cloned stem cells to differentiate into cells of the blood and bone marrow. Autoimmune disorders such as multiple sclerosis and rheumatoid arthritis arise when white blood cells of the immune system, which arise from the bone marrow, attack the body's own tissues. Preliminary studies have shown that cancer patients who also had autoimmune diseases gained relief from autoimmune symptoms after they received bone marrow transplants to replace their own marrow that had been killed by high-dose chemotherapy to treat the cancer. Infusions of blood-forming, or hematopoietic, cloned

stem cells might "reboot" the immune systems of people with autoimmune diseases.

But are cloned cells—or those generated through parthenogenesis—normal? Only clinical tests of the cells will show ultimately whether such cells are safe enough for routine use in patients, but our studies of cloned animals have shown that clones are healthy. In the November 30, 2001, issue of *Science*, we reported on our success to date with cloning cattle. Of 30 cloned cattle, six died shortly after birth, but the rest have had normal results on physical exams, and tests of their immune systems show they do not differ from regular cattle. Two of the cows have even given birth to healthy calves.

The cloning process also appears to reset the "aging clock" in cloned cells, so that the cells appear younger in some ways than the cells from which they were cloned. In 2000 we reported that telomeres—the caps at the ends of chromosomes—from cloned calves are just as long as those from control calves. Telomeres normally shorten or are damaged as an organism ages. Therapeutic cloning may provide "young" cells for an aging population.

A report last July by Rudolf Jaenisch of the Whitehead Institute for Biomedical Research in Cambridge, Mass., and his colleagues gained much attention because it found so-called imprinting defects in cloned mice. Imprinting is a type of stamp placed on many genes in mammals that changes how the genes are turned on or off depending on whether the genes are inherited from the mother or the father. The imprinting program is generally "reset" during embryonic development.

Although imprinting appears to play an important role in mice, no one yet knows how significant the phenomenon is for humans. In addition, Jaenisch and his co-workers did not study mice cloned from cells taken from the bodies of adults, such as fibroblasts or cumulus cells. Instead they examined mice cloned from embryonic cells, which might be expected to be more variable. Studies showing that imprinting is normal in mice cloned from adult cells are currently in press and should be published in the scientific literature within several months.

Meanwhile we are continuing our therapeutic cloning experiments to generate cloned or parthenogenetically produced human embryos that will yield stem cells. Scientists have only begun to tap this important resource.

MORE TO EXPLORE

Human Therapeutic Cloning. Robert P. Lanza, Jose B. Cibelli and Michael D. West in *Nature Medicine,* Vol. 5, No. 9, pages 975–977; September 1999.

Prospects for the Use of Nuclear Transfer in Human Transplantation. Robert P. Lanza, Jose B. Cibelli and Michael D. West in *Nature Biotechnology,* Vol. 17, No. 12, pages 1171–1174; December 1999.

The Ethical Validity of Using Nuclear Transfer in Human Transplantation. Robert P. Lanza et al. in *Journal of the American Medical Association,* Vol. 284, No. 24; December 27, 2000.

The Human Embryo Research Debates: Bioethics in the Vortex of Controversy. Ronald M. Green. Oxford University Press, 2001.

The full text of our article in *e-biomed: The Journal of Regenerative Medicine* can be viewed at **www.liebertpub.com/ebi**

THE AUTHORS

JOSE B. CIBELLI, ROBERT P. LANZA and *MICHAEL D. WEST* are vice president of research, vice president of medical and scientific development, and president and CEO, respectively, of Advanced Cell Technology, a privately held biotechnology company in Worcester, Mass. Cibelli received his D.V.M. from the University of La Plata in Argentina and his Ph.D. from the University of Massachusetts at Amherst. His research led to the creation of the first cloned genetically modified calves in 1998. Lanza has an M.D. from the University of Pennsylvania. He is a former Fulbright scholar and is the author or editor of numerous popular and scientific books, including the text *Principles of Tissue Engineering.* West holds a Ph.D. from Baylor College of Medicine and is particularly interested in aging and stem cells. From 1990 until 1998 he was founder, director and vice president of Geron Corporation in Menlo Park, Calif., where he initiated and managed research programs in the biology of telomeres [the ends of chromosomes, which shrink during aging] and the effort to derive human embryonic stem cells. Carol Ezzell is a staff writer and editor.

Reprinted with permission from *Scientific American,* January 2002, pp. 44-51. © 2002 by Scientific American, Inc. All rights reserved.

A State of the Art
Pregnancy

New prenatal tests detect problems earlier and more accurately. They may even foretell the health of the adult the baby will become. By Karen Springen

WHEN SHE WAS NEARLY halfway into her pregnancy, Lisa Lahti, now 31, got the news that every parent-to-be dreads: a routine blood-screening test showed that she was at increased risk of delivering a child with Down syndrome. To learn conclusively, both Lahti's OB-GYN and a geneticist recommended amniocentesis. In the amnio, a doctor would insert a thin needle through Lahti's abdomen to extract two tablespoons of fluid from the sac holding the fetus. A lab would analyze the fluid, which contains the baby's cells and chromosomes, and make a definitive diagnosis. But Lahti turned down the amnio: she and her husband, Daryl, "wouldn't abort in any situation," she explains. Her son, Jacob, now 18 months, was born completely healthy. It turns out that the $50 blood test she took has a false-positive rate of one in 20.

More than half of the 3.9 million pregnant women in the United States will nevertheless take this blood test, and 125,000 will undergo an amnio. But the popularity of the tests belies their shortcomings. First and foremost: neither the blood-screening test nor amniocentesis can

be done before the second trimester. Amnios performed earlier than 15 weeks into pregnancy put women at higher risk of miscarrying, leaking amniotic fluid and delivering a baby with a severe clubfoot. Even chorionic villus sampling, in which a highly trained doctor extracts tiny parts of the placenta for chromosomal testing, cannot be done earlier than 10 weeks into pregnancy—and results take at least seven days to come back. "If you're going to end pregnancies, earlier is better," says Arthur Caplan, director of the Center of Biomedical Ethics at the University of Pennsylvania. That's why the push is on for more accurate, earlier prenatal tests. They are just one of the high-tech tools that are giving women a better chance than ever of having a safe pregnancy and a healthy newborn.

Parents in the new millennium will trade their current blurry ultrasound pictures for clearer, three-dimensional photos of their fetuses. But the goal isn't to start the baby album with a better picture. Rather, the new 3-D machines should provide more precise images of the fetal brain and heart, and detect hard-to-

spot abnormalities such as cleft lip and palate (one in 930 births) and clubfeet (one in 735).

Ultrasound can also be combined with a blood test for an even clearer crystal ball. Scientists are studying whether the combination can tell if a 10- to 14-week fetus is likely to have either Down syndrome or a form of severe mental retardation called trisomy 18. The ultrasound looks for loose skin in the neck of the fetus, which indicates the presence of three chromosome 21s, and hence Down syndrome. It detects more cases, and can be done earlier, than existing tests for these conditions. "The vast majority of women are going to leave [after the test] feeling good about their pregnancy," says Eugene Pergament, director of reproductive genetics at Northwestern University.

Another test that will be done early in pregnancy analyzes maternal blood. Fetal cells, it turns out, leak into the mother's circulatory system. Although the cells are few and far between, "for the past several years [we have] been trying to find these needles in the haystack," says Mark I. Evans, acting chairman

Ten Tips to a Healthy Start

Most of the 3.9 million women in the United States who gave birth last year had healthy babies.
Here are some steps to increase the excellent odds that you will, too.

1 Nutrition: Sorry, you're still eating for one, not two. An average pregnant woman needs only 300 more calories per day than her usual 2,200. Make every calorie count. Folic acid, starting at least a month before conception, helps prevent neural-tube defects. Get 400 micrograms a day, from leafy greens like spinach (130 micrograms per half cup, boiled) or supplements. To make sure the fetus gets plenty of oxygen, choose iron-rich foods, such as red meat and enriched cereals. Vitamin C helps iron absorption. Try to get 1,000 mg of calcium a day (a cup of nonfat plain yogurt contains 450).

2 Vitamins: Avoid megadoses. More than 10,000 IUs of vitamin A, for example, can cause birth defects.

3 Alcohol: Abstain. No one knows how much alcohol is safe to drink during pregnancy. Alcohol reaches the fetus through the placenta and can restrict growth and cause cardiac defects and facial malformations. It's the most common nongenetic cause of mental retardation.

4 Smoking: Stop. Tobacco users are more likely to miscarry and to deliver small, preterm babies with a higher risk of ear infections, colds, heart problems, upper respiratory infections and sudden infant death syndrome (SIDS).

5 Weight gain: Most women should gain 25 to 35 pounds. Underweight women should gain 28 to 40; overweight women, 15 to 25. Women who gain too little are more likely to have smaller babies.

6 Exercise: Avoid sports such as racquetball that expose the abdomen to potential trauma. Many doctors advise against Rollerblading, skiing or bicycling after 20 weeks, since growing bellies make it easier to fall and damage the uterus. Walk, swim, run. But check your pulse to make sure your heart isn't beating more than 140 times a minute for more than 20 minutes; that can divert too much blood from the fetus.

7 Sex: Enjoy it. Amniotic fluid cushions the fetus.

8 Medicine: Acetaminophen is fine, but ibuprofen in the third trimester may increase the risk of prolonged gestation and labor, and can in rare instances cause pulmonary hypertension in newborns. The acne drug Accutane can cause cleft palate, small ears and brain malformations. Tetracycline in the second half of pregnancy can yellow a baby's teeth.

9 STDs: Get checked for HIV, syphilis and gonorrhea—ideally before conception. Gonorrhea can infect the baby's eyes at birth; syphilis can cause congenital malformations. Medications can significantly cut the risk of transmitting AIDS to a baby.

10 Seat belts: Not wearing them is a leading cause of fetal death. In an accident, a belt is far less likely than a windshield to hurt the baby.

SOURCES: DR. LARRY C. GILSTRAP; ACOG

of OB-GYN at Wayne State University in Detroit. Now researchers are getting better at it. Within a decade, fetal DNA analysis "could replace everything" from blood-screening tests to amnios, says Dr. Ronald Wapner, director of maternal fetal medicine at Jefferson Medical College in Philadelphia. Parents would learn about chromosomal abnormalities weeks earlier than now.

And that's not all they would learn. Fetal DNA holds the child's genetic blueprint, and with a new invention physicians will be able to read it. The device is called a DNA chip, or "biochip." It consists of thousands of strands of DNA. When a sample of blood is dropped onto the chip, DNA in the blood matches up with DNA on the chip. A laser reads the chip, and thus can tell whether the fetus carries virtually any gene that scientists have identified. That means physicians will be able to tell if a fetus is at risk for disorders such as Down syndrome, as well as hundreds of genetic diseases that strike only in adulthood, such as Alzheimer's and cancer. Eventually embryos conceived through in vitro fertilization could be tested before being implanted in the mother-to-be.

Couples could opt not to implant ones at high risk for, say, juvenile diabetes or breast cancer. Yet this "advance" raises troublesome ethical issues. "I could see society saying, 'We don't want to pay [to treat] any babies with genetic diseases. You could have prevented them'," says Caplan.

Even more important than detecting problems is treating them. Highly trained surgeons now operate on fetuses about a dozen times a year, repairing hernias, lung malformations, urinary-tract obstructions and spina bifida, a condition that leaves an opening near the spinal cord and causes paralysis. Working with cameralike "endoscopes" and instruments that pass through the uterine wall without making an incision, doctors hope to correct cleft lip and palate, too. Some surgeons even foresee performing open-heart surgery on fetuses. Still, fetal surgery remains controversial largely because it can cause preterm birth. "It really hasn't revolutionized obstetrics in terms of changing overall outcome for any great number of people," cautions OB-GYN Fredric Frigoletto, chief of obstetrics at Massachusetts General Hospital. But advocates say it's far cheaper to correct birth defects before delivery than to provide a lifetime of care.

When all the tests point to a healthy fetus, just about the only worry left is preterm labor, the No. 1 problem in obstetrics. Some 10 percent of U.S. babies are born less than 37 weeks into pregnancy, which increases the risk of everything from blindness and deafness to cerebral palsy. "The damage that preterm birth causes can last for life," says James McGregor, professor of OB-GYN at the University of Colorado at Denver. "If you can get close to 37 weeks, you're kind of in the clear. You don't get brain damage. You don't get lung damage. You don't have increased risk of cerebral palsy." To avoid all that, a $90 test measures the amount of a form of estrogen called estriol in a pregnant woman's saliva. Estriol levels usually start climbing three weeks before labor. Women at risk for early delivery (because of cramping, illness, a fetal abnormality or a previous early delivery) can now simply provide about a tablespoon of saliva and learn their estriol level within two days. If the level indicates they are about to go into labor, and if it's not time for that, the obstetrician can try to figure out why and treat the cause. To help detect other conditions that can trigger early delivery, some doctors are also performing a $100 test for high levels of a molecule called fibronectin. (They collect it from the cervix with a Q-Tip.) A high level of fibronectin means the uterus is separating from the (probably inflamed) amniotic sac. Moms are vigorously treated for the infection, which can otherwise precipitate early labor.

And who would have guessed that the space program would help prevent preterm deliveries? Scientists at NASA have created a 1 1/2-inch pill-shaped transmitter—implanted into the uterus about 27 weeks into pregnancy—that measures contractions. They're also working on transmitters to measure fetal acidity, temperature and heart rate, all of which reflect the fetus's health. If the transmitter costs $1,000 and saves $300,000 in medical costs from problems caused by a preterm birth, it's well worth it, argues John Hines of NASA's Ames Research Center.

Expect changes even in electronic fetal monitoring, used to detect babies' heart rate during labor. Now the monitors are used on 98 percent of pregnant women. The heart rate supposedly shows whether the baby is getting enough oxygen. If he is not, most obstetricians order an emergency Caesarean section. But a device under development would directly measure how much oxygen the fetus is receiving, rather than making an educated guess based on the heart rate, which can raise false alarms. If the fetus is getting plenty of oxygen after all, despite a high heart rate, the mom could continue natural labor instead of undergoing a C-section. For that's the goal of all these tests anyway: making sure that the fetus is developing normally and setting the mother-to-be's mind at ease.

From *Newsweek*, Spring 1999 Special Issue, pp. 16-23. © 1999 by Newsweek, Inc. All rights reserved. Reprinted by permission.

SHAPED BY LIFE IN THE
WOMB

Scientists used to think that adult illnesses like diabetes, obesity, cardiovascular disease and breast cancer were the result of either unhealthy living or bad genes. No longer. Startling new research suggests that these conditions may have their roots before birth.

BY SHARON BEGLEY

When John Carter was born, 73 years ago, the doctor in the town of Ware just north of London wasn't sure if the little guy would make it: he weighed a mere 3.4 pounds. "They laid me on a hot-water bottle, wrapped me in cotton soaked in cod-liver oil and gave me brandy through the nib of a fountain pen," Carter says. "Surviving was rather a miracle." But the little boy grew to manhood, landing a job as a warehouseman and enjoying normal health—until his early 50s. That's when a physical discovered that Carter had sky-high blood pressure. Another test found that he had adult-onset diabetes.

Carter had no reason to suspect it, but his illnesses may not stem from the usual culprits: genetic defects, unhealthy living or environmental toxins. Cutting-edge research suggests instead that the roots of both his high blood pressure and his diabetes stretch back decades—to his life in the womb. Scientists now think that conditions during gestation, ranging from the torrent of hormones that flow from Mom to how well the placenta delivers nutrients to the tiny limbs and organs, shape the health of the adult that fetus becomes. "Recent research" says Dr. Peter Nathanaielsz of Cornell University, whose new book "Life in the Womb" explores this science, "provides compelling proof that the health we enjoy throughout our lives is determined to a large extent by the conditions in which we developed, [conditions that] can program how our liver, heart, kidneys and especially our brain function." It is no exaggeration to call these findings a revolution in the making. The discovery of how conditions in the womb influence the risk of adult disease casts doubt on how much genes contribute to disease (because what scientists classify as a genetic influence may instead reflect gestational conditions) and suggests that adult illnesses long blamed on years of living dangerously (like dining on pizza and cupcakes) instead reflect "fetal programming." "Two years ago no one was even thinking about this," says Dr. Matthew Gillman of Harvard Medical School. "But now what we are seeing is nothing short of a new paradigm in public health."

What is so startling is that the findings go far beyond the widespread recognition that conditions during gestation shape the health of the newborn. We've known for a while that alcohol reaching the fetus can lead to mental retardation and heart defects and that the stew of toxins in tobacco can cause upper-respiratory-tract and ear infections. But these compounds work by more or less poisoning the baby. The result is often a child who, at birth or soon after, has detectable problems. The new findings are dramatically different. First of all, the gestational conditions scientists are talking about fall far short of toxic. They are, instead, paragons of subtlety. They are conditions that reprogram the fetus's physiology so that, for instance, the child's (and eventually the adult's) metabolism turns just about everything she eats into body fat. This is the woman who needn't bother actually eating the french fries; she might as well just insert them directly into her hips. Second, unlike the toxic influences

A Tragic But Telling Legacy

Doctors are using a horror of war to learn more about the long-term effects of nutrition on fetal development

YOU COULDN'T DESIGN a grimmer experiment. A Nazi blockade of the western Netherlands in September 1944 and an early winter triggered a famine that lasted until the spring of 1945. By January, daily rations in the cities were down to 750 calories, half of what they had been earlier in the war; they would eventually fall below 500 calories. City dwellers were forced into the country to scavenge for food, including tulip bulbs. The "Hunger Winter" had killed 20,000 people by Liberation Day on May 5, 1945, scarring an entire populace—including, scientists later found, generations yet unborn. In the 1960s, husband-and-wife researchers Zena Stein and Mervyn Susser realized that, horrific as it was, the Dutch Hunger Winter offered unprecedented clues to the effects of prenatal nutrition.

Stein and Susser discovered that fetuses exposed to the famine early in gestation, when organs form, had an increased risk of central-nervous-system defects like spina bifida, in which the brain or spine is not fully developed. Other scientists found that a fetus starved early in development during the famine was at high risk for adult obesity. Two decades later, Stein and Susser's son, Ezra Susser, went further. Now a pioneering epidemiologist at Columbia University, Susser examined psychiatric evaluations of adults who were Hunger Winter babies to study the theory that schizophrenia was the result of a defect in neural development. Susser and Hans Hoek in the Netherlands discovered that fetuses who received poor nutrition early in gestation were twice as likely to develop schizophrenia in adulthood as fetuses whose mothers had an adequate diet. Susser is now looking for links between prenatal nutrition and other mental illnesses. It's a sad but revealing legacy of that season of devastation.

JOHN DAVENPORT

Tragic Echoes: *Children relied on relief programs; infants suffered later in life*

whose effects on a fetus are apparent immediately, the effects of fetal programming often show up only decades later. The nine-pound bouncing girl will be perfectly healthy for decades. But the same influences that gave her layers of baby fat—"growth factors" like estrogen's crossing the placenta from Mom—prime her mammary tissue so that exposure to estrogen after puberty gives her breast cancer at 46.

There is one thing the findings do not mean. While they may tempt you to blame Mom for even more of your ills, or make you feel powerless against a fate that was set before you cried your first cry, forget it: how you live your life outside the womb still matters. Since the conditions in which the fetus develops influence adult health, learning what those conditions are (through measurements of length, weight, girth and head size at birth) tells you what extra risks you carry with you into the world. And that suggests ways to keep these risks from becoming reality. If as a newborn your abdomen was unusually small, for instance, then your liver may be too small to clear cholesterol from your

bloodstream as well as it should, and you may have an extra risk of elevated cholesterol at the age of 50. So scrutinize those baby pictures: if your tummy was scrawny compared with the rest of chubby-cheeked you, be careful about controlling your cholesterol levels.

The discovery of fetal programming might never have happened if Dr. David Barker of England's University of Southampton had not noticed, in 1984, some maps that did not seem to make sense. They displayed measures of health throughout England and Wales. Barker saw that neonatal mortality in the early 1900s was high in the same regions where deaths from heart disease were high. That was odd. In general, infant mortality rises in pockets of poverty; heart disease is supposedly a disease of affluence (butter, meat and all that). They shouldn't go together. Barker wondered whether the search for the cause of heart disease should begin in the womb. To embark on his quest, he needed birth records, and lots of them, going back decades, to link conditions at the beginning of life with the health of the

adults he would study. Lending a hand, Britain's Medical Research Council hired an Oxford University historian to scour the country for such records. During a two-year hunt, the historian found records in archives, lofts, sheds, garages, boiler rooms and even flooded basements—but the best records were in Hertfordshire. There, the "lady inspector of midwives" had recorded the weight of every baby born in the shire (including John Carter) from 1911 to 1945. Barker had his data.

Ominous signs:
Michels's study of thousands of American women finds a link between a girl's birth weight and her risk of breast cancer at a relatively young age

---

Soon Barker and his colleagues had their "Aha!" moment. Studying 13,249

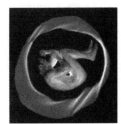

EARLY WIRING: the growth factors that give a newborn fat may prime her mammary tissue, making her more susceptible to breast cancer in her 40s.

The Roots of Health

Disorders such as heart disease and diabetes are not only the result of unhealthy habits or bad genes. The new science of "fetal programming" suggests that as pregnancy progresses, each month in the womb shapes your health for life.

Stress 1

(A) Mother   **(B) Fetus**   **(C) Adult child**

Placenta
Enzyme

Elevated levels of cortisol

Fetus

Active cortisol

Elevated levels of cortisol

High blood pressure

Usually, an enzyme in the placenta deactivates cortisol, a stress hormone. But if the mother does not get proper nutrition, the enzyme fails. Cortisol reaches the fetal brain, increasing susceptibility to stress in adulthood. Cortisol can also raise blood pressure.

Diabetes 3

If a mother-to-be is diabetic, she may expose her fetus to high levels of glucose. This can stress the fetal pancreas, producing diabetes in adulthood. If weight is controlled, however, the risk of adult-onset diabetes decreases.

Obesity 2

Undernutrition during the fetus's first trimester makes obesity more likely in adulthood, perhaps because the appetite-control center in the brain is programmed to overeat.

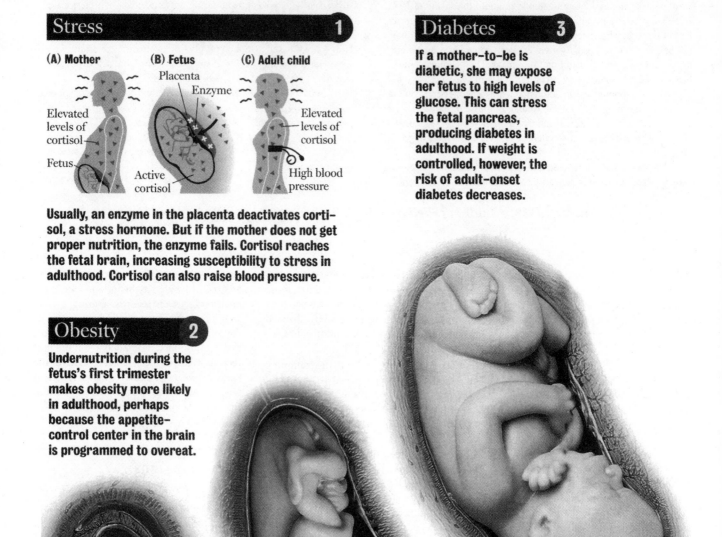

SECOND MONTH

FIFTH MONTH

SEVENTH MONTH

Graphic continued on next page.

men born in Hertfordshire and Sheffield, Barker found that a man who weighed less than 5.5 pounds at birth has a 50 percent greater chance of dying of heart disease than a man with a higher birth weight, even accounting for socioeconomic differences and other heart risks. "Death rates from both stroke and coronary heart disease tended to be highest in men whose birth weight had been low," says Barker, especially when it was low compared with their length or head size (an indication that

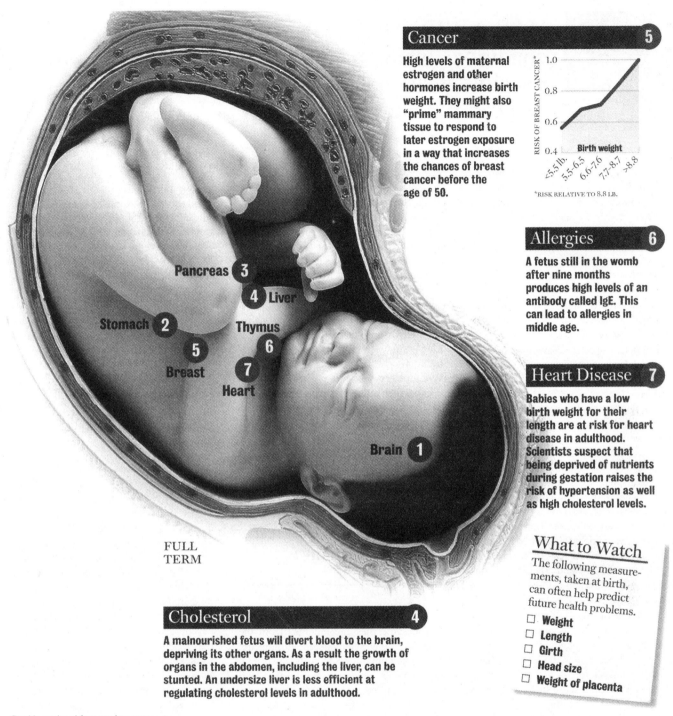

Cancer 5

High levels of maternal estrogen and other hormones increase birth weight. They might also "prime" mammary tissue to respond to later estrogen exposure in a way that increases the chances of breast cancer before the age of 50.

RISK OF BREAST CANCER*

1.0
0.8
0.6
0.4

Birth weight

<5.5 lb.   5.5-6.5   6.6-7.6   7.7-8.7   >8.8

*RISK RELATIVE TO 8.8 LB.

Allergies 6

A fetus still in the womb after nine months produces high levels of an antibody called IgE. This can lead to allergies in middle age.

Heart Disease 7

Babies who have a low birth weight for their length are at risk for heart disease in adulthood. Scientists suspect that being deprived of nutrients during gestation raises the risk of hypertension as well as high cholesterol levels.

Pancreas 3
4 Liver
Stomach 2
5
Breast
Thymus
6
7
Heart
Brain 1

FULL TERM

What to Watch

The following measurements, taken at birth, can often help predict future health problems.

☐ **Weight**
☐ **Length**
☐ **Girth**
☐ **Head size**
☐ **Weight of placenta**

Cholesterol 4

A malnourished fetus will divert blood to the brain, depriving its other organs. As a result the growth of organs in the abdomen, including the liver, can be stunted. An undersize liver is less efficient at regulating cholesterol levels in adulthood.

Graphic continued from previous page.

the baby's growth was stunted). Using other birth records from India, Barker found the same link in a 1996 study. Again, low birth weight predicted coronary heart disease, especially in the middle-aged: 11 percent of 42- to 62-year-olds who weighed 5.5 pounds or less at birth got it, compared with 3 percent of those born chubbier. The link between low birth weight and cardiovascular disease is now one of the strongest in the whole field of fetal programming, holding across conti-

nents as well as genders. Researchers led by Dr. Janet Rich-Edwards of Harvard reported, in 1997, that of 70,297 American women studied, those born weighing less than 5.5 pounds had a 23 percent higher risk of cardiovascular disease than women born heftier.

But it is not smallness per se that causes heart disease decades later. Instead, what seems to happen is that the same suboptimal conditions in the womb that stunt a baby's growth also saddle it with risk fac-

tors that lead to heart disease. "Birth weight is a proxy for something," says Rich-Edwards. "It's a marker for a complex set of factors that influence both growth in the womb and susceptibility to disease later on." Scientists have some suspects. Nathanielsz suggests it may be as simple as having undersized kidneys: these organs help regulate blood pressure, but if they are not up to the task, the result can be hypertension, a leading cause of heart disease. Or, animal studies have shown that if

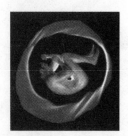

HARD WIRED: A fetus's response to conditions inside the uterus produces permanent physiological changes. But there's still plenty you can fix later.

a fetus does not receive adequate protein, then an enzyme in the placenta loses its punch and can no longer disarm harmful hormones trying to sneak into the fetus. One such hormone is cortisol. Cortisol raises blood pressure, as you are reminded every time stress makes your veins bulge. In the fetus, cortisol seems to raise the set point for blood pressure—irreversibly. "You are talking about hard-wiring the system," says Jonathan Seckl of the University of Edinburgh.

The discoveries are drawing throngs of excited scientists. A year ago the Society for Epidemiologic Research half-filled a small room at its annual meeting for a session on fetal programming. This spring the same subject packed a whole lecture hall. "This whole topic is just now catching fire," says Rich-Edwards. The surge in interest reflects the lengthening list of diseases that scientists are tracing back to the womb. The National Institutes of Health held a conference in January on the link between conditions in the womb and breast cancer; in September, another NIH confab examined the link to cardiovascular disease, kidney disease and other ills. A conference at Harvard will explore the topic in November.

The breast-cancer link is one of the most surprising. The very existence of the disease is bad enough. What terrifies women is that it strikes so many who have no known risk factors—such as age, close relatives with the disease or not bearing a child before 30. Dr. Karin Michels of the Harvard School of Public Health has identified one overlooked cause. After collecting health data from tens of thousands of nurses, Michels and colleagues reported in 1997 that women who had weighed about 5.5 pounds at birth had half the risk of breast cancer compared with women who had weighed about 9 pounds at birth. That was especially true of breast cancers in women 50 or younger. "There is increasing evidence," says Michels, "that breast cancer may originate before birth."

A very high birth weight may be a marker for uterine influences that "prime"

mammary tissue for cancer. Growth factors, living up to their name, make a fetus larger. Such factors include insulin, leptin and estrogen. If the mother has high levels of these substances (being obese raises levels of estrogen, for instance), and if they reach her fetus, the hormones may do more than act like Miracle-Gro on backyard tomatoes: they may alter nascent mammary tissue in such a way that it responds to estrogen during puberty by becoming malignant. This is no reason to starve your girl fetus—stunted fetal growth leads to other problems. But it does suggest that if you were a pudgy newborn you might want to be extra vigilant about breast exams.

Heart of the matter: Barker's discovery that birth weight is linked to cardiovascular disease in adulthood has launched a revolution in public health

The same message emerges from the other links that scientists are turning up. Weight and other traits at birth may offer a map of where your personal disease land mines are buried:

• Cholesterol: The smaller the abdomen at birth, the higher the cholesterol level in adulthood. What may happen is that if the mother is poorly nourished or if a problem with the placenta keeps the fetus from receiving adequate nutrition, then the fetus switches into emergency mode: it shunts blood to the brain, the most vital organ, at the expense of organs in the abdomen. That includes the liver, which plays a key role in regulating cholesterol levels. A smaller liver can't clear cholesterol as well as a hefty one. This suggests an answer to the longstanding puzzle of how some people can eat high-fat and cholesterol-laden

diets with impunity: these lucky folks were programmed as fetuses to process fat and cholesterol as efficiently as a sewage-treatment plant. The others have defective treatment plants. "When a fetus adapts to conditions in the womb," says Southampton's Barker, "that adaptation tends to be permanent."

• Obesity: This was the first trait suspected of reflecting life in the womb. In World War II, the Nazis tried to starve the population of western Holland from September 1944 until the following May (sidebar). Men who were fetuses during all or part of the period showed a telling pattern. If their mothers were starving during the first trimester—from March to May 1945—but got adequate food later, the men were born heavier, longer and with larger heads than babies in normal periods. As adults, they were more likely to be obese. If their mothers went hungry only in the final trimester—if the boys were born in November 1944, say—the men usually stayed svelte. What may happen is this: if food is scarce during the first trimester, the fetus develops a so-called thrifty phenotype. Its metabolism is set so that every available calorie sticks. Or, the availability or scarcity of food may affect the appetite centers in the fetal brain. In that case, undernutrition early in fetal life could dial up the appetite controls to the setting "eat whatever's around: you never know when famine will hit." An abundance of food early keeps the dial at "no need to pig out." Fetuses undernourished later in gestation may develop fewer fat cells (it is in the later months that most cells are added). That makes it harder to become fat after birth.

• Diabetes: Being skinny at birth puts an individual at high risk for diabetes in middle age, finds David Leon of the London School of Hygiene and Tropical Medicine. The effect is powerful: diabetes is three times more common in 60-year-old men who, as newborns, were in the bottom fifth on a scale of plumpness (technically, it's birth weight divided by length cubed) than in more rotund babies. "One explanation is that inadequate nutrition programs the fe-

What Moms Can Do Now

If you're pregnant, take advantage of the latest research to give your babies the best start. They'll thank you later.

OF COURSE THOSE nine months matter. Doctors now say that from the moment the sperm and egg fuse, conditions in your body determine how healthy your baby will be as an adult. Pediatricians can estimate risk for diseases by measuring length, weight, girth and head size at birth. Visit an obstetrician who's up on the latest research before you get pregnant and follow these guidelines:

Preconception care: A doctor can help you avoid medicines that harm embryos. Tell your obstetrician about any diseases or conditions you have that might complicate the pregnancy. If you're diabetic, make sure to take your insulin. To prevent neural-tube defects such as spina bifida, get at least 400 micrograms of folic acid a day from foods like leafy green vegetables and orange juice.

Meal plan: Eat about 300 extra calories a day during pregnancy. Snack or eat small meals throughout the day if you can't take large amounts of food. Your baby needs nutrients to grow normally, and you can't make up for lost calories by eating more later on.

The right stuff: Eat lots of carbohydrates, but don't skimp on fruits, vegetables, low-fat dairy products and lean meats. These foods contain protein, vitamins and minerals that build your baby's blood, bones and muscles.

Weight gain: Try to put on about 25 to 35 pounds if your weight is normal (more if you're on the thin side and less if you're fat). Focus on gaining weight, not watching calories. Your baby needs the extra nutrition to develop properly.

Drugs: Ask your doctor about any medications you take. Anticonvulsants and the acne drug Accutane can cause birth defects. Some antidepressants and painkillers may affect the baby, but don't stop taking them without consulting a doctor. Cocaine can kill a fetus, and babies born addicted to narcotics will suffer withdrawal after birth.

Caffeine: Your blood volume doubles during pregnancy, so a java overdose will dehydrate you when you need water most. Some research has linked excessive doses of caffeine to low birth weight, so limit yourself to a couple of cups a day.

Exercise: Staying in shape may ease labor and speed recovery after delivery. But don't exercise to exhaustion, and stay away from sports that expose your belly to trauma. Swimming and walking should be high on your list.

Stress: Reduce it. Both chronic and sudden, intense stress may increase the risk of premature labor by raising your levels of cortisol, a stress hormone. Try cutting back on work hours or joining a yoga class. And remember to get enough sleep.

Seat belts: Use them; your uterus and amniotic fluid prevent seat belts from injuring the fetus. Wear the lap belt below your belly, and adjust the shoulder strap so it rests between your breasts.

Alcohol: Doctors urge temperance during pregnancy. Excessive alcohol causes facial and heart defects, mental retardation and behavioral problems.

Smoking: Kick the habit now. Smoking contributes to 25 percent of cases of low birth weight and can cause miscarriage and premature birth.

STDs: Get tested. Untreated chlamydia, HIV, gonorrhea, syphilis and herpes cause a wide range of complications during pregnancy and childbirth.

ERIKA CHECK

---

tus to develop a thrifty metabolism," says Leon. "That includes insulin resistance, so the body saves and marshals existing glucose stores." When this metabolism meets junk food, the body is flooded with glucose and becomes diabetic. But diabetes is a prime example of how life in the womb is not an immutable sentence. Although thinness at birth raises the risk of developing diabetes in middle age, finds Leon, that risk is much reduced if you stay thin.

• Brain: Research on how life in the womb influences the brain is only beginning. But already there are hints, from both animal and human research, that something is going on. In a 1997 paper, biologists reported on a study of people with asymmetries in traits like feet, fingers, ears and elbows. IQs were lower in asymmetric people by about as much (percentagewise) as their measurements deviate from perfect symmetry. Some sort of stress during fetal development probably causes asymmetries, suggests Randy Thornhill of the University of New Mexico. The same stress may cause imperfections in the developing nervous system, leading to less efficient neurons for sensing, remembering and thinking. Here, too, asymmetry is a marker for something going wrong in the womb. Thornhill estimates that between 17 and 50 percent of IQ differences reflect in utero causes.

The new science of fetal programming suggests that we may have gone overboard in ascribing traits to genes. "Programming," concludes Nathanielsz, "is equally if not more important than our genes in determining how we perform mentally and physically." Consider one of the standard ways that scientists assess how much of a trait reflects genetic influences and how much reflects environment: they compare twins. If identical twins share a trait more than other siblings do, the trait is deemed to be largely under genetic control. But twins share something besides genes: a womb. Some of the concordance attributed to shared genes might instead reflect a shared uterine environment. The womb may have another effect. Merely *having* a gene is not enough to express the associated trait. The genes must be turned on to exert an effect, otherwise they are silent—just as having a collection of CDs doesn't mean that your home is filled with music unless you play them. In the womb, a flood of stress hormones may actually turn off genes associated with the stress response; the response becomes less effective, which is another way of saying this child is at risk of growing into an adult who can't handle stress. "The script written on the genes is altered by... the environment in the womb," says Nathanielsz.

As fetal programming becomes better understood, it may even resurrect the long-discredited theory known as Lamarckism. This idea holds that traits acquired by an organism during its lifetime can be passed on to children—that if a woman spends the 10 years before pregnancy whipping herself into a bodybuilder physique, her baby will emerge ready to pump iron. Modern genetics showed that inheritance does not work that way. But according to fetal programming, some traits a mother acquires can indeed be visited on her child. If she becomes diabetic, then she floods her fetus with glucose; waves of glucose may overwhelm the developing pancreas so that fetal cells that secrete insulin become exhausted. As a result, the child, too, becomes diabetic in adulthood. When this child becomes pregnant, she too, floods her fetus with glucose, stressing its pancreas and priming it for adult-onset diabetes. This baby will develop diabetes because of something that happened two generations before—a kind of grandmother effect.

In "Brave New World," Aldous Huxley describes how workers at the Central London Hatchery, where fetuses grow in special broths, adjust the ingredients of the amniotic soup depending on which kind of child they need. Children destined to work in chemical factories are treated so they can tolerate lead and cadmium; those destined to pilot rockets are constantly rotated so that they learn to enjoy being upside-down. The quest for the secrets of fetal programming won't yield up such simple recipes. But it is already showing that the seeds of health are planted even before you draw your first breath, and that the nine short months of life in the womb shape your health as long as you live.

With WILLIAM UNDERHILL *in London*

From *Newsweek*, September 27, 1999, pp. 50-57. © 1999 by Newsweek, Inc. All rights reserved. Reprinted by permission.

THE MYSTERY OF FETAL LIFE:
SECRETS OF THE WOMB

JOHN PEKKANEN

In the dim light of an ultrasound room, a wand slides over the abdomen of a young woman. As it emits sound waves, it allows us to see into her womb. The video screen brightens with a grainy image of a 20-week-old fetus. It floats in its amniotic sac, like an astronaut free of gravity.

The fetal face stares upward, then turns toward us, as if to mug for the camera. The sound waves strike different tissues with different densities, and their echoes form different images. These images are computer-enhanced, so although the fetus weights only 14 ounces and is no longer than my hand, we can see its elfin features.

Close up, we peek into the fetal brain. In the seconds we observe, a quarter million new brain cells are born. This happens constantly. By the end of the nine months, the baby's brain will hold 100 billion brain cells.

The sound waves focus on the chest, rendering images of a vibrating four-chambered heart no bigger than the tip of my little finger. The monitor tells us it is moving at 163 beats a minute. It sounds like a frightened bird fluttering in its cage.

We watch the rib cage move. Although the fetus lives in an airless environment, it "breathes" intermittently inside the womb by swallowing amniotic fluid. Some researchers speculate that the fetus is exercising its chest and diaphragm as its way of preparing for life outside the womb.

The clarity of ultrasound pictures is now so good that subtle abnormalities can be detected. The shape of the skull, brain, and spinal cord, along with the heart and other vital organs, can be seen in breathtaking detail.

In this ultrasound exam, there are no hints to suggest that anything is abnormal. The husband squeezes his wife's hand. They both smile.

The fetus we have just watched is at the midpoint of its 40-week gestation. At conception 20 weeks earlier, it began as a single cell that carried in its nucleus the genetic code for the human it will become.

After dividing and redividing for a week, it grew to 32 cells. Like the initial cell, these offspring cells carry 40,000 or so genes, located on 23 pairs of chromosomes inherited from the mother and father. Smaller than the head of a pin, this clump of cells began a slow journey down the fallopian tube and attached itself to the spongy wall of the uterus.

Once settled, some embryonic cells began to form a placenta to supply the embryo with food, water, and nutrients from the mother's bloodstream. The placenta also filtered out harmful substances in the mother's bloodstream. The embryo and mother exchange chemical information to ensure that they work together toward their common goal.

Instructed by their genes, the cells continued to divide but didn't always produce exact replicas. In a process still not well understood, the cells began to differentiate to seek out their own destinies. Some helped build internal organs, others bones, muscles, and brain.

At 19 days postconception, the earliest brain tissues began to form. They developed at the top end of the neural tube, a sheath of cells that ran nearly the entire length of the embryo.

The human brain requires virtually the entire pregnancy to emerge fully, longer than the other organ systems. Even in the earliest stage of development, the fetus knows to protect its brain. The brain gets the most highly oxygenated blood, and should there be any shortage, the fetus will send the available blood to the brain.

Extending downward from the brain, the neural tube began to form the spinal cord. At four weeks, a rudimentary heart started to beat, and four limbs began sprouting. By eight weeks, the two-inch-long embryo took human form and was more properly called a fetus. At 10 to 12 weeks, it began moving its arms and legs, opened its jaws, swallowed, and yawned, Mostly it slept.

"We are never more clever than we are as a fetus," says Dr. Peter Nathanielsz, a fetal researcher, obstetrician, and professor of reproductive medicine at Cornell University. "We pass far more biological milestones before we are born than we'll ever pass after we're born."

Not long ago, the process of fetal development was shrouded in mystery. But through the power of scanning techniques, biotechnology, and fetal and animal studies, much of the mystery of fetal life has been unveiled.

We now know that as the fetus matures it experiences a broad range of sensory stimulation. It hears, sees, tastes, smells, feels, and has rapid eye movement (REM) sleep, the sleep stage we associate with dreaming. From observation of its sleep and wake cycles, the fetus appears to know night from day. It learns and remembers, and it may cry. It seems to do everything in utero that it will do after it is born. In the words of one researcher, "Fetal life is us."

Studies now show that it's the fetus, not the mother, who sends the hormonal signals that determine when a baby will be born. And we've found out that its health in the womb depends in part on its mother's health when she was in the womb.

Finally, we've discovered that the prenatal environment is not as benign, or as neutral, as once thought. It is sensitive to the mother's health, emotions, and behavior.

The fetus is strongly affected by the mother's eating habits. If the mother exercises more than usual, the fetus may become temporarily short of oxygen. If she takes a hot bath, the fetus feels the heat. If she smokes, so does the fetus. One study has found that pregnant women exposed to more sunlight had more-outgoing children.

We now know that our genes do not encode a complete design for us, that our "genetic destiny" is not hard-wired at the time of conception. Instead, our development involves an interplay between genes and the environment, including that of the uterus. Because genes take "cues" from their environment, an expectant mother's physical and psychological health influences her unborn child's genetic well-being.

Factors such as low prenatal oxygen levels, stress, infections, and poor maternal nutrition may determine whether certain genes are switched on or off. Some researchers believe that our time in the womb is the single most important period of our life.

"Because of genetics, we once thought that we would unfold in the womb like a blueprint, but now we know it's not that simple," says Janet DiPietro, an associate professor of maternal and child health at the Johns Hopkins School of Public Health and one of a handful of fetal-behavior specialists. "The mother and the uterine environment she creates have a major impact on many aspects of fetal development, and a number of things laid down during that time remain with you throughout your life."

The impact of the womb on our intelligence, personality, and emotional and physical health is beginning to be understood. There's also an emerging understanding of something called fetal programming, which says that the effects of our life in the womb may be not felt until decades after we're born, and in ways that are more powerful than previously imagined.

Says Dr. Nathanielsz, whose book *Life in the Womb* details the emerging science of fetal development: "It's an area of great scientific importance that until recently remained largely unknown."

"I'm pregnant. Is it okay to have a glass of wine? Can I take my Prozac? What about a Diet Coke?"

Years ago, before she knew she was pregnant, a friend of mine had a glass of wine with dinner. When she discovered she was pregnant, she worried all through her pregnancy and beyond. She feels some guilt to this day, even though the son she bore turned out very well.

Many mothers have experienced the same tangled emotions. "There's no evidence that a glass of wine a day during pregnancy has a negative impact on the developing fetus," says Dr. John Larsen, professor and chair of obstetrics and gynecology at George Washington University. Larsen says that at one time doctors gave alcohol by IV to pregnant women who were experiencing preterm labor; it relaxed the muscles and quelled contractions.

Larsen now sometimes recommends a little wine to women who experience mild contractions after a puncture from an amniocentesis needle, and some studies suggest that moderate alcohol intake in pregnancy may prevent preterm delivery in some women.

Even though most experts agree with Larsen, the alcohol message that most women hear calls for total abstinence. Experts worry that declaring moderate alcohol intake to be safe in pregnancy may encourage some pregnant women to drink immoderately. They say that pregnant women who have an occasional drink should not think they've placed their baby at risk.

What is safe? Some studies show children born to mothers who consumed three drinks a day in pregnancy averaged seven points lower on IQ tests than unexposed children. There is evidence that six drinks a day during pregnancy puts babies at risk of fetal alcohol syndrome (FAS), a constellation of serious birth defects that includes mental retardation. The higher the alcohol intake, the higher the FAS risk.

Are there drugs and drug combinations that women should avoid or take with caution during pregnancy? Accutane (isotretinoin), a prescription drug for acne and psoriasis, is known to cause birth defects. So too are some anticonvulsant drugs, including Epitol, Tegretol, and Valproate. Tetracycline, a widely prescribed antibiotic, can cause bone-growth delays and permanent teeth problems for a baby if a mother takes it during pregnancy.

Most over-the-counter drugs are considered safe in pregnancy, but some of them carry risks. Heavy doses of aspirin and other nonsteroidal anti-inflammatory drugs such as ibuprofen can delay the start of labor. They are also linked to a life-threatening disorder of newborns called persistent pulmonary hypertension (PPHN), which diverts airflow away from the baby's lungs, causing oxygen depletion. The March issue of the journal

Pediatrics published a study linking these nonprescription pain-killers to PPHN, which results in the death of 15 percent of the infants who have it.

OTC DRUGS

In 1998, researchers at the University of Nebraska Medical Center reported dextromethorphan, a cough suppressant found in 40 or more OTC drugs including Nyquil, Tylenol Cold, Dayquil, Robitussin Maximum Strength, and Dimetapp DM, caused congenital malformations in chick embryos. The research was published in *Pediatric Research* and supported by the National Institutes of Health.

Although no connection between dextromethorphan and human birth defects has been shown, the Nebraska researchers noted that similar genes regulate early development in virtually all species. For this reason, the researchers predicted that dextromethorphan, which acts on the brain to suppress coughing, would have the same harmful effect on a human fetus.

Many women worry about antidepressants. Some need them during pregnancy or took them before they knew they were pregnant. A study published in the *New England Journal of Medicine* found no association between fetal exposure to antidepressants and brain damage. The study compared the IQ, temperament, activity level, and distractibility of more than 125 children whose mothers took antidepressants in pregnancy with 84 children whose mothers took no drugs known to harm the fetus.

The two groups of children, between 16 months and eight years old when tested, were comparable in every way. The antidepressants taken by the mothers included both tricyclates such as Elavil and Tofranil and selective serotonin reuptake inhibitors such as Prozac.

Not all mood-altering drugs may be safe. There is some evidence that minor tranquilizers taken for anxiety may cause developmental problems if taken in the first trimester, but there is no hard proof of this. Evidence of fetal damage caused by illegal drugs such as cocaine is widely accepted, as is the case against cigarette smoking. A 1998 survey found that 13 percent of all mothers who gave birth smoked. Evidence is striking that cigarette smoking in pregnancy lowers birth weight and increases the risks of premature birth, attention deficit hyperactive disorder, and diminished IQ.

A long-running study based on information from the National Collaborative Perinatal Project found that years after they were born, children were more apt to become addicted to certain drugs if their mother took them during delivery.

"We found drug-dependent individuals were five times more likely to have exposure to high doses of painkillers and anesthesia during their delivery than their nonaddicted siblings," says Stephen Buka of the Harvard School of Public Health. Buka suspects this is caused by a modification in the infant's brain receptors as the drugs pass from mother to child during an especially sensitive time.

CAFFEINE

Coffee consumption has worried mothers because there have been hints that caffeine may be harmful to the fetus. Like most things in life, moderation is the key. There's no evidence that 300 milligrams of caffeine a day (about three cups of coffee, or four or five cups of most regular teas, or five to six cola drinks) harms a developing baby. Higher caffeine consumption has been weakly linked to miscarriage and difficulty in conceiving.

Expectant mothers concerned about weight gain should be careful of how much of the artificial sweetener aspartame they consume. Marketed under brand names such as NutraSweet and Equal, it's found in diet soft drinks and foods.

The concern is this: In the body, aspartame converts into phenylalanine, a naturally occurring amino acid we ingest when we eat protein. At high levels, phenylalanine can be toxic to brain cells.

When we consume phenylalanine in protein, we also consume a number of other amino acids that neutralize any ill effects. When we consume it in aspartame, we get none of the neutralizing amino acids to dampen phenylalanine's impact. And as it crosses the placenta, phenylalanine's concentrations are magnified in the fetal brain.

If a fetal brain is exposed to high levels of phenylalanine because its mother consumes a lot of aspartame, will it be harmed? One study found average IQ declines of ten points in children born to mothers with a fivefold increase of phenylalanine blood levels in pregnancy. That's a lot of aspartame, and it doesn't mean an expectant mother who drinks moderate amounts of diet soda need worry.

Researchers say consuming up to three servings of aspartame a day—in either diet soda or low-calorie foods—appears to be safe for the fetus. However, a pregnant woman of average weight who eats ten or more servings a day may put her unborn baby at risk. In testimony before Congress, Dr. William Pardridge, a neuroscience researcher at UCLA, said it's likely that the effect of high phenylalanine levels in the fetal brain "will be very subtle" and many not manifest until years later.

One wild card concerns the 10 to 20 million Americans who unknowingly carry a gene linked to a genetic disease called phenylketonuria (PKU), which can lead to severe mental retardation. Most carriers don't know it, because PKU is a recessive genetic disorder, and both mother and father must carry the defective gene to pass PKU on to their child. A carrier feels no ill effects. According to researchers, a pregnant woman who unknowingly carries the PKU gene might place her unborn child at risk if she consumes even relatively moderate amounts of aspartame. There is no hard evidence that this will happen, but it remains a serious concern. PKU can be detected in the fetus by amniocentesis; a restrictive diet can prevent the worst effects of PKU on the child.

How does a mother's getting an infection affect her unborn baby? And should she be careful of cats?

Many experts think pregnant women should be more concerned about infections and household pets than a glass of wine or can of diet drink. There's overwhelming evidence of the potential harm of infections during pregnancy. We've known for a long time that rubella (German measles), a viral infection, can cause devastating birth defects.

More worrisome are recent studies showing that exposure to one of the most common of winter's ills—influenza—may put an unborn child at risk of cognitive and emotional problems. If flu strikes in the second trimester, it may increase the unborn baby's risk of developing schizophrenia later in life. While the flu may be a trigger, it's likely that a genetic susceptibility is also needed for schizophrenia to develop.

Some evidence exists that maternal flu may also lead to dyslexia, and suspicions persist that a first-trimester flu may cause fetal neural-tube defects resulting in spina bifida. The common cold, sometimes confused with the flu, has not been linked to any adverse outcomes for the baby.

"Infections are probably the most important thing for a pregnant woman to protect herself against," says Lise Eliot, a developmental neurobiologist at the Chicago Medical School. "She should always practice good hygiene, like washing her hands frequently, avoiding crowds, and never drinking from someone else's cup." She adds that the flu vaccine has been approved for use during pregnancy.

Some researchers recommend that pregnant women avoid close contact with cats. Toxoplasmosis, a parasitic infection, can travel from a cat to a woman to her unborn child.

Most humans become infected through cat litter boxes. An infected woman might experience only mild symptoms, if any, so the illness usually goes undetected. If she is diagnosed with the infection, antiparasitic drugs are helpful, but they don't completely eliminate the disease. The infection is relatively rare, and the odds of passing it from mother to child are only one in five during the first two trimesters, when the fetal harm is most serious. The bad news is that a fetus infected by toxoplasmosis can suffer severe brain damage, including mental retardation and epilepsy. Some researchers also suspect it may be a latent trigger for serious mental illness as the child grows older.

CEREBRAL PALSY

An expectant mother may not realize she has potentially harmful infections. The prime suspects are infections in the reproductive tract. Researchers suspect most cerebral-palsy cases are not caused by delivery problems, as has been widely assumed. There's strong evidence that some cases of cerebral-palsy may be linked to placental infections that occur during uterine life. Other cerebral-palsy cases may be triggered by oxygen deprivation in early development, but very few appear to be caused by oxygen deprivation during delivery. It's now estimated that only 10 percent of cerebral-palsy cases are related to delivery problems.

Maternal urinary-tract infections have been linked to lower IQs in children. Another infection, cytomegalovirus (CMV), has been linked to congenital deafness. Sexually transmitted diseases such as chlamydia are suspected to be a trigger for pre-term birth. Despite the serious threat posed to developing babies, infections during pregnancy remain poorly understood.

"We just don't know right now when or how the uterine infections that really make a difference to the fetus are transmitted in pregnancy," says Dr. Karin Nelson, a child neurologist and acting chief of the neuro-epidemiology branch of the National Institute of Neurologic Disorders and Stroke at NIH. "Nor do we know all the potential problems they may cause."

Because of this, researchers offer little in the way of recommendations other than clean living and careful sex. They recommend that any woman contemplating pregnancy get in her best physical condition, because a number of studies have found that a woman's general health before she becomes pregnant is vital to fetal health. They also recommend a thorough gynecological exam because it may detect a treatable infection that could harm the fetus.

Rachel Carson was right about pesticides. So if you're pregnant, how careful should you be about what you eat?

In her book *Silent Spring,* author Rachel Carson noted that when pregnant mammals were exposed to synthetic pesticides, including DDT and methoxychlor, the pesticides caused developmental abnormalities in offspring. Carson, a scientist, noted that some pesticides mimicked the female hormone estrogen and caused the male offspring to be feminized.

About the time of Carson's 1962 book, another story was emerging about diethylstilbestrol (DES), a man-made female hormone administered in the 1940s and '50s to prevent miscarriages. In the 1960s it became clear that many young daughters of DES mothers were turning up reproductive malformations and vaginal cancers. Sons born to DES mothers suffered reproductive problems, including undescended testicles and abnormal sperm counts.

ENDOCRINE DISRUPTERS

Over the years, suspicion grew from both animal and human studies that something in the environment was disrupting fetal development. In the 1990s it was given a name—endocrine disruption. The theory was that DES and the pesticides cited by Carson caused defects in offspring because they disrupted the normal endocrine process. They did this by mimicking hormones inside the human body.

It's now clear that DDT and DES are the tip of the iceberg. Today more than 90,000 synthetic chemicals are used, most made after World War II. New chemicals are produced every week. They are used in everything from pesticides to plastics.

How many of these man-made chemicals might act as endocrine disrupters? More than 50 have been identified, and hundreds more are suspects.

To understand the threat from endocrine disrupters, it helps to understand what human hormones do. Secreted by endocrine glands, these tiny molecules circulate through the bloodstream to the organs. They include estrogen, adrenalin, thyroid, melatonin, and testosterone. Each is designed to fit only into a specific receptor on a cell, like a key that fits only one lock. When a hormone connects with the cell receptor, it enters the cell's nucleus. Once there, the hormone acts as a signaling agent to direct the cell's DNA to produce specific proteins.

During fetal life, the right type and concentration of hormones must be available at the right time for normal fetal development to occur. Produced by both mother and fetus, hormones are involved in cell division and differentiation, the development of the brain and reproductive organs, and virtually everything else needed to produce a baby.

"We know from animal experiments and wildlife observations that periods in development are very sensitive to alterations in the hormone levels," says Robert Kavlock, director of reproductive toxicology for the Environmental Protection Agency.

The damage is done when chemical mimickers get into cells at the wrong time, or at the wrong strength, or both. When this happens, something in the fetus will not develop as it should.

After years of witnessing the harmful impact on wildlife, we now know that humans are not immune to endocrine disrupters. More troubling, because of the pervasiveness of these chemicals, is that we can't escape them. We get them in the food we eat, the water we drink, the products we buy.

One of the most dramatic examples came to light in the 1970s when researchers wanted to find out why so many babies born in the Great Lakes region suffered serious neurological defects. They found the answer in polychlorinated biphenyls (PCBs), organic chemicals once used in electrical insulation and adhesives. Heavy PCB contamination of Great Lakes fish eaten by the mothers turned out to be the cause.

It is not clear how PCBs cause fetal brain damage, but it's believed to happen when they disrupt thyroid hormones. Severe thyroid deficiency in pregnancy is known to cause mental retardation. Another study found reduced penis size in boys born to mothers exposed to high levels of PCBs.

The U.S. manufacture of PCBs ended in 1977. PCB levels found in the mothers and the fish they ate suggested at the time that only very high exposure caused a problem for developing babies. Now we know this isn't true.

Because PCBs don't break down, they've remained a toxin that continues to enter our bodies through the food we eat. They have leached into soil and water and are found in shellfish and freshwater fish and to a smaller degree in ocean fish. Bottom-feeding freshwater fish, such as catfish and carp, have the highest PCB concentrations.

PCBs store in fat tissue and are found in dairy products and meats. Fatty meats, especially processed meats like cold cuts, sausages, and hot dogs, are usually heaviest in PCBs. They get into these products because farm animals graze on PCB-contaminated land. However, eating fish from PCB-contaminated water remains the primary way we get these chemicals into our systems. In pregnant women, PCBs easily cross the placenta and circulate in the fetus.

PCBs are ubiquitous. They've been detected in the Antarctic snow. If you had detection equipment sensitive enough, you'd find them in the milk at the supermarket.

What concerns experts are findings from studies in the Netherlands and upstate New York that found even low maternal PCB exposures pose risk to a fetus.

The Dutch study followed 418 children from birth into early childhood. In the final month of pregnancy, researchers measured the maternal PCB blood levels, and at birth they measured PCB levels in the umbilical cord. None of the mothers was a heavy fish eater or had any history of high PCB exposure, and none of their PCB levels was considered high by safety standards.

At 3 1/2 years of age, the children's cognitive abilities were assessed with tests. After adjusting for other variables, the researchers found that maternal and cord blood PCB levels correlated with the children's cognitive abilities. As the PCB blood levels went up, the children suffered more attention problems and their cognitive abilities went down. It should be noted that the brain damage in these Dutch children was not devastating. They were not retarded or autistic. But on a relative scale, they had suffered measurable harm.

The Dutch researchers concluded that the in utero PCB exposure, and not any postnatal exposure, caused the children's brain damage. The study also revealed that these children had depressed immune function.

"All we can say now," says Deborah Rice, a toxicologist at the EPA's National Center for Environmental Assessment in Washington, "is we have strong evidence that PCB levels commonly found among women living in industrialized society can cause subtle neurological damage in their offspring." But one of the difficulties, according to Rice, is that we really don't yet know what an unsafe maternal PCB level might be.

"I think the bottom line is that women should be aware of PCBs and aware of what they're putting in their mouth," adds Rice.

The Dutch study is a warning not only about the potential impact of low levels of PCBs but about the potential harm from low levels of other endocrine disrupters.

More news arrived in March when the results from the federal government's on-going Fourth National Health and Nutrition Examination Survey (NHANES) became public. The survey of 38,000 people revealed that most of us have at least trace levels of pesticides, heavy metals, and plastics in our body tissues. In all, NHANES tested for 27 elements.

The survey found widespread exposure to phthalates, synthetic chemicals used as softeners in plastics and other products. Phthalates are one of the most heavily produced chemicals and have been linked in animal studies to endocrine disruption and birth defects. The likely sources of human exposure are foods and personal-care products such as shampoos, lotions, soaps, and perfumes; phthalates are absorbed through the skin.

Dr. Ted Schettler, a member of the Greater Boston Physicians for Social Responsibility, suspects endocrine disrupters may be linked to increases in the three hormone-driven cancers—breast, prostate, and testicular. The rate of testicular cancer among young men has nearly doubled in recent years, and the rates of learning disabilities and infertility also have increased.

"We can't blame all that is happening on toxic chemicals," says Schettler, who coauthored *In Harm's Way,* a report on how chemical contaminants affect human health. "But we need to ask ourselves if we're seeing patterns that suggest these chemicals are having a major impact on fetal development and human populations. We also need to ask what level of evidence we're going to need before we take public-health measures. That's a political question."

The EPA's Kavlock says, "We don't know the safe or unsafe levels for many of these chemicals." Nor do we know how many of the thousands of man-made chemicals in the environment will turn out to be endocrine disrupters or cause human harm. The EPA received a mandate from Congress in 1996 to find the answers, but it will be a long wait.

"If we devoted all the toxicology testing capacity in the entire world to look for endocrine-disrupting chemicals, we couldn't do all the chemicals. There's just not enough capacity," Kavlock says. "So we are focusing on 500 to 1,000 chemicals that are the major suspects. It will take many years and a lot of money just to understand how they interact with hormonal-system and fetal development."

What is all this bad stuff we can get from eating fish or from microwaving food in plastics? Do vitamins help?

Methylmercury is a heavy metal that can cause fetal brain damage. NHANES revealed that 10 percent of American women of child-bearing age—a representative sample of all American women—had methylmercury blood and hair levels close to "potentially hazardous levels." The EPA and some nongovernment experts consider these existing methylmercury levels already above what is safe.

Dr. Jill Stein, an adolescent-medicine specialist and instructor at Harvard Medical School, has studied methylmercury's toxicity. She says the acceptable levels of methylmercury in the NHANES report were too high and that many more women are in the danger zone. "The NHANES data tells me that more than 10 percent of American women today are carrying around enough mercury to put their future children at risk for learning and behavior problems," she says.

Like PCBs and other toxic chemicals, mercury is hard to avoid because it is abundant in our environment. It comes from natural and man-made sources, chiefly coal-fired power plants and municipal waste treatment. Each year an estimated 160 tons of mercury is released into the nation's environment. In water, mercury combines with natural bacteria to form methylmercury, a toxic form of the metal. It is easily absorbed by fish. When a pregnant woman consumes the contaminated fish, methylmercury crosses the placenta and the fetal blood-brain barrier.

The world became aware of methylmercury's potential for harm more than 40 years ago in the fishing village of Minamata in Japan. People there were exposed to high levels of the heavy metal from industrial dumping of mercury compounds into Minamata Bay. The villagers, who ate a diet heavy in fish caught in the bay, experienced devastating effects. The hardest hit were the unborn. Women gave birth to babies with cerebral-palsy-like symptoms. Many were retarded.

MERCURY

Fish are the major source of mercury for humans. The Food and Drug Administration recommends that pregnant women not eat swordfish, king mackerel, shark, and tilefish. These fish are singled out because large oceangoing fish contain more methylmercury. Smaller ocean fish, especially cod, haddock, and pollock, generally have low methylmercury levels. A whitefish found off the coast of Alaska, pollock is commonly found in fish sticks and fast-food fish. Salmon have low methylmercury levels, but they are a fatty fish and apt to carry higher levels of PCBs.

Like the Dutch PCB studies, recent studies of maternal methylmercury exposure have turned up trouble. They've shown that the so-called "safe" maternal levels of the metal can cause brain damage during fetal development.

One study was carried out in the 1990s by a Danish research team that studied 917 children in the Faroe Islands, where seafood is a big part of the diet. Children were grouped into categories depending on their level of maternal methylmercury exposure; they were assessed up to age seven by neurological tests. None of the children's methylmercury exposure levels was considered high, yet many of the children had evidence of brain damage, including memory, attention, and learning problems.

"Subtle effects on brain function therefore seem to be detectable at prenatal methylmercury exposure levels currently considered safe," the study concluded. In a follow-up report published in a 1999 issue of the *Journal of the American Medical Association,* the authors said the blood concentrations of methylmercury found in the umbilical cord corresponded with the severity of the neurological damage suffered by the children.

In a study of 237 children, New Zealand researchers found similar neurological harm, including IQ impairment and attention problems, in children whose mothers' exposure to methylmercury came from fish they ate during pregnancy.

"The children in these studies were not bathed in methylmercury," notes Rita Schoeny, a toxicologist in the EPA's Office of Water. "Can people in the U.S. be exposed to the same levels of mercury in the course of their dietary practice? We think so."

Jill Stein and other experts worry that the more scientific studies we do, the more we'll realize that in fetal development there may be no such thing as a "safe" maternal level for methylmercury, PCBs, and scores of other synthetic chemicals.

"We keep learning from studies that these chemicals are harmful to fetal development at lower and lower doses," Stein says. "It's what we call the declining threshold of harm."

What about canned tuna? It has been assumed to contain low methylmercury levels because most of it comes from smaller fish. The FDA offers no advisories about it. But according to EPA researchers, a recent State of Florida survey of more than 100 samples of canned tuna found high levels of methylmercury. The more-expensive canned tuna, such as albacore and solid white tuna, usually carried higher methylmercury levels, according to the survey. This apparently is because more expensive canned tuna comes from larger tuna. In some of the canned tuna, the methylmercury levels were high enough to prevent their export to several countries, including Canada.

Some of the methylmercury levels were "worrisomely high," according to Kathryn Mahaffey, a toxicologist and director of the division of exposure assessment at the EPA. They were high enough to cause concern for pregnant women.

"A big problem is the tremendous variability out there in the tuna supply," adds Stein. "You have no idea when you're eating a can of tuna how much methylmercury you're getting."

"Even if you ate just a small serving of some of these canned tunas each day," says Mahaffey, "you'd be substantially above a level we would consider safe."

Mahaffey and Stein agree that an expectant mother who ate even a few servings a week with methylmercury levels found in some of the canned tuna would put her developing baby at risk of brain and other neurological damage.

Now that we know a developing fetus is sensitive to even low levels of toxic chemicals, women can exercise some basic precautions to help protect their developing babies.

Don't microwave food that is wrapped in plastic or is still in plastic containers. "There are endocrine-disrupting chemicals in these plastics," Schettler says, "that leach right into the food when it's microwaved. This has been well documented and measured." Studies suggest that even at very low levels these chemicals can have an adverse effect on the fetus's hormonal system.

The EPA's Kavlock considers the fruits and vegetables you buy at the supermarket to be safe in pregnancy, but Schettler says you should try to eat organic foods to avoid even trace amounts of pesticides. Wash fruits and vegetables before eating them. Avoid pesticides or insecticide use around the house during pregnancy as well as the use of chemical solvents for painting or remodeling.

Herbicides and pesticides have leached into reservoirs that supply home drinking water, and filtration plants can't remove them all. Some are known to be endocrine disrupters. Home water filters can reduce contaminants; the best ones use active charcoal as a filtering agent.

Experts agree that a pregnant woman, or a woman who may get pregnant, can eat fish but should be careful about the kind she eats and how much of it. EPA's Rice cautions any woman who is pregnant or thinking of becoming pregnant to avoid eating any sport fish caught in a lake or river.

VEGETABLE FATS
Rice adds that the PCB risk with fish can be reduced. "Trim the fish of fat and skin, and broil or grill it," see says. "That way you cook off fat and minimize your PCB exposure." There is not much you can do to reduce the methylmercury levels in fish because it binds to protein.

"Fat is important for a baby's neurological development before and after birth, so pregnant women should consider vegetable fats like olive oil and flaxseed oil as a source," Rice adds. She says low fat dairy and meat products carry fewer PCBs than higher-fat ones.

The EPA has issued a PCB advisory for the Potomac River in the District, Virginia, and Maryland, citing in particular catfish and carp. You can go to *www.epa.gov/ost/fish/epafish.pdf* for EPA advisories on PCB and methylmercury environmental contamination. From there you can connect to state Web sites for advisories on local waters and specific fish.

Women can help prevent neurological and other birth defects by taking vitamin supplements before pregnancy. A daily dose of 400 micrograms of folic acid can reduce the risk of such problems as spina bifida by more than 70 percent as well as prevent brain defects and cleft lip and palate. Indirect evidence from a study published last year in the *New England Journal of Medicine* suggests that folic acid may also help prevent congenital heart defects.

To be effective, folic acid should be taken before pregnancy to prevent developmental defects. Folic acid comes in multivitamins and prenatal vitamins and is found naturally in legumes, whole-wheat bread, citrus fruits, fortified breakfast cereal, and leafy green vegetables. Despite the proven value of folic acid, a recent March of Dimes survey found that only 32 percent of American women of childbearing age—including pregnant women—took folic-acid supplements.

What can a fetus learn in the womb? And does playing Mozart make a baby lots smarter?

Developmental psychologist Anthony DeCasper wanted to answer two questions: What does a fetus know, and when does it know it?

DeCasper's aim was to find out if a fetus could learn in utero and remember what it learned after it was born. He enlisted the help of 33 healthy expectant mothers and asked each to tape-record herself reading passages from Dr. Seuss's *The Cat in the Hat* or from another children's book, *The King, the Mice, and the Cheese*. The mothers were randomly assigned to play one of these readings, each of which lasted two or three minutes, to their unborn children three times a day during the final three weeks of their pregnancies.

DeCasper, a professor of developmental psychology at the University of North Carolina at Greensboro, could do the experiment because it was known that fetuses could hear by the third trimester and probably earlier. DeCasper had shown earlier that at birth, babies preferred their mother's voice to all other voices. Studies in the early 1990s found that fetuses could be soothed by lullabies and sometimes moved in rhythm to their mother's voice. Fetuses hear their mother's voice from the outside, just as they can hear any other voice, but they hear the mother's voice clearer and stronger through bone conduction as it resonates inside her.

A little more than two days after birth, each of the newborns in DeCasper's study was given a specially devised nipple. The device worked by utilizing the baby's sucking reflex. When the baby sucked on the nipple, it would hear its mother's voice. But if it paused for too long a time between sucks, it would hear another woman's voice. This gave the baby control over whose voice it would hear by controlling the length of its pause between sucks.

DeCasper also placed small earphones over the infant's ears through which it could hear its mother's voice read from the books.

"Now two days or so after it was born, the baby gets to choose between two stories read by its own mother," DeCasper said. "One was the story she'd recited three times a day for the last three weeks of pregnancy, and the other is one the baby's never heard before, except for the one day his mother recorded it. So the big question was: Would the babies prefer the story they'd heard in the womb, or wouldn't they? The answer was a clear yes—the babies preferred to hear the familiar story."

DeCasper did a second experiment by having women who were not the baby's mothers recite the same two stories. The babies again showed a strong preference for the story they'd heard in the womb.

"These studies not only tell us something about the fidelity with which the fetal ear can hear," DeCasper says, "but they also show that during those two or three weeks in the womb, fetal learning and memory are occurring."

British researchers observed expectant mothers who watched a TV soap opera. The researchers placed monitors on the mother's abdomens to listen in on fetal movements when the program aired. By the 37th week of pregnancy, the babies responded to the show's theme music by increasing their movements, an indication they remembered it.

Soon after the babies were born, the researchers replayed the theme music to them. This time, instead of moving more, the babies appeared to calm down and pay attention to the music. The researchers considered this a response to familiar music.

FETAL MEMORY

"The fact that we find evidence of fetal memory doesn't mean fetuses carry conscious memories, like we remember what we ate for breakfast," explains Lise Eliot, author of *What's Going On in There?*, a book on early brain development. "But we now know there is a tremendous continuity from prenatal to postnatal life, and the prenatal experience begins to shape a child's interaction with the world it will confront after birth. Babies go through the same activity patterns and behavioral states before and after birth. Well before it is born, the baby is primed to gravitate to its mother and its mother's voice."

Some researchers speculate a baby's ability to remember in the womb may be a way of easing its transition from prenatal life to postnatal life. A baby already accustomed to and comforted by its mother's voice may be reassured as it enters a new world of bright lights, needle pricks, curious faces, and loud noises.

The question arises: Can the uterine environment affect a baby's intelligence? Twins studies have shown that genes exert an all-powerful influence on IQ. The role of environment in IQ has traditionally meant the nurturance and stimulation the baby receives after birth.

Bernie Devlin, a biostatistician and assistant professor of psychiatry at the University of Pittsburgh, did an analysis of 212 twins studies on intelligence. In a paper published in *Nature,* he concluded that the accepted figure of 60 to 80 percent for IQ heritability is too high. It should be closer to 50 percent, he says, which leaves more room for environmental factors. Devlin says the one environmental factor that's been missing in understanding human intelligence is time in the womb.

"I'm surprised that the impact of fetal life on a child's intelligence had not been accounted for in these IQ studies," Devlin says. "I know it's very complicated, but it's surprising that people who study the heritability of intelligence really haven't considered this factor."

What is the impact of life in the womb on intelligence? Devlin thinks it's equal to if not greater than the impact of a child's upbringing. In other words, it's possible a mother may have more influence over her child's intelligence before birth than after.

As the brain develops in utero, we know it undergoes changes that affect its ultimate capacity. Nutritional and hormonal influences from the mother have a big impact. And twins studies show that the heavier twin at birth most often has the higher IQ.

A number of studies from the United States and Latin America also found that a range of vitamins, as well as sufficient protein in the mother's prenatal diet, had an impact on the child's intelligence.

Links between specific vitamins and intelligence have been borne out in two studies. An animal study conducted at the University of North Carolina and published in the March issue of *Developmental Brain Research* found that rats with a choline deficiency during pregnancy gave birth to offspring with severe brain impairments. Choline, a B-complex vitamin involved in nerve transmission, is found in eggs, meat, peanuts, and dietary supplements.

The August 1999 issue of the *New England Journal of Medicine* reported that expectant mothers with low thyroid function gave birth to children with markedly diminished IQs as well as motor and attention deficits. The study said one cause of hypothyroidism—present in 2 to 3 percent of American women—is a lack of iodine in the American diet. Women whose hypothyroidism was detected and treated before pregnancy had children with normal test scores. Hypothyroidism can be detected with a blood test, but expectant mothers who receive little or late prenatal care often go undiagnosed or are diagnosed too late to help their child.

Although most American women get the nutrition they need through diet and prenatal vitamins, not all do. According to a National Center for Health Statistics survey, more than one in four expectant mothers in the U.S. received inadequate prenatal care.

Devlin's *Nature* article took a parting shot at the conclusions reached in the 1994 book *The Bell Curve,* in which Richard J. Herrnstein and Charles Murray argued that different social classes are a result of genetically determined, and therefore unalterable, IQ levels. The lower the IQ, the argument goes, the lower the social class.

Not only does the data show IQ to be far less heritable than that book alleges, Devlin says, but he suspects improvements in the health status of mostly poor expectant mothers would see measurable increases in the IQs of their offspring.

Devlin's argument is supported by Randy Thornhill, a biologist at the University of New Mexico. Thornhill's research suggests that IQ differences are due in part to what he calls "heritable vulnerabilities to environmental sources of developmental stress." In other words, vulnerable genes interact with environmental insults in utero resulting in gene mutations that affect fetal development. Thornhill says environmental insults may include viruses, maternal drug abuse, or poor nutrition.

"The developmental instability that results," Thornhill says, "is most readily seen in the body's asymmetry when one side of the body differs from the other. For example, on average an individual's index fingers will differ in length by about two millimeters. Some people have much more asymmetries than others."

But the asymmetries we see on the outside also occur in the nervous system. When this happens, neurons are harmed and memory and intelligence are impaired. Thornhill says the more physical asymmetries you have, the more neurological impairment you have. He calculates that these factors can account for as much as 50 percent of the differences we find in IQ.

Thornhill adds that a fetus that carries these genetic vulnerabilities, but develops in an ideal uterine environment, will not experience any serious problems because the worrisome mutations will not occur.

"The practical implications for this are tremendous," Thornhill says. "If we can understand what environmental factors most disrupt fetal development of the nervous system, then we'll be in a position to remove them and have many more intelligent people born."

Studies on fetal IQ development suggest that the current emphasis on nurturance and stimulation for young children be rethought. The philosophy behind initiatives such as Zero to Three and Early Head Start makes sense. The programs are based on evidence that the first three years are very important for brain development and that early stimulation can effect positive changes in a child's life. But Devlin and Thornhill's research suggests a stronger public-health emphasis on a baby's prenatal life if we are to equalize the opportunities for children.

Does that mean unborn babies need to hear more Mozart? Companies are offering kits so expectant mothers can play music or different sounds to their developing babies—the prenatal "Mozart effect." One kit promises this stimulation will lead to "longer new-born attention span, better sleep patterns, accelerated development, expanded cognitive powers, enhanced social awareness and extraordinary language abilities." Will acceptance to Harvard come next?

"The number of bogus and dangerous devices available to expectant parents to make their babies smarter constantly shocks me," says DiPietro. "All these claims are made without a shred of evidence to support them."

Adds DeCasper: "I think it is dangerous to stimulate the baby in the womb. If you play Mozart and it remembers Mozart, is it going to be a smarter baby? I haven't got a clue. Could it hurt the baby? Yes, I think it could. If you started this stimulation too early and played it too loud, there is evidence from animal studies that you can destroy the ear's ability to hear sounds in a particular range. That's an established fact. Would I take a risk with my fetus? No!"

DeCasper and other researches emphasize that no devices or tricks can enhance the brainpower of a developing baby. Their advice to the expectant mother: Take the best possible care of yourself.

"The womb is a quiet, protective place for a reason," DiPietro concludes. "Nature didn't design megaphones to be placed on the abdomen. The fetus gets all the stimulation it needs for its brain to develop."

Mr. Pekkanen is a contributing editor to The Washingtonian. *From* "Secrets of the Womb," *by John Pekkanen,* The Washingtonian, *August 2001, pages 44–51, 126–135.*

From *Current*, September 2001, pp. 20-29. © 2001 by Current.

UNIT 2

Development During Infancy and Early Childhood

Unit Selections

Key Points to Consider

- What are the four new ways of thinking about infant development that all parents and caregivers should know?

- Of vision, hearing, taste, touch, and smell, which sense is most developed at birth? Which is least well developed?

- What is "normal" in the development of physical and socioemotional milestones?

- What purpose is served by involving babies in hectic activity schedules and introducing them to academics as early as possible?

- What is the "Mozart effect"? What does it have to do with cognitive development?

- How should caregivers respond to little children's sexual behaviors and questions?

- When should children know right from wrong? How is it learned?

 **Links: www.dushkin.com/online/**
These sites are annotated in the World Wide Web pages.

Aggression and Cooperation: Helping Young Children Develop Constructive Strategies
http://ericps.crc.uiuc.edu/eece/pubs/digests/1992/jewett92.html

Children's Nutrition Research Center (CNRC)
http://www.bcm.tmc.edu/cnrc/

Early Childhood Care and Development
http://www.ecdgroup.com

Zero to Three: National Center for Infants, Toddlers, and Families
http://www.zerotothree.org

Hundreds of thousands of studies have linked various environmental variables to development during infancy and early childhood. With new technologies (e.g., gene splicing, behavioral genetics, diagnostic imaging, computational biology, possibly stem cell replacements and cloning), hundreds of new studies are sure to link various biological variables to childhood development during the twenty-first century. The articles selected for inclusion in this unit reflect both the known influences of nurture (environment) and nature (biology) and the relationships and interactions of multiple variables and child outcomes about which we hope to know more in the new millennium.

Newborns are quite well developed in some areas, and incredibly deficient in others. Babies' brains, for example, already have their full complement of neurons (worker cells). The neuroglia (supportive cells) are almost completely developed and will reach their final numbers by age one. In contrast, babies' legs and feet are tiny, weak, and barely functional. Look at newborns from another perspective, however, and their brains seem somewhat less superior. The neurons and neuroglia present at birth must be protected. We may discover ways to make more neurons regenerate in the future, but such knowledge now is in its infancy and does not go very far. By contrast, the cells of the baby's legs and feet (skin, fat, muscles, bones, blood vessels) are able to replace themselves by mitosis indefinitely. Their numbers will continue to grow through early adulthood; then their quantity and quality can be regenerated through advanced old age.

The developing brain in infancy is a truly fascinating organ. At birth it is poorly organized. The lower (primitive) brain parts (brain stem, pons, medulla, cerebellum) are well enough developed to allow the infant to live. The lower brain directs vital organ systems (heart, lungs, kidneys, etc.). The higher (advanced) brain parts (cerebral hemispheres) have all their neurons, but the nerve cells and cell processes (axons, dendrites) are small, underdeveloped, and unorganized. During infancy, these higher (cerebral) nerve cells (that allow the baby to think, reason, and remember) grow at astronomical rates. They migrate to permanent locations in the hemispheres, develop myelin sheathing (insulation), and conduct messages. Many twentieth-century researchers, including Jean Piaget, the father of cognitive psychology, believed that all brain activity in the newborn was reflexive, based on instincts for survival. They were wrong. New research has documented that fetuses can learn and newborns can think as well as learn.

The role played by electrical and chemical activity of neurons in actively shaping the physical structure of the brain is particularly awe-inspiring. The neurons are produced prenatally. After birth, the flood of sensory inputs from the environment (sights, sounds, smells, tastes, touch, balance, and kinesthetic sensations) drives the neurons to form circuits and become wired to each other. Trillions of connections are established in a baby's brain. During childhood the connections that are seldom or never used are eliminated or pruned. The first 3 years are critical for establishing these connections. Environments that provide both good nutrition and lots of sensory stimulation really do produce richer, more connected brains.

The first article in this section on infancy explains what mothers, fathers, and all other infant caregivers need to know immediately upon birth of their precious baby. The Human Genome Project gives new life to attempts to integrate all the separate pieces of knowledge about infant development from biology and psychology. Joanna Lipari articulates the old thinking with its counterpoint new thinking.

The second selection describes the five sensory windows on the world for newborns: vision, hearing, taste, touch, and smell. It describes the rapid growth and development of both sensory and perceptual neuronal circuitry. Understanding how the infant experiences the world gives caregivers a more sympathetic understanding of their abilities.

The last selection on infancy asks and answers the question, "Who's Raising Baby?" Anne Pierce discusses the challenges to modern day parenting from a mother's-eye view. Contemporary parents seem to be on a competitive merry-go-round to have their offspring involved in as many "enriching" activities as their neighbors, friends, coworkers, etc. What is the purpose of all this activity? The article cites the opinions of renowned child psychologists such as David Elkind and Stanley Greenspan that this race for supremacy is not healthy. In infancy, emotional learning and the ability to relate to others are more important than literacy. Home life is valuable. The author believes lessons learned at home supercede those obtained in daycare.

The selections about toddlers and preschoolers included in this anthology continue looking at development physically, cognitively, and socioemotionally. Each of the articles, while focusing on one topic more than others, views the whole child across all three domains, considering both hereditary and environmental factors.

The first early childhood article addresses the "Mozart effect." This topic has gotten a great deal of mileage in the media. Is it desirable to play classical music to children in their cribs? What other kinds of cognitive stimulation can improve the quality and quantity of neuronal interconnections? Should children go to school by age 3, 4, 5, or 6? Sharon Begley sums up the pros and cons of various programs that promise to boost early intelligence. She also emphasizes the importance of emotional learning.

Alice Honig, in the next early childhood selection, reviews what is known about the sexual thoughts and behaviors of preschool-aged children. She deals with masturbation, sex questions, use of sex words, gender stereotypes, gender-differentiated play, and gender discrimination. She gives a list of tips for caregivers to promote healthy psychosexual development.

The last article in this unit discusses how parents can instill and nurture moral values and behaviors in young children. Although states vary in the ages that they hold children legally accountable for knowing right from wrong, child developmentalists believe that preschoolers can grasp, and should be taught, moral values.

FOUR THINGS YOU NEED TO KNOW ABOUT RAISING BABY

New thinking about the newborn's brain, feelings and behavior are changing the way we look at parenting

BY JOANNA LIPARI, M.A.

Bookstore shelves are crammed with titles purporting to help you make your baby smarter, happier, healthier, stronger, better-behaved and everything else you can imagine, in what I call a shopping-cart approach to infant development. But experts are now beginning to look more broadly, in an integrated fashion, at the first few months of a baby's life. And so should you.

Psychological theorists are moving away from focusing on single areas such as physical development, genetic inheritance, cognitive skills or emotional attachment, which give at best a limited view of how babies develop. Instead, they are attempting to synthesize and integrate all the separate pieces of the infant-development puzzle. The results so far have been enlightening, and are beginning to suggest new ways of parenting.

The most important of the emerging revelations is that the key to stimulating emotional and intellectual growth in your child is your own behavior—what you do, what you don't do, how you scold, how you reward and how you show affection. If the baby's brain is the hardware, then you, the parents, provide the software. When you understand the hardware (your baby's brain), you will be better able to design the software (your own behavior) to promote baby's well-being.

The first two years of life are critical in this regard because that's when your baby is building the mental foundation that will dictate his or her behavior through adulthood. In the first year alone, your baby's brain grows from about 400g to a stupendous 1000g. While this growth and development is in part predetermined by genetic force, exactly how the brain grows is dependent upon emotional interaction, and that involves you. "The human cerebral cortex adds about 70% of its final DNA content after birth," reports Allan N. Schore, Ph.D., assistant clinical professor of psychiatry and biobehavioral sciences at UCLA Medical School, "and this expanding brain is directly influenced by early environmental enrichment and social experiences."

Failure to provide this enrichment during the first two years can lead to a lifetime of emotional disability, according to attachment theorists. We are talking about the need to create a relationship and environment that allows your child to grow up with an openness to learning and the ability to process, understand and experience emotion with compassion, intelligence and resilience. These are the basic building blocks of emotional success.

Following are comparisons of researchers' "old thinking" and "new thinking." They highlight the four new insights changing the way we view infant development. The sections on "What To Do" then explain how to apply that new information.

1 FEELINGS TRUMP THOUGHTS

It is the emotional quality of the relationship you have with your baby that will stimulate his or her brain for optimum emotional and intellectual growth.

OLD THINKING: In this country, far too much emphasis is placed on developing babies' cognitive abilities. Some of this push came out of the promising results of the Head Start program. Middle-class families reasoned that if a little stimulation in an under-endowed home environment is beneficial, wouldn't "more" be better? And the race to create the "superbaby" was on.

Gone are the days when parents just wished their child were "normal" and could "fit in" with other kids. Competition for selective schools and the social pressure it generates has made parents feel their child needs to be "gifted." Learning exercises, videos and educational toys are pushed on parents to use in play with their children. "Make it fun," the experts say. The emphasis is on developing baby's cognitive skills by using the emotional reward of parental attention as a behavior-training tool.

THE NEW THINKING: Flying in the face of all those "smarter" baby books are studies suggesting that pushing baby to learn words, numbers, colors and shapes too early forces the child to use lower-level thinking processes, rather than develop his or her learning ability. It's like a pony trick at the circus: When the pony paws the ground to "count" to three, it's really not counting; it's simply performing a stunt. Such "tricks" are not only not helpful to baby's learning process, they are potentially harmful. Tufts University child psychologist David Elkind, Ph.D., makes it clear that putting pressure on a child to learn information sends the message that he or she needs to "perform" to gain the parents' acceptance, and it can dampen natural curiosity.

Instead, focus on building baby's emotional skills. "Emotional development is not just the foundation for important capacities such as intimacy and trust," says Stanley Greenspan, M.D., clinical professor of psychiatry and pediatrics at George Washington University Medical School and author of the new comprehensive book *Building Healthy Minds*. "It is also the foundation of intelligence and a wide variety of cognitive skills. At each stage of development, emotions lead the way, and learning facts and skills follow. Even math skills, which appear [to be] strictly an impersonal cognition, are initially learned through the emotions: 'A lot' to a 2-year-old, for example, is more than he would expect, whereas 'a little' is less than he wants."

It makes sense: Consider how well you learn when you are passionate about a subject, compared to when you are simply required to learn it. That passion is the emotional fuel driving the cognitive process. So the question then becomes not "what toys and games should I use to make my baby smarter?" but "how should I interact with my baby to make him 'passionate' about the world around him?"

WHAT TO DO: When you read the baby "milestone" books or cognitive development guides, keep in mind that the central issue is your baby's *emotional* development. As Greenspan advises, "Synthesize this information about milestones and see them with emotional development as the central issue. This is like a basketball team, with the coach being our old friend, emotions. Because emotions tell the child what he wants to do—move his arm, make a sound, smile or frown. As you look at the various 'milestone components'—motor, social and cognitive skills—look to see how the whole mental team is working together."

Not only will this give you more concrete clues as to how to strengthen your emotional relationship, but it will also serve to alert you to any "players" on the team that are weak or injured, i.e., a muscle problem in the legs, or a sight and hearing difficulty.

2 NOT JUST A SCREAMING MEATLOAF: BIRTH TO TWO MONTHS It's still largely unknown how well infants understand their world at birth, but new theories are challenging the traditional perspectives.

OLD THINKING: Until now, development experts thought infants occupied some kind of presocial, precognitive, preorganized life phase that stretched from birth to two months. They viewed newborns' needs as mainly physiological—with sleep-wake, day-night and hunger-satiation cycles, even calling the first month of life "the normal autism" phase, or as a friend calls it, the "screaming meatloaf" phase. Certainly, the newborn has emotional needs, but researchers thought they were only in response to basic sensory drives like taste, touch, etc.

THE NEW THINKING: In his revolutionary book, *The Interpersonal World of the Infant,* psychiatrist Daniel Stern, Ph.D., challenged the conventional wisdom on infant development by proposing that babies come into this world as social beings. In research experiments, newborns consistently demonstrate that they actively seek sensory stimulation, have distinct preferences and, from birth, tend to form hypotheses about what is occurring in the world around them. Their preferences are emotional ones. In fact, parents would be unable to establish the physiological cycles like wake-sleep without the aid of such sensory, emotional activities as rocking, touching, soothing, talking and singing. In turn, these interactions stimulate the child's brain to make the neuronal connections she needs in order to process the sensory information provided.

WHAT TO DO: "Take note of your baby's own special biological makeup and interactive style," Greenspan advises. You need to see your baby for the special individual he is at birth. Then, "you can deliberately introduce the world to him in a way that maximizes his delight and minimizes his frustrations." This is also the time to learn how to help your baby regulate his emotions, for example, by offering an emotionally overloaded baby some soothing sounds or rocking to help him calm down.

3 THE LOVE LOOP: BEGINNING AT TWO MONTHS At approximately eight weeks, a miraculous thing occurs— your baby's vision improves and for the first time, she can fully see you and can make direct eye contact. These beginning visual experiences of your baby play an important role in social and emotional development. "In particular, the mother's emotionally expressive face is, by far, the most potent visual stimulus in the infant's environment," points out UCLA's Alan Schore, "and the child's intense interest in her face, especially in her eyes, leads him/her to track it in space to engage in periods of intense mutual gaze." The result: Endorphin levels rise in the baby's brain, causing pleasurable feelings of joy and excitement. But the key is for this joy to be interactive.

OLD THINKING: The mother pumps information and affection into the child, who participates only as an empty receptacle.

THE NEW THINKING: We now know that the baby's participation is crucial to creating a solid attachment bond. The loving gaze of parents to child is reciprocated by the baby with a loving gaze back to the

parents, causing their endorphin levels to rise, thus completing a closed emotional circuit, a sort of "love loop." Now, mother (or father) and baby are truly in a dynamic, interactive system. "In essence, we are talking less about what the mother is doing to the baby and more about how the mother is being with the baby and how the baby is learning to be with the mother," says Schore.

The final aspect of this developing interactive system between mother and child is the mother's development of an "emotional synchronization" with her child. Schore defines this as the mother's ability to tune into the baby's internal states and respond accordingly. For example: Your baby is quietly lying on the floor, happy to take in the sights and sounds of the environment. As you notice the baby looking for stimulation, you respond with a game of "peek-a-boo." As you play with your child and she responds with shrieks of glee, you escalate the emotion with bigger and bigger gestures and facial expressions. Shortly thereafter, you notice the baby turns away. The input has reached its maximum and you sense your child needs you to back off for awhile as she goes back to a state of calm and restful inactivity. "The synchronization between the two is more than between their behavior and thoughts; the synchronization is on a biological level—their brains and nervous systems are linked together," points out Schore. "In this process, the mother is teaching and learning at the same time. As a result of this moment-by-moment matching of emotion, both partners increase their emotional connection to one another. In addition, the more the mother fine-tunes her activity level to the infant during periods of play and interaction, the more she allows the baby to disengage and recover quietly during periods of nonplay, before initiating actively arousing play again."

Neuropsychological research now indicates that this attuned interaction—engaged play, disengagement and restful nonplay, followed by a return to play behavior—is especially helpful for brain growth and the development of cerebral circuits. This makes sense in light of the revelation that future cognitive development depends not on the cognitive stimulation of flashcards and videos, but on the attuned, dynamic and emotional interactions between parent and child. The play periods stimulate baby's central nervous system to excitation, followed by a restful period of alert inactivity in which the developing brain is able to process the stimulation and the interaction.

In this way, you, the parents, are the safety net under your baby's emotional highwire; the act of calming her down, or giving her the opportunity to calm down, will help her learn to handle ever-increasing intensity of stimulation and thus build emotional tolerance and resilience.

WHAT TO DO: There are two steps to maximizing your attunement ability: spontaneity and reflection. When in sync, you and baby will both experience positive emotion; when out of sync, you will see negative emotions. If much of your interactions seem to result in negative emotion, then it is time to reflect on your contribution to the equation.

In these instances, parents need to help one another discover what may be impeding the attunement process. Sometimes, on an unconscious level, it may be memories of our own childhood. For example, my friend sings nursery rhymes with a Boston accent, even though she grew up in New York, because her native Bostonian father sang them to her that way. While the "Fah-mah in the Dell" will probably not throw baby into a temper tantrum, it's a good example of how our actions or parenting style may be problematic without our realizing it.

But all parents have days when they are out of sync with baby, and the new perspective is that it's not such a bad thing. In fact, it's quite valuable. "Misattunement" is not a bioneurological disaster if you can become attuned again. The process of falling out of sync and then repairing the bond actually teaches children resilience, and a sense of confidence that the world will respond to them and repair any potential hurt.

Finally, let your baby take the lead. Schore suggests we "follow baby's own spontaneous expression of himself," which lets the child know that another person, i.e., mom or dad, can understand what he is feeling, doing, and even thinking. Such experiences, says Schore, assist in the development of the prefrontal area, which controls "empathy, and therefore that which makes us most 'human.'"

4 THE SHAME TRANSACTION Toward the end of the first year, as crawling turns to walking, a shift occurs in the communication between child and parents. "Observational studies show that 12-month-olds receive more positive responses from mothers, while 18-month-olds receive more instructions and directions," says Schore. In one study, mothers of toddlers expressed a prohibition—basically telling the child "no"—approximately every nine minutes! That's likely because a mobile toddler has an uncanny knack for finding the most dangerous things to explore!

Yesterday, for example, I walked into the living room to find my daughter scribbling on the wall with a purple marker. "NO!" shot out of my mouth. She looked up at me with stunned shock, then realized what she had done. Immediately, she hung her head, about to cry. I babbled on a bit about how markers are only for paper, yada-yada and then thought, "Heck, it's washable." As I put my arm around my daughter, I segued into a suggestion for another activity: washing the wall! She brightened and raced to get the sponge. We had just concluded a "shame transaction."

OLD THINKING: Researchers considered all these "no's" a necessary byproduct of child safety or the socialization process. After all, we must teach children to use the potty rather than wet the bed, not to hit another child when mad, to behave properly in public. Researchers did not consider the function of shame vis-à-vis brain development. Instead, they advised trying to limit situations in which the child would feel shame.

NEW THINKING: It's true that you want to limit the shame situations, but they are not simply a necessary evil in order to civilize your baby. Neurobiological studies indicate that episodes of shame like the one I described can actually stimulate the development of the right hemisphere, the brain's source of creativity, emotion and sensitivity, as long as the shame period is short and followed by a recovery. In essence, it's not the experience of shame that can be damaging, but rather the inability of the parent to help the child recover from that shame.

WHAT TO DO: It's important to understand "the growth-facilitating importance of small doses of shame in the socialization process of the infant," says Schore. Embarrassment (a component of shame) first emerges around 14 months, when mom's "no" results in the child lowering his head and looking down in obvious sadness. The child goes from excited (my daughter scribbling on the wall) to sudden deflation (my "NO!") back to excitement ("It's okay, let's wash the wall together"). During this rapid process, various parts of the brain get quite a workout and experience heightened connectivity, which strengthens these systems. The result is development of the orbitofrontal cortex (cognitive area) and limbic system (emotional area) and the ability for the two systems to interrelate emotional resiliency in the child and the ability to self-regulate emotions and impulse control.

What is important to remember about productive shame reactions is that there must be a quick recovery. Extended periods of shame result in a child learning to shut down, or worse, become hyperirritable, perhaps even violent. It's common sense: Just think how you feel when someone embarrasses you. If that embarrassment goes on without relief, don't you tend to either flee the situation or rail against it?

From these new research findings, it's clear that successful parenting isn't just about intuition, instinct and doing what your mother did. It's also not about pushing the alphabet, multiplication tables or violin lessons. We now believe that by seeing the newborn as a whole person—as a thinking, feeling creature who can and should participate in his own emotional and cognitive development—we can maximize the nurturing and stimulating potential of our relationship with a newborn baby.

Joanna Lipari is pursuing a Psy.D. at Pepperdine University in Los Angeles.

READ MORE ABOUT IT

The Irreducible Needs of Children: What Every Child Must Have to Grow, Learn and Flourish, T. Berry Brazelton, M.D., and Stanley Greenspan, M.D. (Perseus Books, 2000).

Building Healthy Minds, Stanley Greenspan, M.D. (Perseus Books, 1999).

Reprinted with permission from *Psychology Today*, July/August 2000, pp. 38-43. © 2000 by Sussex Publishers, Inc.

The World
Of the
Senses

From the moment of birth, babies respond to their mothers' voices, distinguish shapes and have definite taste and aroma preferences.

By Joan Raymond

IT'S TUESDAY AFTERNOON AT THE Epsteins' Philadelphia apartment. Seven-month-old Ana Natalia is sitting up, smiling, waiting for her favorite midafternoon activities: snack time, featuring a lovely sweet-potato purée, accompanied by a gentle back rub. When her mother, Lucia, puts some world music on the CD player, Ana Natalia arches her 15-pound body in delight. Life doesn't get any better than cool times, good food and a massage.

REACH OUT
At birth the sense of touch is so developed that a baby will prefer soft flannel to coarse burlap.

Even babies—especially babies—know that. They revel in their senses and almost intuitively know what looks, tastes, feels, sounds and smells good. They love skin-to-skin touching, which can inhibit the release of stress hormones and heighten immune responses. They respond to their mothers' voices and can distinguish them (thanks to hearing her voice

through the walls of the womb) from all others. They are fascinated by shapes and moving objects. And they definitely know what they like to eat. All of these talents reflect the fact that at birth a baby's sensory system is well developed, even though the neural pathways that underlie perception still need years of fine-tuning. In the first years of life neurons in the brain—the master sense organ—form circuits that will enable a child to distinguish the smell of lilacs from gasoline, the sight of cerulean from mauve, the sounds of her native tongue from all others.

A baby's journey through the realm of the senses begins in the womb. By the seventh month, nerves connecting the eye and the brain's visual cortex have begun to function in a rudimentary way, transmitting visual information in the form of electrical impulses (but not very efficiently). Nerves that relay touch perceptions appear on the skin of the fetus by about the 10th week. By the fourth month, the somatosensory cortex—the part of the brain that registers tactile perceptions—is coming online; a gentle massage of Mom's belly will likely stimulate fetal movement. By about 28 weeks, the fetus will respond to loud noises. Taste buds make an appearance at a remarkably early seven weeks.

And although the fetus doesn't smell in the conventional sense, it can absorb odors in the amniotic fluid by the 24th week of gestation.

Children fine-tune their sensory apparatus through the critical first years of life. "Infants and toddlers give their senses a tune up every time they are exposed to new stimuli," says pediatric neurologist Dr. Max Wiznitzer of Cleveland's Rainbow Babies & Children's Hospital. Each new stimulus sets off a cascade of brain events; in fact, in the first three months of life the regions of the brain with the highest metabolic rate are those processing sights, sounds and touches, as if the nascent circuits within the gray matter were burning the midnight oil to take in everything they could about their new world.

Sensory information doesn't just stop with perception; it also interacts with other functions and regions of the brain. In adults, the sense of smell can be a powerful trigger to memory (with the aroma of roses, perhaps, triggering memories of a long-ago romance), and such connections start to be forged in the first weeks of life. Right from birth a baby's ability to detect odors is well developed. That makes sense, since smell is processed in one of the most primitive and (evolutionarily) oldest parts

MAKING SENSE OF IT

Five Windows on the World

Although babies come into the world wired for vision, hearing, touch, smell and taste, their experiences in infancy and throughout childhood complete the neuronal circuitry.

Touch It's such a crucial sense that the area of the brain responsible for touch perceptions—the primary sensory cortex—can process tactile sensations by the fourth month of gestation. Skin nerves appear at week 10.

Vision It's the slowest sense to develop. Although the rudimentary visual cortex can receive signals from the fetus's eye at seven months' gestation, neurons in the vision pathway remain immature for months after birth. Much of the world looks fuzzy to babies.

Smell Even while in utero, babies perceive the smell of the amniotic fluid; at birth they can distinguish their mother's smell from all others. Olfaction seems to be tightly linked to memories and emotions.

PRIMARY SENSORY CORTEX

TASTE CORTEX

PRIMARY AUDITORY CORTEX

PRIMARY VISUAL CORTEX

OLFACTORY BULB

THE CEREBRAL CORTEX: This outermost layer of the brain processes signals from the peripheral nervous system

Taste Preferences are shaped so early that even newborns have definite likes and dislikes. The 10,000 or so taste buds on the tongue and soft palate begin to appear a mere seven weeks after conception. Each responds most strongly to salty, sour, sweet or bitter. In general, newborns prefer sweet. But the specific tastes that the fetus is exposed to before birth, through what Mom eats and through breast milk—whose taste also reflects Mom's previous meals— shape which ones he will prefer and which he will reject.

Hearing Just as prenatal exposure to tastes shapes a baby's preferences, so the sounds penetrating the womb leave a lasting effect. By 28 weeks' gestation, the brain's auditory cortex, which receives input from nerve cells in the inner ear, can perceive loud noises. At birth, a baby can usually distinguish her mother's voice, the one she has been hearing for the last 12 or so weeks of gestation, and prefers it to all others. Newborns can perceive every phoneme in the world's languages, an ability that's lost within the first year.

---

of the brain. A newborn can distinguish her mother's fragrance from all others and, since it is generally associated with pleasant things like food and comfort, comes to prefer it. When a baby smells his mother's skin, the olfactory signal reaching the brain triggers the formation of neuronal links between it and the brain's memory and emotion centers. As a result, the baby remembers Mom's smell and associates it with pleasant events.

LOOKIN' GOOD
The world looks fuzzy to newborns, but within 3 months they can track moving objects

As early as the second month, babies learn to distinguish between more types and intensities of aromas. Their repertoire continues expanding, with the result that toddlers form even more sophisticated

neuronal links between aromas and memories. Smelling a flower, for instance, sends signals to the brain's limbic system, a site of memory storage. Presto: emotion-laden memories—happy (if the toddler was having a lovely day with Mom when he picked the rose) or not (it was a prize-winning bloom, and plucking it led to a very, very long timeout).

Vision is the last sense to reach full capacity. At birth, the neurons of the visual cortex (which receive visual information from the eye) are still not "myelinated," or coated with the fatty substance that keeps nerve signals from leaking out like electricity from badly insulated transmission lines. As a result of the faulty lines, newborns see little more than light and shadow. They focus best on objects eight to 15 inches away—about the distance to the face of the person feeding them—and even with their fuzzy vision can tell circles from squares and prefer the former. They love to look at faces.

By 3 months a baby can track objects that move toward him, and soon after that

can follow moving objects smoothly. By 4 to 7 months a child develops full color vision; this is when brightly colored toys will capture his attention. By 6 months his depth and distance perception work reliably—convenient for a little being just starting to scoot around. By 2, most children have 20/60 vision, which will gradually improve over the next three years to 20/25. Vision will continue to sharpen until the age of 9 or so, when a child sees as clearly as a normal adult. But this progression is far from inevitable: visual stimulation is crucial to the developing child. When deprived of visual stimulation, the ocular columns in the brain's visual cortex fail to wire up correctly. That means those mobiles over the bed do more than just look pretty. They help your child focus and improve his vision (though everyday interactions and a caring environment are perfectly adequate to stimulate visual development).

Hearing depends on experience, too. Newborns have a well-developed auditory system, and can distinguish loud from quiet. But they can pick up higher-pitched sounds better than they can lower-frequency ones, which may be why they are entranced by the high-pitched coos and singsong of "parentese." Adults' practice of speaking to babies in a higher pitch therefore matches their auditory abilities. By 2 to 3 months a baby can distinguish the source of a sound, and follow it, which makes tracking the conversations around them possible.

FLAVOR CRAVER
Taste buds appear at seven weeks' gestation. Babies have an acute sense of taste, and prefer sweet.

Perhaps the most impressive aspect of newborns' auditory abilities is their enviable talent for hearing the phonemes of every language, from that odd (to an English speaker) French "eu" to the "r" and "l" that a Japanese adult can't distinguish. But by the age of 1, infants lose the ability to hear sounds not present in the language they hear every day, finds Patricia Kuhl, professor of speech and hearing at the University of Washington. A baby raised amid the sounds of English literally loses the ability to hear the sound of, say, a Swedish vowel;

if auditory neurons that once had the ability to detect it are never exposed to it, they essentially give up and find a job detecting sounds that the baby *is* exposed to. The brain becomes deaf to other phonemes, which is why native Japanese speakers have trouble telling "l" from "r."

Even newborns revel in their senses; they seem to intuitively prefer sweet to bitter and high tones to low

At birth, the sense of touch is developed enough that a baby will prefer a soft piece of flannel to coarse burlap. There is growing evidence that touch is crucial to an infant's cognitive and physical development. Tiffany Field, director of the Touch Research Institutes at the University of Miami, has shown that premature infants massaged three times a day for 15 minutes gained weight 47 percent faster than preemies who were not massaged. She also finds that infants showed fewer signs of stress, such as grimacing or fist clenching, and had lower levels of stress hormones following a massage with oil.

Newborns' sense of taste is acute enough that some reject breast milk after

Mom has eaten a heaping plate of broccoli. They can tell salty from sweet and bitter from acidic because amniotic fluid acts as a kind of "flavor bridge," says Julie Mennella, a biopsychologist at Philadelphia's Monell Chemical Senses Center. That bridge seems to lead babies to definite, and early, taste preferences. Earlier this year Mennella reported the findings of an experiment designed to trace the origins of babies' likes and dislikes. The old wives' tale about breast milk's influence on a child's taste preferences holds true, she found. When she gave 6-month-olds cereal prepared with either water or carrot juice, the infants who were exposed to carrot juice either prenatally or in breast milk strongly preferred the carrot-juice porridge to the water version. The other infants showed no preference, suggesting that if women eat a varied diet during pregnancy and while nursing, their babies are more likely to accept new foods. Scientists have confirmed another bit of folk wisdom: babies are born with a sweet tooth, probably because breast milk is sweet. In our drive to survive, we have a natural preference for the taste of that first food. (Formula manufacturers try to mimic the sweet taste of human breast milk.) A baby's sensory development starting in the months before birth is nothing short of extraordinary, says Field. "Children are little hedonists," she says. "That's how they learn about their world."

From *Newsweek* Special Issue, Fall/Winter 2000, pp. 16-18. © 2000 by Newsweek, Inc. All rights reserved. Reprinted by permission.

WHO'S RAISING BABY?

Challenges To Modern-Day Parenting

Anne R. Pierce

Drive through the empty streets of our neighborhoods and ask yourself not merely where the children have gone but where childhood has gone. It is most unlikely you will see such once-familiar scenes as these: a child sitting under a tree with a book, toddlers engaged in collecting leaves and sticks, friends riding bikes or playing tag, parents and their offspring working together in the yard, families (in no hurry to get anywhere) strolling casually along. Today's children are too busy with other things to enjoy the simple pleasures children used to take for granted. Preoccupied with endless "activities" and diversions, they have little time for simply going outside.

Where are the children and what are they doing? They are in day-care centers, now dubbed "learning centers." They are in "early childhood programs" and all-day kindergarten. They are acquiring new skills, attending extracurricular classes, and participating in organized sports. They are sitting in front of the computer, the TV, and the Play Station. They are not experiencing the comfortable ease of unconditional love, nor the pleasant feeling of familiarity. They are not enjoying a casual conversation, nor are they playing. They are working—at improving their talents, at competing with their peers, at "beating the enemy" in a video game, at just getting by, at adapting to the new baby-sitter or coach, at not missing Mom or Dad. They, like their computers, are "on." Being, for them, is doing, adjusting, coping. Parenting, for us, is providing them with things to do.

Young children expend their energy on long days in group situations, in preschool and after-school programs, in music and athletic lessons. For much-needed relaxation, they collapse in front of the TV or computer, the now-defining features of "homelife." Relaxation no longer signifies quiet or repose. The hyperactive pace of children's television shows and video games, always accompanied by driving music, exacerbates and surpasses the fast pace of modern life. Children stare at the screen, though the inanity, violence, and doomsday sociopolitical messages of the programming are anything but reassuring.

From doing to staring, from staring to doing. There is little room in this scenario for idle contentment, playful creativity, and the passionate pursuit of interests. Alter-

natives to this framework for living are provided neither in thought nor in deed by busy parents who, themselves, end their rushed days with television and escapism.

Before nursery school starts, most children who can afford it have attended "classes," from gymnastics to ballet, piano, or swimming. Infant "swim lessons," in which an instructor in diving gear repeatedly forces screaming babies underwater so that they are forced to swim, are now commonplace. Day-care centers claim to give toddlers a head start in academic advancement and socialization. Increasing numbers of bright young children spend time with tutors or at the learning center to attain that ever-elusive "edge."

Children in elementary school now "train" and lift weights in preparation for their sports. Football and track are new options for first-graders. A recent trend in elementary athletic programs is to recruit professional coaches, due to the supposed competitive disadvantage of amateur coaching done by parents. It is more common for young children to "double up," participating in two team sports at a time. A constantly increasing selection of stimulating activities lures modern families, making downtime more elusive.

What used to be "time for dinner" (together) is, more often than not, time for family members to rush and scatter in different directions. A typical first-grade soccer team practices two evenings a week, from 6:00 to 7:30. The stress involved in getting six-year-olds fed and in gear by practice time and, after practice, bathed and in bed at an appropriate hour is obvious. And yet, if you attend a first-grade soccer game, you'll likely find parents eager to discover the activities of other people's children and anxious to sign their children up for—whatever it might be. Some parents appear to be jealous of the activities others have discovered.

THE NEW CONFORMISM—AFRAID OF MISSING OUT

In asking scores of parents about the purpose of all this activity, I have never received a clear or, to my mind, satisfactory answer. The end, apparently, is unclear apart from the idea, often expressed, that if one's child starts activities later than other children, he (or she) will be "left behind." Some of the more cohesive explanations I have received are these: A mother described herself as being "swept along by the inevitable"; she didn't want her young daughter to be "the only one missing out." A couple explained their determination to expose their toddler to a wide variety of opportunities so that he would know which sports he excelled in "by the time things get competitive." A father said, simply, that he saw his role in terms of making sure his children were "the best at something," and with all the other kids starting activities at such an early age, this meant that his kids "had to start even earlier."

In effect, this is the "do what everyone else does, only sooner and more intensely" theory of child rearing. This theory creates a constant downward pressure upon children of a younger and younger age. This was evident to me when my youngest son entered kindergarten and I discovered he was within a small minority of boys who had not *already* participated in team sports. Only five years earlier, my oldest son was within the sizable majority of kindergartners whose parents had decided kindergarten was a little too early for such endeavors. (First grade was then the preferred starting point.)

The more families subscribe to this "lifestyle," the more there is another reason for pushing kids off to the races: If no children are around to play with, then, especially for only children, organized activities become their only opportunity to "play" with other kids. Playing is thus thoroughly redefined.

The philosophy of child rearing as a race and of homelife as oppressive for women compels families toward incessant action. Love, nurture, and, concomitantly, innocence have been demoted as compared to experience and exposure. The family is viewed as a closedness to experience, the nurturing role within the family as the most confining of all. Indeed, busyness supplants togetherness in many modern families.

One legacy of Freud, Piaget, Pavlov, and the behaviorists, neodevelopmentalists, and social scientists who followed them has been the decreasing respect for the child's being and the increasing emphasis upon his "becoming." The child is seen as "socializable" and is studied as a clinical object whose observable response to this or that "environmental stimulus" becomes more important than his deeper, more complicated features. With the clinical interpretation of childhood, social engineering projects and "activities" that make the child's world more stimulating gain momentum.

In addition to the advantage that all this activity supposedly gives children, there is also the element of convenience. If parents are too busy to supervise their children, it behooves them to keep the kids so busy and under the auspices of so many (other) adults that they are likely to "stay out of trouble." Such is the basis of many modern choices. Children spend much of their time exhausted by activities, the purposes of which are ill construed.

Conformism, convenience, and new interpretations of childhood are, then, contributing factors in the hectic existence and the premature introduction to academics that parents prescribe for their children.

Conformism, convenience, and new interpretations of childhood are, then, contributing factors in the hectic existence and the premature introduction to academics that parents prescribe for their children. For example, before the 1960s, it was generally believed that placing young children in out-of-home learning programs was harmful. The concern for the harmfulness of such experiences was abandoned when these learning programs became convenient and popular.

EDUCATION AS 'SOCIALIZATION'

In *Miseducation: Preschoolers at Risk*, David Elkind expressed dismay at the fact that age-inappropriate approaches to early education have gained such momentum despite the undeniable evidence that pushing children into formal academics and organized activities before they are ready does more harm than good. He lamented, "In a society that prides itself on its preference for facts over hearsay, on its openness to research, and on its respect for 'expert' opinion, parents, educators, administrators, and legislators are ignoring the facts, the research and the expert opinion about how young children learn and how best to teach them.... When we instruct children in academic subjects, or in swimming, gymnastics, or ballet, at too early an age, we miseducate them; we put them at risk for short-term stress and long-term personality damage for no useful purpose."

Elkind pointed to the consistent result of reputable studies (such as that conducted by Benjamin Bloom) that a love of learning, not the inculcation of skills, is the key to the kind of early childhood development that can lead to great things. These findings, warned Elkind, point to the fallacy of early instruction as a way of producing children who will attain eminence. He noted that with gifted and talented individuals, as with children in general, the most important thing is an excitement about learning: "Miseducation, by focusing on skills to the detriment of motivation, pays an enormous price for teaching infants and young children what amounts to a few tricks."

He further observed that those advocating early instruction in skills and early out-of-home education rely upon youngsters who are very disadvantaged to tout early education's advantages. "Accordingly, the image of the competent child introduced to remedy the understimulation of low-income children now serves as the rationale for the overstimulation of middle-class children."

Dr. Jack Westman of the Rockford Institute, renowned child psychiatrist Dr. Stanley Greenspan, and brain researcher Jane Healy are among the many unheeded others who warn of the implications of forcing the "childhood as a race" approach upon young children. Laments Westman, "The result is what is now referred to as the 'hothousing movement' for infants and toddlers devoted to expediting their development. This is occurring in spite of the evidence that the long-term outcomes of early didactic, authoritarian approaches with younger children relate negatively to intellectual development."

In an interview for Parent and Child magazine, Dr. Greenspan insisted that young children suffer greatly if there is inadequate "emotional learning" in their daily lives.

In an interview for *Parent and Child* magazine, Dr. Greenspan insisted that young children suffer greatly if there is inadequate "emotional learning" in their daily lives. Such learning, he explained, is both a requisite for their ability to relate well with others and the foundation of cognitive learning. "Emotional development and interactions form the foundation for all children's learning—especially in the first five years of life. During these years, children abstract from their emotional experiences constantly to learn even the most basic concepts. Take, for example, something like saying hello or learning when you can be aggressive and when you have to be nice—and all of these are cues by emotions."

In *Endangered Minds: Why Children Don't Think and What We Can Do About It*, Healy states the case for allowing young children to play with those who love them before requiring them to learn academic skills. She intones, "Driving the cold spikes of inappropriate pressure into the malleable heart of a child's learning may seriously distort the unfolding of both intellect and motivation. This self-serving intellectual assault, increasingly condemned by teachers who see its warped products, reflects a more general ignorance of the growing brain.... Explaining things to children won't do the job; they must have the chance to experience, wonder, experiment, and act it out for themselves. It is this process, throughout life, that enables the growth of intelligence."

Healy goes so far as to describe the damaging effect on the "functional organization of the plastic brain" in pushing too hard too soon: "Before brain regions are myelinated, they do not operate efficiently. For this reason, trying to 'make' children master academic skills for which they do not have the requisite maturation may re-

sult in mixed-up patterns of learning.... It is possible to force skills by intensive instruction, but this may cause a child to use immature, inappropriate neural networks and distort the natural growth process."

Play is a way for children to relish childhood, prepare for adulthood, and discover their inner passions.

Play is important for intellectual growth, the exploration of individuality, and the growth of a conscience. Play is a way for children to relish childhood, prepare for adulthood, and discover their inner passions. Legendary psychoanalyst D.W. Winnicott warned us not to underestimate the importance of play. In *The Work and Play of Winnicott*, Simon A. Grolnick elucidates Winnicott's concept of play.

> Play in childhood and throughout the life cycle helps to relieve the tension of living, helps to prepare for the serious, and sometimes for the deadly (e.g., war games), helps define and redefine the boundaries between ourselves and others, helps give us a fuller sense of our own personal and bodily being. Playing provides a trying-out ground for proceeding onward, and it enhances drive satisfaction.... Winnicott repeatedly stressed that when playing becomes too drive-infested and excited, it loses its creative growth-building capability and begins to move toward loss of control or a fetishistic rigidity.... Civilization's demands for controlled, socialized behavior gradually, and sometimes insidiously, supersedes the psychosomatic and aesthetic pleasures of open system play.

When we discard playtime, we jeopardize the child's fresh, creative approach to the world. The minuscule amount of peace that children are permitted means that thinking and introspection are demoted as well. Thought requires being, not always doing. Children who are not allowed to retreat once in a while into themselves are not allowed to find out what is there. Our busy lives become ways of hiding from the recesses of the mind. Teaching children to be tough and prepared for the world, making them into achieving doers instead of capable thinkers, has its consequences. Children's innate curiosity is intense. When that natural curiosity has no room to fulfill itself, it burns out like a smothered flame.

In an age when "socialization" into society's ideals and mores is accepted even for babies and toddlers, we should remember that institutionalized schooling even for older children is a relatively new phenomenon. Mass education was a post-Industrial Revolution invention, one that served the dual purposes of preparing children for work and freeing parents to contribute fully to the industrial structure. No longer was work something that families did together, as a unit.

The separation of children from the family's work paved the way for schools and social reformers to assume the task of preparing children for life. This is a lofty role. As parents, we need to inform ourselves as to what our children are being prepared *for* and *how* they are being prepared.

Although our children's days are filled with instruction, allowing them little time of their own, we seem frequently inattentive as to just what they are learning. As William Bennett, Allan Bloom, and others have pointed out, recent years have been characterized by the reformulation of our schools, universities, and information sources according to a relativist, left-leaning ideology saturated with cynicism. This ideology leaves students with little moral-intellectual ground to stand on, as they are taught disrespect not only for past ideas and literary works but for the American political system and Judeo-Christian ethics. Such works as *The Five Little Peppers and How They Grew* and *Little Women* are windows into the soul of a much less cynical (and much less hectic) time.

Teaching children about the great thinkers, writers, and statesmen of the past is neglected as the very idea of greatness and heroism is disputed. Thus, the respect for greatness that might have caused children to glance upward from their TV show or activity and the stories about their country's early history that might have given them respect for a time when computer games didn't exist are not a factor in their lives. The word *preoccupied* acquires new significance, for children's minds are stuffed with the here and now.

THE DEVALUATION OF HOMELIFE

The busyness of modern child rearing and the myopia of the modern outlook reinforce each other. The very ideas that education is a race and that preschool-age children's participation in beneficial experience is more important than playing or being with the family are modern ones that continually reinforce themselves for lack of alternatives. Our busy lives leave insufficient time to question whether all this busyness is necessary and whether the content of our childrens' education is good.

The possibility that children might regard their activities less than fondly when they are older because these activities were forced upon them is not addressed. The possibility that they may never find their own passionate interests is not considered. (I came across an interesting television show that discussed the problem middle-school coaches are having with burned-out and unenthusiastic participants in a wide range of sports. The coaches attributed this to the fact that children had already been doing these sports for years and were tired of the pressure.)

One needs time to be a thinker, freedom to be creative, and some level of choice to be enthusiastic. Families can bestow upon children opportunities for autonomy while at the same time giving them a stable base to fall back upon and moral and behavioral guidelines. Having a competitive edge is neither as important nor as lasting as the ability to lead a genuine, intelligently thought-out, and considerate life.

Some of the best learning experiences happen not in an institution, not with a teacher, but in a child's independent "research" of the world at hand.

Some of the best learning experiences happen not in an institution, not with a teacher, but in a child's independent "research" of the world at hand. As the child interprets the world around her, creates new things with the materials available to her, and extracts new ideas from the recesses of her mind, she is learning to be an active, contributing participant in the world. She occupies her physical, temporal, and intellectual space in a positive, resourceful way. Conversely, if she is constantly stuffed with edifying "opportunities," resentment and lack of autonomy are the likely results.

In *The Erosion of Childhood*, Valerie Polakow insists upon the child's ability to "make history" as opposed to simply receiving it. Lamenting the overinstitutionalization of children in day care and school, she warns, "Children as young as a year old now enter childhood institutions to be formally schooled in the ways of the social system and emerge eighteen years later to enter the world of adulthood having been deprived of their own history-making power, their ability to act upon the world in significant and meaningful ways." She adds, "The world in which children live—the institutional world that babies, toddlers and the very young have increasingly come to inhabit and confront—is a world in which they become the objects, not the subjects of history, a world in which history is being made of them."

Day care provides both too much stimulation of the chaotic, disorganized kind, which comes inevitably from the cohabitation of large numbers of babies and toddlers, and too much of the organized kind that comes, of necessity, from group-centered living. It provides too little calm, quiet, space, or comfort and too little opportunity to converse and relate to a loving other.

Imagine, for example, a parent sitting down with her child for a "tea party." As she pours real tea into her own cup and milk into her child's, the "how to do things" is taken seriously. The child is encouraged to say "thank you" and to offer cookies to his mother, and their chat begins. Although they are pretending to be two adults, the ritual is real; it occurs in a real home setting; it provides the child with real food and a real opportunity for "mature" conversation. The mother says, "I'm so glad to be here for tea. How have you been?" The child, enjoying the chance to play the part of his mother's host, answers, "Fine! Would you like another cookie?" "Oh yes, thank you," answers his mother. "These cookies are delicious!" The child is learning about civilized behavior.

Children living in the new millennium need a refuge from the impersonal, the mechanical, and the programmed. We must provide them with more than opportunities for skill learning, socialization, and competition.

Then, picture the toy tea set at the learning center. Two children decide "to have tea." They fight over who has asked whom over. When one child asks, "How have you been?" the other loses interest and walks away. Too much of this peer-centered learning and not enough of adult-based learning clearly has negative implications for social development. The child simply cannot learn right from wrong, proper from improper, from other children who themselves have trouble making these distinctions.

Homelife that provides a break from group action has innumerable advantages for older children as well. Think of the different learning experiences a child receives from sitting down at the dinner table with his family and from gulping down a hamburger on the way to a nighttime game. In one case, the child has the opportunity to learn about manners and conversation. In the other, he is given another opportunity to compete with peers. (This is not to deny the benefits of being part of a team but simply to state that homelife itself is beneficial.) I hear many parents of high-school students complain about the compet-

itive, selfish manner of today's students. And, yet, most of these students have not a moment in their day that is not competitive.

How can we expect children to value kindness and cooperation when their free time has been totally usurped by activities wherein winning is everything? At home, winning is not everything (unless the child expends all his time trying to "beat the enemy" in a video game). At home, a child is much more likely to be reprimanded for not compromising with his siblings than for not "defeating" them. If homelife provides children with time to define their individuality and interact with family members (and all the give-and-take implied), then it is certainly an invaluable aspect of a child's advancement.

Children living in the new millennium need a refuge from the impersonal, the mechanical, and the programmed. We must provide them with more than opportunities for skill learning, socialization, and competition. Otherwise, something will be missing in their humanness. For to be human is to have the capacity for intimate attachments based upon love (which can grow more intimate because of the closeness that family life provides); it is to reason and to have a moral sense of things; it is to be capable of a spontaneity that stems from original thought or from some passion within.

We must set our children free from our frenetic, goal-oriented pace. We must create for them a private realm wherein no child-rearing "professional" can tread. Within this secure space, the possibilities are endless. With this stable base to fall back upon, children will dare to dream, think, and explore. They will compete, learn, and socialize as the blossoming individuals that they are, not as automatons engineered for results.

Anne R. Pierce is an author and political philosopher who lives in Cincinnati with her husband and three children. As a writer, she finds that bringing up children in the modern world gives her much food for thought.

From *The World & I,* February 2002, pp. 306-317. © 2002 by The World & I, a publication of The Washington Times Corporation. Reprinted by permission.

Wired for Thought

Babies know more, and know it sooner, than researchers ever suspected. There is a mind in the crib, requiring stimulation to thrive.

By Sharon Begley

WHEN ALISON GOPNIK GOT HOME from the lab one day, she was overcome with the feeling that she was a lousy teacher, an incompetent scientist and a bad mother. A student had argued with a grade, a grant proposal had been rejected and the chicken legs she'd planned for dinner were still in the freezer. So the University of California, Berkeley, developmental psychologist collapsed on the couch and started to cry. Her son, almost 2, sized up the situation like a little pro. He dashed to the bathroom, fumbled around for what he needed and returned with Band-Aids—which he proceeded to stick all over his sobbing (and now startled) mother, figuring that eventually he would find the place that needed patching. Like most 2-year-olds, the little boy had just reached the point where he could not only exhibit empathy (even babies bawl when they hear another baby cry), but also try to soothe another's pain.

For decades scientists studying the blossoming of children's minds had been pretty much blind to this and other talents of the sandbox set. That's changing: researchers today have a lot more respect for what a child's mind is capable of. Babies know more, and know it earlier, than

the founders of the field of child development ever guessed. Even 1-month-olds learn whether their parents respond to them quickly or slowly. From 4 to 6 months, babies come to understand that some things (Dad's clothes) change, but others (his face) do not. Between 7 and 10 months they may learn to carry out sequences of actions to reach a goal, like piling up pillows so they can clamber up and see onto Mom and Dad's bed. By 18 months they can form intentions and understand the intentions of others.

Pint-size scientists
Babies actively seek out information through observations and experiments, changing their brains

---

How children come to achieve these and other cognitive milestones has proved the real revelation. The sequence of brain development is genetically programmed, with the brain stem coming online first to control basic bodily func-

tions like respiration. The cerebellum and basal ganglia follow, to control movement. The limbic system, for emotion and memory, comes next, and the cerebral cortex, for higher-order thinking, matures last. "The *quality* of neural development, however, is shaped by a child's experiences," says neurobiologist Lise Eliot of Chicago Medical School. Like miniature scientists, babies are sponges for information, learning through "mini-experiments with pots and pans, and by playing peekaboo and other everyday games," says developmental psychologist Andrew Meltzoff of the University of Washington. "A baby doesn't just grow into a 3-year-old without external stimulation, like a caterpillar into a butterfly. A baby contributes to cognitive growth by actively seeking information, through observations, play and baby-size experiments. This information changes the baby's mind."

Literally. Brains change as a result of the experiences they live. At birth the brain is packed with an estimated 100 billion neurons. But newborn brains should be labeled SOME ASSEMBLY REQUIRED. Although genes rough out where the brain's visual centers will be and where the auditory centers will nestle, where the regions that govern emotion will lie and where the center of higher thought will sit, the fine details are left to experience. This discovery of the importance of experience led in the 1990s to a proliferation of products and services offering "brain stimulation" for babies, marketed to parents frantic that failing to introduce number concepts in infancy will doom their child to a 400 on the SAT. But the formative experiences scientists have in mind don't involve flashcards. A new report from the National Academy of Sciences called "The Science of Early Childhood Development" puts it this way: "Given the drive of young children to master their world… the full range of early childhood competencies can be achieved in typical, everyday environments. A cabinet with pots and pans… seems to serve the same purpose as a fancy, 'made for baby' musical instrument."

How powerful are everyday interactions? Scientists have recently found that the way a parent talks to children can make them better at some tasks than others. It is a peculiarity of the Korean language that verb endings convey so much information that a mother can talk about the world to her baby without using many nouns. English, in contrast, uses comparatively more nouns and fewer verbs. The result? Korean babies use more verbs in their speech, and English-speaking babies more nouns. But the effects go beyond language. Korean babies, scientists at UC, Berkeley, found in a recent study, learn to solve action problems, like using a long-handled rake to retrieve out-of-reach objects, months before English-speaking kids do. But English hearers learn the concept of categories before Korean-speaking children do, apparently reflecting a language that emphasizes objects. The difference between the languages that babies hear seems to make one kind of problem easier than another.

No one is suggesting that parents adopt a different language depending on how they want their child to think: playing to children's strengths is enough to nurture little minds. Scientists learned how badly they had underestimated babies when Meltzoff discovered that just 40 minutes after birth, babies can imitate facial expressions. That might not seem like such a big deal, but it's actually pretty impressive. A newborn has never seen her own face, yet still knows that she has cheeks she can raise to mimic Dad's smile, and a tongue she can poke out to match what her brother is doing. From the first, babies know that they are like other people, an insight they will build on as they play imitating games with you.

36% of parents
of young children say they plan to start sending their child to school by the age of 3; an additional
29% say they'll do so at 4

It is babies' capacity for "abstract mental representation," as Eliot calls it, that has really taken scientists by surprise. At the tender age of 4 weeks, many babies can transfer data taken in by one sense over to another sense. After they have been sucking on a nubby pacifier, for instance, they can pick it out of a lineup: shown a smooth one and the nubby one, they look longer at the nubby one, an indication that they recognize how something should look from how it feels. Their capacity for abstract thinking extends even to physics. When scientists rig things so a block appears suspended in midair, even 3-month-olds stare at it as if in disbelief that the law of gravity has been repealed. Perhaps the most dramatic evidence of infants' capacity for abstract thinking comes from a 1992 experiment in which 5-month-olds watched scientists place dolls one by one behind a screen. If six dolls went in, but the screen was raised to reveal only four, the babies appeared startled. The kid can't sit, but she's caught you in a mathematical error.

Babies have an innate understanding of the world of things that the simplest games can encourage. A 5-month-old will follow a ball with his eyes as it rolls behind a screen, then scan ahead to the far edge, expecting the ball to emerge. But his grasp of where and when an object should be found has limits. If you show a 6-month-old a little toy, then cover it with a cloth, his face is a mask of befuddlement. A 9-month-old, though, can find the toy, and loves playing hide-and-seek games with objects.

When babies turn 1, they begin to look where people point. This suggests that their minds grasp not only the physical world but other minds. "Like imitation, pointing implies a deep understanding of yourself and other people," says Gopnik, coauthor with Meltzoff and Patricia Kuhl of the 1999 book "The Scientist in the Crib." The baby now grasps that two minds can share an intention—to turn the eyes in the indicated direction. At this age, pointing games are not only a blast but a way to encourage the neural connections underlying this nascent understanding.

Also by their 1st birthday, babies begin to grasp the idea of shared feelings. If Mom peeks into one box and looks disgusted, then peeks into another box and looks delighted, and next pushes the two boxes toward her baby, the child will shun the first box but gleefully reach into the second. He is learning to judge what is good and bad in the world by others' reactions, which means that a look of disgust when your in-laws arrive can leave a lasting impression. Even a 9-month-old can learn how the world works by watching how others make it work. When Meltzoff ran an experiment in which he touched his forehead to a box rigged to light up when touched, babies were mesmerized. When the kids returned to the lab a week later, they immediately touched their own foreheads to the box and turned the lights on.

This is not just a "stupid baby trick." It shows, rather, that "babies can use other people to figure out the world," says Meltzoff. This is the age when they are adept little mimics, an age when parents have a clear shot at teaching babies how the world works by holding books, hugging older siblings and otherwise acting as they hope their children will.

Before they are 1, most babies can grasp only broad categories. If a blue ball rolls behind a screen and a yellow truck comes out, they're not surprised: the category "rolling object" covers both ball and truck. Once children reach their 1st birthday, though, a blue truck's turning into a yellow duck elicits definite surprise. This is about the age when kids sort objects into sensible groups, like grouping toy horses with toy horses and pencils with pencils. At 2 or 3, children go beyond superficial appearances. They know that baby tigers, though they look like kittens, belong to the same category as grown tigers. And, showing that they are ready for the era of the genome, they seem to know about heredity: ask a preschooler if a pig raised by cows will have a curly tail or a straight one, and he doesn't hesitate to answer curly. Young children take to category games like pigs to pokes.

Fun with physics
Even a 3-month-old stares in disbelief at objects that defy gravity, like balls dangling in midair

---

It was only a generation ago that psychologists proclaimed that newborns have no cortex, the thinking part of the brain. They thought of babies as slightly mobile vegetables—"carrots that cry." Now we know that babies come prewired to learn. Although many parents (and marketers) have interpreted that as a clarion call to bombard them

with "stimulation," in fact the best science we have today says that children learn about causes and categories, self and other, through listening and watching, and through games no fancier than hide-and-seek and peekaboo. "If you make a child feel loved, connected, purposeful and inquisitive, brain development will follow," says Peter Gorski of Harvard Medical School. "Our role as parents is not to perfect brain circuitry, but to foster the development of healthy, sane and caring human beings." We are a social species. Our babies learn in social environments, from people who love them, who delight in their little triumphs and pick them up when they slip, who recognize the mind behind the brain.

From *Newsweek* Special Issue, Fall/Winter 2000, pp. 25-30. © 2000 by Newsweek Inc. All rights reserved. Reprinted by permission.

Psychosexual Development in Infants and Young Children

Implications for Caregivers

Alice Sterling Honig

Psychosexual development in young children is a topic that early childhood educators often ignore in the belief that children are not sexual beings. Yet young children show behaviors that indicate awareness of sexual organs and pleasuring very early.

Four-year-old Rosie took the orange Koosh ball I had been tossing back and forth with her and thrust it between her legs. Holding it there firmly, she announced to me, "I have a penis!"

At first, not understanding her symbolic act, I replied mildly, "Rosie, you have a vagina. Boys have a penis."

"No, not a vagina; I have a penis," she affirmed with a satisfying assured tone as she set the Koosh ball more securely between her legs over her dress and kept it in place there between her thighs.

"Oh, the Koosh ball is like an orange penis for you. You are making it into an orange penis."

Satisfied with my confirmation of her desire and my understanding of her symbolism, Rosie whispered confidentially to me, "Some boys have a vagina."

"No way," I assured her. "Boys have a penis. Girls have a vagina."

Rosie looked up at me uncertainly and replied, "I was in a boy's bathroom once and saw a boy who had a vagina."

I explained to her that maybe the boy had such a little penis that she could not see it and thought he had a vagina. But *only* girls have a vagina. Then I explained to Rosie how lucky girls are to have a vagina, because after a girls grows up, if she wants to get married and have a baby, the vagina is the place a baby can come out when it is born.

Once Rosie had played out her sexual wish and had it fully acknowledged and accepted, she no longer seemed interested in showing me that she could make a penis for herself. (Brave girl! She did not depend on anyone else to get a penis for her!)

Rosie went on then to chat with me about some boys who can pee sitting down. We both agreed that boys could do this, but a boy would have to hold his penis way down so that no pee-pee would get on the floor.

After I matter-of-factly talked about this with Rosie, she told me a dream she'd had. In the dream two friends, both boys, went into the bathroom in her house near her bedroom and "peed *all* over the room!" I told her there sure would be a lot of cleaning up that the boys would have to do!

Rosie ignored my remark and said with great satisfaction that they would "get a licking on their backside." She leaned forward, thrust her backside out, and then gestured with her hand to show me how and where the boys would get a spanking. In her view, boys have a penis and she does not. But a boy can get into trouble with a penis!

Other little girls do not get a sympathetic hearing for their longing to have a penis. How would *you* have responded to Rosie's confidence that she could make herself a penis of her very own?

Preschoolers are often puzzled by sexual anatomical differences

Teachers need to be careful that they do not misinterpret as sexual prurience children's deep curiosity about each other's body.

After the preschoolers had finished toileting and were milling about in the bathroom, Jonah came over to Mirra and slowly lifted up her dress. The teacher's eyes widened anxiously. She was afraid that a sexually charged episode was about to occur. But Jonah kept lifting Mirra's dress until he reached her belly button. With wonder, he gently put his finger in her belly button. She had one too! Just like his!

Child care personnel need to help parents understand children's ideas about sexual organs and behaviors. Yet many child care professionals themselves are puzzled by young children's naive conceptualizations, and especially by little girls' wish for the power that a penis could presumably bring them.

Another teacher telephoned me to say that parents had contacted her for advice. They were very upset about their little girl, Jennie.

Grandma had called long distance to ask what Jennie wanted for Christmas.

"Grandma, I would like a penis," Jennie answered promptly and enthusiastically.

Grandma was horrified and scolded Jennie on the phone. "But Grandma," Jennie replied anxiously, thinking this precious gift she had asked for might perhaps be too expensive, "it's all right. You could buy me a *little* one."

I reassured the teacher that such longings were very common among little girls. Boys have this visible, extensible organ that they can see easily and even waggle up and down. Girls cannot even see where their urine comes from. Little boys can urinate standing up and even make different fountain designs with pee on the grass! Sometimes little girls are envious of this ability.

Five-year-old Melody was grumpy. She complained that all the boys boasted that they could pee standing up. "I can do it too," she declared to me. "I'll show you!"

We walked into the bathroom and Melody straddled the toilet. With great effort she kept her legs far apart and managed to "pee like a boy." I agreed that she surely could do that, but probably she would find it more comfortable to sit down while she was urinating.

Once I had accepted her indignation at boys' teasing about their greater powers, Melody readily agreed that sitting on the toilet was easier and more comfortable.

Many infants and young children are not so lucky when they confide in adults. Their caregivers bring ancient fears and shame about sexuality into the children's lives very early. Some caregivers do not address a child's

worry that little girls are "missing" a penis because they were "naughty" and it was cut off. Such dread and anxiety should be directly addressed. Give clear, simple descriptions of the anatomical differences between boys and girls in a conversational and reassuring tone to help young children give up fears that one could lose a penis. Caregiver shame and confusion about sexuality can send negative messages to young children.

"Girls don't but women do have breasts. Boys never do, not even when they're men."

The teacher watched carefully as her older toddlers settled in for naptime. "I make them put their hands outside the covers," she explained to me. "I don't want them touching themselves."

Good observation skills reveal how frequent and natural it is, when babies are free of diapers during changing times, for them to caress a penis or finger their genitals. When adults are anxious and guilty about sexuality themselves, they can create havoc with young children's ideas of reality.

> One day in a child care center where the parents had insisted on thick swinging doors to close off each toilet, five-year-old Louis came running. "Teacher, teacher, Leanne lost her wee-wee!" he wailed in a panic.
>
> Apparently, the swinging door had closed sufficiently slowly that Louis had glimpsed Leanne sitting on the toilet seat with legs spread apart and no penis in view at all! Feeling embarrassed, the teacher called her director to handle this matter.
>
> The director reassured Louis that all boys have a penis and girls do not have a penis. Girls have a uterus so that when they are grown up and married, if they decide to have a child, the baby can grow in the uterus. And girls have a vagina, a canal through which a newborn baby will come out when it is born.
>
> Louis listened in awe and amazement. "Do you have a vagina, too, Ms. Smith?" he inquired.
>
> She assured him she was built just like every other girl and woman, including his own mama.
>
> His next question was, "Can I see it, Ms. Smith?"
>
> The director smiled and explained gently that sexual parts of the body are private parts and we do not show them off to others.

What Louis asked of his mom when he reached home from child care that day we shall never know!

Children need names for sexual parts

Humans are sexual beings. Girls discover genital differences between 16 and 19 months of age (Galenson 1993). Infants and toddlers find it soothing to rub a penis or stroke a vulva. During bath time many little ones are curious about their genitals. Yet a parent or caregiver who cheerfully sings out, "I am washing your pretty arms; now I was your pretty toes," often neglects to name genitalia that are washed. Thus, many children do not know the names for sexual body parts.

Indeed, caregivers use euphemisms of all sorts when referring to a penis, such as *faucet, tinkle,* or *wee-wee.* Adults even warn children, "Do not touch yourself *down there,*" as if the genital region is so dangerous, one cannot even give it a name!

Occasional masturbation is normal

Many young children rub their genitals dreamily as a prelude to napping. One little girl patted her vulva rhythmically while her grandpa, who was visiting, read her a bedtime story. He was very shocked and upset. Mother

had to explain to her preschooler that she could pat her vulva just fine *after* Grandpa had finished reading the story, because it made Grandpa uncomfortable. Waiting till the lights were out to do this activity would make it easier for Grandpa to read to her at bedtime during his visit.

When the teacher reads a story to a group of young children, some may put their hands into their pants and peacefully pat their genitals, as if this good feeling helps them concentrate better on the story that the adult is reading. This is normal.

Masturbation that is compulsive and goes on all day is not normal. This can indicate great stress, an infection in the urethra or the genital region, that a child has been exposed to explicit adult sexual activity or pornography, or that sexual abuse has occurred.

For example, a toddler was enrolled in an early childhood program by his mom after she had angrily left the father in another country and come back to live with her mother in the United States. The child was uncertain and bewildered at so many life changes. During the day he sucked and pulled on the thumb of one hand, and with his other hand he held on to his penis as if grasping for security. This made it quite difficult for teachers to engage the boy in play with toys! The child's anxious behavior continued for three months, until he felt more secure with the now-familiar, loving caregivers and grew to become more and more interested in the play potential of toys in the toddler classroom (Honig 1977).

Freudian stages in psychosexual development

Freud theorized that humans are born with sexual life energy, which he called *libido.* During the first year of life, this sexual energy is presumed to be associated more with the mouth and needs for sensual gratification (as well as nutrition) through sucking.

During the second and third years, Freud postulated, libidinal energy is more strongly focused on the rectal/anal area, especially since caregivers often focus much attention on this area while toilet learning is being urged. Because the anus is literally behind a child, this area often seems mysterious and associated with shameful or forbidden activities. Indeed, toddlers sometimes smear bowel movements.

Sometimes young children use the rectal/anal area as a way to represent defiance of adult standards or strict requirements. Thus, some toddlers joyously call out, "Doody, doody, doody," as if by naming bowel movements they are carrying out brave, adult-defying acts. And many caregivers have struggled with perplexity when some older toddlers react with extreme opposition to adult attempts to get them to use a potty.

> A graduate student had asked the secretary downstairs to watch her three-year-old daughter

Lana (who had recently learned to use the potty) while the student went upstairs to work with me on her research paper. The secretary soon came rushing up to say she needed to speak to me.

I closed the door, and the secretary in agitation told me that the little girl had taken down her panties and was bending over, holding wide apart the cheeks of her backside to exhibit her anus for all the world to see.

Walking downstairs, I remarked firmly and cheerfully to Lana, "You sure wanted to show us your backside and your behind hole. You sure have shown them to us! Now it is time to pull up your panties. And you can choose some crayons to color a picture while I work with your mama."

Hearing me affirm her need, Lana no longer needed to use her anal powers, as it were, to hold the adult world at bay! Quite cooperatively, she pulled up her panties and turned to choosing crayons for drawing a picture for her mama.

Freud taught that during the brief period of the preschool years, libidinal energy becomes focused on the genitals. He theorized that during the early school years (which he called the *latency period)* children would be involved in peer relations and learning activities, and he assumed (without much evidence) that sexual interest in the genitals would recede for a while until the adolescent years.

The Oedipus complex: What is it?

Freudian theory conceptualized that between about three years and six to seven years of age, a child begins to want to "possess" and become closer to the parent of the opposite sex. A boy may push away his father who has come close to kiss and hug the mother. A little girl may insist on going into the bathroom to watch in fascination as her papa holds his penis and urinates.

Lila, three and a half years old, asked her father seriously one day, "Daddy, when I grow up and sleep in the big bed with you, where will poor Mommy sleep?" Lila looked troubled. Then she brightened and exclaimed, "I know, Daddy! She can sleep in my little bed!"

The father, a human development professional, told me he was nonplussed, even though in textbooks he certainly had read much about Oedipal wishes and jealousies of preschool-age children.

Near the mirror in the dress-up corner of the center, Evie was twirling and admiring herself in the "wedding gown" she had put on. Mr. Joe came over and knelt down to her level. "Are you a bride?" he asked.

"Yes, and I'm going to get married!" proudly replied Evie.

"Oh! And whom are you going to marry?" asked her young teacher.

"My daddy, of course!" she answered happily as Mr. Joe in surprise fell backward onto the floor.

Caregivers as well as parents need to know about the Oedipal period and the sometimes surprising expectations that preschoolers have as they grow through this period toward emotional resolution of their desire to rival the same-sex parent. Soon enough, children who indeed do love the parent of the same sex learn to want to grow up to be like the parent of the same sex rather than a "competitor."

Play choices of boys and girls can differ

Psychoanalyst Erik Erikson (1963) studied dramatic scenarios constructed by young children. Boys tended to make tall block configurations and then told stories full of bold actions. Girls created more peaceful, enclosed, domestic scenes. Gender differences in interactive play styles begin to appear from 10 to 14 months of age and are well established by the time children are 36 months old. Fagot (1988) reports that

Girls engage in more doll play and domestic rehearsal, more art activities, and dressing up. Boys play more with transportation toys, with blocks and with carpentry toys. Boys also engage in more aggressive activities and play more in larger peer groups. Girls spend more time talking and spend far more time with teachers than do boys. (p. 134)

Sexual identity and gender role

The term *sexual identity* refers to the biological reproductive patterns of a person's behavior. *Gender identity* is the self-awareness and acceptance of being either a female or a male. *Gender role* refers to a person's acceptance and adoption of *behaviors* socially defined as belonging to one sex or the other. Thus, "A little boy may know that he is a boy, and feel comfortable about it, but still enjoy some activities such as playing house or pretending to nurse a doll tenderly" (Honig 1983, 58). A little girl may love to climb trees and dream of becoming a tractor driver but be very glad she is a girl.

Sometimes persons who show extremely sex-stereotypic behavior and attitudes about what is appropriate for a boy or for a girl "may actually be more insecure in their gender identity than others who are less rigid in their beliefs and values about sex-appropriate behaviors" (Honig 1983, 58).

Boys and girls are equally sophisticated in their *cognitive* understandings of gender identity. Toddlers between one and one-half to two years of age can label their peers correctly by sex. Gesell's work in the 1940s revealed that about three-quarters of older toddlers (three years old) answered with certainty the question, "Are you a little girl or a little boy?" Yet preschoolers are just beginning to understand that gender identity is stable and consistent across time. Not until the end of the preschool years do children realize that they cannot change their sexual identity simply by putting on clothes worn by children of the opposite sex or by acting out behaviors of the opposite sex, such as pretending to be Batman or any superhero.

> Roy was visiting with Grandma and playing with his cuddly toy monkey while Mother was in the bedroom nursing the new baby. Roy lifted up his T-shirt and pretended peacefully to nurse his furry monkey. Grandma remarked lovingly that his mama had nursed him too when he was a baby. She also explained that boys cannot grow up to make milk and nurse babies; only girls can grow up to nurse a baby.
>
> "Oh yes, I will too be able to nurse when I grow up!" Roy asserted indignantly.

Preschoolers struggle to understand that sex ascription is stable; they still believe that in the future they can carry out biological roles of the other sex (Honig 1998). The concepts of gender stability and gender constancy develop along with other cognitive competencies. Between five and seven years of age, when other constancies, like conservation of length, number, and mass, are learned, children start to understand that girls will grow up to become women and boys will grow up to become men. Children then usually come to *value* same-sex oriented objects, toys, and activities. It should be noted, however, that some children do show a strong wish for cross-dressing very early and caregivers need to protect children from peer ridicule.

Why do children prefer single-sex play groups?

On the playground or in a classroom of young children, it is not unusual to find girls playing together and boys playing with other boys. How do we explain the groupings by sex?

Biological explanations

Across cultures, boys show a higher level of activity and engage in more physically vigorous play than do girls, whether indoors or outdoors. Even children's humor expression differs by sex. Young school-age boys are more likely than girls to clown playfully and, laughing vigorously, throw themselves on the floor (Honig 1988).

The tendency of young children from three years onward to play in same-sex groups may possibly be attributable to different gender *styles* in play and in fearfulness. Boys show higher levels of rough-and-tumble play, so toddler females may prefer to play with girls, whose styles are less bumptious. Thus, the basic biological primate pattern, that males are both more active and more aggressive than are females, may in part be responsible for early choices for sex-segregated play.

Cognitive developmental explanations

Cognitive ability level partly explains the sex separations seen in play. A child's self-definition as a girl or boy is part of the growing ability and need to categorize persons in order to understand social relationships. Some children are boys, some are girls. Maccoby (1990) suggests that young children must even exaggerate gender roles to get them cognitively clear.

Sex stereotyping in toy preference

Toddlers start segregating themselves by toy preference, so that boys age 14 to 22 months prefer to play with trucks and cars, while girls prefer soft toys and dolls (Smith & Daglish 1977; Huston 1985). Boys often prefer war toys, while many girls prefer Barbie dolls (Goldstein 1994). Boys also avoid feminine toys far more than girls avoid "boy" toys (Etaugh & Liss 1992). During the elementary school years, sex stereotypes in toy preference, as expressed in children's letters asking Santa Claus for gifts, become even more pronounced (Richardson & Simpson 1982).

Peer influences on sex stereotyping during elementary school

Peers are a powerful influence. By age six children become far more rigid and intolerant; they view violations of conventional sex-appropriate behaviors and use of toys as serious transgressions (Nucci & Nucci 1982). Males impose more pressure on their peers to conform. Sometimes they may seem even menacing or jeering if they notice any hint of male peer appreciation or enjoyment of activities and toys perceived as "female" (Liss 1981; Honig 1998). Indeed, boys tend to ignore teachers or other girls, but their male peers give them "constant feedback on both appropriate play styles and appropriate playmates" (Fagot 1988, 135).

> "Daniel, I hate girls! Do you hate girls too?" inquired Christopher of his six-year-old peer who lived down the block and was visiting in Chris's yard.

"This horse is named Bagina. I mean Andy, who has a bagina because he's a girl horse."

Anxious to please his friend, Daniel hesitantly answered, "Yes. All except Natalie."

"Who is Natalie?" asked the frowning Chris.

"She's my new baby sister," whispered Daniel bravely.

Thus, if males want to be accepted into the world of male peer play, they seem driven to avoid liking girls and girl toys or play. Such behaviors challenge caregivers and teachers to devise subtle and clear ways to enlarge the sphere and scope of acceptable play roles in the classroom.

Television emphasizes female-male differences

Television is a powerful force for children's learning about sexual life roles. Women can be seen as doctors as well as nurses, as detectives and managers as well as secretaries. Yet research shows that quite rigid sex role stereotypes are often promoted on TV shows. Television commercials specifically target children's interest in conforming to social perceptions of gender identity in order to sell more toys or food (Van Hoorn et al. 1993). During children's television programs, commercials have overwhelmingly more male characters than female. Males express more high excitement than do females, and they dominate during commercial voiceovers (Honig & Hake no date).

Boys are more likely to enact fictional TV superhero roles they have seen. Girls prefer to portray family characters (Paley 1986). Compared to Teenage Mutant Ninja Turtles with 100 acts of violence per hour, the Power Rangers average more than 200 such acts. Furthermore, the program splices footage of real-life actors with special animation effects, thus blurring the boundaries of real

and film characters for young children. Preschool teachers report that the Power Rangers are powerful role models who "encourage more violent play, interfere with imaginative, cooperative play, and... squelch creativity in play" (Levin & Carlsson-Paige 1995, 69).

Decades ago Bandura, Ross, and Ross (1963) demonstrated that male preschoolers are far more likely than female preschoolers to imitate aggressive acts of a powerful adult model, particularly an adult male. TV works toward widening sex differences so that males increasingly act out violent, antisocial behaviors.

Some adults overemphasize sex differences

Caregivers sometimes anticipate that boys will be naughtier than girls. Even when both sexes are mostly compliant with teacher requests, teachers respond significantly more to the noncompliant male toddler responses (Wittmer & Honig 1987).

Parental expectations from birth onward provide powerful incentives, both as direct reinforcers and as models, for sharply divergent gender role behaviors (Brooks-Gunn & Matthews 1979; Schan et al. 1980; Block 1983; Honig 1983; Archer 1992). Fathers are more likely to punish play that is not gender stereotyped. Mothers, however, actively join in and "interact with sons when playing with feminine-typed toys" (Golombok & Fivush 1994, 116).

The sexes diverge in developing interpersonal skills in contrast to dexterity in manipulation of objects in the physical world. Girls tend to value and be more adept at the former; boys at the latter (Honig 1998).

When four-year-olds were paired with playmates of their same sex, the children mostly enacted the roles of mother and father (Matthews 1981). Boys playing wife roles acted as if wives are inept and helpless. As "fathers," boys enacted leadership roles and did little housekeeping participation. Girls, in contrast, played mother roles as nurturant, generous, and highly managerial. But they too portrayed wives as helpless and incompetent! The role of mother is viewed as positive in play; the role of wife is not.

Teachers need to use their skills to widen the creative, imaginative scope of sociodramatic play to decrease sex role stereotyping (Smilansky & Shefatya 1986).

Tips for caregivers to promote healthy psychosexual development

How can teachers respect children's psychosexual development and learning of gender roles and yet promote more egalitarian respect for each sex? Teachers can

•Name body parts for young children, including penis, nipples, vulva, and testicles. Let's give children naming power for anatomical parts, just as we do with all objects, toys, foods, and people in their environments.

• Talk about sex discrimination on TV. If a TV program shows little girls as passive and boys as rescuers, talk about the plot and remind children of scenarios that are the other way around! Talk about the ways males and females act on different shows or in cartoons and how realistic these portrayals may be. A four-year-old may think rape on a TV program is OK. When a child watches such fare, an adult needs to help the child understand the feelings of persons of either sex if violence occurs (Honig 1983).

• Help boys and girls to become both competent/agentic *and* nurturant in their social interactions. As teachers we need to reexamine our prejudices that only little girls can be tender and empathic and become ballet stars and only little boys can romp and bravely play the role of cowboy or truck driver.

• React calmly if children come up with bizarre dreams or scenarios such as believing that boys have vaginas or girls have "lost a penis!"

• Give children the words to refuse to allow touching or exhibition of their sexual parts. One teacher coached a child so she could determinedly say to peers urging her yet again to take down her panties, "You've seen my 'gina enough, and I've seen your penis enough!"

• Use bibliotherapy. Read books with young children that matter-of-factly teach about gender differences and how a baby grows inside a mama's uterus and then gets born as a boy or a girl (Gordon 1991; Gordon & Gordon 1992). Read books in which girls are heroines, like *The Paper Bag Princess* by Robert N. Munsch.

• Work on your own attitudes, fears, shames about sexuality. Learn to accept your body and its functions as a great gift, a natural gift, a gift that can be used for enjoyment and for being more fully human. Sexuality is a great mystery and can be a force for making the world a more loving and interesting place.

• Remember that what looks like sexual curiosity in a young child more likely may be general curiosity about similarities and differences between children. Children are genuinely curious about each other, but this does not mean that your preschoolers are obsessed with sex!

• For show-and-tell bring into the classroom adults who are active role models against gender stereotypes. Let a father describe his experiences with diapering and rocking the new baby to soothe colic. A mother can describe how she fixed a dripping faucet or uses a soldering iron to create jewelry.

• Learn to recognize the signs of possible sexual abuse. Inflammation of genital and anal areas, fearfulness of being touched, nervous furtiveness in sexual "showing" games, compulsive masturbation, or ability to describe or act out adult sex acts—clearly all of these are urgent signs to alert a teacher to a child's possible sexual abuse or premature exposure to adult sexual behaviors.

• Use creativity in planning and organizing activities that minimize strong sex differentiation in play patterns. Some children are indeed more comfortable playing with same-sex peers and with stereotypic toys. But taking down barriers between the housekeeping corner and the block area may make it easier for boys and girls to use construction materials as well as kitchen make-believe appliances in playing house.

• Talk with the children about how girls and boys sometimes choose the same and sometimes different toys and activities. Accept children's choices and also lure them into trying new roles and play themes. Teach tolerance of each child's choices rather than allow children to bully peers who prefer nonstereotypic toy or play choices.

• Provide a library of materials for parents so that they can learn more about psychosexual development (Child Study Association of America 1970; Gordon & Gordon 2000).

• Affirm and acknowledge the wonder and rightness of each child's being a little boy or girl whose special gifts and unique self you respect and enjoy in the classroom.

References

Archer, J. 1992. Childhood gender roles: Social context and organization. In *Childhood social development: Contemporary perspectives*, ed. H. McGurk. Hove, UK: Erlbaum.

Bandura, A., D. Ross, & S.S. Ross. 1963. Imitation of film-mediated aggressive models. *Journal of Abnormal and Social Psychology* 66: 3–11.

Block, J.H. 1983. Differential premises arising from differential socialization of the sexes: Some conjectures. *Child Development* 54: 1335–54.

Brooks-Gunn, J., & W.S. Matthews. 1979. *He and she: How children develop their sex-role identity*. Englewood Cliffs, NJ: Prentice Hall.

Child Study Association of America. 1970. *What to tell your children about sex*. New York: Simon & Schuster.

Erikson, E. 1963. *Childhood and society*. New York: Norton.

Etaugh, C., & M.B. Liss. 1992. Home, school, and playroom: Training grounds for adult gender roles. *Sex Roles* 26: 639–48.

Fagot, B.I. 1988. Toddlers, play, and sex stereotyping. In *Play as a medium for learning and development: A handbook of theory and practice*, ed. D. Bergen, 133–35. Portsmouth, NH: Heinemann.

Galenson, E. 1993. Sexual development in preoedipal females: Arrest versus intrapsychic conflict. In *The vulnerable child*, vol. 1, eds. T.B. Cohen & M.H. Etezady. Madison, CT: International Universities Press.

Goldstein, J.H. 1994. *Toys, play, and child development.* New York: Cambridge University Press.

Golombok, S., & R. Fivush. 1994. *Gender development.* New York: Cambridge University Press.

Gordon, S. 1991. *Girls are girls and boys are boys. So what's the difference?* Amherst, NY: Prometheus.

Gordon, S., & J. Gordon. 1992. *Did the sun shine before you were born?* Amherst, NY: Prometheus.

Gordon, S., & J. Gordon. 2000. *Raising a child responsibly in a sexually permissive world.* 2d ed. Holbrook, MA: Adams Media.

Honig, A.S. 1977. The Children's Center and the Family Development Research Program. In *Infant education: A guide for helping handicapped children in the first three years,* eds. B. Caldwell & D. Stedman, 81–99. New York: Walker.

Honig, A.S. 1983. Research in Review. Sex role socialization in young children. *Young Children* 38: 57–70.

Honig, A.S. 1988. Research in Review. Humor development in children. *Young Children* 43 (4): 60–73.

Honig, A.S. 1998. Sociocultural influences on sexual meanings embedded in playful experiences. In *Play from birth to twelve and beyond: Contents, perspectives, and meanings,* eds. D.P. Fromberg & D. Bergen, 338–47. New York: Garland.

Honig, A.S., & D. Hake. Nd. Sex differences in commercials during children's television programming. Manuscript in preparation.

Huston, A.C. 1985. The development of sex typing: Themes from recent research. *Developmental Review* 5: 1–17.

Levin, D.E., & N. Carlsson-Paige. 1995. The Mighty Morphin Power Rangers: Teachers voice concern. *Young Children* 50 (6): 67–74.

Liss, M.B. 1981. Patterns of toy play: An analysis of sex differences. *Sex Roles* 7: 1143–50.

Maccoby, E.E. 1990. Gender and relationships: A developmental account. *American Psychologist* 45: 513–20.

Matthews, W.S. 1981. Sex role perception, portrayal, and preferences in the fantasy play of young children. *Sex Roles* 1 (10): 979–87.

Nucci, L., & M.S. Nucci. 1982. Children's social interactions in the context of moral and conventional transgressions. *Child Development* 53: 403–12.

Paley, V. 1986. *Boys and girls: Superheroes in the doll corner.* Chicago: University of Chicago Press.

Richardson, J.G., & C.H. Simpson. 1982. Children, gender, and social structure: An analysis of the contents of letters to Santa Claus. *Child Development* 52: 429–36.

Schan, C.G., L. Kahn, J.H. Diepold, & F. Cherry, 1980. The relationships of parental expectations and preschool children's verbal sex-typing to their sex-typed toy play behavior. *Child Development* 51: 266–70.

Smilansky, S., & L. Shefatya. 1991. *Facilitating play: A medium for promoting cognitive, socio-emotional, and academic development in young children.* Gaithersburg, MD: Psychosocial & Educational Publications.

Smith, P.K., & L. Daglish. 1977. Sex differences in parent and infant behavior in the home. *Child Development* 46: 1250–54.

VanHoorn, J., P. Nourot, B. Scales, & K. Alward. 1993. *Play at the center of the curriculum.* New York: Macmillan.

Wittmer, D.S., & A.S. Honig. 1987. Do boy toddlers bug teachers more? *Canadian Children* 12 (1): 21–27.

Alice Sterling Honig, Ph.D., is professor emerita of childhood development of Syracuse University in Syracuse, New York. She has published hundreds of articles and chapters, and her books include Playtime Learning Games for Young Children, Talking with Your Baby: Family as the First School *(with H. Brophy), and* Behavioral Guidelines for Infants and Toddlers.

This article was a presentation at the NAEYC Annual Conference, 19 November 1998, in Toronto.

From *Young Children,* September 2000, pp. 70-77. © 2000 by the National Association for the Education of Young Children. Reprinted by permission.

Raising a Moral Child

For many parents, nothing is more important than teaching kids to know right from wrong. But when does a sense of morality begin?

By Karen Springen

NANCY ROTERING BEAMS AS she recalls how her 3-year-old son Jack recently whacked his head against a drawer hard enough to draw blood. It's not that she found the injury amusing. But it did have a silver lining: Jack's wails prompted his 2-year-old brother, Andy, to offer him spontaneous consolation in the form of a cup of water and a favorite book, "Jamberry." "Want 'Berry' book, Jack?" he asked. Nancy loved Andy's "quick-thinking act of sympathy." "I was thrilled that such a tiny person could come up with such a big thought," she says. "He stepped up and offered Jack refreshment—and entertainment—to take his mind off the pain."

All parents have goals for their children, whether they center on graduating from high school or winning the Nobel Prize. But for a great many, nothing is more important than raising a "good" child—one who knows right from wrong, who is empathetic and who, like Andy, tries to live by the Golden Rule, even if he doesn't know yet what it is. Still, morality is an elusive—and highly subjective—character trait. Most parents know it when they see it. But how can they instill and nurture it in their children? Parents must lead by example. "The way to raise a moral child is to be a moral person," says Tufts University psychologist David Elkind. "If you're honest and straightforward and decent and caring, that's what children learn." Humans seem innately inclined to behave empathetically; doctors talk about "contagious crying" among newborns in the hospital nursery. And not all children of murderers or even tax cheats follow in their parents' footsteps. "What's surprising is how many kids raised in immoral homes grow up moral," says New York psychiatrist Alvin Rosenfeld.

81% of mothers and 78% of fathers say they plan eventually to send their young child to Sunday school or some other kind of religious training

Parents have always been preoccupied with instilling moral values in their children. But in today's fast-paced world, where reliable role models are few and acts of violence by children are increasingly common, the quest to raise a moral child has taken on new urgency. Child criminals grow ever younger; in August, a 6-year-old California girl (with help from a 5-year-old friend) smothered her 3-year-old brother with a pillow. Such horrific crimes awaken a dark, unspoken fear in many parents: Is my child capable of committing such an act? And can I do anything to make sure that she won't?

There are no guarantees. But parents are increasingly aware that even very young children can grasp and exhibit moral behaviors—even if the age at which they become "morally accountable" remains under debate. According to the Roman Catholic Church, a child reaches "the age of reason" by 7. Legally, each state determines how old a child must be to be held responsible for his acts, ranging from 7 to 15. Child experts are reluctant to offer a definitive age for accountability. But they agree that in order to be held morally responsible, children must have both an emotional and a cognitive awareness of right and wrong—in other words, to know in their heads as well as feel in their hearts that what they did was wrong. Such morality doesn't appear overnight but emerges slowly, over time. And according to the latest research, the roots of morality first appear in the earliest months of an infant's life. "It begins the day they're born, and it's not complete until the day they die," says child psychiatrist Elizabeth Berger, author of "Raising Children with Character."

It's never too early to start. Parents who respond instantly to a newborn's cries lay an important moral groundwork. "You work to understand what the baby's feeling," says Barbara Howard, a specialist in developmental behavioral pediatrics at the Johns Hopkins University School of Medicine. "Then the baby will work to understand what other people are feeling." Indeed, empathy is among the first moral emotions to develop. Even before the age of 2, children will try to comfort an upset child—though usually in an "egocentric" way, says Marvin Berkowitz, professor of character education at the University of Missouri-St. Louis: "I might give them *my* teddy even though your teddy is right there." To wit: Andy Rotering brought his brother his own favorite book.

Morality consists of not only caring for others but also following basic rules of conduct. Hurting another child, for instance, is never OK. But how you handle it depends on your child's age. If a 1-year-old is hitting or biting, "you simply say 'no' firmly, and you remove the child from the situation," says Craig Ramey, author of "Right From Birth." But once a child acquires language skills, parents can provide more detail. "You can say, 'We don't hit in this family'," says David Fassler, chairman of the American Psychiatric Association's council on children, adolescents and their families. "You can say, 'Everyone feels like hitting and biting from time to time. My job is to help you figure out what to do with those kinds of feelings'." Suggest alternatives—punching a pillow, drawing a sad picture or lying quietly on a bed.

Children grow more moral with time. As Lawrence Kohlberg of Harvard University has said, kids go through progressive stages of moral development. Between 1 and 2, children understand that there are rules—but usually follow them only if an adult is watching, says Barbara Howard. After 2, they start obeying rules—inconsistently—even if an adult isn't there. And as any adult who has ever driven faster than 65mph knows, people continue "circumstantial" morality throughout life, says Howard. "People aren't perfect, even when they know what the right thing to do is."

Though all children are born with the capacity to act morally, that ability can be lost. Children who are abused or neglected often fail to acquire a basic sense of trust and belonging that influences how people behave when they're older. "They may be callous because no one has ever shown them enough of the caring to put that into their system," says Howard. Ramey argues that "we come to expect the world to be the way we've experienced it"—whether that means cold and forbidding or warm and loving. According to Stanford developmental psychologist William Damon, morality can also be hampered by the practice of "bounding"—limiting children's contact with the world only to people who are like them—as opposed to "bridging," or exposing them to people of different backgrounds. "You can empathize with everyone who looks just like you and learn to exclude everyone who doesn't," says Damon. A juvenile delinquent may treat his sister gently—but beat up an old woman of another race. "The bridging approach ends up with a more moral child," says Damon.

No matter how hard you try, you can't force your child to be moral. But there are things you can do to send him in the right direction:

If you're honest, straightforward, decent and caring, that's what children learn'

• Decide what values—such as honesty and hard work—are most important to you. Then do what you want your children to do. "If you volunteer in your community, and you take your child, they will do that themselves," says Joseph Hagan, chairman of the American Academy of Pediatrics' committee on the psychosocial aspects of child and family health. "If you stub your toe, and all you can say is the F word, guess what your child is going to say when they stub their toe?"

Always help your child see things from the other person's point of view

---

• Praise children liberally. "You have to ignore the behaviors you don't want and highlight the behaviors you do want," says Kori Skidmore, a staff psychologist at Children's Memorial Hospital in Chicago. Rather than criticizing a toddler for his messy room, compliment him on the neat corner, recommends Darien, Ill., pediatrician Garry Gardner. Use "no" judiciously, otherwise "a child starts to feel like 'I'm always doing something wrong'," says the APA's Fassler. "If you're trying to teach a child to share, then praise them when they share. Don't just scold them when they're reluctant to."

• Take advantage of teachable moments. When Gardner's kids were 3 and 4, they found a $10 bill in front of a store. Gardner talked to them about the value of the money—and they agreed to give it to the shopkeeper in case someone returned for it. They mutually decided "finders keepers" shouldn't apply to anything worth more than a quarter. "Certainly you wouldn't go back and say, 'I found a penny'," says Gardner. Parents can also use famous parables, like "The Boy Who Cried Wolf," or Bible stories to illustrate their point.

• Watch what your child watches. TV and computer games can glorify immoral behavior. "If children are unsupervised, watching violence or promiscuity on TV, they're going to have misguided views about how to treat other people," says Karen Bohlin, director of Boston University's Center for the Advancement of Ethics and Character. "Children by nature are impulsive and desperately need guidance to form good habits. That can come only from a loving caregiver who's by their side, teaching them how to play nicely, safely, fairly, how to take turns, how to put things back where they belong, how to speak respectfully."

• Discuss consequences. Say, " 'Look how sad Mary is because you broke her favorite doll'," explains Berkowitz. Parents can also ask their children to help them pick fair punishments—for example, no TV. "They're learning that their voice is valued," says Berkowitz. Allowing kids to make choices—even about something as trivial as what to have for lunch—will enable them to make moral ones later. "If they don't learn peanut butter and jelly at 2, how are they going to decide about drinking when they're 14?" asks family physician Nancy Dickey, editor in chief of Medem, an online patient-information center.

• Always help them see things from the other person's point of view. If a child bops his new sibling, try to reflect the newborn's outlook. Say, " 'Oh, my, that must hurt. How would you feel if someone did that to you?'" says Howard. Gardner encourages parents whose kids find stray teddy bears to ask their children how sad they would feel if they lost their favorite stuffed animal—and how happy they would be if someone returned it. "It's one thing to hear about it at Sunday school," he says. And another to live the "do unto others" rule in real life.

In the end, the truest test of whether a parent has raised a moral child is how that young person acts when Mom or Dad is not around. With a lot of love and luck, your child will grow up to feel happy and blessed—and to want to help others who aren't as fortunate. Now, *that's* something to be proud of.

From *Newsweek* Special Issue, Fall/Winter 2000, pp. 70-73. © 2000 by Newsweek, Inc. All rights reserved. Reprinted by permission.

UNIT 3

Development During Childhood: Cognition and Schooling

Unit Selections

Key Points to Consider

- What can cognitive psychologists learn from neuroscience to improve the ways in which children are taught?

- Why has Piaget's cognitive theory changed the way we educate children? What are some of these changes?

- Should metacognitive strategies be taught to children? Why?

- Is achievement testing justified? Why do some educators support it, while others vehemently oppose it?

- Will computer-technology change the way students are educated? How?

- How can children be inspired to choose learning in school?

- What is the next wave in education? Is online distance learning efficient?

- Can teachers assist children in managing their devastation after terrorist attacks and other traumas?

 **Links: www.dushkin.com/online/**
These sites are annotated in the World Wide Web pages.

Children Now
http://www.childrennow.org

Council for Exceptional Children
http://www.cec.sped.org

Educational Resources Information Center (ERIC)
http://www.ed.gov/pubs/pubdb.html

Federation of Behavioral, Psychological, and Cognitive Science
http://federation.apa.org

The National Association for the Education of Young Children (NAEYC)
http://www.naeyc.org

Project Zero
http://pzweb.harvard.edu

Cognition is the mental process of knowing. It includes aspects such as sensing, understanding, associating, and discriminating. Many kinds of achievement that require superb cognitive processes (awareness, perception, reasoning, judgment) cannot be measured with intelligence tests or with achievement tests. Intelligence is the capacity to acquire and apply knowledge. It is usually assumed that intelligence can be measured. The ratio of tested mental age to chronological age is expressed as an intelligence quotient (IQ). For years, school children have been classified and tracked educationally by IQ scores. This practice has been both obsequiously praised and venomously opposed. The links between IQ scores and school achievement are positive, but no significant correlations exist between IQ scores and life success. Consider, for example, the motor coordination and kinesthetic abilities of former baseball player Cal Ripken, Jr. He had an intelligence about the use of his body that surpassed the capacity of most other athletes and nonathletes. A Harvard psychologist, Howard Gardner, has suggested that there are at least eight different kinds of intelligences. Kinesthetic intelligence includes the body movement skills of athletes such as Ripken, of actors, and of dancers. The seven other types of intelligences are linguistic, logical/mathematical, spatial, naturalist, self-understanding, and social understanding. Naturalist intelligence is a new addition to Gardner's eight intelligences. Psychological research frequently addresses the last two types of intelligences: self-understanding and social understanding.

Some psychologists have suggested that uncovering more about how the brain processes various types of intelligences will soon be translated into new educational practices. Today's tests of intelligence only measure abilities in the logical/mathematical, spatial, and linguistic areas of intelligence, which is what schools now teach. Jean Piaget, the Swiss founder of cognitive psychology, was involved in the creation of the world's first intelligence test, the Binet-Simon Scale. He became disillusioned with trying to quantify how much children knew at different chronological ages. He was much more intrigued with what they did not know, what they knew incorrectly, and how they came to know the world in the ways in which they knew it. He started the Centre for Genetic Epistemology in Geneva, Switzerland, where he began to study the nature, extent, and validity of children's knowledge. He discovered qualitative, rather than quantitative, differences in cognitive processes over the life span. Infants know the world through their senses and their motor responses. After language develops, toddlers and preschoolers know the world through their language/symbolic perspectives. Piaget likened early childhood cognitive processes to bad thought, or thought akin to daydreams. By school age, children know things in concrete terms, which allows them to number, seriate, classify, conserve, think backwards and forwards, and think about their own thinking (metacognition). They also begin to develop social cognition. However, Piaget believed that children do not acquire the cognitive processes necessary to think abstractly and to use clear, consistent, logical patterns of thought until early adolescence. Their moral sense and personal philosophies of behavior are not completed until adulthood.

The first article in this unit, "Intelligence: The Surprising Truth," lays out 12 interesting facts about intelligence. Stephen

Ceci's subject matter includes the idea that there are plural intelligences, not just one IQ. He explains why IQ scores are going up with every generation in developed countries. Ceci also addresses the roles played by factors such as birth date, birth order, school attendance, family size, head size, speed of physiological processing, breast-feeding, and nutrition on intelligence. Not every one of these factors are positively related to IQ.

The second selection introduces the reader to a glimpse of the life of Piaget, the founder of the field of cognitive science. Einstein called him a genius. His discoveries about how children think have revolutionized educational practices. Right versus wrong answers should not be stressed in childhood. Rather, children should be allowed to form theories and test out answers for themselves: learn by doing. He suggested that there may be different ways of arriving at knowledge. This is being embraced today by scientists who are looking at women's versus men's ways of knowing and at culturally different ways of acquiring information.

The third cognition selection deals with metacognitive knowledge, the mental process of reflecting on, monitoring, and regulating what one knows. Deanna Kuhn explains why metacognition is an important developmental and educational goal. She traces its origins in childhood to its performance in adulthood, suggesting how it could be optimized. This article stimulates great discussions about the major concepts of critical thinking.

The first article in the schooling subsection of this unit addresses the issue of defining and testing academic performance for purposes of school placement and educational programming. Politicians play with rhetoric about what our children should and should not learn in school. Peter Schrag, a very strong writer, discusses the backlash against proficiency testing in "High Stakes Are for Tomatoes." In most cases parents, students, and teachers have had little control over the tests. To what extent is this accountability in math, science, and English discriminating against other children who demonstrate high motivation and potential to achieve but have different types of intelligences?

The second school-related article, "The Future of Computer Technology in K–12 Education," discusses the power of computers in the new millennium. How will this emerging technological force change education? Frederick Bennett believes that exceptionally good teachers are in the minority, and many teachers are not talented in teaching. So far computers in schools have not improved the quality of academics very much either. Dr. Bennett's alternate solution is to allow computers to tutor students directly and individually. He cites the successes of some school systems that have tried this radical approach. Teachers would not be eliminated, nor downgraded, but would assume new roles as group leaders, guides, and leader-teachers.

The last article in the school section of this compendium discusses social education, particularly teaching about tragedy. Written in the wake of the September 11, 2001, World Trade Center bombing in New York and the Pentagon bombing in Washington, it has important implications for all social education. There are many other situations where students experience trauma. School teachers can help them cope by integrating crisis counseling into the formal curriculum.

INTELLIGENCE: THE SURPRISING TRUTH

Stephen Ceci, Ph.D., lays out 12 facts about intelligence that may astound even the experts.

By Stephen Ceci, Ph.D.

Every culture has a word for "smart," and for "stupid." And everyone feels entitled to have an opinion about intelligence. Unlike, say, brain surgery, intelligence is not an area of expertise that is considered off-limits. Because it's something that our society particularly values, just about everyone has taken a test that measures intelligence, whether it's billed as an IQ test or not. Will you be assigned to the radar corps or the mess tent?

OVER THE PAST TWO DECADES, A NATIONAL DEbate has raged about intelligence: what is it, who has it and how do we measure it? The argument is fueled by findings from two camps of research. There are the psychometricians, who look at the statistics and biology of IQ and try to determine how much of intelligence is innate. And then there are the cultural ecologists, who focus on environment and point out the mutability of intelligence and the unfairness of IQ tests. Unfortunately, the two lines of study seldom meet because their methods are so different. Rarely does one camp communicate with the other.

Birth order doesn't predict IQ, and there is no causal role for family size in determining a child's IQ.

That leaves most ordinary citizens on the outside of the debate, free to cling to their personal beliefs about intelligence. The only trouble is our theories of intelligence are too narrowly constructed. They tend to ignore real data, even though a voluminous literature exists on the topic.

At the very least, intelligence can be defined as the ability for complex thinking and reasoning. One thing the research shows for sure: much of the ability for complex reasoning depends on the situation. A person can be a genius at the racetrack but a dolt in the stock market, even though both pursuits require comparable mental activities. But the knowledge is organized in the mind differently in different domains, so what a person knows about the track can lie fallow on Wall Street.

I would like to present a dozen research-supported facts about intelligence that most people, including some IQ experts, might find surprising:

The truth is that smart people tend to have small families, but it is not small families per se that make people smart.

FACT 1: IQ correlates with some simple abilities

Glance at the two lines below in Figure 1 and decide which is longer; now decide whether the two letters in each pair of figure 1b have the same name or are physically identical. Finally, name the number in 1c. Simple, huh?

No one with a measurable IQ has difficulty answering that the line on the right is longer. But those with a higher IQ respond to the question faster.

Even individuals with an IQ below 70 can do this task at a high level of accuracy, but they need up to five times longer than subjects with a higher IQ. This may be because such tasks require a series of physiological processes, and the nervous systems of individuals with low

Figure 1.

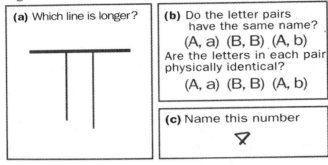

IQs are less efficient, requiring longer, visual displays. Whether you accept this explanation, studies show that IQ is modestly related to the speed at which you do some pretty simple things.

FACT 2: IQ is affected by school attendance

Although intelligence does influence the decision to stay in school, staying in school itself can elevate IQ. Or, more accurately, prevent it from slipping. Each additional month a student remains in school may increase his IQ above what would have been expected had he dropped out. The idea that schooling increases IQ may surprise anyone who views it as a measure of innate intelligence.

The earliest evidence comes from the turn of the last century, when the London Board of Education studied children who had very low IQ scores. The report revealed that the IQ of children in the same family decreased from the youngest to the oldest. The youngest group—ages 4 to 6—had an average IQ of 90, and the oldest children—12 to 22—had an average of only 60. This suggests that factors other than heredity are at work. The older children progressively missed more school, and their IQs plummeted as a result.

A few other facts about school attendance:

- IQ is affected by delayed schooling. Researchers in South Africa studied the intellectual functioning of children of Indian ancestry. For each year of delayed schooling, the children experienced a decrement of five IQ points. Similar data has been reported in the U.S.
- IQ is affected by remaining in school longer. Toward the end of the Vietnam War, a draft priority was established by lottery. Men born on July 9, 1951, were picked first so they tended to stay in school longer to avoid the draft; while men born July 7 had no incentive to stay in school longer because they were picked last in the lottery. As a result, men born on July 9 not only had higher IQs, they also earned more money—approximately 7% more.

- Dropping out of school can also diminish IQ. In a large-scale study, 10% of all males in the Swedish school population born in 1948 were randomly selected and given an IQ test at age 13. Upon reaching age 18 (in 1966), 4,616 of them were tested again. For each year of high school not completed, there was a loss of 1.8 IQ points.
- IQ is affected by summer vacations. Two independent studies have documented that there is a systematic decline in IQ scores over the summer months. With each passing month away from school, children lose ground from their end-of-year scores. The decline is pronounced for children whose summers are least academically oriented.

FACT 3: IQ is not influenced by birth order

The idea that birth order influences personality and intelligence is long-standing. First-borns are allegedly smarter and more likely to become leaders than are later-born siblings. Recently, however, this belief has come up against scrutiny. The idea that large families make low-IQ children may be unfounded because researchers have discovered that low-IQ parents actually make large families.

The truth is that smart people tend to have small families, but it is not small families per se that make people smart. Hence, birth order doesn't predict IQ, and there is no causal role for family size in determining a child's IQ.

Also, no structural aspects of family size influence a child's IQ. Otherwise two siblings closer in age would have more similar IQs than two siblings spaced far apart. But this is not the case.

FACT 4: IQ is related to breast-feeding

My colleagues and I were skeptical when we first heard claims that breast-fed infants grew into children with higher IQs than their siblings who were not breast-fed. There are factors that differ between breast-fed and non-breast-fed children, such as the amount of time mother and child spend together through nursing and the sense of closeness they gain from nursing.

It turns out, however, that even when researchers control for such factors, there still appears to be a gain of 3 to 8 IQ points for breast-fed children by age three. Exactly why is unclear. Perhaps the immune factors in mother's milk prevent children from getting diseases that deplete energy and impair early learning. Breast milk may also affect nervous system functioning. Mother's milk is an especially rich source of omega-3 fatty acids that are building blocks of nerve cell membranes and crucial to the efficient transmission of nerve impulses.

FACT 5: IQ varies by birth date

Most states have restrictions on the age of students entering schools, as well as policies mandating attendance until age 16 or 17. School attendance drops off for students born during the final three months of the year, as they are more likely to enter school a year later. When these individuals come of age, they have been in school one year less than their classmates.

For each year of school completed, there is an IQ gain of approximately 3.5 points.

Researchers have shown that for each year of schooling completed, there is an IQ gain of approximately 3.5 points. Students born late in the year, as a group, show a lower IQ score. Given the random processes involved in being born early versus late within a given year, we can assume that the genetic potential for intelligence is the same in both groups.

FACT 6: IQ evens out with age

Imagine interviewing two biological siblings, adopted by two different middle class families, at age five and again at 18. Will their IQs be more alike when they are younger and living in the homes of their adoptive parents, or when they are older and living on their own? Many people reason that IQs will be more alike when they're younger because they are under the influence of their respective middle class parents. Once they are on their own, they may diverge as they become exposed to different experiences that may influence their intelligence differently.

IQ has risen about 20 points with every generation.

But according to data, this isn't true. As these siblings go out on their own, their IQ scores become more similar. The apparent reason is that once they are away from the dictates of their adoptive parents, they are free to let their genotypes express themselves. Because they share approximately 50% of their segregating genes, they will become more alike because they are propelled to seek similar sorts of environments. Genes may be more potent in making siblings alike than similarities in home environments.

FACT 7: Intelligence is plural, not singular

Regardless of their views about the existence and the strength of so-called general intelligence, researchers agree that statistically independent mental abilities exist—such as spatial, verbal, analytical and practical intelligence.

The rise in IQ has been attributed to many factors, such as better nutrition, more schooling and better-educated parents.

In 1995, Yale psychologist Robert Sternberg and colleagues developed new evidence that practical and analytical intelligence are two different things. They demonstrated that the skills of practical intelligence, such as common sense, were important in predicting life outcomes, but were not associated with IQ-type analytic intelligence. There may even be at least seven or eight different kinds of intelligence, says researcher Howard Gardner of Harvard, including interpersonal, intrapersonal, linguistic, motoric and musical intelligence.

FACT 8: IQ is correlated with head size

The relationship between head size and IQ has long been a subject of controversy. Popular writers such as Stephen J. Gould have rightly objected to the crude and biased means 19th-century scholars used to establish this correlation, which were based on head size and contour. But modern neuroimaging techniques demonstrate that cranial volume is correlated with IQ. Evidence also comes from studies of the helmet sizes of members of the Armed Services, whose IQs were measured during basic training. The correlations, however, are quite small.

FACT 9: Intelligence scores are predictive of real-world outcomes

People who have completed more school tend to earn more—over a lifetime, college graduates earn $812,000 more than high school dropouts, and those with professional degrees earn nearly $1,600,000 more than the college grads. But more schooling can't be the only factor in earning differences, because at every level of schooling, there is a variety of intellectual ability.

Research appears to confirm our mothers' wisdom that diet influences brain functioning.

As Figure 2 shows, even among those with comparable levels of schooling, the greater a person's intellectual ability, the higher that person's weekly earnings. Workers with the lowest levels of intellectual ability earn only two-thirds the amount workers at the highest level earn. Because differences in schooling are statistically controlled, the rise in earning must be due to other factors, such as intelligence.

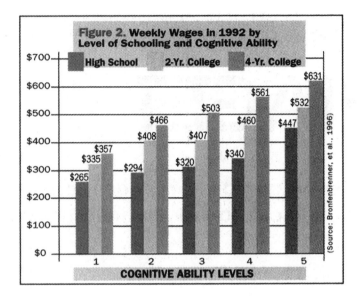

Figure 2. Weekly Wages in 1992 by Level of Schooling and Cognitive Ability

(Source: Bronfenbrenner, et al., 1996)

FACT 10: Intelligence is context-dependent

The setting in which we measure intelligence matters. In 1986, a colleague and I published a study of men who frequented the racetracks daily. Some were excellent handicappers, while others were not. What distinguished experts from non-experts was the use of a complex mental algorithm that converted racing data taken from the racing programs sold at the track. The use of the algorithm was unrelated to the men's IQ scores, however. Some experts were dockworkers with IQ scores in the low 80s, but they reasoned far more complexly at the track than all non-experts—even those with IQs in the upper 120s.

In fact, experts were always better at reasoning complexly than non-experts, regardless of their IQ scores. But the same experts who could reason so well at the track were often abysmal at reasoning outside the track—about, say, their retirement pensions or their social relationships.

FACT 11: IQ is on the rise

IQ has risen approximately 20 points with every generation, a steady increase called the "Flynn Effect," after New Zealand political scientist James Flynn. If people taking an IQ test today were scored with the norms of their grandparents' performances 50 years ago, more than 90% of them would be classified as "geniuses," while if our grandparents were scored today, most of them would be classed as "borderline mentally retarded." No one believes that real intelligence has risen as swiftly as IQ—if our grandparents were born today, they'd do just as well on IQ tests as they did a half century ago.

The rise in IQ has been attributed to many factors, such as better nutrition, more schooling, better-educated parents and more complex spatial environments thanks to smart toys and computers. The rise in IQ suggests that whatever it is that IQ tests test, it is not some inherent quality of the mind.

Immune factors in mother's milk may prevent children from getting diseases that deplete energy and impair early learning.

FACT 12: IQ may be influenced by the school cafeteria menu

Recent research appears to confirm our mothers' wisdom that diet influences brain functioning. Eat your fish; it's brain food.

In one large-scale analysis of approximately 1 million students enrolled in the New York City school system, researchers examined IQ scores before and after preservatives, dyes, colorings and artificial flavors were removed from lunch offerings. They found a 14% improvement after the removal. And the improvement was greatest for the weakest students. Prior to the dietary changes, 120,000 of the students were performing two or more grade levels below average. Afterward, the figure dropped to 50,000.

Intelligence, IQ, heredity and ecology are intertwined in complex and intriguing ways. Technical journals are awash with data, and one should consider the facts before leaping to conclusions about what is and what is not intelligence. We should all challenge the implicit theories of intelligence; otherwise we are in danger of misinterpreting the truth.

READ MORE ABOUT IT:

On Intelligence: A Bio-ecological Treatise on Intellectual Development, Stephen J. Ceci, Ph.D. (*Harvard University Press, 1996*)
Resolving the debate of birth order, family size and intelligence, Rodgers, J.L., et al. (*American Psychologist, 2000*)

Stephen J. Ceci, Ph.D., is the Helen L. Carr Professor of Developmental Psychology at Cornell University.

From *Psychology Today*, July/August 2001, pp. 46-48, 50, 52-53. © 2001 by Sussex Publishers, Inc. Reprinted with permission of the author.

CHILD PSYCHOLOGIST

JEAN PIAGET

He found the secrets of human learning and knowledge hidden behind the cute and seemingly illogical notions of children

BY SEYMOUR PAPERT

Jean Piaget, the pioneering Swiss philosopher and psychologist, spent much of his professional life listening to children, watching children and poring over reports of researchers around the world who were doing the same. He found, to put it most succinctly, that children don't think like grownups. After thousands of interactions with young people often barely old enough to talk, Piaget began to suspect that behind their cute and seemingly illogical utterances were thought processes that had their own kind of order and their own special logic. Einstein called it a discovery "so simple that only a genius could have thought of it."

Piaget's insight opened a new window into the inner workings of the mind. By the end of a wide–ranging and remarkably prolific research career that spanned nearly 75 years—from his first scientific publication at age 10 to work still in progress when he died at 84—Piaget had developed several new fields of science: developmental psychology, cognitive theory and what came to be called genetic epistemology. Although not an educational reformer, he championed a way of thinking about children that provided the foundation for today's education-reform movements. It was a shift comparable to the displacement of stories of "noble savages" and "cannibals" by modern anthropology. One might say that Piaget was the first to take children's thinking seriously.

ARCHIVES JEAN PIAGET
PIAGET IN '23: REVERED BY GENERATIONS OF TEACHERS

"[He is] one of the two towering figures of 20th century psychology."

JEROME BRUNER, Founder of the Harvard Center for Cognitive Studies

Others who shared this respect for children—John Dewey in the U.S., Maria Montessori in Italy and Paulo Freire in Brazil —fought harder for immediate change in the schools, but Piaget's influence on education is deeper and more pervasive. He has been revered by generations of teachers inspired by the belief that children are not empty vessels to be filled with knowledge (as traditional pedagogical theory had it) but active builders of knowledge—little scientists who are constantly creating and testing their own theories of the world. And though he may not be as famous as Sigmund Freud or even B.F. Skinner, his contribution to psychology may be longer lasting. As computers and the Internet give children greater autonomy to explore ever larger digital worlds, the ideas he pioneered become ever more relevant.

BORN Aug. 9, 1896, in Switzerland
1907 Publishes first paper at age 10
1918 Obtains doctorate in zoology, studies psychoanalysis
1920 Studies children's intelligence in Paris
1923 First of nearly 60 scholarly books published
1929 Appointed director, International Bureau of Education
1955 Establishes Center for Genetic Epistemology
1980 *Dies in Geneva*

Piaget grew up near Lake Neuchâtel in a quiet region of French Switzerland known for its wines and watches. His father was a professor of medieval studies and his mother a strict Calvinist. He was a child prodigy who soon became interested in the scientific study of nature. When, at age 10, his observations led to questions that could be answered only by access to the university library, Piaget wrote and published a short note on the sighting of an albino sparrow in the hope that this would influence the librarian to stop treating him like a child. It worked. Piaget was launched on a path that would lead to his doctorate in zoology and a lifelong conviction that the way to understand anything is to understand how it evolves.

After World War I, Piaget became interested in psychoanalysis. He moved to Zurich, where he attended Carl Jung's lectures, and then to Paris to study logic and abnormal psychology. Working with Théodore Simon in Alfred Binet's child-psychology lab, he noticed that Parisian children of the same age made similar errors on true-false intelligence tests. Fascinated by their reasoning processes, he began to suspect that the key to human knowledge might be discovered by observing how the child's mind develops.

Back in Switzerland, the young scientist began watching children play, scrupulously recording their words and actions as their minds raced to find reasons for why things are the way they are. In one of his most famous experiments, Piaget asked children, "What makes the wind?" A typical Piaget dialogue:

Piaget: What makes the wind?
Julia: The trees.
P: How do you know?
J: I saw them waving their arms.
P: How does that make the wind?
J (waving her hand in front of his face): Like this. Only they are bigger. And there are lots of trees.
P: What makes the wind on the ocean?
J: It blows there from the land. No. It's the waves...

Piaget recognized that five-year-old Julia's beliefs, while not correct by any adult criterion, are not "incorrect" either. They are entirely sensible and coherent within the framework of the child's way of knowing. Classifying them as "true" or "false" misses the point and shows a lack

PIAGET FAMILY/ARCHIVES JEAN PIAGET

PIAGET'S SUBJECTS INCLUDED HIS OWN THREE CHILDREN

of respect for the child. What Piaget was after was a theory that could find in the wind dialogue coherence, ingenuity and the practice of a kind of explanatory principle (in this case by referring to body actions) that stands young children in very good stead when they don't know enough or have enough skill to handle the kind of explanation that grownups prefer.

Piaget was not an educator and never enunciated rules about how to intervene in such situations. But his work strongly suggests that the automatic reaction of putting the child right may well be abusive. Practicing the art of making theories may be more valuable for children than achieving meteorological orthodoxy; and if their theories are always greeted by "Nice try, but this is how it really is... " they might give up after a while on making theories. As Piaget put it, "Children have real understanding only of that which they invent themselves, and each time that we try to teach them something too quickly, we keep them from reinventing it themselves."

Disciples of Piaget have a tolerance for—indeed a fascination with—children's primitive laws of physics: that things disappear when they are out of sight; that the moon and the sun follow you around; that big things float and small things sink. Einstein was especially intrigued by Piaget's finding that seven-

year-olds insist that going faster can take more time—perhaps because Einstein's own theories of relativity ran so contrary to common sense.

Although every teacher in training memorizes Piaget's four stages of childhood development (sensorimotor, preoperational, concrete operational, formal operational), the better part of Piaget's work is less well known, perhaps because schools of education regard it as "too deep" for teachers. Piaget never thought of himself as a child psychologist. His real interest was epistemology—the theory of knowledge—which, like physics, was considered a branch of philosophy until Piaget came along and made it a science.

Piaget explored a kind of epistemological relativism in which multiple ways of knowing are acknowledged and examined nonjudgmentally, yet with a philosopher's analytic rigor. Since Piaget, the territory has been widely colonized by those who write about women's ways of knowing, Afrocentric ways of knowing, even the computer's ways of knowing. Indeed, artificial intelligence and the information-processing model of the mind owe more to Piaget than its proponents may realize.

The core of Piaget is his belief that looking carefully at how knowledge develops in children will elucidate the nature of knowledge in general. Whether this has in fact led to deeper understanding remains, like everything about Piaget, controversial. In the past decade Piaget has been vigorously challenged by the current fashion of viewing knowledge as an intrinsic property of the brain. Ingenious experiments have demonstrated that newborn infants already have some of the knowledge that Piaget believed children constructed. But for those, like me, who still see Piaget as the giant in the field of cognitive theory, the difference between what the baby brings and what the adult has is so immense that the new discoveries do not significantly reduce the gap but only increase the mystery.

M.I.T. professor Seymour Papert, creator of the Logo computer language, worked with Piaget in Geneva

From *Time*, March 29, 1999, pp. 104-107. © 1999 by Time Inc. Magazine Company. Reprinted by permission.

Metacognitive Development

Abstract

Traditional developmental research in memory and reasoning, as well as current investigations in such disparate areas as theory of mind, epistemological understanding, knowledge acquisition, and problem solving, share the need to invoke a meta-level of cognition in explaining their respective phenomena. The increasingly influential construct of metacognition can be conceptualized in a developmental framework. Young children's dawning awareness of mental functions lies at one end of a developmental progression that eventuates in complex metaknowing capabilities that many adults do not master. During its extended developmental course, metacognition becomes more explicit, powerful, and effective, as it comes to operate increasingly under the individual's conscious control. Enhancing (a) metacognitive awareness of what one believes and how one knows and (b) metastrategic control in application of the strategies that process new information is an important developmental and educational goal.

Keywords
metacognition; development; knowledge acquisition

Deanna Kuhn[1]
Teachers College, Columbia University, New York, New York

Metacognition—that is, cognition that reflects on, monitors, or regulates first-order cognition—was characterized by Flavell in 1979 as a "promising new area of investigation" (p. 906). He appears to have been on the right track. The claim that metacognition is "where the action is" in understanding intellectual performance would meet with approval in many (though not all) circles today. If so, what do we need to know about this construct? The answer is, a great many things, but here I focus on two fundamental questions that have lacked clear answers: Where does metacognition come from and what kinds of it are there? In addition, I examine the relation between metacognition and cognition. Do they work together closely, or is the relation a more distant and formal one, akin to that between metaphysics and physics?

The answer I propose to the first question is that metacognition develops. It does not appear abruptly from nowhere as an epiphenomenon in relation to first-order cognition. Instead, metacognition emerges early in life, in forms that are no more than suggestive of what is to come, and follows an extended developmental course during which it becomes more explicit, more powerful, and hence more effective, as it comes to operate increasingly under the individual's conscious control. Placing metacognition in this developmental framework helps to clarify its nature and significance.

DEVELOPMENTAL ORIGINS OF METACOGNITION IN THEORY OF MIND

Over the past decade, the wave of research on children's understanding of the mind has been valuable in highlighting the earliest forms of metacognition. By age 3, children have acquired some awareness of themselves and others as knowers. They distinguish thinking about an object from actually perceiving it, and begin to refer to their own knowledge states, using verbs such as *think* and *know* (Flavell, 1999). By age 4, they understand that others' behavior is guided by beliefs and desires and that such beliefs may not match their own and could be incorrect. This so-called false belief understanding is a developmental milestone because it connects assertions to their generative source in human knowers. These early years are also a period of rapidly developing awareness of how one has come to know that what one claims is so—that is, awareness of the sources of one's knowledge.

These early metacognitive achievements serve as foundations for much of the higher-order thinking that appears later. Understanding knowledge as the product of human knowing is a critical first step in the development of epistemological thinking, which is metacognitive in the sense of constituting an implicit theory of how things are known and increasingly is becoming recognized as influential in higher-order thinking (Hofer & Pintrich, 1997). Scientific thinking is another form of higher-order thinking whose roots lie in early metacognitive achievements (Kuhn & Pearsall, 2000). Awareness of the sources of one's knowledge is critical to understanding evidence as distinct from and bearing on theories—an understanding that lies at the heart of scientific thinking. In skilled scientific thinking, existing understandings are coordinated with new evidence, and new knowledge is thereby acquired, in a highly deliberate, rule-governed, and therefore metacognitively controlled process.

DEVELOPMENTAL ORIGINS OF METASTRATEGIC AWARENESS AND CONTROL

Are there different kinds of metacognition? A long-standing distinction in cognitive psychology is that between declarative (knowing that) and procedural (knowing how) knowing. If these two kinds of knowing are fundamentally different, perhaps meta-level operations on them also differ. Specifically, I propose, we would expect meta-level operations to have their greatest influence on procedural knowing. Meta-level awareness of strategies for comprehending a chapter in a textbook, for example, may influence comprehension efforts, whereas explicit meta-level awareness of the declarative knowledge gained from the chapter ("knowing that I know") has less obvious effects on the knowledge itself.

I have proposed *metastrategic knowing* as a separate term to refer to metaknowing about procedural knowing, reserving *metacognitive knowing* (addressed in the preceding section) to refer to metaknowing about declarative knowing. Metastrategic knowledge can be further divided into *metatask* knowing about task goals and *metastrategic* knowledge about the strategies one has available to address these goals (Kuhn & Pearsall, 1998).

How and when does metastrategic cognition originate? Central to Vygotsky's (1962) view of cognitive development is the child's acquisition of

voluntary control in initiating or inhibiting actions, with Vygotsky attributing a major role to meta-level awareness in this achievement. More recently, Zelazo and his associates have investigated early origins of what they call executive control in the execution of a simple object-sorting task. To perform the task, an executive function is called on to select which of two previously learned rules (sort by shape or by color) to apply. Three-year-olds, these researchers have found, have difficulty selecting the called-for rule, even though they can easily execute either rule. The requisite executive control of cognitive functions, it is proposed, is acquired gradually and undergoes multiple developmental transitions (Zelazo & Frye, 1998).

META-LEVEL CONSTRUCTS IN THE STUDY OF DEVELOPMENTAL PROCESS

Why do metastrategic and metacognitive functions warrant our attention? One reason is that they help to explain how and why cognitive development both occurs and fails to occur (Kuhn, in press). Developmentalists have long been criticized for failing to address the core question of how change occurs. The picture has changed with the advent of microgenetic methods, in which the process of change is observed directly as individuals engage in the same task repeatedly. The consistent finding of microgenetic studies is that people possess a repertory of multiple strategies of varying adequacy that they apply variably to the same problem. Development, then, rather than constituting a single transition from one way of being to another, entails a shifting distribution in the frequencies with which more or less adequate strategies are applied, with the inhibition of inferior strategies as important an achievement as the acquisition of superior ones (Kuhn, 1995; Siegler, 1996).

This revised conception of the developmental process has important implications in the present context because it suggests a critical role for meta-level processes. If shifts in strategy usage cannot be satisfactorily explained at the

level of performance (e.g., frequency of prior use dictates the probability of a strategy's appearance), the explanatory burden shifts from the performance level to a meta-level that dictates which strategies are selected for use on a given occasion. The meta-level directs the application of strategies, but feedback from this application is directed back to the meta-level. This feedback leads to enhanced meta-level awareness of the goal and the extent to which it is being met by different strategies, as well as enhanced awareness and understanding of the strategies themselves, including their power and limitations. These enhancements at the meta-level lead to revised strategy selection. These changes in strategy usage in turn feed back to further enhance understanding at the meta-level, in a continuous cycle in which the meta-level both directs and is modified by the performance level.

Such a model privileges the meta-level as the locus of developmental change. Developmentally, then, increasing meta-level awareness and control may be the most important dimension in terms of which we see change (Kuhn, in press). In addition, the model makes it clear why efforts to induce change directly at the performance level have only limited success, indicated by failures of a newly acquired strategy to transfer to new materials or contexts. Strategy training may appear successful, but if nothing has been done to influence the meta-level, the new behavior will quickly disappear once the instructional context is withdrawn and individuals resume meta-level management of their own behavior.

EXTENDING THE SCOPE OF METACOGNITION RESEARCH

A second reason that metacognition warrants our attention has to do with the phenomena to which it is applied. In the era in which Flavell wrote his 1979 article, almost all the research on metacognitive development was confined to metamemory—the study of what children and adults know about how to remember and about their own memory functions and how such knowledge relates to memory performance. Today, metacognition is conceptualized and studied in a much broader context. Meta-cognitive and metastrategic functions are being investigated within domains of text comprehension, problem solving, and reasoning, as well as memory. Meta-cognition in the year 2000, then, is "about" more than it was in 1979.

It thus becomes more feasible to construct and evaluate alternative theories of the role that meta-level processes play in regulating and advancing cognitive development (Crowley, Shrager, & Siegler, 1997; Kuhn, in press). It is a reasonable hypothesis that the nature of strategy-metastrategy relations shows some generality across different kinds of cognition, specifically in the ways in which meta-level processes operate to select and regulate performance strategies. Studies of these phenomena across different kinds of cognitive strategies stand to inform one another.

ENDPOINTS OF METACOGNITIVE DEVELOPMENT

A third reason that metacognition warrants attention has to do with the later rather than early portions of its developmental course. Despite the centrality of knowledge acquisition as a topic of theoretical and practical significance, we lack sufficient research observing individuals engaged in the process of acquiring new knowledge. Microgenetic methods allow us to study this process of "knowledge building" (Chan, Burtis, & Bereiter, 1997) during which existing understandings are modified in the course of their interaction with new information. In addition, we can examine how knowledge-acquisition strategies are themselves transformed in the course of their continuing application. Such studies point to the critical role of metacognitive and metastrategic processes in regulating knowledge-acquisition processes.

Adults show more skill in these respects than do children (Kuhn, Garcia-Mila, Zohar, & Andersen, 1995), but the performance of adults is far from optimum. Their beliefs are frequently modified by the new information they encounter, to be sure, and they may become more certain of these beliefs over time, but they often lack awareness of why they are certain (i.e., of the process of theory-evidence coordination that has transpired), and they apply knowledge-acquisition and inference strategies in a selective way to protect their own, often erroneous, beliefs. Enhancing (a) meta-cognitive awareness of what one believes and how one knows and (b) meta-strategic consistency in application of the strategies that select and interpret evidence is thus both a developmental and an educational (Olson & Astington, 1993) goal.

SUPPORTING METACOGNITIVE DEVELOPMENT

In sum, competence in metaknowing warrants attention as a critical endpoint and goal of childhood and adolescent cognitive development. Young children's dawning awareness of their own and others' mental functions lies at one end of a developmental progression that eventuates in complex metaknowing capabilities not realized before adulthood, if they are realized at all. Linking these diverse attainments within a developmental framework makes it possible to investigate ways in which earlier attainments prepare the way for later ones.

As I suggested in the introduction, much remains to be learned about meta-cognition. We need to know more about how it develops and how it comes to regulate first-order cognition, or, very often, fails to do so. The fact that such failure is a common occurrence raises what is perhaps the most consequential question in need of more investigation: How can meta-cognitive development be facilitated?

Flavell (1979) expressed a broad vision in this respect:

It is at least conceivable that the ideas currently brewing in this area could someday be parlayed into a method teaching children (and adults) to make wise and thoughtful life decisions as well as to comprehend and learn better in formal educational settings. (p. 910)

Although it has yet to be realized, this vision conveys the potential significance of achieving meta-level control of one's knowing processes. A promising approach to fostering metacognitive development focuses on the idea of exercising, at an external, social level, the cognitive forms we would hope to become operative as well at the individual level. One of a number of researchers who have pursued this approach is Brown (1997), whose "community of learners" curriculum relies on

the development of a discourse genre in which constructive discussion, questioning, querying, and criticism are the mode rather than the exception. In time, these reflective activities become internalized as self-reflective practices. (p. 406)

There would seem few more important accomplishments than people becoming aware of and reflective about their own thinking and able to monitor and manage the ways in which it is influenced by external sources, in both academic, work, and personal life settings. Metacognitive development is a construct that helps to frame this goal.

Recommended Reading

Crowley, K., Shrager, J., & Siegler, R. (1997). (See References)

Hofer, B., & Pintrich, P. (1997). (See References)

Kuhn, D. (1999). A developmental model of critical thinking. *Educational Researcher, 28,* 16–25.

Kuhn, D. (1999). Metacognitive development. In L. Balter & C. Tamis-LeMonda (Eds.), *Child psychology: A handbook of contemporary issues* (pp. 259–286). Philadelphia: Psychology Press.

Kuhn, D. (in press). How do people know? *Psychological Science.*

Olson, D., & Astington, J. (1993). (See References)

Note

1. Address correspondence to Deanna Kuhn, Box 119, Teachers College, Columbia University, New York, NY 10027.

References

Brown, A. (1997). Transforming schools into communities of thinking and learning about serious matters. *American Psychologist, 52,* 399–413.

Chan, C., Burtis, J., & Bereiter, C. (1997). Knowledge-building as a mediator of conflict in conceptual change. *Cognition and Instruction, 15,* 1–40.

Crowley, K., Shrager, J., & Siegler, R. (1997). Strategy discovery as a competitive negotiation between metacognitive and associative mechanisms. *Developmental Review, 17,* 462–489.

Flavell, J. (1979). Metacognition and cognitive monitoring: A new area of cognitive-developmental inquiry. *American Psychologist, 34,* 906–911.

Flavell, J. (1999). Cognitive development: Children's knowledge about the mind. *Annual Review of Psychology, 50,* 21–45.

Hofer, B., & Pintrich, P. (1997). The development of epistemological theories: Beliefs about knowledge and knowing and their relation to learning. *Review of Educational Research, 67,* 88–140.

Kuhn, D. (1995). Microgenetic study of change: What has it told us? *Psychological Science, 6,* 133–139.

Kuhn, D. (in press). Why development does (and doesn't) occur: Evidence from the domain of inductive reasoning. In R. Siegler & J. McClelland (Eds.), *Mechanisms of cognitive development: Neural and behavioral perspectives.* Mahwah, NJ: Erlbaum.

Kuhn, D., Garcia-Mila, M., Zohar, A., & Andersen, C. (1995). Strategies of knowledge acquisition. *Society for Research in Child Development Monographs, 60* (4, Serial No. 245).

Kuhn, D., & Pearsall, S. (1998). Relations between metastrategic knowledge and strategic performance. *Cognitive Development, 13,* 227–247.

Kuhn, D., & Pearsall, S. (2000). Developmental origins of scientific thinking. *Journal of Cognition and Development, 1,* 113–129.

Olson, D., & Astington, J. (1993). Thinking about thinking: Learning how to take statements and hold beliefs. *Educational Psychologist, 28,* 7–23.

Siegler, R. (1996). *Emerging minds: The process of change in children's thinking.* New York: Oxford University Press.

Vygotsky, L.S. (1962). *Thought and language.* Cambridge, MA: MIT Press.

Zelazo, P., & Frye, D. (1998). Cognitive complexity and control: II. The development of executive function in childhood. *Current Directions in Psychological Science, 7,* 121–125.

From *Current Directions in Psychological Science*, October 2000, pp. 178-181. © 2000 by the American Psychological Society. Reprinted by permission.

"High Stakes Are for Tomatoes"

Statewide testing of students, with penalties for failure, has run into opposition from parents across the political spectrum

by Peter Schrag

By now it's hardly news that as education has risen to the top of the national agenda, a great wave—some would say a frenzy—of school reform has focused on two related objectives: more-stringent academic standards and increasingly rigorous accountability for both students and schools.

In state after state, legislatures, governors, and state boards, supported by business leaders, have imposed tougher requirements in math, English, science, and other fields, together with new tests by which the performance of both students and schools is to be judged. In some places students have already been denied diplomas or held back in grade if they failed these tests. In some states funding for individual schools and for teachers' and principals' salaries—and in some, such as Virginia, the accreditation of schools—will depend on how well students do on the tests. More than half the states now require tests for student promotion or graduation.

But a backlash has begun.

- In Massachusetts this spring some 300 students, with the support of parents, teachers, and community activists, boycotted the Massachusetts Comprehensive Assessment System MCAS tests ("Be a hero, take a zero") and demanded that if students had good enough records or showed other evidence of achievement, they be allowed to graduate even if they hadn't passed the test. Last November, after a strong majority of students failed the test, the state board of education lowered the score for passing to the level that the state designates as "needs improvement."

- In Wisconsin last year the legislature, pressed by middle-class parents, refused to fund the exit examination that the state had approved just two years earlier. After an extended battle with Governor Tommy Thompson, who has been a national leader in the push for higher standards and greater ac-

countability, a compromise was reached under which student achievement will be assessed on a variety of criteria. Failing the exam will not result in the automatic denial of a diploma.

- In Virginia this spring parents, teachers, and school administrators opposed to the state's Standards of Learning assessments, established in 1998, inspired a flurry of bills in the legislature that called for revising the tests or their status as unavoidable hurdles for promotion and graduation. One bill would also have required that each new member of the state board of education "take the eighth grade Standards of Learning assessments in English, mathematics, science, and social sciences" and that "the results of such assessments... be publicly reported." None of the bills passed, but there's little doubt that if the system isn't revised and the state's high failure rates don't decrease by

2004, when the first Virginia seniors may be denied diplomas, the political pressure will intensify. Meanwhile, some parents are talking about Massachusetts-style boycotts.

- In Ohio, where beginning next year fourth-graders who fail the Ohio Proficiency Tests will be held back, a growing coalition of parents and teachers—members of the Freedom in Education Alliance, Parents Against Unfair Proficiency Testing, and other groups—are circulating petitions to place a referendum on the ballot to amend or repeal the state's testing laws.

- In New York a policy requiring that all students pass Regents examinations in a variety of subjects in order to graduate is increasingly the subject of controversy. Three former members of the State Board of Regents who helped to develop the policy issued a position paper earlier this year saying that they had never expected that all students would be held to a single standard, and calling for a re-examination of the policy. "The thinking [when I voted for the test requirement] was that everyone would take the exams," one of them told *The New York Times*, "but you could get a diploma through other channels."

THE backlash, touching virtually every state that has instituted high-stakes testing, arises from a spectrum of complaints: that the focus on testing and obsessive test preparation, sometimes beginning in kindergarten, is killing innovative teaching and curricula and driving out good teachers; that (conversely) the standards on which the tests are based are too vague, or that students have not been taught the material on which the tests are based; that the tests are unfair to poor and minority students, or to others who lack test-taking skills; that the tests overstress young children, or that they are too long (in Massachusetts they can take thirteen to seventeen hours) or too tough or simply not good enough. In Massachusetts, according to students protesting MCAS, some students designated as needing improvement out-

scored half their peers on national standardized tests. "Testing season is upon us," says Mickey VanDerwerker, a leader of Parents Across Virginia United to Reform SOL, "and a lot of kids are so nervous they're throwing up." In Oakland, California, a protest organizer named Susan Harman is selling T-shirts proclaiming HIGH STAKES ARE FOR TOMATOES.

Some of the backlash comes from conservatives who a decade ago battled state-imposed programs that they regarded as anti-family exercises in political correctness. Although she has always thought of herself as a "bleeding-heart liberal," Mary O'Brien, a parent in Ohio who calls herself "an accidental activist" and is the leader of the statewide petition drive against the Ohio Proficiency Tests, complains that the state has no business trying to control local school curricula. In suburban Maryland this spring some parents kept their children out of school on test days, because they regard the Maryland School Performance and Assessment Program as a waste of time. They complain that it is used only to evaluate schools, not students—thereby objecting to almost precisely what parents in some other states are demanding. "It's more beneficial to have my child in his seat in the fifth grade practicing long division," one Maryland parent told a *Washington Post* reporter.

But many more of the protesters—parents, teachers, and school administrators—are education liberals: progressive followers of John Dewey, who believe that children should be allowed to discover things for themselves and not be constrained by "drill-and-kill" rote learning. They worry that the tests are stifling students and teachers. Most come from suburbs with good, even excellent, schools. Instead of the tests they want open-ended exercises—portfolios of essays, art and science projects, and other "authentic assessments"—that in their view more genuinely measure what a student really knows and can do. They have gotten strong reinforcement from, among others, FairTest, of Cambridge, Massachusetts, which opposes standardized testing; Senator Paul Wellstone, of Minnesota, who is sponsoring an anti-testing bill in Congress; Alfie Kohn, a prolific writer and polemicist who ar-

gues that the standards movement is a travesty that has "turned teachers into drill sergeants" in the traditionalist belief that "making people suffer always produces the best results"; and Gerald Bracey, an education researcher and a critic of the widespread belief that U.S. students are far behind their peers overseas, which has given impetus to the standards movement.

> In most cases tests and standards were imposed with little input from teachers or parents.

The anti-testing backlash is beginning to cohere as an integrated national effort. Earlier this year some 600 test critics attended a national conference on high-stakes testing, at Columbia University's Teachers College, to discuss effects, alternatives, and strategies: how to get the attention of legislators, what kinds of cases would be suited to civil-rights litigation, what assessments ensure accountability, how to achieve higher standards without high-stakes tests. Some on the left believe that the whole standards movement is a plot by conservatives to show up the public schools and thus set the stage for vouchers. All believe that poor and minority kids, who don't test well, are the principal victims of the tests and the standards movement. They contend (correctly) that almost no testing experts and none of the major testing companies endorse the notion of using just one test to determine promotion or graduation or, for that matter, the salaries of teachers and principals. But so far legislators and governors haven't paid much attention.

Among the most articulate critics of the tests are the boycotting students, who complain about narrowing opportunities and shrinking curricula. The most exciting ninth-grade course in his school, says Will Greene, a high school sophomore in Great Barrington, Massachusetts, is a science-and-technology class with a lot of hands-on experimentation. In the 1998–1999 school year, when students could take the class without worrying about MCAS, eighty students enrolled; this past year enrollment fell to thirty. Greene says that students feel the course will not help them pass the test, and failing the test next year could mean they don't get a diploma. "At least create a test," wrote Alison Maurer, an eighth-grader in Cambridge, Massachusetts, "that doesn't limit what students learn, something that shows what we have learned, not what we haven't."

THE movement is a long way from achieving critical mass. The two most prominent lawsuits brought to date—one in Texas, challenging the test as racially biased; the other in Louisiana, arguing that students hadn't had a chance to learn the material—have failed. The boycotts are still small, and polls, by Public Agenda and other organizations, continue to show that 72 percent of Americans—and 79 percent of parents—support tougher academic standards and oppose social promotion "even if [the outcome is] that significantly more students would be held back." Those numbers seem to reinforce the argument of Diane Ravitch, an education historian, an education official in the Bush Administration, and a strong supporter of standards, who has described the protesters as "crickets"— few in number, but making a disproportionate amount of noise. "There's tremendous support" for tests, Ravitch says, "among elected officials and in the business community." She may also be correct when she says that a great many of those who profess to oppose the high-stakes tests oppose all testing and all but the fuzziest standards. They are the same people, Ravitch argues, who in the end cheat kids by demanding too little and forever blaming children's inability to read or to do elementary math on the shortcomings of parents, neighborhoods, and the culture. Scrap the tests and we're back to the same neglect and indifference, particularly toward poor, marginal students, that we had before. Letting students who can't read, write, or do basic math graduate is doing no one a favor.

Yet even Ravitch is concerned about what she calls the "test obsession" and the backlash it could create if large

numbers of students fail and the whole system unravels. The accountability structure in Virginia has been set up in such a way that even if the vast majority of students pass the tests, a large percentage of schools could fail the accompanying Standards of Accreditation. Under the SOA, any school in which more than 30 percent of students fail in 2007 will be subject to loss of accreditation. That, according to a study by the conservative Thomas Jefferson Institute for Public Policy, in Springfield, Virginia, is a formula that fosters public distrust of both the schools and the system. The study points out that because high-scoring students are concentrated in just a handful of districts, only 6.5 percent of Virginia schools met the SOA in 1999, when 35 percent of all Virginia students passed all the required SOL tests.

The Jefferson Institute study illustrates a wider set of problems underlying the new standards and tests. In an effort to look like the toughest guy on the block, some states have imposed standards that will be difficult if not impossible for many students and schools to meet. Members of the Virginia Board of Education are negotiating over allowing students to graduate without necessarily passing a standardized test. As noted, Massachusetts has already lowered the passing score on MCAS. A policy in Los Angeles to hold back all failing students has been modified. And merit-scholarship systems have been created in Michigan and California to keep top students from blowing off the test. The states that have had the least trouble with backlash are those, like Texas, that set standards low enough (and the Texas standards are far too low, in the view of some critics) that a large percentage of students can pass the tests.

Some protesters complain that students are being constrained by "drill-and-kill" rote learning.

It is, of course, in the public ambivalence about where the bar should be set

that the larger uncertainty about the standards movement lies. Robert B. Schwartz, the president of Achieve, an organization created in 1996 by governors and business executives to defend the standards movement (at that time mostly against conservative attacks), recognizes that despite the polls, "not enough has been done to bring the public along." In most cases the tests and standards were imposed from the top down, with little input either from teachers—often regarded as the problem rather than the solution—or from parents (who in Arizona and California are not even allowed to see old test questions). What's needed now, Schwartz says, is to bolster public understanding and "capacity building," including professional development for teachers, to make the whole system work. "The good news," he told a reporter from *Education Week* in April, is that "states are not simply stopping with raising the bar, and shouting at kids and teachers to jump higher, but are moving to address the support question."

The question, as Schwartz knows, is whether resources—and particularly the quality of teaching in inner cities—will catch up with the demands on students. Since April, Schwartz has also acknowledged that as the day of reckoning approaches for millions of American students, the backlash will spread and intensify. "It's easy to assent in the abstract," he told me recently. "When it's my kid, it's something different." In the mid-1990s Delaware threw out a testing program because, in the words of Achieve, the legislature "had been unprepared for high rates of student failure."

In his state of education speech in February the U.S. Secretary of Education, Richard Riley, a strong advocate of accountability and standards, seemed to recognize the danger. "Setting high expectations," he said, "does not mean setting them so high that they are unreachable except for only a few.... If all of our efforts to raise standards get reduced to one test, we've gotten it wrong. If we force our teachers to teach only to the test, we will lose their creativity.... If we are so consumed with making sure students pass a multiple-choice test that we throw out the arts and civics then we will be going backwards instead of forward."

And yet the line between the political drive to be tough and indifference to standards in the name of creativity and diversity sometimes seems hard to draw. Diane Ravitch says that a person much missed in this debate is the late Albert Shanker, a longtime president of the American Federation of Teachers, who was relentless in his push for high standards for both students and teachers. But Shanker also pointed out that if only one standard for graduation exists, it will necessarily be low, because the political system can't support a high rate of failure. Shanker suggested two criteria: a basic competency level required of everyone, combined with honors diplomas, by whatever name, for students who do better and achieve more. The issue of the tradeoff between minimum competency and what is sometimes called "world-class standards" is rarely raised in any explicit manner, but it has bedeviled this debate since the beginning. As the standards requirements begin to take effect, and as more parents face the possibility that their children will not graduate, pressure to lower the bar or eliminate it entirely will almost certainly increase. Conversely, as more people come to understand that the "Texas miracle" and other celebrated successes are based on embarrassingly low benchmarks, those, too, will come under attack. The most logical outcome would be the Shanker solution. But in education politics, where ideology often reigns, logic is not always easy to come by.

From *The Atlantic Monthly*, August 2000, pp. 19-21. © 2000 by Peter Schrag. Reprinted by permission.

The Future of Computer Technology in K–12 Education

American business was not able to take advantage of the power of computer technology until many of its basic practices changed, Mr. Bennett points out, and this is equally true in education. Until schools can permit a major alteration in the way teaching is carried on, they must necessarily continue to miss out on the improvement that computer technology can bring.

BY FREDERICK BENNETT

IN A PIECE published in February 2001, syndicated columnist George Will used Hippocrates and Socrates to illustrate the difficulties in contemporary American schooling. "If you were ill and could miraculously be treated by Hippocrates or by a young graduate of Johns Hopkins medical school, with his modern technologies and techniques, you would choose the latter. But if you could choose to have your child taught either by Socrates or by a freshly minted holder of a degree in education, full of the latest pedagogical theories and techniques? Socrates, please."

Teaching has always been more art than science and depends heavily on the talents of the practitioner. Some teachers are outstanding; some are not. In medicine, Hippocrates probably had more innate abilities than many of the new physicians, but his successors have the advantage of modern technology. Teachers, however, rely on basically the same approach that instructors have used throughout history, and, consequently, they must count on their own native skills. This situation presents a difficulty for education because exceptional instructors are in the minority. We see this easily if we think back over the teachers that we ourselves had in our school career. The number we remember as superb is not large.

THE PRESENT

Education today, as always, depends on the luck of the draw—who gets the good teachers and who gets the others? Meanwhile, technology has become a powerful force in the world. Theoretically, it might change education, just as it has made the new physician better equipped than

Hippocrates and has brought dazzling benefits to innumerable other areas of society. Education authorities apparently hoped for comparable results because they have placed millions of computers in schools. By 1999, there

was one computer for every six children.[1] Yet despite this massive infusion of technology, overall improvements in education have been minimal.

Scores on the National Assessment of Educational Progress point up this lack of advancement. Results for 1999 showed no significant change in reading, mathematics, or science for the three age groups tested—9-year-olds, 13-year-olds, and 17-year-olds—from 1994 through 1999.[2] During this five-year period, schools acquired huge numbers of computers and hoped earnestly that this influx of technology would improve education.

Since few people want to despair and conclude that K–12 education seems to be about the only major field that technology cannot benefit, authorities have sought reasons for the current failure. The most frequently suggested explanation is that teachers have not learned how to employ technology in their classrooms. Therefore, if schools could train teachers, the argument goes, technology would finally deliver major benefits to education. President Clinton joined those who wanted additional teacher training when in June 2000 he announced $128 million in grants to instruct teachers in the use of technology.

Lack of teacher training, however, is a myth. In 2000 the U.S. Department of Education issued a study in which half of all teachers reported that college and graduate work had prepared them to use technology. In addition, training continues after formal schooling. The same government document pointed out that, from 1996 to 1999, 77% of teachers participated in "professional development activities in the use of computers or the Internet."[3] Thirty-three percent to 39% of teachers responding to two surveys in 1999 said that they felt well prepared to use computers.[4] Although not the full universe of teachers, this percentage of well-prepared instructors ought to have brought some improvement if technology were going to lift education to a higher plateau.

The failure of test scores to change after schools have added millions of computers, after teachers have received considerable training, and after many years of computer usage leads to a troubling question: Is it possible that technology as currently used can never fundamentally improve today's K–12 education? I believe that such hopelessness is indeed warranted, for one obvious reason: the power of electronic interaction is necessarily diminished because of the way computers must be used in schools today.

Interaction takes place when the instructor and the student react directly to each other's contributions. Interaction between child and teacher has always been found in good instruction. It can make learning enjoyable, can adjust to the varied abilities of different students, and is effective with children of all ages. Very possibly, one of the attributes of the teachers that we remember as being superb was their ability to develop a high degree of interaction with us.

Computer games show the power of electronic interaction. The secret to a large portion of this technology's success in maintaining its iron grip on the attention of game players is the unparalleled ability of the machine to interact

continually with the participant. Theoretically, this same interactive power ought to make computers a potent force in education. When computers are used in classrooms today, however, interaction between the computer and the student cannot be strong and ongoing. This is because the teacher, not the computer, must control and direct instruction. Individual teachers must decide how they will use computer instruction in the dissemination of classroom material—how much the machine will teach the student and how much instruction the teacher will provide. These conditions are unalterable in the present system of education, and they drastically curtail interaction between the computer and the student.

BUSINESS AND COMPUTERS

American education, however, is not unique in its poor initial results with computers. Corporate America had a similar experience. For several years, businesses added large numbers of computers, but overall productivity did not improve. Many workers acquired the machines for their desks. They used them for important jobs such as word processing and spreadsheets, but the basic manner in which companies carried on their activities did not change. This kind of computer usage was bound to fail. In time, corporations made the necessary structural changes and thus altered the basic way they carried on their business. When that happened, productivity increased dramatically. In an extensive article about the increase in productivity that technology has brought to business, Erik Brynjolfsson and Lorin Hitt point out, "Investments in computers may make little direct contribution to overall performance of a firm or the economy until they are combined with complementary investments in work practices, human capital, and firm restructuring."[5]

Education is in a position today akin to that of American business in those early days. Despite the millions of computers in schools, teaching has not changed. In the encompassing evaluation of technology in schools mentioned above, the Department of Education notes, "According to the literature, the advent of computers and the Internet has not dramatically changed how teachers teach and how students learn."[6]

AN ALTERNATIVE

There is an alternative to the way we use computers in schools, an alternative that would take advantage of the power of interaction. We could allow computers to tutor children individually and directly, without a teacher in the usual role. This approach seems radical when first considered. Nonetheless, a few schools have tried it for some students or subjects. The usual students in these computerized classes are those who are at risk of dropping out of school. In many cases, these students have been so difficult to teach that authorities have allowed this new approach. The results have been uniformly good.

Several companies have developed fitting teaching software. Among these are Plato Learning, Inc., Scientific Learning, and NovaNet Learning, Inc. All three have Web pages on which the results of their programs are posted.[7]

Lakeland High School in Florida, Lawrence High School in Indianapolis, and Turner High School in Carrollton, Texas, provide three interesting examples of Plato programs. In retests in Lakeland, student FHSCT (Florida High School Competency Test) scores increased dramatically, and the school identified a significant positive relationship between some Plato student performance data and the FHSCT scores. Authorities at Lawrence implemented an extensive remediation program in 1998–99 to increase the passing rate of their students taking the state-mandated competency exam, ISTEP (Indiana Statewide Testing for Educational Progress). At the beginning of the year, 406 students failed either the math or the English component. At the end of the year, only 74 of those pupils continued to fail the exam. At Turner, the pass rate on TAAS (Texas Assessment of Academic Skills) reversed a trend and improved from 69% in 1998 to 83% in 2000.

Scientific Learning has concentrated on reading and comprehension, especially with students who are behind in these vital areas. Pretest and posttest results with standardized, nationally normed tests showed significant gains with various levels of students from kindergarten through grade 12.

Dillard High School in Fort Lauderdale, Florida, provides an example of the results of using NovaNet software. In this program there were 123 students, all of whom were below the 20th percentile on state standards. After three months of using the program, all pupils had made gains. Moreover, half of the students had advanced at least one full grade, and 27 of those pupils had improved by either two or three grade levels.

Although schools have used this form of computerized education primarily with at-risk children, there are other programs that teach average and bright students, and they have recorded equally exciting gains. For example, researchers at Carnegie Mellon University created software to teach algebra through computers. They installed the program in a number of high schools, including some in their hometown of Pittsburgh. The authors made a study of freshmen at three schools, none of whom had taken the subject in middle school. Approximately 470 students enrolled in 21 computer classes. At the end of the year the schools assessed results and compared math achievement for these students with that of a comparable group of 170 ninth-grade students in standard math courses. The results showed the power of the computerized learning. The computer students scored 15% better on standardized tests. Moreover, they scored 100% better on the more difficult questions that "focused on mathematical analysis of real-world situations and the use of computational tools."[8]

In all these successful programs the electronic instruction takes advantage of many of the strengths of computers: children are taught individually and at their own pace, and the software develops interaction between the computer and the student. Moreover, the electronic instructor never retires or gets sick, and programmers can continually improve the software. Teachers continue to be essential, but with a role that differs from our accustomed conception of what teachers do.

Careful consideration of results from these and other studies makes it seem possible that, if this type of computerized education were adopted universally, technology could begin to make real and beneficial changes for students, teachers, and schools. Under this scenario, not only would there be interaction between the computer and the student, but also each pupil would have, in effect, a private tutor throughout his or her educational career. Like a human tutor, the electronic instructor would teach the child at his or her learning level. For example, superior students would constantly have new vistas and challenges opened to them, with continual opportunities for advancement. With sub-par students, the computer would provide appropriate material but would also move at a speed that would fit each pupil's capacity for progress.

Through constant testing and continual interaction, the electronic instructor would be aware of the child's needs and would immediately provide proper material to correct any problems and to encourage and help the student to advance. Students who had more difficulty learning would never be overwhelmed because the class had proceeded beyond their level of scholarship. Moreover, there would be no embarrassment if the computer had to take longer to cover a given lesson for a particular student. The child's classmates would not know. Only the computer and the authorities receiving the computer reports would have this information. At the other end of the learning spectrum, students who were capable of advancing more rapidly would find new excitement and challenges, and much of the boredom that has always engulfed these students would be removed.

Moreover, the electronic instructor could be programmed to emulate the approaches that good teachers have always used with their students. It would point out errors and praise and reinforce all gains. Positive feedback helps the student and makes learning enjoyable, as all teachers recognize. In a classroom of 15 or 20 students, teachers are often unable to give each student individual encouragement. The computer, however, with only one child to attend to, would always be quick to praise his or her accomplishments. Since the computer would interact directly with the child, it could concentrate its power exclusively on the needs of the individual student without affecting the requirements of other children in the class. They would all have their own private tutors.

TEACHERS

Computerized education would change the role of teachers but would neither eliminate nor downgrade them. On the contrary, human instructors would remain extremely important but with a radically different focus. This possibility often frightens teachers, but computerization would actually enhance their position. Many of the tedious, boring duties that they must endure today, such as preparing daily lesson plans and correcting tests, would vanish. That would leave them more time to function in their true and essential position as educators. There are two basic roles that I foresee for teachers in computerized education: continuing to conduct group activities and acting as "leader teachers."

Many teachers today conduct a variety of group sessions, such as workshops, seminars, and discussions. In computerized education, these duties would not only continue but would take on more importance than in today's schools. In addition, some aspects of today's group meetings would change. The computer would handle the basic necessities of the assigned curriculum, giving teachers greater freedom to choose topics for a group setting and the prospect of dealing more deeply with those topics than is possible today. Group projects might continue for several class periods or for several days. Despite the length of time used in these activities, the students would not miss any of their computer classes because the computer would begin again exactly where the last lesson ended. Today, teachers usually have all the students from their own classes in their groups and no one else. In computerized education, preset conditions would not determine attendance. Students could choose the workshops that most interested them, and teachers could establish prerequisites for attendance. For a teacher, this type of group would form the ideal teaching environment.

One of the fears sometimes voiced about children learning extensively from computers is that they would lose the valuable human give-and-take that currently happens in classes. In actuality, because of the need for discipline, less interplay among students goes on in today's classrooms than is often imagined. But group sessions in computerized education would provide many legitimate opportunities for student interaction.

Another vitally important activity for humans in the education of children would be to function as leader teachers.[9] Every student at every age level would have a leader teacher whom the pupil and his or her parents would choose and who would be responsible for leading the child as he or she pursued an education. This relationship between student and teacher would last for at least a year at a time and might continue for several years. The student would meet this mentor privately and on a regular basis. These meetings would vary, depending on the age and needs of the child. For example, the leader teacher of a student in the first grade might see and talk with the child several times every day. The leader teacher of a student in high school might meet with the youth only once every couple of weeks if that seemed appropriate.

All children, however, at all age levels would sit down regularly with their teachers, who would have access to their computer records. Time would be available for the instructors to get to know the children well. This system would make directing the education of the children easier and more productive for the teachers and make the children comfortable with this kind of direction. In today's education system, many students go months or even years without meeting privately with a teacher. That could never happen if computers were teaching and leader teachers had both the responsibility of directing children's education and the time to carry out that responsibility.

Parents would have another advantage because a leader teacher directed their child. They would find it easier to arrange parent/teacher conferences. They would need to meet with only one instructor, who would have a thorough knowledge of the student and of all the subjects he or she was studying.

THE FUTURE

Can schools ever take advantage of true computerized education? When corporate America learned how it could use computers to improve productivity, the central role of the computer in business was assured. The need for improvement in education is present, as even such staunch defenders of today's schools as the Sandia National Laboratories and Gerald Bracey point out. Moreover, everybody would be delighted if there could be additional gains even among today's best schools.

Emulating the successful employment of computers by business, however, is not simple. There are unique difficulties in education. For example, school boards must alleviate the fears of teachers that they will lose their jobs. In addition, since education is much more involved in the political world, proportionately more people must take part in the process of making changes. The numbers of citizens who must become aware of the potential of computerization in education will be larger than in business, where the decision makers are fewer. In corporate America, when software companies developed programs to enhance productivity, individual businesses bought that software because they wanted to improve and did not fear changes. Education, with some exceptions, has a history of resisting serious change. This tendency lessens the incentive for software companies to develop the necessary programming.

The solution, therefore, must be twofold. First, educators, politicians, parents, and concerned citizens must understand how schools can use computers more effectively to improve education and to benefit students and teachers. Second, commercial companies must create suitable software.

These seem to be monstrous tasks, but both are possible. Many teachers, parents, and administrators want improvements and are engaged in an ongoing search for answers. They will need to examine and debate the value of true computerization as they carry out their quest. If these many searchers for improved education decide that computerization can supply an important portion of the answer, then it will be up to the private corporations to do their part. Some of these are already developing programming, as noted above, and they and other companies could turn more of their resources and ingenuity toward developing outstanding and effective educational software. The potential market is huge, and software corporations will produce the programming as soon as they see that education will accept these changes.

Although there are differences in the paths of education and business in developing the use of computerization, there is one major similarity. American business was not able to take advantage of the power of computer technology until many of its basic practices changed. This is equally true in education. Until schools can permit a major alteration in the way teaching is carried on, they must necessarily continue to miss out on the improvement that computer technology can bring.

NOTES

1. Becky Smerdon et al., *Teachers' Tools for the 21st Century: A Report on Teachers' Use of Technology* (Washington, D.C.: National Center for Education Statistics, 2000), p. 5.
2. Jay R. Campbell, Catherine M. Hombo, and John Mazzeo, *NAEP 1999 Trends in Academic Progress: Three Decades of Student Performance* (Washington, D.C.: National Center for Education Statistics, 2000), Figure 1.
3. Smerdon et al., p. iii.
4. Ibid.; and Market Data Retrieval, "New Teachers and Technology: Examining Perceptions, Habits, and Professional Development Experiences," survey conducted in 1999.
5. Erik Brynjolfsson and Lorin M. Hitt, "Computing Productivity: Firm-Level Evidence," p. 2, available at http://grace.wharton.upenn.edu/~lhitt/ cpg.pdf.
6. Smerdon et al., chap. 7.
7. Plato Learning, Inc.: http://www.plato.com; Scientific Learning: http://www.scilearn.com; and NovaNet Learning, Inc.:http://www.nn.com.
8. Kenneth R. Koedinger et al., "Intelligent Tutoring Goes to School in the Big City," *Journal of Artificial Intelligence in Education*, vol. 8, no. 1, 1997, p. 31.
9. Frederick Bennett, *Computers as Tutors: Solving the Crisis in Education* (Sarasota, Fla.: Faben, 1999), chap. 19.

FREDERICK BENNETT *is a retired psychologist and the author of* Computers as Tutors: Solving the Crisis in Education *(Faben, 1999). He lives in Sarasota, Fla.* E-mail address: bennett@fabenbooks.com

From *Phi Delta Kappan,* April 2002, pp. 621-625. © 2002 by Phi Delta Kappa International. Reprinted by permission of the author.

Choosing to Learn

Students in all classrooms have always had the power to make the most basic choice about their learning: they may choose to engage in learning or to disengage. Our goal, the authors point out, is to inspire them to choose to engage. In short, we want students to choose to learn and choose in order to learn.

BY BOBBY ANN STARNES AND CYNTHIA PARIS

HIGH SCHOOL English and Spanish teacher Susan Moon stood near a thick pad of chart paper. Her class of juniors and seniors sat casually around the room. On the chalkboard were the state curriculum mandates. They had been through this process before, so they were prepared.

"Okay," Susan said, "this is what we have to demonstrate that we know. Any ideas how we are going to do that?"

With almost no lapse, the kids began to throw out ideas and to argue the merits of each proposal until they identified a project they believed would permit each student to meet the state requirements. Once Susan felt confident that their choices would allow them to do well, she asked, "Okay, you're going to need money to do this. How are you going to get it?"

Once again, the kids took over. Before I left, they had identified how they would meet or exceed state mandates, raise

money to support their plans, and demonstrate what they had learned. They were energized. I was exhausted from trying to keep up with them.

Will they meet their goals? If their history bears out, they will.... Typically, kids in Susan's classes score in the 90th percentile on state achievement tests. And this is no wealthy suburban school district. It is a rural school serving a population in which teen pregnancy and dropout rates are high. It is a school where one might not expect to find this kind of teaching and learning going on.

—Trip Log, September 1996

Some might say that Susan is unique, that she is part of an elite club of exceptional teachers, or that hers is a one-of-a-kind classroom. But our experience has shown us that there are many Susans in many schools around the country—places

where, without fanfare and often where one might least expect it, teachers go about their work and do remarkable things in spite of challenges and barriers. Foxfire works with some of these teachers—in both small schools and massive urban campuses in 37 states, from the border town of Calexico, California, to a school at the end of the road in Elk City, Idaho; from South Central Los Angeles to rural Alabama; from the suburbs of Princeton, New Jersey, to the inner-city neighborhoods of Seattle, Washington. Across grade levels, across content areas, across cultures and races and economic levels, these teachers create dynamic learning environments.

Like Susan, many teachers believe learners will meet high expectations when they are actively involved in making meaningful choices about how they will learn. Such teachers have worked in isolation, in small groups, and in regional or national networks to define, develop, and construct means to put their beliefs into practice. Through their efforts and their individual and collective decisions, they have found ways to provide their students opportunities to succeed academically and, at the same time, to engage in classroom experiences that make them active decision makers and partners in their own educations.

To achieve success, these teachers balance the demands of their school systems and their own deeply held beliefs. They involve learners in making significant decisions about how they will learn, how they will assess what they learn, and how they will use what they have learned in meaningful ways. In this way, they create active, learner-centered teaching and learning steeped in the ideas and ideals of democratic principles. Moreover, their work together creates rich, interactive relationships between teachers, learners, and the curriculum.

Regardless of experience or the school context, they adapt their work in proactive ways, creating learning environments that are unique, yet similar. And though they share these powerful beliefs, most of these teachers have never met or talked, or even know there are others with whom they share a vision.

Including learners in making decisions that affect them and *still* meeting high academic standards strikes many in the popular and professional media as incompatible, if not mutually exclusive. Yet, these teachers know they are not. They know that including learners increases their determination to do well, to meet high standards. Our work has taught us that learners of all ages can and will make good choices and contribute meaningfully when they are regularly given—with proper preparation and within developmentally-appropriate boundaries—the opportunity to participate in making the decisions that affect them. The climate that emerges from a decision-making classroom allows the learners, in collaboration with the teacher, to solve emerging problems as they address the curriculum. In this way, learners are supported in the development of their ability to solve problems and accept responsibility. At the same time, teachers who share these beliefs accept their responsibility to ensure that the academic integrity of all classroom experiences is clear. These teachers share their high expectations, taking away the mystery of what they are "supposed" to learn. Then, through collaborative planning, students engage in learning experiences that allow them to meet or exceed the mandates.

We know that access to educational, economic, and career opportunities is more available to those who have mastered a set of basic academic skills in such areas as reading, writing, speaking, math, and science. Therefore, teachers have a moral and ethical responsibility to ensure that learners acquire these skills and develop the traits that provide access to a broad array of life choices.

Teachers who include their students in devising a learning plan for the class that ensures that all learners achieve academic success have the ability to integrate these two, seemingly divergent ideals. Through the experiences of such teachers, we have learned that, taken together, these practices contribute to the development of independent, self-assured, self-directed citizens with the intelligence and personal power to think and act independently, both as individuals and as members of a larger community.

"Taken together" is both the key and the challenge. One without the other diminishes the richness and possibility of education. To permit learners to make choices that deprive them of the opportunity to build the skills they need in order to obtain access to learning opportunities is to act irresponsibly. To slight learners' development as good decision makers or self-governing young adults is just as irresponsible.

Yet the history of our profession has been one of either/ors and pendulum swings from "soft" progressivism to "tough" back-to-basics movements. It is not surprising, then, that many teachers see academic integrity and learner choice as incompatible. And teachers who see them as incompatible but value both are faced with an interesting dilemma. Some teachers resolve the conflict by retaining for themselves decisions regarding the curriculum, discipline, grades, and classroom learning activities. Learners are left to make small choices, such as whether they use green paint or red. Other teachers resolve this conflict by providing choice during free time or after the "work" is done.

John Dewey leads us to see the spaces between these either/ors as places of possibility. In such spaces, we can explore the ways in which learner choice creates conditions in which academic integrity can flourish. And we can do so with a confidence bred of our own experience and that of many others.

Over half a century ago, this kind of dynamic interdependence between choice and academic integrity was explored in the

The Foxfire Core Practices

1. The work teachers and learners do together is infused from the beginning with learner choice, design, and revision.
2. The role of the teacher is that of facilitator and collaborator.
3. The academic integrity of the work teachers and learners do together is clear.
4. The work is characterized by active learning.
5. Peer teaching, small-group work, and teamwork are all consistent features of classroom activities.
6. Connections between the classroom work, the surrounding communities, and the world beyond the community are clear.
7. There is an audience beyond the teacher for learner work.
8. New activities spiral gracefully out of the old, incorporating lessons learned from past experiences, building on skills and understandings that can now be amplified.
9. Imagination and creativity are encouraged in the completion of learning activities.
10. Reflection is an essential activity that takes place at key points throughout the work.
11. The work teachers and learners do together includes rigorous, ongoing assessment and evaluation.

Eight-Year Study (Aiken, 1942). This study confirmed that students who had attended schools in which they were partners in curriculum planning met and even exceeded expectations for academic achievement in college. Teachers and learners in those schools engaged in creating curricula that were grounded in the learners' interests and experiences and directed toward the achievement of academic goals. Projects and theme studies focusing on learners' concerns were the vehicles for acquiring the necessary academic skills and knowledge.

Alfie Kohn's (1993) synthesis of more recent classroom research has demonstrated the applicability of the findings of the Eight-Year Study's findings to education today. Among other things, Kohn found that learners given opportunities to make choices about how they would learn worked longer, produced more creative work, missed fewer days of school, and scored higher on standardized tests.

In the sections that follow, we examine the concepts of learner choice and academic integrity as teachers and learners who use the Foxfire approach have come to understand them over the years. Using excerpts from logs we have kept of classroom visits over the years as well as published remarks, we hope to show that learner choice and academic integrity are, by necessity, interwoven concepts.

Learner Choice

... [T]he choice thing just doesn't work with these kids.... [I agree] kids should be allowed to make choices... but these kids make bad choices....

"The other day I was working with a reading group, and I told the rest of the class they could choose what to do. One boy chose to crawl around the room and make loud whooping noises. We couldn't get our work done because he was making so much noise. But it was his choice, so I couldn't do anything about it."

I was stunned.

—Trip Log, September 1996

The most damaging misinterpretation of the notion of learner choice is that adopting it leads to an "anything goes" classroom. Of course, such an interpretation invites anarchy. If students are permitted to make decisions without boundaries, without coaching, and without respect for the rights of others, effective learning, the development of democratic principles, and the developmental process are seriously impaired.

Still, confusion about the difference between democratic principles and anarchy is not unusual. It may be difficult for those with limited experience participating in environments shaped by democratic principles to see the differences between freedom and license and to see the need for boundaries within which choices must be made.

Over the years, teachers have documented learners' engagement, achievement, and pride in mastering skills that permit them to complete tasks they have set for themselves and helped design. Through their reports, we have come to understand the nature and implications of making student choice a pivotal piece of teaching practice. Typical of these reports is Carol Coe's (1997) description of students in her sophomore composition class

after they decided they would write a book in order to meet their required curriculum goals:

> The book idea had definitely captured their interest and without any of my ideas appearing to light the class fire.... I noticed an immediate surge in energy and mood among the students, with ideas bubbling forth.... Students willingly volunteered their time and talents.... Why hadn't I noticed this wealth of creative energy and talent before? Clearly it had been there all along, but I hadn't seen it. This previously untapped potential now became a driving force propelling us forward.[3]

With their interests engaged and potential revealed, Coe's students completed this challenging academic task.

John Dewey offers us some insight into what might be at work here. He claimed that there are conditions that must be met for school activities to be truly educative. The first is interest. An activity must "lay hold on the emotions and desires" and "offer an outlet for energy that means something to the individual."[4] Such an activity "arouses curiosity, strengthens initiative, and sets up desires and purposes sufficient to carry a person over the dead places."[5]

Potential "dead places" litter the path to learning. They may be the seemingly endless revisions before a piece of writing meets the author's standards, or they may be the necessary but often tedious and frustrating struggle to master skills necessary to accomplish a task. Clearly, neither Dewey nor teachers we write about here are saying that *everything* learners do must be solely their choice. Both acknowledge the significance and reality of dead places.

Diane Sanna describes a child whose personal interests and desires carried him through these places:

> I was having a difficult time finding a way to reach Craig. Then it happened one day; Craig found something that was uniquely meaningful to him, the spark that would launch him forward academically... a children's book about the *Titanic*.... Although the book was at a reading level that was challenging for him, Craig stuck with it for two days, reading every chance he got.... Eager to discover the magic the book had for Craig, I asked him why it was interesting to him. He told me he had once watched a TV program about the *Titanic* with his father. Craig was connecting... something that was interesting to him [in school] to his life outside the classroom.[6]

This is all well and good, but professional wisdom and humility require us to concede that we cannot know what engages the interest of each and every one of our students. Nor can we presume to know what life has offered or demanded of each learner in our increasingly diverse classrooms. Well-meaning attempts to anticipate learners' interests and purposes with flashy teaching units on teddy bears or dinosaurs or poetry introduced through rap music often miss the mark. If we hope to arouse and engage learners' interests, we must help *them* discover and pursue what *they* care about, what excites *them,* and what arouses *their* curiosity. We cannot guess it for them.

Craig's teacher summed up her story with this thought: "The best we can do is provide meaningful experiences and wait and watch their eyes light up and they're off and running, and determined and motivated to learn."[7]

Now, all interests, in and of themselves, are not educative. Neither are all choices. Good choices are those that have a purpose or what Dewey refers to as an "end view."[8] Good choices are purposeful on at least two levels. Good choices allow learners to pursue interests of personal significance, while building on past knowledge and experience, stretching toward greater understanding and skill, and meeting required learning objectives.

Making good choices is an acquired skill. It demands, among other things, the higher-order thinking skills to evaluate options against standards. When choices are offered to learners, the question posed is seldom "What shall we learn?" Curricular mandates most often guide the "what." Rather, the question is "How shall we learn?" Together, teachers and learners construct a plan for meeting the requirements that allows all learners to be involved at their individual achievement levels of and that includes opportunities for individual choice.

"Together" is key here. Choices are made *in collaboration* with the teacher—a mature, responsible decision maker who deliberately models decision making for learners and coaches them in the skills of making good choices.

This point can best be illustrated by taking a close look at Harold Brown's sophomore English classroom. He has carefully prepared his students, and, although he remains outside the discussion reported here, he is a fully attentive and active member of the decision-making activity.

This is a really big day in Harold Brown's sophomore English class near the California-Mexico border. It is the day he turns over decision making to his students for the first time. Harold spent a semester preparing the students for this day—helping them learn to make good choices, providing opportunities for them to assess their work, creating a learning community, setting high standards, and making the curriculum mandates explicit.

Standing in front of the room, he begins. "These are the givens," he says pointing to a long list. Moving his hand down the list, he continues by identifying those requirements mandated by the state and school, those determined by his teaching team, those he will require, and those that the class has developed.

"Now the question is," he says, "how are we going to make sure that we meet these requirements in the next nine weeks? Your job today is to figure out how we do that."

Before moving their chairs into the discussion circle, the students briefly review the class norms. Finally, Harold explains that he will not participate in the discussion. "You will need to talk to each other to solve the problem," he explains.

The students are silent. This is a bigger challenge than Harold has posed before. Some seem skeptical that they will really be given so much responsibility.

Once in the circle, they sit quietly for a few moments. Then one takes the lead. Another goes to the chalkboard to write their ideas. For the next 30 minutes, the students talk among themselves, making decisions about homework, journal entries, use of class time, responsibility. At first timidly, students begin to take charge. By the end of the discussion period, they are on the edge of their seats, even the most skeptical waving his hand wildly to add to the conversation.

Early in the discussion, Harold's role was tested. "Mr. Brown," one student asked, "Can we decide to do our journal entries for homework?" Harold remained silent, raising his arms to point back at the group. After a pause, the student looked away from Harold to the group and asked, "So, can we decide to do the journals for homework?"

Harold's only comment during the discussion came after the students' first vote. "Remember, now, that although almost all of you agree, some people do not." The students take the cue, and a discussion begins that gives time for those with minority opinions to speak their minds. Sometimes

the minority sways the group. Other times they re convinced to go along. But in each case, those with divergent views are heard and respected.

This is the first such meeting for this class. There will be many more. These students are now crafters of their own learning experiences. For months before this meeting, they learned to choose. Now they are choosing to learn.

—Trip Log, January 1998

During the study, Harold and his students will revisit the plan periodically, assess its effectiveness, and make revisions based on the plan's success in meeting objectives. Issues may arise that challenge the ability of the teacher and learners to implement their plans. Whether students are dealing with unforeseen obstacles (e.g., school closings that make deadlines unattainable) or management problems (e.g., inappropriate or nonproductive behavior disrupting others' efforts), any issues that affect the learners will be solved collaboratively. Throughout the planning and implementation of learning experiences, emphasis will be placed on providing opportunities for learners to make individual and group choices about how they will address curricular mandates. Through this process, learners will construct experiences that build on their personal and group concerns and interests.

Such carefully constructed experiences lead learners to assume responsibility for their learning and to see a clear purpose in all they do. As they see that they can make good decisions and that their participation in planning and implementing learning experience is valued, learners become more connected to the content. Through this process, they become ever more capable of participating in the development of learning experiences. By assuming more ownership, their commitment to meeting curricular objectives rises, and their sense of personal power and their concern for the group increase. As a result, it becomes possible to build a true community of learners.

Learners will often not bring with them well-developed decision-making skills. They may see decision making as the teacher's responsibility. Nevertheless, learners can develop decision-making skills. Still, it is important for teachers to assess learners' developmental levels and match the complexity of decisions to be made to the learners' abilities. Just as teachers work to move curricular skills to higher levels, so do they work to build and move to higher levels individual and group decision-making skills.

When learners in Harold Brown's class make significant choices about how they will learn the required curriculum, how they will use what they learn, and how they will assess what they have learned, they are able to engage the personal interests, curiosities, questions, goals, and experiences that will support solid academic learning. Furthermore, they are given opportunities to develop the abilities necessary to take an active, informed role in making important life decisions.

Academic Integrity

Susan explained that she had made some leaps of faith—that the kids could learn basic Spanish skills by following the plan they had devised: planning lessons and teaching Spanish to younger children. It felt risky, and she worried all year long. As the teacher across the hall finished chapter after chapter in the Spanish textbook, her anxiety grew. At the end of the year, the kids took the state Spanish tests. Her kids scored first in the state in Spanish 2 and second in Spanish 1.

—Trip Log, September 1996

In spite of Susan Moon's success and the success of her students, the lingering suspicion that Spanish should be learned by covering chapters plagues her. She struggles against a taken-for-granted notion that good teaching and learning must rise from one of two choices: either "soft" liberalism or "tough" conservatism. For some reason and in spite of evidence to the contrary, there is a persistent notion that to fall into one of these camps ensures "good teaching" and to fall into the other ensures failure. We believe this notion is false; effective and ineffective teachers reside in both camps.

We propose a discussion of academic integrity that transcends the black-and-white definitions. Simply stated, we believe that teaching and learning with academic integrity can only mean that learners achieve at consistently high levels, meeting and even exceeding mandated goals. Regardless of the approach used, teaching that does not provide learners with the skills they need to make choices for their futures or prepare them to be fully participating citizens is unacceptable.

To teachers who embrace the practice of integrating choice and academic standards, merely fulfilling curriculum mandates is not enough. They believe that education requires more. They recognize that the rich experiences they create open doors to a wide variety of learning opportunities that build strong, assertive, and self-directed learners who know how to learn and how to use what they learn.

The classrooms of teachers who integrate choice and high academic expectations are highly conceptualized and operate to meet the unique interests and needs of the teachers and learners who inhabit them. Yet, a striking commonality among these teachers is the explicit nature of expectations and mandates. As in Harold Brown's classrooms, learners know they are required to learn. By making the curricular and teacher "givens" explicit, teachers can involve learners in building exciting learning opportunities within which, in collaboration with the teacher and to the extent appropriate, the learners assume responsibility and are accountable for their own learning.

Most often, teachers present curriculum requirements and teacher expectations to the class or to individual learners and work with them to develop the means for meeting these givens. When learners and teachers make decisions about learning experiences, they do so with curricular goals and objectives clearly in mind. While many options may be proposed, teachers and learners weigh each one carefully and jointly select those that are most likely to lead to mastery of curriculum goals. By making the expectations and mandates explicit, the appropriateness of potential learning activities can be measured against the givens.

A curriculum with academic integrity, then, not only teaches mandated skills. It also teaches a rich array of life skills, from decision making to responsibility, from respect for self to respect for others, and from strong individuality to a powerful sense of belonging to a group larger than the self.

In keeping with this expanded definition of academic integrity, learning can be seen to spring from and lead back to learners' own homes and communities. It is so alive and vital that learners can readily see uses for it in their own lives. Emphasis is placed on helping learners to identify the ways in which the subject matter relates to their lives, to their communities, and to the world beyond. Learners are helped to see the curriculum as an integrated whole. Skills learned in one content area open doors for new explorations in other areas of the curriculum. Students learn to articulate how their current focus of study relates to other content areas. They are aware of what they are learning, why they are learn-

ing it, and how mastering the curriculum will affect their lives outside the classroom.

Early in the century, Alfred North Whitehead (1929) warned against an education that presents learners with "inert ideas" handed down by teachers in small disconnected portions, a theorem here, a historical fact there. Life, he argued, is conducted each day as a whole, drawing on skills and knowledge from various subject areas simultaneously. And life—the here-and-now lives of learners—should be the context, motivation, and proving ground for learning. Whitehead argued that expecting learners to participate in studies for which they can imagine no purpose in their immediate experience couldn't lead to true and lasting learning. Instead, this kind of learning leads to a mere performance of meaningless and trivial "intellectual minuets."[9]

Teachers and learners share responsibility for meeting and exceeding curriculum goals and for connecting the curriculum with learners' lives and across disciplinary lines. Learners experience the difference between freedom and license and learn responsibility for the decisions they make. These experiences support social and emotional growth and create the basis for the development of skilled, active, and responsible membership in society, be it the society of the school, the community, or the country.

Keeping the Faith

In spite of research that documents the broad gains learners make when they are given power to make choices about their learning, a group of learners lacking decision-making skills can create a dilemma for teachers. Sometimes teachers feel they must "play it safe" and revert to more teacher-directed practices. But teachers who persist testify to the rewards of "keeping the faith." To them, trusting the process and focusing on teaching children to choose wisely is so fundamental that meeting the challenges of learners unprepared to choose to learn is one they accept. Judy Bryson's story provides a final example of how involving learners in the decisions that affect them, even if slowly at first, leads to significant educational gains, along with growth in responsibility, involvement, creativity, and attitude. And, coincidentally, it improves test scores.

In an article title "Learning in a Forest," Judy Bryson (1996, pp. 22–26) tells the

story of one of her most challenging classes. She was an accomplished and experienced teacher when she faced her new fourth grade class that year. Still she struggles as she begins the year with an especially difficult class, and she wondered whether they would ever be able to learn to choose or choose to learn. Kentucky's state testing requirements are rigorous, and schools are judged by the students' performance on a battery of performance and portfolio assessments. The fourth grade is a key year for these tests. If schools don't meet expectations, a series of punitive measures can be imposed up to and including the state taking over the schools' operation.

…"I had never heard such a squabbling and bickering group of students. They got off the bus quarreling and left my room at the end of the day [the same way] and probably continued all the way home."

The group wasn't able to make decisions at a level Judy had anticipated. Focusing on helping them become decision makers, rather than reverting to a more teacher-directed approach, seemed risky. But, with the stubbornness common to teachers like Judy, she chose to take the time to help the students learn to choose. The process required all of her patience and grit.

"We began with small decisions which grew larger almost every day. Once the students became confident that I truly valued their ideas; they tried even harder to come up with bigger and better plans."

Finally, the students were challenged to consider ways they might meet science requirements. They took up the challenge and decided to study a nearby old-growth forest. By the end of the year, students had completed an impressive array of learning experiences, all using the forest as a basis for study. They had met their science, social studies, and writing requirements. But the final evaluation of Judy's move to create a community of decision makers would come when her class faced the state tests.

"Our overall writing scores were up.… The proctor was impressed with the way the group of students attacked their group [performance] task, [how they] distributed jobs within their groups and worked together to find solutions.… Beyond all of the wonderful student-initiated learning, I believe the changes within the students themselves were the most remarkable."

Student attendance was up, there were few discipline issues, every student could find important and meaningful ways to contribute to the group while doing work appropriate to her or his own academic and social needs and strengths.

"At the end of the year I was as proud as a mother hen with her brood of chicks under her wings. This group had been, without a doubt, the most quarrelsome, most frustrating, hardest-working, and most productive class I'd ever had."[10]

Learners in all classrooms have always had the power to make the most basic choice about their learning: they may choose to engage in learning or to disengage. We cannot remove that choice. Our goal is to inspire students to choose to engage. When they do, we know they can and will make good choices about how they learn, how they use what they learn, and how they assess their learning. And we can help them exceed all expectations. In short, we want students to choose to learn and choose in order to learn.

Notes

1. Wilfred Aiken, *The Story of the Eight-Year Study with Conclusions and Recommendations* (New York: Harper & Row, 1942).

2. Alfie Kohn, "Choices for Children: Why and How to Let Students Decide," *Phi Delta Kappan,* September 1993, pp. 8–20.

3. Carol Coe, "Turning over Classroom Decision Making," *The Active Learner: A Foxfire Journal for Teachers,* August 1997, pp. 7–9.

4. John Dewey, *How We Think* (Lexington, Mass.: D.C. Heath, 1933), p. 218.

5. John Dewey, *Experience and Education* (New York: Simon & Schuster, 1938), p. 38.

6. Diane E. Sanna, "Waiting for Magical Moments," *The Active Learner: A Foxfire Journal for Teachers,* Winter 1998, pp. 18–19.

7. Ibid.

8. Dewey, *Experience and Education,* p. 67.

9. Alfred North Whitehead, *The Aims of Education and Other Essays* (New York: Macmillan, 1929), p. 10.

10. Condensed from Judy Bryson, "Learning in a Forest," *The Active Learner: A Foxfire Journal for Teachers,* August 1996, pp. 22–26.

BOBBY ANN STARNES is president of the Foxfire Fund, Mountain City, Ga. (foxfire@foxfire.org). CYNTHIA PARIS is an associate professor of education at Rider University, Lawrenceville, N.J. (parisc@rider.edu). © 2000, The Foxfire Fund, Inc.

Originally from *Phi Delta Kappan,* January 2000, pp. 392-397. © 2001. This is a revised edition by Bobby Ann Starnes, president of The National Center for Collaborative Teaching and Learning and assoc. professor of education at Montana State Univ. Northern (bstarnes@msun.edu) and Cynthia Paris, associate professor of education at Rider Univ. and The National Center for Collaborative Teaching and Learning Director of Programs. Reprinted by permission.

The Trauma of Terrorism:
HELPING CHILDREN COPE

ILENE R. BERSON AND MICHAEL J. BERSON

SEPTEMBER 11, 2001, began for many as an ordinary Tuesday morning throughout the United States. In some parts of the country, students were in school, some adults were at work or engaged in their daily routines, and others were still in peaceful slumber, unaware of the horrific series of events about to unfold. At about 8:45 a.m., the tragic assault on the country began. Within moments, the nation became a collective witness to and victim of a violent atrocity.

Elie Wiesel has stated, "More than anything—more than hatred and torture—more than pain—do I fear the world's indifference."[1] The intensity of the response to this assault on the nation has awakened the compassion of our citizens. We have lived in a long period of peace, and this event has been a sudden jolt. The immediacy of the news accounts and images made everyone not only witnesses, but also participants in the tragedy. Unlike in times past, when travelers spread news of atrocities months after the event, firsthand knowledge of threat and potential for risk heightens the intensity of our response. Even those individuals who are far from the disaster sites cannot remain emotionally distant.

The terrifying aspect of this violence is the realization that we are not just bystanders to aggression but also the target of it. Violence is not a unique occurrence here, but mass destruction of human life still stirs fear and uneasiness across America. Because mass violence often appears to happen at a safe distance, we have remained detached from the reality that civilians are the sometimes accidental and often intentional victims of attacks. In recent conflicts, civilians account for almost 75 percent of resulting deaths.[2] Terrorism involves a violent lawlessness in which aggression intrudes into the ordinary existence of people.

The horrors of conflict and organized violence have not escaped touching the lives of the young. A year is comprised of 525,600 minutes, but it takes only one moment to make a lasting impact on children and young adults. The powerful images of this event affected many students throughout the country, and the enduring influence is intensified as their imaginations are fed by the memory of the violence.

> By fostering coping skills and drawing on the strength of the collective community, we can help students begin to heal.

In fact, the end of the twenty-first century has been burdened by images of brutality. Conflicts are characterized by atrocity, and recent history attests to an abandonment of any "rules of war, starting with the abandonment of respect for any distinction between combatants and civilians, or the innocence of children."[3] In the United States, the shock of direct attacks on our own soil has left us to deal with the aftermath. We have little empirical research to guide our responses to this form of tragedy because so few terrorist attacks have occurred in the United States. The most recent event, the Oklahoma City bombing, provides the most updated understanding of the reaction of children.[4] We have learned from other tragic incidents that the meaning we assign to events and the messages we highlight are crucial to the healing process. Terrorism is insidious in infiltrating the collective psyche with fear and the pervasiveness of our horror. Children and young adults are especially vulnerable to the psychological impact. Adults must guide the response of children and youth to an awareness that "the world needn't be evil simply because some people are. It is only evil when we let the evil happen."[5]

Social studies teachers in particular are confronted with how to respond to these acts of violence as they enveloped the nation. Gripping current events provide an important opportunity to expand students' global understanding of the world while integrating these important topics into the formal curriculum. While assisting students in managing devastation and loss, teachers can also see the experience as a segue into such content as the beliefs of Islam, the geography of Afghanistan, the history of U.S.-Middle East relations, security strategies, antiterrorist operations, and tolerance activities. Many teachers recognize not only the importance of the events, but also the natural connection between these events and the social studies curriculum. Nonetheless, teachers need guidance on how to infuse these events into instruction.[6]

Because young children relate events to themselves, they will be most worried about their own safety and the well-being of those they care about.

In the ensuing weeks, teachers must shift the focus from "What happened?" to "Where do we go from here?" How do we restore the faith of young people in the promise of their future as Americans who can live in safety and security? How can we triumph over our fears and prejudice? How do we use our strength and character as a nation not only to deal with the tragedy, but also to grow and seek out peace? The following suggestions can guide social studies teachers in addressing such important questions. Through these actions, teachers will seed the hope for the future.

Students' Exposure to Terrorist Attacks

Acts of terrorism infringe on our basic sense of safety and often leave us questioning whom to trust. "Human degradation and misery are intensified in the experience of the child whose innocence may be consumed by the horrid realities which disturb so many lives."[7]

Selected Web-Based Resources

- **American Academy of Child & Adolescent Psychiatry**
  www.aacap.org
- **American Academy of Pediatrics**
  aap.org
- **American School Counselor Association**
  www.schoolcounselor.org
- **ChildTrauma Academy**
  www.childtrauma.org
- **Educators for Social Responsibility**
  www.esrnational.org
- **Emergency Services & Disaster Relief, Center for Mental Health**
  www.mentalhealth.org/cmhs/emergencyservices
- **ERIC Clearinghouse for Social Studies/Social Science Education**
  www.indiana.edu/~ssdc/eric_chess.htm
- **Federal Emergency Management Agency (FEMA)**
  www.fema.gov
- **Federal Emergency Management Agency FEMA for Kids**
  www.fema.gov/kids
- **George Mason University Psychological First Aid Kit**
  www.gmu.edu/departments/psychology
- **National Association of School Psychologists**
  www.nasponline.org
- **National Center for Post-Traumatic Stress Disorder**
  www.ncptsd.org/what_is_new.html
- **National Institute of Mental Health: Helping Children & Adolescents Cope with Violence & Disasters**
  www.nimh.nih.gov/publicat/violence.cfm
- **National Institute of Mental Health Post-Traumatic Stress Disorder (PTSD), Trauma, Disasters, & Violence**
  www.nimh.nih.gov/anxiety/ptsdmenu.cfm
- **National Council for th Social Studies: Teachable Moments—Resources for Teachers and the Media**
  www.socialstudies.org/resources/moments
- **National School Safety and Security Services**
  www.schoolsecurity.org/terrorist_response.html
- **National Victim's Assistance Organization**
- www.try-nova.org
- **PBS: America Responds: Classroom Resources**
  www.pbs.org/americaresponds/educators.html
- **Purdue Extension: Terrorism and Children**
  www.ces.purdue.edu/terrorism/children/index.html
- **The Dougy Center for Grieving Children**
  www.grievingchild.org
- **Tolerance.org: A Project of the Southern Poverty Law Center**
  www.tolerance.org
- **University of Virginia Youth Violence Project**
  youthviolence.edschool.virginia.edu
- **U.S. Department of Education**
  www.ed.gov/inits/september11/index.html

American students could not escape the horrific images of the terrorist attack. Child victims of atrocities are particularly vulnerable and may require careful intervention to restore their sense of safety and security. Nonetheless, even in the face of devastating trauma, children and young adults have the potential to exhibit resiliency, courage, and an enduring vitality. By fostering coping skills and drawing on the strength of the collective community, we can help students begin to heal.

Behavioral and Emotional Effects of Exposure

Links between an exposure to violence and negative behaviors in children and young adults exist across all age ranges. Exposure to a traumatic experience has short- and long-term consequences in a student's life and can contribute to physical and mental health problems as well as educational impairments.[8] Even children and young adults who have been exposed to a single terrorizing event can exhibit clinical indicators of Posttraumatic Stress Disorder, including fears, repetitive nightmares, thought reenactments, and thought suppression. The children and young adults with greater proximity to the event tend to experience more intense symptoms.[9] It may seem obvious that relatives of the victims or direct witnesses to the disaster may have strong responses, but other children and young adults may also have less obvious connections to the events, which similarly heightens their sensitivity to the trauma. These connections include students who have visited the buildings that were affected, whose parents fly frequently, who have recently suffered another loss, or who have experienced other forms of trauma. Students in the last two categories may have expended their coping resources in dealing with their daily problems and may not be equipped to handle further adversity in their lives.

The numbing effect of the trauma, combined with fear and depression, may make it hard for teachers to identify students in crisis

---

Although responses to the events will be unique to individual students, ranging from total disinterest to chronic obsession and panic attacks, the age and developmental levels of a student are important in determining his or her ability to deal with the events. Young children under age six will typically look to adults to guide their response. The powerlessness and anxiety of parents and teachers may be apparent to the young, who often observe others around them for cues on how to act. Because young children relate events to themselves, they will be most worried about their own safety and the well-being of those they care about. Subsequently, they may become clingy and concerned about the whereabouts of parents and family members. Generalized fears may become more intense; loud noises, including sirens and the sounds of airplanes, may result in fearful reactions. Children may have greater difficulty sleeping and may be plagued by dreams of monsters and other creatures during their rest periods.

Although crying and fussiness may appear more frequently, young children may have difficulty identifying feelings because they lack the vocabulary to express their emotions. Children may exhibit regressive symptoms and lose previously acquired skills. Conversely, if adults have successfully monitored their reactions and limited their children's exposure to media images of the tragedy, some young children may be relatively unaware of the attack. Other children may have repeated exposure to horrific images and misinformation about the event; they may presume, for example, that each viewing on television represents a separate incident in which a building is attacked, leaving the impression that hundreds of planes struck many structures.

Elementary-age children may express similar feelings of anxiety, appear fearful or worried, and cling to teachers or parents. They may be irritable in class, indicate concern about ongoing violence, and complain of headaches or stomach aches. In their play, elementary children may repeatedly reenact the event or discuss elements of the attack. Teachers may observe changes in children's behavior, with increased acting out, heightened aggression, angry outbursts, withdrawal, poor concentration, and impaired performance on school work. They may also hear children discussing death and dying.

Middle school students will exhibit comparable symptoms of anxiety. In addition, middle school concerns may include a generalized fear about school violence and war. In repeated discussions of the events, these students may share horrific details and focus on acts of revenge. Middle school students may struggle with accepting others who are different and may be more suspicious of diverse perspectives. Changes in school behaviors include defiance, as well as an increase in absenteeism or withdrawal from extracurricular activities. Some students may indicate that the terrorism has had no effect on them at all.

In the high school, students may not only be fearful and exhibit many of the signs of trauma noted in younger children, but may also feel vulnerable to death. They may try to numb this vulnerability with drugs or alcohol. Some students may become so transfixed on issues of death and dying, combined with a sense of hopelessness, that suicidal thoughts enter their minds. Other adolescents will appear unaffected by the atrocity. For some, this denial is a self-protective coping mechanism. For others, who by age eighteen have witnessed over 800,000 real and imaginary deaths on the television, they have already been desensitized to these acts (see www.childtrauma.org).

The Impact of Violence on Social Studies Teachers

At the very time when students turn to their teachers for stability and support, teachers may be equally traumatized. The numbing effect of the trauma, combined with fear and depression, may make it hard for teachers to identify students in crisis. These adults may be more irritable and less responsive than usual. Some teachers may have less tolerance for student misbehavior, and their punitive response may leave students feeling withdrawn or perceiving themselves as bad. Other teachers, fearful of their reactions or lacking answers to students' questions, may avoid discussing the events. Teachers may worry about exacerbating the negative emotions of the students. Thus, while experiencing their own traumatic response, teachers' ability to play a stabilizing role and support students' resilience may be compromised.

At a time when students need structure and routine, teachers may have trouble concentrating on planning for lessons. Fear of being ill-equipped to handle controversial or emotionally laden content may result in a denial of the importance of the event. Some teachers may also become incapacitated with fear of physical harm in the school setting, exhibiting a hypervigilance to their surroundings.

Support offered within the school and throughout the broader community can help combat the sense of isolation and the saturation of the senses that overwhelms coping responses. Many students will sense the fear, tension, and confusion of teachers who are distracted by worry. Teachers need to reach out to their colleagues and use employee assistance programs when they are overwhelmed by their emotions and reactions. But supportive conversations among staff should be conducted outside the purview of students to protect them from reexposure to frightening interactions. It is important for children to know that even though their teachers may be upset by the events, they are still capable of teaching and caring for them and meeting their needs in the classroom.

Discussions of Events and Feelings

A safe and supportive environment in which to address concerns and feelings helps combat the sense of isolation and validate the presence of a caring community. The ability to deal with complex issues can be empowering to young people who must integrate into their experience a barrage of facts, images, and diverse perspectives. Teachers need to understand that students' reactions to these events will vary. Young people who are experiencing other crises in their lives, including preexisting mental health and behavioral problems, may have intensified anxiety. Others will appear unaffected. These variations of feelings may also relate to the developmental stage of the student: young children are concerned about separation and safety, older elementary school students focus on fairness and caring for others, and adolescents grapple with the ethical dilemmas about violence and the resolution of conflict. Teachers can help children and adolescents cope with this disaster by attending to their words and actions and observing signs of distress.

Social studies teachers in particular can serve as important informants to children whose perspective on the tragedy may be influenced by rumors, speculation, and misunderstanding. Students need to express their feelings and to make sense of the events. Competing values and ethics may create stress as students wrestle with antiviolent sentiments, which have been promoted in schools, and revenge-oriented ideology, which provides a simplistic mechanism for coping.

Regardless of the age of the students, young people need reassurance that they are safe and secure. This message needs to be reinforced over time, especially as new developments reintroduce concerns. A sense of security is communicated through consistent class routines and the fair application of rules of the classroom, which provide students with a sense that they have control of their environment. Flexibility in scheduling is also important, however, to allow students to process their thoughts and feelings and to receive accurate information. Because of television and other technologies, students who were not geographically present at the event became eyewitnesses and, in that sense, victims. Controlling student contact with disturbing images and adult conversations is important to limit exposure to vicarious traumatization. False assurances, however, are unsettling to students who experience a cognitive dissonance between the reality of the situation and the information they receive.

Teachers may find it helpful to structure a limited period of time for discussions, although they need to respond to students' questions that arise throughout the day directly and honestly, with a guided transition back to the class activity. Teachers should emphasize that it is the responsibility of adults to create safety for children. They should also give students an appropriate overview of school plans to address emergencies, including a review of school safety guidelines. Although we want students to recover the security and routine of their daily lives, we must also assist them in learning from this tragedy. Wallowing in fear is not productive; neither is living in a state of terror. But the complexity and enormity of this event may necessitate repeated discussions.

Anger management activities should be infused into class discussions. Students can describe how they successfully managed past frightening situations and identify effective coping strategies for dealing with stress. They often feel empowered when they realize that they have overcome hardships in the past. Relaxation exercises, creative activities (i.e., listening to music, reading stories, singing), and moments of quiet reflection are soothing to students. Students will also be comforted by knowing that over time, they will be able to cope with their strong feelings better. This is a crucial time to maintain open communication with parents and other school personnel about students' functioning. Mental health professionals in the school and community are a valuable resource for students who continue to experience strong emotions without relief.

Young children need repeated assurances that adults are working together to keep them safe and cared for. Young children may need extra assistance with transitions from home to school, with a warm greeting in the morning and a nurturing school environment during the day. In addition to verbal assurances, physical comfort—smiling faces, extra hugs, and hand-holding—is important. Because children will imitate teachers and parents, adults should model good coping skills. The complexity of information necessitates repeated clarification of information, including discussions of who is responsible for the event. Some children will believe that they are to blame for tragic events because of their misbehavior. Others will have inaccurate information about events. Teachers need to provide honest and realistic responses.

Young children also need to improve their "feeling vocabulary" so they can verbalize their distress. Teachers need to be aware of nonverbal cues that indicate fear, anger, or grief. For young children, hands-on activities are helpful for expressing feelings. These activities include watching puppet shows, drawing pictures, reading books, doing art projects, writing letters, making music, and taking action to help. Young children may need to reenact the experience to gain control over the event. Rescue materials, building blocks, and puppets can help children express their fear and anger.

In the elementary years, children may notice that adults are concerned and upset, but they need to know that the significant adults in their lives can still take care of them and guide them through the scary and angry feelings. Not talking about it makes children feel that the topic is taboo. Teachers can initiate the conversation with opening questions about the children's knowledge of the event and then let children guide the discussion. Strong feelings, such as anger, fear, anxiety, and grief, can be difficult emotions for children under any circumstances. Teachers should anticipate that children who feel overwhelmed and fearful might struggle with concentrating, sleeping, and controlling aggression. Maintaining routines can help. Children also need assistance in labeling their feelings and differentiating between angry emotions and angry behaviors.

Reenactment in play may help, but if children are unable to acquire a sense of control, this process may not be productive. During play, teachers can help students explore alternative endings and guide them to find words to explain their actions. Elementary students also may benefit from writing about their experiences, dis-

cussing other examples of disasters in literature, and observing that most people in their lives are caring and helpful.

Older students may not directly express their concerns but still grapple with fears about a reoccurrence of the event, the loss of a loved one, separation from the family, isolation, and loneliness. In addition to having access to adults who are receptive to questions, adolescents need guidance in developing constructive responses and alternative solutions. Class activities might emphasize constructing answers to questions together to demonstrate an orderly way to solve a problem. Sensitivity to the reactions of others may help identify other young people who are relying on self-destructive mechanisms (i.e., drugs, alcohol, aggression) to cope. Teachers should carefully observe student behavior to redirect students before angry outbursts escalate into conflict.

As events continue to unfold, teachers will need to provide additional updates on basic facts and check on students' evolving understanding and ability to cope. (Prompts to guide discussions are available at www.apa.org.) Teachers can model for their students how to express feelings in an appropriate manner by acknowledging the variety of their emotions and by managing expressions of anger and intense fear.

Building Students' Resilience to Trauma

We need to safely steer students through the onslaught of emotions and images that have touched them since September 11. The creativity and vibrancy of childhood is violated by those images depicting an attack on the communities that are supposed to nurture their development.[10] The most important factor in restoring that sense of safety is a strong relationship with a competent, caring, positive adult. Students are comforted through the reassurance of significant adults and the engagement in normal routines. Specific discussions about safety and victim assistance will calm their fear. Children want to be assured that they and their family and friends will be OK. They need permission to laugh and play and explore their childhood. Vulnerability and powerlessness disappear when a child discovers joy and self-efficacy.

Celebrate Diversity and Promote Tolerance

In times of crisis, we are bound by the commonality of our experience, yet there remains the threat of isolating individuals on the basis of racial, ethnic, or religious differences. Now is an important time to ensure that the curriculum infuses tolerance-building activities that explore the rights of people throughout the world, consider historical examples of ethnic discrimination and stereotyping, and examine resources and organizations promoting tolerance and the elimination of terrorism. Lessons on religious understanding, with a particular focus on Islamic teachings, are important to counter mis-perceptions about Muslims and their beliefs. Students need to know that violent acts that target civilians are not Islamic in origin and "there is no justification in Islamic scriptures and jurisprudence for indiscriminate killings or assassinations of local or foreign citizens by either Sunni or Shiite Muslims."[11]

> Survival does not mean insulating our youth from further trauma, but rather providing them with skills to make a positive impact on their lives and the lives of others.

As fear over the event transforms to anger, the intensification of hatred can feed stereotypes and prejudice. In such an environment, atrocity and counter-atrocity flourish.[12] Dehumanization of the perpetrators of the event minimizes children's stress,[13] but teachers of adolescents must be wary of the danger of mis-socializing students with fear, violence, and hatred. Adults should be role models of acceptance and community.

In classrooms, we often have a tendency to present isolated details of events without an in-depth analysis of the conflict or exploration of multiple perspectives. In fact, students may experience confusion when the messages of patriotism replace thoughtful observation and discussion.[14] Teachers need to promote an understanding not only of patriotism for our own country, but also of the love that others feel for their countries.[15] An exploration of the efforts of world leaders to respond to terrorism can reduce hatred and violence on local, national, and global levels.

Celebrate the Helpers

K–12 students can focus on the unity of communities in the wake of a tragedy. Moreover, students can affirm the actions of so many individuals who are committed to assisting the victims, consoling families, investigating the tragedy, or working to ensure the continued safety of our nation.

A powerful counterresponse to powerlessness is action. Although the tragedy of September 11 has caused deep sorrow, we observe the heroic acts of so many generous and courageous people. Students should be encouraged not only to observe and celebrate the efforts of others, but also to engage in outreach and participatory

service in their schools and communities. Memorials can also provide an opportunity for young people to share their feelings, and a range of service activities can offer students a chance to bond as a community and combat isolation and vulnerability.

Final Thoughts

Acts of terrorism instill fear and helplessness in a society. Coping with the intense stress and trauma of these events can be overwhelming for our youth, who may feel especially vulnerable. To function optimally, each student has a basic need for safety and security.[16] Although many are still coping with the trauma of the terrorist attacks, teachers have the opportunity to transform students' shock into action. Already, many heroic individuals have modeled lessons of unity and strength. Survival does not mean insulating our youth from further trauma, but rather providing them with skills to make a positive impact on their lives and the lives of others. "The basic law of terrorism is that even the smallest threat can ripple out to touch those a thousand miles away."[17] Our youth can instigate a counterresponse that spreads compassion, understanding, and hope throughout our nation and the global community.

Notes

1. L. Ullmann, "Forward" in *No Place to be a Child: Growing up in a War Zone*, eds. J. Garbarino, K. Kostelny, and N. Dubrow (San Francisco: Jossey-Bass, 1991), x.
2. M. Black, "War against Childhood" in *In the Firing Line: War and Children's Rights* (London: Amnesty International United Kingdom, 1999), 11–29.
3. Black, 12.
4. B. Pfefferbaum, S. Nixon, P. Tucker, R. Tivis, V. Moore, R. Gurwitch, R. Pynoos, and H. Geis, "Posttraumatic Stress Response in Bereaved Children after Oklahoma City Bombing," *Journal of American Academy of Child and Adolescent Psychiatry* 38 (1999): 1372–1379; B. Pfefferbaum, T. Seale, N. McDonald, E. Brandt, S. Rainwater, B. Maynard, B. Meierhoefer, and P. Miller, "Posttraumatic Stress Two Years after the Oklahoma City Bombing in Youths Geographically Distant from the Explosion," *Psychiatry* 63 (2000): 358–370.
5. Ullmann, xi.
6. M. M. Merryfield, "Responding to the Gulf War: A Case Study of Instructional Decision Making," *Social Education* 57, no. 1 (1993): 33–41.
7. Ilene R. Berson and Michael J. Berson, "An Introduction to Global Child Advocacy: Historical Action, Contemporary Perspectives, and Future Directions," *International Journal of Education Policy, Research, and Practice* 1, no. 1 (2000): 1–12.
8. Ilene R. Berson and Michael J. Berson, "Introduction: Galvanizing Support for Children's Issues through Awareness of Global Advocacy," in *Cross-cultural Perspectives Child Advocacy*, ed. Ilene R. Berson, Michael J. Berson, and B.C. Cruz (Greenwich, CT: Information Age Publishing, 2001).

9. J. L. Horn and P.K. Trickett, "Community Violence and Child Development: A Review of Research," in *Violence against Children in the Faintly and the Community*, eds. P.K. Trickett and C.J. Schellenbach (Washington, D.C.: American Psychological Association, 1998), 103–138.

10. Berson and Berson, 2001.

11. M. Hanif,, "Islam: Sunnis and Shiites," *Social Education* 58 (1994): 343.

12. Beasley, 1999.

13. J. Garbarino, K. Kostelny, and N. Dubrow, *No Place to be a Child: Growing Up in a War Zone* (San Francisco: Jossey-Bass, 1998).

14. T. Knowles, "A Missing Piece of Heart: Children's Perceptions of the Persian Gulf War of 1991," *Social Education* 57 (1993): 19–22.

15. L. K. Egendorf, *Terrorism: Opposing Viewpoints* (San Diego, CA: Greenhaven Press, 2000).

16. Michael J. Berson, "Rethinking Research and Pedagogy in the Social Studies: The Creation of Caring Connections through Technology and Advocacy," *Theory and Research th Social Education* 28 (2000): 5.

17. See www.apa.org.

Ilene R. Berson is a Research Assistant Professor in the Department of Child and Family Studies at the Louis de la Parte Florida Mental Health Institute at the University of South Florida in Tampa. She is a cofounder of the American Educational Research Association SIG Research in Global Child Advocacy. Her research focuses on creating safe, supportive school environments for child victims and investigating preventative interventions for child safety and prosocial development in cyberspace. She can be contacted at berson@mirage.fmhi.usf.edu

Michael J. Berson is Associate Professor of Social Science Education in the Department of Secondary Education at the University of South Florida. He is a cofounder of the American Educational Research Association SIG Research in Global Child Advocacy. His research explores technology in social studies education and global child advocacy. He can be contacted at berson@tempest. coedu.usf.edu

From *Social Education,* October 2001, pp. 341-343, 385-387. © 2001 by National Council for the Social Studies. Reprinted by permission.

UNIT 4

Development During Childhood: Family and Culture

Unit Selections

Key Points to Consider

- What contributes to raising emotionally happy, cognitively achieving children in the new millennium?

- Why is childhood obesity threatening our youngsters? What can be done?

- What is dyssemia? How do adults recognize dyssemia in children? How can dyssemic children be helped to fit in?

- Why are so many boys feeling alienated and confused today? Are boys the weaker sex emotionally?

- What are the effects of maltreatment on children? How can adults help children develop resiliency?

- What is "normal" behavior for students in the wake of September 11, 2001?

 **Links: www.dushkin.com/online/**
These sites are annotated in the World Wide Web pages.

Childhood Injury Prevention Interventions
http://depts.washington.edu/hiprc/

Families and Work Institute
http://www.familiesandworkinst.org

The National Parent Information Network (NPIN)
http://ericps.crc.uiuc.edu/npin

Parentsplace.com: Single Parenting
http://www.parentsplace.com/

Most people accept the proposition that families and cultures have substantial effects on child outcomes. Do they? New interpretations of behavioral genetic research suggest that genetically predetermined child behaviors may also be having substantial effects on how families parent, how children react, and how cultures evolve. Nature and nurture are very interactive.

If parents and societies have a significant impact on child outcomes, is there a set of cardinal family values? Does one culture have more correct answers than another culture? This became an often debated question after Osama bin Laden and other Middle Eastern spokesmen called the Western culture corrupt and decadent. Laypersons often assume that children's behaviors and personalities have a direct correlation with the behaviors and personality of the person or persons who provided their socialization during infancy and childhood. Are you a mirror image of the person or persons who raised you? How many of their beliefs, preferences, and virtuous behaviors do you reflect? Did you learn their hatreds and vices as well? Do you model your family, your peers, your culture, all of them, or none of them?

During childhood, a person's family values get compared to and tested against the values of schools, community, and culture. Peers, schoolmates, teachers, neighbors, extracurricular activity leaders, religious leaders, and even shopkeepers play increasingly important roles. Culture influences and is influenced by children through holidays, styles of dress, music, television, world events, movies, slang, games played, parents' jobs, transportation, exposure to sex, drugs, and violence, and many other variables. The ecological theorist Urie Bronfenbrenner calls these cultural variables exosystem and macrosystem influences. The developing personality of a child has multiple interwoven influences: from genetic potentialities through family values and socialization practices to community and cultural pressures for behaviors.

The first article discusses "Raising Happy Achieving Children in the New Millennium." Alice Honig gives advice on how parents and teachers can build child self-esteem, how parents and teachers can cooperate in education, how to discipline positively, how to apply insights from the new brain research, and how parents can partner with professionals to increase children's happiness and achievement.

The second article suggests that 6 million American children are threatened by the multiple health risks of obesity. Lack of exercise, the rise of fast foods, technology, and other social forces combine to make this one of the fastest growing menaces of childhood. One-third of our youth are overweight. The research suggests that lifestyle is a major factor, more to blame than genes. The article suggests positive incentives to help children eat wisely and lose weight without developing eating disorders.

The third article focuses on "Kids Who Don't Fit In." Eric Harris and Dylan Klebold said they executed the massacre in Littleton, Colorado, to get revenge on the students who teased them because they did not fit in. This fomented controversy about bullying and the maltreatment of students whose behaviors are different. The theme of this essay is that early and appropriate help for children with dyssemia (difficulty with social skills) is more beneficial than punishment of the children who tease them. Ad-

vice is given on how to recognize dyssemia and where to turn for help. Emotional intelligence can be learned. Families can help.

The first article in the culture subsection of this unit asks and partially answers the question, "Are Boys the Weaker Sex?" Anna Mulrine describes America's struggle with its sons: impulsivity, aggressivity, vulnerability, and inefficiency. She quotes a Boston pediatrician, Eli Newberger, who believes that today's boys are growing up without the emotional tools they need to succeed. Some sex differences are biologically based. Knowledge of sex-based brain differences, however, can lead to better ways to educate boys and more understanding of how and why they emote the way they do.

The last article in this subsection deals with the question of maltreatment of children. It reviews some of the neurological effects of abuse, neglect, and other traumatic events that affect about 4 million American children each year. Prolonged abuse is known to change regions of the brain that are responsible for memory, learning, and emotional stability. Barbara Lowenthal suggests several measures that can promote resiliency in child victims of maltreatment. Among her suggestions are availability of alternate caregivers, social support interventions, informal support systems, formal support systems, and intervention programs. Each of these supports are described in greater detail.

Raising Happy Achieving Children in the New Millennium*

ALICE STERLING HONIG—*Syracuse University (Received 12 April 2000)*

Key words: Children, happy, achieving

Raising happy achieving children is a tall order. The recipe is complicated. The ingredients are awesomely many! Some of the ingredients involve educators and the training of high quality caregivers and teachers. Some of the recipe requirements involve political advocacy for the poor. Some ingredients are challenging—such as how to provide sexual information and information about unwanted pregnancies and AIDS and how to provide internship opportunities for practicing excellent caregiving within a high school model childcare—for teens who need clear and helpful knowledge and skills. These recipe requirements mean changes in offering school courses in junior high and senior high school. Required courses in positive communication techniques and required courses in family life education are as urgent as studying the invasions of Ghenghis Khan or the history of the Norman invasion in England and its effect on enriching the vocabulary of the English language.

Changes in the way education is offered for medical, nursing, and legal professionals to include more knowledge about children's interests and needs must also be part of the complex societal recipe to support children's flourishing. Thus, part of the recipe lies in enhancing the training of obstetricians and nurses caring for pregnant first time parents. Sensitivity training and knowledge, in dealing with birthing situations for single parents and high-risk teens, are important for professionals involved with childbirth. They will be more likely then to provide nurturance to promote early bonding with the newborn and to support breast feeding for those who may be physically able to nurse but have no clue as to how or why.

Another political ingredient in this recipe will mean much wider monetary support for home visitation personnel who work with at-risk pregnant women PRIOR to the birth of the baby. Honig and Morin's (2000) research has shown that IF high-risk teens who dropped out of an intensive home visitation program had about 7 home visits, then they still had much lower rates of confirmed neglect/abuse several years later. These rates were actually comparable to rates for high risk teen moms who stayed in program for 18 to 24 months regardless of whether program teens' entry was prebirth or postbirth. High risk teens who started program after the birth of the baby and then dropped out had markedly higher confirmed abuse/neglect rates.

LOVING, KNOWLEDGEABLE, SKILLED CAREGIVERS: THE PRICELESS INGREDIENT

The priceless ingredient in the recipe for a happy achieving child is a strong and loving family foundation and highly competent caregivers in group care. Parents are young children's most precious resource. No other caregiver and no material resources can take the place of parents who genuinely treasure their children and are deeply committed to nourish their children's growth and optimal development. The dream of every family is a child who is able to grow up independent yet lovingly related to family and achieving work success and satisfaction in life. We still cannot improve on this formula of the old master, Sigmund Freud!

After their needs for food and comforting, for protection from distress and from danger are taken care of, young children most need a special person whom they know in their deepest self is their loving protector, teacher, and friend. This fundamental security base, this unpaid worker who puts in countless overtime hours without pay and often without much recognition from society, is a PARENT. Thus, this presentation will focus particularly on positive parental ingredients for raising happy achieving children.

Many excellent enrichment programs such as Head Start, Even Start, HIPPY, and Parent Child Development Centers actively work to enlist parental help in young children's learning. Yet sometimes programs that attempt to work with low-income, low education parents, or very young parents or upper class dual career busy parents, report frustrations they were not prepared to cope with. Often the program staff goal is to assist new parents in positive ways to deepen the love relationship with a child, become primary educators of their preschoolers and to encourage parents to work actively in partnership with child care providers. Yet staff report low turnout for meetings, missed appointments for home visits, and lack of parent attunement to program messages.

...quality parenting is the secret indispensible ingredient to provide the inner core of self-love and self-esteem that sustains each growing child.

What are the sources of difficulties? Part of the problem lies in the stressful lives of parents with limited time and often with aggravating lack of means of transportation to program sites. Some families may not have learned in their own families of origin the ability to empathize with child neediness. Struggling to cope with their own adult problems, some parents are not even aware of how important early consistent tender nurturing is in order to promote early child emotional attachment to parents. Chaos, drug abuse, spousal or partner abuse, depression and current lack of family supports account for some of the frustrations for families and for program staff. The deep reverberations of what Fraiberg (1980) calls "ghosts in the nursery"—angers, jealousies, resentments over being rejected or unloved or terrorized in own's own childhood—

intrude in dangerous ways into the parent's current relationship with a young child. Some staff frustrations stem from lack of access to technical skills, such a specific therapeutic techniques, book reading techniques, anger management skills, etc. on the part of staff. Sometimes staff is strong on wishing to do good but not trained thoroughly enough in sensitivity to client needs nor community mores. This can lead, for example, to family outreach workers becoming discouraged with parents and gradually working more and more directly with the child even though the program goals were to empower parents to become their children's most special enrichment person.

Part of the problem also results when service providers lack materials for parents with low literacy skills or for immigrant parents from different culture groups. Programs need to be proactive and create lending libraries that contain both videos (on infant massage and well-baby care, for example) and materials written in easy to read words or in a family's native language. Many publications available for encouraging optimal parenting are geared toward families with more resources, higher literacy, and fewer stresses.

Family support and information programs for parents need to brainstorm creatively to find ways to engage parents with their children. For example, a home visiting program can provide a weekly xeroxed "How to play the game" sheet with suggestions for **varying** an interactive learning game if a child needs more help OR, if a child needs more challenge (Honig, 1982b). And of course, staff needs to affirm steadily for parents how priceless is their role in supporting their children's emotional and intellectual learning.

PARENTS AND TEACHERS BUILD CHILD SELF ESTEEM

A caring adult committed to children's secure well-being is a person every society should honor or cherish. There could not be enough "awards" or medals for such special persons! Responsive caregivers permit hope that the fabric of society will not be rent with violence, alienation, school dropouts, suicides, drug abuse, and other tragic attempts by youngsters attempting to deaden their personal pain or to carve out a feeling of power. Watch the new films about kids in high school, for example. So many "in" youngsters in school cliques behave in ruthlessly ridiculing ways. Girls who aren't considered "sexy" or "beautiful" are called unkind names and treated with contempt socially. Boys who are shy or intellectual are labelled "nerds". Teachers need specialized training in working on cutting out bullying in classrooms, corridors, rest rooms and playing fields! In Norway, thanks to the work of Olweus on the noxious effects of school bullying, teachers are trained to address this issue and are responsible for proactive handling of bullying. Teaching as a profession needs more respect from society, and more in-depth training on how to enhance emotional intelligence as well as intellectual intelligence and knowledge! Teaching staff in childcare has very high turnover each year. Many caregivers earning minimum wage also have minimum training. We need to enhance the respect for quality caregiving. We need to support campaigns for worth wages! An even more intriguing question is how to help parents to see how important a quality child care provider in each child's life—not as paid servant but as a concerned, talented, hardworking extra "parenting" person in that young child's life.

Children need parents who provide for them as the parents in the fairy tale of the Three Bears, where the porridge was not too hot and not too cold, but just right!

Because of the hazards of changing providers and inconsistent care, we must still emphasize that quality parenting is the secret indispensable ingredient to provide the inner core of self-love and self-esteem that sustains each growing child. As Erik Erikson taught us long ago, this consistent core of cherishing permits that child in turn to grow up to care for others in ways that sustain family and community. As a young one is given unto, so does that little one grow up learning how to become a giver. Such caring gives inner courage to cope with problems so that the child can both lead a productive personal life as well as contribute to society (Honig, 1982a). Parents are the **mirror** wherein young children find their inner true selves reflected as either essentially lovable or sadly unworthy (Briggs, 1975).

In a women's dress store, a toddler wandered among the clothes. As she walked around, babbling "Da" and touching clothing, the mother called out over and over either "No! No! Don't touch!". Mostly she kept saying "I don't want you. I don't want you!" The toddler looked bewildered and started to cry. "It must feel frustrating to be among all these clothes racks while the grown ups are busy shopping" I remarked sympathetically to the mother. "Yeah, I've been frustrated with her every minute since she's born!" replied the mother as she reluctantly picked up the tiny tot and continued down the store aisle.

Just giving birth to a child is not the same as parenting! Bettelheim (1987) and Winnicott (1987), wise psychia-

trists, remind us, however, the young children do not need perfect parents to thrive. They will do very well with a "good enough parent". There is no "How-to" book that works for every child in every life situation.

Parents with profound good will for their children remember that cherishing does not mean smothering or intrusiveness.

A teen mother was waiting in the well-baby clinic for the pediatrician to see her child. The toddler, playing with a ring stack set (provided with other toys by a caring nursing staff in a play corner in the waiting room) put the rings on haphazardly. "That's not how you do it", the mom remarked with contempt. She snatched the ring stack from her child and put the rings on in graduated sizes. "There, that's the right way", she announced triumphantly as she handed back the toy to her child. The toddler took the ring stack, and turned it upside down as she let all the rings tumble in disarray to the floor. She gave her mother an angry look and walked silently away from her.

Insightful adults understand developmental stages. They understand that wanting a child to do well cannot be forced but must be supported. They let children have the leisure to try toys on their own. They don't constantly intrude with trying to force the child's attention. They LURE kids to new experiences. But they do not dominate the play situation. Rather they are responsive to children's cues, to children's curiosity, to children's explorations when the child seems calm and engrossed in play. If a toy seems too frustrating, they may move in quietly to provide a bit of unobtrusive support (such as steadying the elbow of a child trying to stack boxes), a quiet suggestion, a turning of a puzzle piece so that the child can better notice where it goes. TEMPO is an important skill in childrearing and in lovemaking! We need to talk more about tempo just as we need to address power issues more in society, with respect to marriages and childrearing as well as in business and politics!

Keeping the see-saw of daily life from bumping down too hard for some children is a major challenge!

Havighurst, a half-century ago, wrote about the developmental tasks of childhood. As a theorist he may be out of fashion nowadays. But he observed wisely that many adults need to become more aware emotionally that a young child first needs to be **allowed to be dependent** and kept safe in order to grow up brave enough to become **independent** and separate from the parents. Youth who feel they must belong to a gang, must cut classes and smoke and drink to be "cool" and grownup, who must act violent with a sex partner are NOT independent persons. They are acting out ancient wounds and scenarios. Their immature and scary actions show how much they lack skills for being independent, contributing helpful adults in society. As one adult remarked quietly to me about her teen years:

> I cut out emotionally. My parents were both quarreling a lot. They were so busy with their careers. They did not seem to have time really to talk with me or to see that their intellectual interest were not the same as my interests in music and sports. So I gave up caring about their world. I turned to peers and to drugs so my friends became my "family" support. It took me years to become my own person.

Parents and teachers together need to notice how special and *individual* each child is in a family. Children do not have the same temperament or wishes or abilities as a parent or as another youngster. A child who is very shy may be quite unlike a gregarious younger sibling. Children need parents who provide for them as the parents in the fairy tale of the Three Bears, where the porridge was not too hot and not too cold, but just right!

Too Much Enmeshment or Too Much Isolation Emotionally Withers The Souls of Young Children

What a strange job parenting is! We cherish and protect, worry over sniffles, blow noses, tie shoelaces, read stories, help with homework, patiently teach moral values and courtesies toward others (Lickona, 1983). Yet we do the job of parenting so that children can grow up to make their own choices and be able to live calmly and effectively on their own without parental help. If the job of parenting is done well, it is done so that parents work themselves OUT of a job!

Flexibility and Adaptability Help Caregivers and Parents Survive

Caregiving requirements change with children's ages and stages. Caregivers who are perceptive will note when to drop the baby talk that so delighted the 10-month-old and truly encouraged her to try words. Now they will use clearly pronounced adult words like "water" rather than "wa-wa" with their toddler whose vocabulary is growing by leaps and bounds. Adults will note that a toddler expresses fierce independence about what he wants, how much he wants and how he wants it right away. They

cannot let that child run in the street or go out without clothes on a winter morning! But, they will also note that a No-saying defiant toddler who tries adult patience in the household still needs his thumb or pacifier and definitely needs the reassurance of his parent's lap when tired, crabby, or coming down with a cold. Parents who are perceptive will note that the five-year-old can feed and dress herself rather well now and can even be allowed to choose clothes to lay out the night before going to kindergarten.

The mystery of growth and development is not steady or predictable. Perceptive caregivers balance firmness with sensible tuning in to a child's stages and needs. They work hard to figure out where each child is at in each domain in his or her learning career. Some children love tinkering with tools and are good at helping Mom or granddad with a repair job. But they may have many frustrations with reading and math in school work. Ridicule and nagging only increase a child's smoldering resentment or stubborn refusal to cooperate at home or school. Finding a warm caring tutor and also exploring the community for an excellent vocational high school may open the path to real job satisfaction later in life for this youngster. Adults need to be good noticers and good balancers in order to promote each child's well being. Keeping the see-saw of daily life from bumping down too hard for some children is a major challenge!

PARENTS AS TEACHERS: TEACHERS AS PARENT SUPPORTERS

Parents and caregivers must both be the emotional teachers of young children. They can teach empathy (sensitivity to feelings—of one's own and of other persons) and trustfulness; or they can teach mistrust and anger, insensitivity and uncaring.

> On the toddler playground, Donny pushed at another boy and snatched his shiny toy auto. Mama came over, kneeled down, held his hands and firmly reminded him of the social rules: "Donny, no pushing or hitting." The toddler nodded and added tearfully "And no biting and kicking!" Self-control is so hard to learn. But with the help of his mother's clear and patient teachings, Donny was learning.

Authoritative parents (as opposed to permissive parents or to authoritarian "Do as I say because I say so!" parents) bring up children who are easiest to live with at home and teachers report that they are a pleasure to have in the classroom (Baumrind, 1977). Such parents show genuine interest in their children. They provide firm clear rules and reasons for rules. And they need, of course, to be flexible about rules. A feverish school child may be ex-cused from family chores. A child just starting a new day-care placement needs more lap time and more tolerance for his crankiness until he feels more secure in the new environment. A teenager who comes home with a really difficult and long set of homework problems feels grateful when a concerned parent offers to take on the teenager's chore of loading the dishwasher to free up some extra study time that evening. Teach generosity by being generous. Teach kindness by showing kindness.

Thus, every child needs caring adults who will promote emotional intelligence (Goleman, 1995). How to be assertive as differentiated from angry and hostile is a challenging emotional task. Children and parents need to focus on how to reframe daily hassles as opportunities to strengthen positive emotional skills, such as: giving a peer a chance to explain, being able to articulate well your point of view and trying to see another's point of view as well; searching for win-win reasonable solutions to social hassles; asking for help in ways that affirm the role of the helper, whether teacher or parents. Some folks believe that the job of teacher and the job of parent are totally different. Those of you who have cared for infants and toddlers know so well that diaper changing, holding a frightened tiny person, feeding, and soothing are intimate ministrations. The roles are indeed blurred when we care for the youngest little persons. Maybe a high school teacher can be sarcastic and put down a student in front of the class. Maybe that student will not feel resentment and anger. Maybe. Sometimes an adolescent with strong family supports achieves ego serenity and resilience and can handle such classroom stresses fairly well. The provider of care for your children is working with a small person whose ego is gradually building. Be sure that all the builders are cooperating, caring and knowledgeable or the structure being built will have troublesome flaws!

Learning Values

Parents are also on the frontiers of a child's learning values in the family. If parents deal their own problems by screaming and lashing out, or being sharply jeering and critical of weaknesses or mistakes made by a family member, then children will **model** their folks and learn those ways to cope with frustrations. If parents struggle to keep a family organized and functioning, then even though financial resources are limited, if they cherish children through hard times and good, their children will learn courage and caring (Honig, 1982a).

Children's empathy flows from experiencing their own parent's empathic response to their early fears and emotional upsets. Research by Yarrow and Zahn-Waxler reveals that during the first two years of life, the parent who shows empathy by soothing a child's hurt after a scare or a kneebruising fall, and who, in addition, clearly does not allow a child to hurt others as a way of solving social disagreements, will have a socially empathic child who is more likely to tune into and try to help other children who are hurt or scared (Pines, 1979).

If families provide models for punitive and vengeful actions, they need to realize that their children may gloat over the misfortune of others or else be indifferent to others' pain. Parents need to become aware of the emotional response that the old master, Sigmund Freud, called "Identification with the aggressor".

> In a rigidly organized household with innumerable rules posted on the refrigerator, the ten-year-old was being punished. She had tried to add her cuddly teddy bear, her comfort object for years, to her school backpack. The parents were angry. The toy animal could have been lost at school or taken by another child. They "punished" the child by having her sit for several hours at an empty dining room table without moving. The five-year-old in the family declared that her older sister "deserved" her punishment and announced that she "did not care" if her sister felt sad.

Parents Prime the Pump of Learning

How does a parent become the first, best teacher who ensures the child's early learning success? Varied are the programs that have been developed to teach parents how best to help their children learn. Some involve parents in groups together. Some programs invite parents as aides into classrooms. Some programs provide Home Visitation in order to promote parenting skills (see Honig, 1979 for an in-depth description of types of parent involvement programs).

Respect for the child is the foundation of good teaching. As parents notice early skills just emerging, they **scaffold, support, and lure** the child to a slightly more difficult accomplishment, to a slightly more subtle level of understanding, to a somewhat higher and more mature level of skill. I have called this technique "Dancing developmental ladders of learning" (Honig, 1982b). In each area of learning, the parent takes CUES from the child: Is the baby making new babbling sounds? Talk delightedly with a cooing baby. Express genuine interest in what baby seems to be trying to communicate. Turn-taking-talk primes language learning (Honig, 1985a). Does the baby smile when he sees animals? Snuggle together and point to pictures of animals during picture book story time with your little one and be sure to label objects baby points to.

Is your year-old child trying to feed herself? Provide Cheerios on the high chair tray to facilitate thumb and forefinger precise pincer prehension. Is your five-year old asking questions about where babies come from? Be an askable parent and provide simple, short calm explanations easy for that young child to understand (Gordon,

1983). Is your six-year-old determined to learn to ride a two-wheeler? Be sure that she is skillful with her tricycle; then advance to training wheels.

Facilitate learning by creating easy "steps" upward toward skill mastery. Figure out the **prerequisites** for success in any area of learning. If a parent provides more toeholds on the ladders of learning, children are more likely to succeed as they push upward in their growth toward achievements.

Preparations ahead of time boost the effectiveness of parent efforts to prime new learning, to scaffold opportunities for learning. Provide lots of discarded paper and crayons for children to draw. Keep assorted "beautiful junk" in a special place; empty egg cartons, pine cones collected on a walk, bubble paper from packaging, old greeting cards, and paper towel rolls plus some paste, blunt scissors, and Magic Markers are good ingredients for rainy day art activities.

> Every parent needs a large repertoire of [discipline] techniques to use at different ages and stages of a child's growing up. Not all techniques work all the time with all youngsters!

Take children on small outdoor walks and to parks often. Give them opportunities to learn to swing, climb, balance, and coordinate their bodies with ease and grace. Also, teach them the names of weeds and flowers (dandelions and daisies are great!) growing by the roadside. Encourage children to notice and feel with their fingers the contrasting roughness and smoothness of the bark of different trees, such as a maple and a beech. Delight in the way clouds and sunshine light the land, the way cool air rustles and sways a flower stem, the way the earth smells fresh after a rain.

Express joy! Your own joy in the glories of the natural world sparks in your young child a deep pleasure, awareness, and appreciation for the world's beauty.

Creativity Turns Living Experiences into Learning Opportunities

Caregivers with limited financial resources need to scout their living space to use every opportunity to turn a household chore or routine into a learning experience. Store-bought toys may be too expensive; but adult cre-

ativity transforms every homey experience into a learning adventure (Honig, 1982b; Honig & Brophy, 1996). *Laundry time* can be used to teach colors, shapes, comparative sizes (of socks and of washcloths and towels), and the names for different materials and garments. Kids will love to feel important as they measure out laundry detergent up to the one-cup line and pour it into a wash tub or machine.

Cooking and baking times are a wonderful opportunity to increase hand dexterity skills in rolling, kneading, shaping, and measuring. And the tastes afterward are an extra reward for the helping youngster.

Grocery shopping is a superb perceptual and language learning experience for young children. Meat, dairy and fruit/vegetable departments give children opportunities to form conceptual categories. Why are peppers and celery and broccoli all in bins near one another? Where would hamburger be found? What items will need refrigeration? Which cartons or cans are heavier than others?

Encourage numerical estimations. As children grow and learn about numbers and letters, many take pride in being able to find a nutritious cereal box by the special letter on the box. They like to help stuff a plastic bag with string beans for supper. Many children by early school age can do estimates; they add up a dollar for this item (rounded off) and three dollars for that item, and so forth, and then come up with a fairly close estimate of how much the groceries will add up to. How proud your child feels. And how much practice in addition such estimates give her!

Teach children about money. People work to earn money. When money is in short supply, a child learns early that food and rent come first. Money, whether in pounds or dollars, for extras such as toys or snacks must be carefully budgeted.

Learning categories and learning gradations (such as little, big, bigger, biggest) are important cognitive tasks of the early years. The real world of shopping, cooking, clean-up times, and yard work provides rich opportunities for learning about number, shape, color, weight, bulk, categories of object, and other cognitive concepts. **Reframe** ordinary household experiences. Transform them into potential lesson times.

POSITIVE DISCIPLINE IDEAS: A GIFT FOR EVERY CAREGIVER AND PARENT

All parents, not just parents with limited resources, need help in acquiring discipline techniques beyond the dreary "hit" and "scold" and "go to your room" many folks learned in their families of origin. Every parent needs a large repertoire of techniques to use at different ages and stages of a child's growing up. Not all techniques work all the time with all youngsters!

Most of the time, a young child is just acting like a child, not thinking in logical sequences, acting in-the-present time rather than planning ahead.

Parents who were raised by being belted or whipped in turn sometimes show powerful urges to use physical punishment. They hated the type of discipline they received but often believe it was justified. They need support to learn more appropriate child management skills. Sometimes young children's boisterous or overly intrusive games spark a feeling of rage in an adult. Grim and hostile parents are reflecting the anger they felt from adults far back in their own childhoods, when family members, furious with some of their behaviors, punished them harshly and branded them as "bad!"

Research has shown that **severe physical punishment (SPP)** was the major discipline method of parents whose youngsters ended up convicted of juvenile crimes. And, the worst crimes (as judged by independent professionals) were committed by the youths who had received the most SPP! (Welsh, 1976).

Let us cull from clinicians and researchers useful ideas about positive discipline that parents CAN use in order to raise responsible and cooperative children without instilling fear and deep anger against parental power (Briggs, 1975; Crary, 1990; Gordon, 1975; Honig, 1985b, 1996; Lickona, 1983). For example, the **redirection technique** helps a parent avoid willful battles with a toddler intent on messing up his big brother's model airplane. The parent invests a different, appropriate activity, such as wooden train tracks or a puzzle, or a jack-in-the-box, with interest so that the toddler turns toward the new and safer game.

Below are some further ideas to help adults re-think what discipline is about and how to use effective teaching techniques and avoid a punishment perspective.

Positive Attributions

Build up self esteem by generous use of **positive attributions** (Honig, 1996). Tell children what you admire about their behaviors and interactions.

Anger Management Techniques

Anger management techniques (such as counting to ten, or using words instead of fists) help children achieve self-control (Eastman & Rozen, 1984).

Teach Sharing

During a play group time, if two toddlers are struggling for a toy, supply an additional toy so each can play with a truck or have a supply of blocks. Talk about taking turns as a reasonable way to share a toy. Tell each child you will help with the taking turns by reminding each child in turn when the toy has been played with for an agreed upon number of minutes. Use a back rub and caress to soothe that child who has snatched a toy from another and as well the aggrieved child who is crying. Thus, you teach both the children that gentleness and kindness are necessary and important for each child.

Time Out as "Teach In"

Use time-out sparingly, and as a **"teach-in"** technique so that children can re-evaluate their inappropriate interactions and choose other ways to get their needs met (Honig, 1996).

Reframe a Problem in Terms of a Developmental Perspective

Adults can take a giant step toward devising new coping skills when they look at certain behaviors in terms of the stage a child is at or the curiosity a child has, or the need the child has to keep moving and exploring. Then certain behaviors, sometimes regarded as "bad" begin to seem just developmentally ordinary, such as a toddler's joy in jumping off a couch (find him someplace else that is appropriate and safe to jump off) or an infant's squeezing a banana through her fingers while watching in wonder.

How can a caregiver steer a child into more appropriate ways to experience vigorous body motions or to experience textures and squish clay?

Be Mindful of the Importance of Practising New Skills

Remember that children have to learn the initial steps for every new learning (and then practice that new skill). This helps an adult be tolerant even of toileting accidents or clumsy spills while a toddler pours juice. Perhaps a two-year-old cannot sit still but needs to run about a lot. He may not have the words for "poop" and "pee" yet. He may get intensely absorbed in his play and forget totally any signals coming from bladder or bowel. Punishing a two-year-old for a toileting accident when that particular child may not be ready to give up diapers for another year shows a lack of awareness of developmental norms for sphincter control. Toilet learning takes several years for some children to master. Male children have higher rates of enuresis. Little boys need particular understanding from parents who want compliance with their toilet training efforts (Honig, 1993).

Develop Realistic Expectations

More realistic expectations of young children's development supports a better understanding of how and when to discipline, and best of all, how to **prevent** discipline problems from arising. Expecting a newly cruising-about baby not to touch breakables or garbage in a bag left on a floor is more than the young one is capable of managing (Honig & Wittmer, 1990). Baby proofing a room full of interesting breakable art objects is a wise idea when curiosity is in full bloom. A toddler has little understanding of the difference between a shiny toy OK to play with and a shiny porcelain vase. Quite possibly, parental yelling if a toddler touches a treasured and fragile knick-knack on a coffee table will surely endow that particular item with increasing fascination and interest as a potential play toy.

Remind yourself that no baby, no school child, no parent, no spouse can ever be "perfect".

> After hearing me at a morning public lecture talk about what children need from their folks, a beautiful young teen mom with a nine-month-old child came to me with tears in her eyes. "Dr. Honig, you seem to know so much about little children. Teach me how to make my baby perfect so I won't have to hit her so much?"

Avoid Hostile Blame

Another danger sign among adults is when they assume that a child is doing unwanted or disapproved actions "on purpose" to displease or act mean to the adult. Babies soak their diapers. Preschoolers love to get all muddy and splash in puddles. They do not "mean" to cause more laundry work for a parent. Beware the dangers of **Projecting Evil** (a Freudian defense mechanism) onto young children. Parental rage is too often fueled in abuse cases by the adult's feeling that a small child deliberately set out to "hurt" or "defy" the adult. If we expect that young children have the same thinking skills as adults we will be very mad at some of their actions and "blame" them—for being children! Most of the time, a young child is just acting like a child, not thinking in logical sequences, acting in-the-present time rather than planning ahead. This focused-on-own-needs small person is sometimes messy, sometimes in short supply of inner controls, sometimes needing to dawdle or say "No". A year-old baby cannot comply perfectly with "No-no". A young preschooler finds it very hard to sit still comfortably for hours without a toy or books or playmates in a dentist's waiting room or at a religious ceremony.

Professionals must help parents gain more **realistic expectations** and understandings of young children's growth needs. Projecting evil onto children is a danger that regrettably leads to violence and inappropriate pun-

ishments rather than behavior guidance to help a youngster gain more mature behaviors.

IMPORTANCE OF THE NEW BRAIN RESEARCH

Apply Insights From the New Brain Research Findings

New brain research reveals that toddlers by 24 months have twice as many brain synapses as adults. Somewhere during the early school years, and by 10 years of age, nature starts to prune away brain connections that have not been wired well by frequent teaching and learning experiences. The motto for rich neural connections is "Use it or lose it!"

It is interesting that in England, compared with the United States, far fewer children are labelled "ADHD" (Attention Deficit and Hyperactivity Disorder) and British teachers are more likely to use behavior modification techniques rather than advocate the use of drugs.

Many families do not realize how early they CAN teach their little ones many kinds of lessons. By three weeks, if a baby has been talked to regularly, and a caregiver has waited with loving calmness for baby to respond with cooing throaty vowels, a baby can keep on cooing back in response to the caregivers' slow delighted talk with the baby held in "en face" position about one foot from the adult's face. The latest brain research reveals that **Parentese** (talk with babies using long drawn out vowels, short phrases, and a high pitched voice) is great for wiring in many rich neuron connections in the brain. This news means that to become good "teachers of the brain", caregivers need to have rich conversations with kids, read picture books frequently, sing songs, and offer their children experiences and adventures such as trips to the zoo, the public library, the supermarket, and local museums.

Figure Out Who Owns A Problem

Decide who owns a particular discipline problem. A teenager who dawdles in the mornings so long that she misses the school bus owns her problem. If a baby tears plant leaves from a favorite plant left on a low ledge, the parent owns the problem. If a parent expects a child with learning disabilities to do as well in school as an older brother who got high grades, the parent owns the problem. A parent's strong disapproval rather than support may contribute to possible school failure, and low child self esteem.

Some problems, of course, are owned by both parent and child. Have family meetings where each person can say what is bothering him about a rule, or an interaction, or a discipline in the family. When such meetings let each person have a say honestly about the week's positives and negatives, then such problems can be identified and hashed out with good will and a desire for reasonable compromise (Gordon, 1975).

Offer Choices

Toddlers who are contrary will often settle more easily into cooperation if offered a choice: "Do you want apple juice or orange juice? Do you want to sleep with your head at this end of the crib or the other end?" (when a tot has trouble setting into nap time). "You go choose two story books that you want me to read to you tonight". Offering choices often heads off a potential problem of crankiness or non-cooperation.

Think Through Household and Classroom Rules

How clear are your rules? Some children are scared that they will do something "wrong" inevitably because of the long lists of strict rules their folks insist on. Have few and clear house rules and be sure there are good reasons for the rules. Drinking milk is not a "must". A child can get calcium and Vitamin A from yellow cheese and from yoghurt. But not hurting a sibling IS a must in a family. *Make sure young children really understand your rules.* Ask a child who is not following a rule of the family to repeat to you what the household rule was. If the child is confused, he may not be aware of his "misbehavior."

Children have to learn about equity as well as fairness. Equity means taking into account special needs at special times for each person.

Adults get weary but need dogged persistence in explaining rules and the reasons for them over and over, especially for toddlers just learning to share, or children just learning how to balance homework responsibilities with their desire to rush out to play after school. "Don't need to wash my hands for supper 'cause they are clean" may mean that the preschooler needs to learn more about germs and the importance of keeping safe from sickness.

Do Not Ignore When Children Harm Others

Ignoring misbehavior only works for minor infractions. For example, if two children are verbally fussing or arguing, they may well be able to settle by themselves who gets to pull the wagon with blocks first. Aggression that is ignored will often escalate; it will not go away. If a child hits or kicks another, and the adult ignores this, the undesirable actions will not decrease but continue. Children then assume that the adult thinks hurting another child is allowed. Be firm about not allowing children to hurt others; but express that firmness without modeling physical hurt yourself. Talk so your child will listen; and be sure to listen so your child will open up to you (Faber & Mazlish, 1980).

Respect Each Child As A Person

Every person, big or little has a viewpoint and feelings of his or her own. A child is not personal property like furniture! Don't make comparisons between kids that make one child feel unloved, unpretty, or untalented compared with another. Screaming at or cursing a child, telling him he is rotten—these behaviors reflect parental anger and anguish, but in no way show that the adult remembers that this little child is a person and deserves to be treated with courtesy even when being disciplined.

Teach To Each Child's Temperament S3tyle

Respect also means that the adult needs to tune into a child's personality style and cluster of temperament traits. Children differ in their threshold of tolerance for distress. They differ in whether they approach or avoid the NEW—whether babysitters or foods or an unknown visiting relative.

Children may be impulsive or quietly reflective. Some are very active, always on the go. Others are quieter. Perceptive parents do not lump all children together. They notice the small differences in mood, in shyness or worrying, in adaptability or rigidity among their children and they are generous in tailoring their demands for more mature behaviors to the temperaments and abilities of each UNIQUE child. It is interesting that in England, compared with the United States, far fewer children are labelled "ADHD" (Attention Deficit and Hyperactivity Disorder) and British teachers are more likely to use behavior modification techniques rather than advocate the use of drugs.

Is a child shy and slow to warm up to new events, people and experiences? Is a child triggery and intense in responding to frustrations? Is a child's mood mostly upbeat and does the child bounce back fairly quickly from upsets? *Tuning into temperament helps you head off potential tantrums* and gives you better clues to guide your child into more peaceable ways of interacting with others (Honig, 1997).

Break Up Tasks Into Manageable Parts

Nobody likes being dictated to. When we give a vague order such as "Go clean up your messy room" a child may have no clear idea how and where to begin. But he sure feels that he cannot succeed and he may grumble and show morose resentment of his folks. Suggest smaller parts of this big task so that the child realizes what has to be done specifically. If you break the task down into manageable bits (put clothes in the hamper; stack books on the shelves; put away toy trucks and cars into the toybox) then a child feels more hopeful about being able to carry out small portions of a task that seemed initially so huge and vague.

Find Out How A Child Reasons When He Or She Misbehaves

When children seem unreasonable in their requests, try to require reasons. Sometimes young children give amusing reasons, such as "I should get four cookies because I am four." "I should go first because I am bigger." As children grow, let them know that you expect them to **think** about their actions and to think through reasons for how they are choosing to act.

Children's acting out gives a strong message that they have "empty" insides and deep needs for adult acceptance and caring.

Adults have to help young children actively learn how to reason and to think causally and sequentially. By asking children for reasons without putting them down, we encourage them to think more clearly: "Can you think of a **different** idea to get Bobby to let you hold his pet puppy?" "Can you think why Grandpa asked you to hold his hand before crossing this wide avenue?" "Can I get dinner ready and read to you at the same time? I can find

time to read to you **after** I have all the food cooking on the stove?" Children learn "polar opposities", such as "before" and "after" "same" and "different" more easily when they are actively utilized in real life discipline situations.

Offer Appropriate Incentives

If your school-age child wants you to take him to the park to play with some friends later in the day, think out loud together (Camp & Bash, 1985). He can finish his homework first and read his little brother a picture book story while you get dinner ready early so that you can then take the time off to go to the park with the children. "After you clean up your room we can play a game of checkers." "If you can take turns with Tanisha playing with the new dump truck or if you can figure out a way to play together, then you can have more play dates with her." This technique is sometimes called *"Grandma's Rule"*. That is, a low preferred activity, such as cleaning up, is followed by a highly preferred activity, such as a privilege or a treat. This timing pattern is more likely to result in an increase in the low-preferred activity. Unfortunately, many parents switch the timing. "Honey, be sure to do your homework after you come back from playing soccer!" is far less likely to result in completed homework!

Teach Ideas of Fairness

Introduce the language of fairness into your talks with children in their play with peers or siblings: "Each child needs to get a turn. Every child in the game needs to play by the same rules. Games will end up in fighting and they will not be fun if children do not follow the rules." Still, fairness may not always work. If one child has disabilities or is ill, then that child may need special attention and care. Children have to learn about **equity as well as fairness. Equity means taking into account special needs at special times for each person.**

Fantasy and Truth are Fuzzy Ideas For Preschoolers

Children have such strong longings and they often believe sincerely and strongly in the reality of fantasy characters, such as Ninja Turtles or He-Man. They sometimes have trouble distinguishing reality from their own wishes. A six-year old reported enthusiastically that she was a terrific swimmer, when she could barely take a few strokes in the water. In Menotti's Christmas opera about the three Wise Men, "Amahl and the night visitors", the boy Amahl tells his mother excitedly that he has seen a star with a tail as long as the sky. Parents may need to ask their children: "Is that a true-true story or a true-false one?" Do not be quick to brand a child as a "liar" when she makes up a fanciful tale or declares her imaginary playmate is sitting on the couch just where visiting Uncle Jim is about to seat himself. Remember how vivid children's imaginations are. Many young children are scared of "monsters" under the bed or in the closet. Many still blend fantasy and reality in ways adults find difficult to imagine!

Some make-believe tall tales of children represent deep longings. If your child pretends to others that she has a fabulously rich uncle who has promised her a pony, you may want to spend more real time doing loving activities together to help your youngster feel more at peace with the real world.

Be A Good Gatekeeper with TV

Be careful and judicious in the use of television. Some programs are prosocial. They give messages about how to handle impulsiveness or mean or mad feelings. Other television programs aimed at youngsters are incubators for teaching violent means of solving social problems. The cartoons are colorful. The animation is awesome. But the messages are pernicious. Sending kids to the television as a babysitter constantly is like using a narcotic to keep a child still. Enjoy activities, even peeling green peas or baking bread, or stripping the bed—together! Caring adults are good gatekeepers for choosing nourishing foods instead of junk food for children. Adults also need to be good gatekeepers for choosing programs that support self-reflectivity, positive solutions to social problems, and mistrust of easy or violent solutions. For example, in the United States there have recently been all too many violent solutions to ostracism and feelings of social rejection in schools with children shooting other children. Television programs with the Aardvark Arthur, the Teletubbies characters, Mr. Roger's Neighborhood neighbors, and the dragons in Dragon Tales all promote positive messages in solving social problems or personal issues. Be sure you are a good gatekeeper for television. Don't nag. Do arrange viewing situations, whether programs or videos or for positive learning.

Try To Figure Out What Is Worrying or Angering A Child

Anger, jealousy, resentment, and fear lead to acting out and misbehavior. Understanding your child's negative emotions may help you figure out how to approach and help your child.

Be careful about deciding what "causes" angry actions or misbehavior. Some families think a child should know right from wrong long before a child's thinking skills are well developed. Some children who were drug addicted in the womb show unmotivated and sudden aggressive actions, such as coming up behind an adult and biting the leg hard. Some children struggle with subtle thinking or perceptual deficits, a legacy from alcohol or drug addiction before they were born.

Blaming the Other Parent is Not a Useful Discipline Technique

Some folks blame the other parent. They say "The child gets his bad temper from his father. It's in his genes." Blaming the other parent for a child's troubling behaviors is guaranteed not to bring peace and good feelings in a family.

Use Victim-Centered Discipline Talk

Help children understand how others feel if they are attacked or hurt. Describe in vivid short sentences how a punch, a nasty word, a bite, a sneering remark hurts another's body and feelings. Galvanize your child to feel how it would be if the hurt had been done to him or her. Be firm in not accepting hurting as a means for your child to solve social conflicts. We do not shame children. They are not bad because they have a toileting accident sometimes or clumsily spill juice when they are toddlers. But if a child hurts another deliberately during the preschool years, we need to summon Eriksonian guilt. A child who understands how she would feel if someone hurt her or how he would feel if someone was mean to him is ready for you to lay your discipline talk on thick! Combine loving kindness with victim-centered discipline talk so that gradually the child comes to understand how kind ways help ease social difficulties far more than hurting ways. With your help, children learn inner self-control.

Use Empathic Listening

"Reflective Listening", sometimes called "Active listening" to the child's emotional message of aggravation, is a powerful tool that communicates an important message to your child: "My parent cares about me. My feelings are important to my folks. My parents want to help me figure out how to resolve my troubles rather than preaching at me or just getting angry." Simple "door-openers" help children open up and pour out their troubles. Try: "Looks like you had a rough day today, honey" (Gordon, 1975).

As you listen to a child's aggravations and woes with a peer or a parent or a teacher, try to reflect back to the child as best you can the genuine feelings you catch when he acts troubled or upset. Ridicule, put-downs, impatience—these are the swords that drive deep into children's hearts to make them feel that adults do not truly care about their feelings. Listen to your child's miseries. Listen and try to express your empathy with the child's upset feelings even when you do not agree with the scenario or think she or he is being childish.

Suppose Ricky is sad because his favorite friend now prefers a neighbor child as playmate and Ricky feels he has no one to play with. This problem seems as serious to a preschooler as adult problems seem to a parent. A teenage girl's worries about her weight or her popularity seem overblown to a parent, but desperately important to that girl. Don't suffer with her. Empathize and try to listen in a caring and supportive way.

Show Genuine Interest in Each Child

Be available and truly interested in talking with children in your care. Give them your full attention. Children hunger so deeply for personal attention. If adults are too involved in their own lives and needs, children express this emptiness in a variety of ways. They may turn away from parents and run with gangs of peers. They will sometimes steal coins out of parents' pockets. Sometimes they fight terribly with siblings or classmates. Children's acting out gives a strong message that they have "empty" insides and deep needs for adult acceptance and caring. Children have deep **emotional hunger for focused adult attention and emotional acceptance. Unconditional acceptance of each person heals the soul.** Can you think of a person in your own life who gave you that precious gift? Hopefully, a parent, a teacher, a spouse, a childcare provider, a religious leader in your faith community. And this gift makes a profound difference in healing past hurts.

Help Children Consider the **Consequences** of Their Actions

Many a youngster has never thought through exactly what will happen IF he hits Johnny or tears up his big brother's homework. It is really important for parents to probe and ask a lot: "What do think will happen next if you do that?" If Johnny fights with Billy over a toy, you may send Billy home and then Johnny will have nobody to play with the rest of the rainy weekend afternoon. Kids need encouragement to THINK, out loud, about what might happen IF they act in a certain way. When children are challenged to think of the consequences they often themselves decide that their action or idea is not helpful for themselves (Shure, 1994).

Challenge Children To Think Up Alternatives to Fighting

Help children get used to making a plan before a social problem arises. Encourage children to think up other ways of handling their social conflicts besides "not playing" with another child, or "hitting him". The more that teachers daily encouraged children to think up *alternative solutions* to their peer problems, the more likely they have been found to solve their social problems more appropri-

ately after three months of such classroom work (Shure & Spivack, 1978).

Find Community Resources, Books, and Programs That Support Families

To cope with the complex stresses and forces in society today, families need a lot of skills, a lot of insights, a lot of supports. Job loss, divorce, a child born with disabilities, death and illness, all impact on the family. Teachers and social service personnel can reach out to offer supports and services to increase peaceable family functioning and enhance children's lives.

Encourage Excellence, Not Perfection

Expect children to try hard. They know they can never be perfect and may deliberately fail or act clumsy if they feel very anxious that adults expect perfection. Praise good trying. Appreciate hard work and good efforts even when a child's grades are not as high as you would wish or even when she is clumsy when she gets to bat in a ball game.

Find Each Child's Gifts: Play as a Wonderful Discovery Channel for Learning a Child's Skills!

Sometimes a parent wants a child to be a terrific ball player because that was the parent's secret desire as a child. Or parents are so anxious about a child doing well in science and math that they do not realize that this child is talented in art but not as gifted for science. Learn the gifts of each child. The child who draws and doodles a lot in class may not be showing disrespect to the teacher. He may be showing a budding gift for cartooning or drawing. Children whose parents ignore their gifts and push other agendas on them (such as getting into a prestigious college 12 years later!) may start to lie and even to cheat on tests in school.

Some children do need help to develop their learning skills. Perhaps a child's family has moved and changed classrooms often. That child may not be able to keep up with school work. Be aware of when a child needs tutoring in school. Other children have more stable schooling situations, but they may have dyslexia or difficulties with reading or math. For example, some school age children reverse letters. They have troubles with figure-ground relationships (of black print on a white page) and do not see words clearly against the background of the page. Other children have perceptual-motor difficulties that make using a pencil to write clearly a very arduous task. Search for professional help when you see a clear need.

But also learn to appreciate the gifts your children do have. Some young children carry a tune flawlessly (Honig, 1995). Some kids can run with fleet feet. Some can recognize the model of every car that passes on the road.

Some kids can tell you the baseball batting statistics of every player on their favorite team. Some kids can soothe a playmate's upset by kind words. Be a not-so-secret admirer of your child and discover each gift with joy and gladness. If you watch your children at play with peers, you may catch their ingenuity at solving a social problem, such as trying to enter a peer group already playing house or pretending to be explorers on Mars.

Promote Children's Play

Provide rich play experiences by arranging for play dates and for quality preschool experiences. And then become a tuned-in NOTICER of the world of play. Read Vivien Paley's books, such as "The boy who would be a helicoptert" or "You can't say you can't play" to get more insights into the power of the world of play to socialize children just as the family is powerful in socializing children. Never permit bullying! Never permit catty clique behaviors. Talk about kindness with others and practice it yourself.

Don't Denigrate The Child's Other Parent

More and more marriages end in divorce, and second marriages tend to end even more frequently in divorce. In separations and divorce, parental bitterness and resentment belong to the adult, but so often heavy negative emotions spill over onto the children. Parental anger should not be sent as an arrow through the soul of a child where there has been a separation or divorce. Professionals need to help parents work through rage and grief so that these sorrowful poisons do not afflict children unduly. Already, young children in divorce often feel that it was their fault. Parents who feel betrayed or abandoned sometimes try to influence a child to turn against and hate the other parent. When possible, children need to feel that they are still loved by the other parent and they have total permission to love each parent. Enrolling children embroiled in divorce/custody issues in the "Banana Splits" programs social workers run in many schools is a good idea. Try to provide books and other materials to answer children's questions (Rofes, 1982). When mothers raise children alone, they may not realize that fathers are very precious to children (Biller & Meredith, 1975). Fathers are the preferred playmates of babies, and loss of affection from a divorced and absent father can cause long-lasting distress for children. Try to promote a climate of surety about each parent's caring for the children even when the parents cannot manage to live with each other.

Use Bibliotherapy

When children feel scared of the dark or worried about starting in a new school, stories have a wonderful power to heal. With stories, you find a way to reassure children so they feel more secure. Children identify with the loyal elephant in Dr. Seuss' "Horton hears a who". They do not always have to act out their resentments or disappointments. They can also identify with kind characters in stories.

In addition, children love mischievous characters, such as Pippo the monkey. They grin at the "Cat in the Hat". Everything gets fixed up just fine at the end of that Dr. Seuss story. Yet the Cat in the Hat surely acted naughty for a while!

Children sometimes misbehave when they want more attention. They act out with misbehavior in order to get attention, even when that attention is negative, such as yelling and spanking! A neighborhood library has good books about children's troubles. If you are going through a troubled time in your family, search for books such as "The boy who could make his mother stop yelling", for example.

Some children misbehave because they desperately want to feel powerful or exact revenge (for example, because they felt unwanted and unimportant when the new baby was born). Many problems hurt a child's soul, such as loss of a grandparent, or living with an alcoholic parent who humiliates the child so that he is afraid ever to invite a friend over to the home. Some children feel abandoned when a parent remarries and the stepparent obviously does not want the child around and never offers any affection to the child. The local library has many books you can read to help your child identify with a story child who has lived through such a problem and has managed to cope despite sorrow and worries.

Read stories that resonate for a child over and over. One youngster loved me to read daily for weeks Dr. Seuss' "The king's stilts". This is a story of a courageous little boy who digs up the king's buried stilts and returns them to the monarch (who loves to play on them at the end of a work day) and thus returns the king's joy and ability to govern well. That message, that a child could be scared of a mean and menacing adult (the king's prime minister in the story) and still finally become brave enough to do the right thing, seemed to resonate so deeply for this child. Another child, much younger, loved me to read "The enormous turnip" over and over. Somehow, naming all the family members as helpers in getting that huge turnip out of the ground was so satisfying. And he loved to point out that even Petya, the tiny beetle really helped too.

Toddlers love the Sam books too. Sam and Lisa quarrel over a toy car. Each one wants it. Each one smacks the other. Mama comes with another car so that each has a car to play with and they play together. These books resonate for toddlers who are learning, struggling, with the idea of sharing and taking turns. Choose your books to help children wrestle with such issues at every level. Choose books with cadences and poetry so that preschoolers can learn the refrains as in the book "Something from nothing". Preschoolers enthusiastically join in saying "Grandpa can fix it!". This is the positive refrain of the little boy Jacob every time his mama wants him to throw out something old and torn.

Create Your Own Stories to Reassure Worried Children

If a child has terrors or fears, for example, about starting kindergarten, make up stories about a little child (who very much resembles your child) who had a similar problem and how a healing, reassuring, good ending happened in that situation (Brett, 1986).

When parents are separating and getting a divorce, children often feel torn in pieces. They are afraid that something they did caused the breakup. They worry that if one parents has left, they may also be abandoned by the other parent. Make up stories that have endings clearly showing how each parent loves the child and showing the child where she will be living and how she will be kept safe and secure.

Help Siblings Get Along More Peacefully

Jealousy, the green-eyed monster, is often alive and well in families. Tattling and reporting important news are different. Make a distinction to your children between 1) tattling to hurt a sibling to get even or as one way to show jealousy, and 2) the importance of telling information to parents if there is a really important trouble where an adult **must** get involved. Praise each time that the siblings try to talk courteously and not trade sneering put downs. Talk with your children about the far future when they are all grown up and will have each other as the only close family persons. Share a good book about jealous siblings and how they dealt with the green eyed monster. Try to find time alone for meeting the special needs of each child. Take one grocery shopping while a friend or relative watches the other children. Bring one down to the laundry room to work together while the others are busy doing homework.

Use relaxation and vivid imagination techniques to help children relax, especially where there is sibling jealousy and too much rush and tension in the children's lives. Deep breathing exercises and conjuring peaceful scenes sometimes help bring down child tensions (Hendricks & Wills, 1975).

Assign Required and Admired Chores

Be sure that chores are not assigned just to get daily jobs done the parents don't want to do! Chores should depend on the age and ability of each child. Children should not feel that they are their parents' "slaves" but family helpers pitching in to make the household work easier. Give children a feeling that when they do their chores they are important, contributing members of the family so they feel proud to be useful and helpful. "I am a big helper. I clear the table after dinner. My papa needs me to hold the nails and hand him a nail as he repairs the ripped porch screens." Swan and Stavros' work among poor inner-city families showed that children with required chores, whose parents praised their participation and gave them genuine admiration and appreciation felt very secure in the bosom of the family and performed with high achievement in the kindergarten and first grade classroom. "Me a big helper" is a proud and splendid boast from an older toddler!

Be a Good Matchmaker

Make the tasks you expect from each child be ones that the child can do. Encourage efforts and support early attempts to master new tasks in accordance with each child's ability (Honig, 1982b).

In a research study in New Orleans, Swan and Stavros (1973) found that low-income parents who required helpfulness (not coerced, but required) had children who were successful as kindergarten learners and in their social relationships with peers. They noted that fathers were mostly present in these low-income families with self-motivated learners. Parents had neat clean living environments, read daily to their young children, ate meals and talked together at dinner time, and found their children genuinely interesting persons.

Express Personal Pleasure With Each Child

Tell a child that you love him, that you love her. Hug that child frequently. Caress a child with warm (rather than cold or disapproving) voice tones. Shine your eyes at a child so that the sunshine of your smile and the pleasure in your tone of voice warm the deepest corners of your child's self.

Talk About Peer Pressure With Children

Peer pressure is very powerful in coercing some youngsters to misbehave. Sometimes peer pressure to have special sneakers or clothes or possessions will lead to children's stealing another's prized clothing item to gain peer admiration. Peer pressure can lead a teenager to drink immoderately, try drugs, or engage in unsafe sex. Families must talk frankly about peer pressure and how their child feels about it. A youngster can accept and more likely live by family values and family circumstances. IF the child feels a strong sense of rootedness and reassurance within the family rather than from the peer group.

Avoid the Use of Shame

Shame is an acid that corrodes the soul. Shame is often twinned with rage that fuels serious misbehavior. Do not shame your children or they may well feel that they need to get revenge on you and on the world. Perhaps a child acts defiant just to show that you cannot really make him eat a food he detests, you cannot make him fall asleep at a too-early bedtime for him. To get even, he will lie awake angry for hours. Power and revenge games are dangerous. They destroy a child's feelings of security and trust in responsible adults.

Encourage Competence

Even very young children need to feel they "can do it"—put a peg into a pegboard, roll a ball, pick up a wiggly spaghetti strand to feed themselves, throw a used Kleenex in the wastebasket, or other simple skills. Let them try, even if they are not expert, to accomplish tasks they are capable of doing, such as putting on a coat, or setting a table or pouring out dog food into the bowl on the floor. Children who give up easily or feel that they can never do their homework, never learn to ride a bide, for example, are **discouraged** children. Try patiently to support their small accomplishments. Figure out ways to decrease their discouraged feelings.

> Felicia asked for a wastebasket right by the table where she struggled nightly with homework math problems. She did not want all the papers with wrong answers and scribbles to pile up in front of her, almost accusing her of being "stupid". But with the handy wastebasket nearby, she was willing to struggle anew with a fresh sheet to try her math homework.

Provide Positive Attributions

Give praise for **specific** actions. Cheerfully tossing off "You're terrific!" or "That's wonderful!" makes a child feel uncomfortable. She knows how much she still has to learn, and how many times she goofs up. Notice specific times when praise can really boost self-esteem and brighten a child's day. For example, an adult could say: "You are a really good friend to Robbie. Did you notice how happy he was when you shared your markers with him. You know how to make another child feel comfortable and welcome here!"

Work Alongside A Young Child

By expecting too much, too fast, we sometimes force children to act incompetent to get out from under the disapproval they feel will be inevitable if they aren't superior (Dinkmeyer & McKay, 1982). When a job seems overwhelming to a young child, make sure you work alongside. "Clean up your room" may send a child into a temper tantrum or into trying to avoid the job entirely. But if you tackle the task cheerfully **together**, the child will enjoy your company and feel pride as he works to-

gether with you. When you break a task into smaller manageable bits, you **scaffold** the task for a youngster: "Which do you want to pick up first—the toys on the floor that go into your toy box or the clothes that go into the wash hamper?"

PROFESSIONALS AS PARTNERS WITH PARENTS

Professionals who work together with parents are not only teachers with a lot of information to share. They sometimes act as therapists. Sometimes they become caring friends of the family. Sometimes, as in Fraiberg's kitchen therapy model of home visitation, they become caring surrogate parents. They re-parent new parents whose ghosts of anguish and violence from the past are strongly impacting on the children in the present. Teachers especially need to "partner" with parents to form a strong team to support a child's early learning.

Sometimes, with very young mothers, professionals need to assist them in the process of **reflectivity**. The more that a new mother can reflect on her family of origin and how much during childhood she resented or was scared of harsh discipline, and decide that she does not want those feelings for her baby, the more affectionate and close will be her relationship with the new baby (Brophy & Honig, 1999).

In addition to support and knowledge, what other functions can personnel carry out to enhance positive family functioning?

Help Parents Find Ways To Give Themselves A Lift

Parents who feel happier with their own lives discipline more effectively and can share their happiness with children. Something as simple and inexpensive as a long bubble bath may relax an adult. Cleanup as a team after dinner with an adult partner helps any parent feel appreciated.

In a family with limited material resources, encourage parents to enlist imagination rather than material objects in order to bring special highlights into the family's day and into life. When rainy days in a row have resulted in short tempers, a family can plan to serve supper as a picnic on the living room floor. The children help make sandwiches. They spread the tuna salad and peanut butter on bread slices and wrap each sandwich. The family places all the picnic fixings in a basket and pretends they are walking to the picnic grounds—an old green sheet spread on the floor. Pretend games can break into the crankiness or hassles of daily living where severe financial constraints do not permit entertainments that "cost money".

Making collages out of bits of plastic egg cartons and other collected throw-aways can brighten an afternoon and provide art decorations to display on a refrigerator door so that children feel how proud you are of their talents.

Help Families to Network

Professionals need to introduce parents to others sometimes so they can form a support group when families feel isolated and alone. They could meet together at one another's home to talk about child issues with professional help or they can choose parenting materials to discuss. Help families feel comfortable in the world of the free public library or in a "Please Touch" museum. Introduce families to a drop-in store front center that welcomes families with respite child care, opportunities to swap children's used clothing and shopping coupons, as well as providing parenting classes and guitar lessons.

Find Respite Care For Overwhelmed Parents

Arrange for respite care when a parent is overwhelmed with caring for a disabled or emotionally disturbed child. Safe and secure respite care that a parent can count on and trust is one of the greatest gifts to give an exhausted parent. In a neighborhood, maybe parents can give each other coupons for helping out with childcare for each other. Such barter systems can provide needed respite without any money changing hands.

Assist Parents Trying to Join the Work Force

Help in finding job training and help in acquiring a high school diploma are other precious supports that families need as the bottom line in order to qualify for work positions to support their children. A resource room in a school or clinic can set out easy-to-read materials that focus on job training and on agencies that can help families in their search to become self sufficient.

Galvanize Specialist Help

When parents are behaving in seriously dysfunctional ways with children you need to act quickly and pinpoint the agencies and service to mobilize. Stresses can unnerve and make life difficult for parents. The five kinds of abuse that do occur in some families are: physical abuse, sexual abuse, physical neglect, emotional hostility, and emotional unavailability. Sometimes counseling and insight from child development experts and therapists can help. In urgent cases, when legal systems are threatening to remove a child from a home, then more strenuous professional help, such as Homebuilders provides (Kinney, Haapala & Booth, 1991), may be required. Homebuilders is an emergency service whereby a caseworker spends a great many hours for about six weeks in the home teaching the family members Gordon's (1975) Active Listening and I-statement techniques so that they can manage their

severe difficulties and get along more positively. Specialists in anger management can be enlisted to "tame the dragon of anger" in children and parents (Eastman & Rozen, 1994).

CONCLUSIONS

Enhancing parent involvement and training a highly skilled childcare provider workforce must become priority goals for nations if we are to improve children's lives and learning careers. As we support parents, particularly parents whose lives include undue stress from limited resources and chaotic and inappropriate role models from the past, we will be ensuring a brighter future not only for the families and children served but for our entire society. And as we support teachers in schools and care providers in nurseries and preschools with money, prestige, training, and our deep appreciation, we will also be ensuring that our children grow up to be happy, responsible, achieving citizens.

References

Baumrind, D. (1977). Some thoughts ab[...] Cohen and T. Comiskey (Eds.), *Chi[...] porary perspectives* (pp. 248–258). Ita[...]

Bettelheim, B. (1987). *A good enough parer[...]* New York: Random House.

Biller, H. and Meredith, D. (1975). *Father[...] fathering and how it can bring joy and freedom to the whole family.* New York: McKay.

Brett, D. (1986). *Annie stories.* Australia: Penguin.

Briggs, D. C. (1975). *Your child's self esteem.* New York: Doubleday.

Brophy-Herb, H. E. and Honig, A. S. (1999). Reflectivity: Key ingredient in positive adolescent parenting. *The Journal of Primary Prevention, 19* (3), 241–250.

Camp, B. N. and Bash, M. A. (1985). *Think aloud. Increasing social and cognitive skills—a problem solving program for children.* Champaign, IL: Research Press.

Crary, E. (1990). *Pick up your socks and other skills growing children need: A practical guide to raising responsible children.* Seattle, WA: Parenting Press.

Dinkmeyer, D. and McKay, G. D. (1982). *The parent's handbook: STEP. Systematic training for effective parenting.* Circle Pines, MN: American Guidance Service.

Eastman, M. and Rozen, S. C. (1994). *Taming the dragon in your child: Solutions for breaking the cycle of family anger.* New York: John Wiley.

Erikson, E. (1970). *Childhood and society.* New York: Norton.

Faber, A. and Mazlish, E. (1980). *How to talk so kids will listen and listen so kids will talk.* New York: Rawson Wade.

Fraiberg, S. (Ed.) (1980). *Clinical studies in infant mental health: The first year of life.* New York: Basic Books.

Goleman, D. (1995). *Emotional intelligence.* New York: Basic Books.

Gordon, S. (1983). *Parenting: A guide for young people.* New York: Oxford.

Gordon, T. (1975). *Parent effectiveness training.* New York:

Hart, B. and Risley, T. R. (1995). *Meaningful differences in the everyday experiences of young American children.* Baltimore, MD: Paul H. Brookes.

Henricks, G. and Wills, R. (1975). *The centering book: Awareness activities for children, parents, and teachers.* Engelwood Cliffs, NJ: Prentice Hall.

Honig, A. S. (1979). *Parent involvement in early childhood education.* Washington, DC.: National Association for the Education of Young Children.

Honig, A. S. (1982a). The gifts of families: Caring, courage, and competence. In N. Stinnett, J. Defrain, K. King, H. Hingren, G. Fowe, S. Van Zandt, and R. Williams (Eds.), *Family strengths 4: Positive support systems* (pp. 331–349). Lincoln, NE: University of Nebraska Press.

Honig, A. S. (1982b). *Playtime learning games for young children.* Syracuse, NY: Syracuse University Press.

Honig, A. S. (1985a). The art of talking to a baby. *Working Mother,* **8** (3), 72–78.

Honig, A. S. (1985b). Research in review; Compliance, control and discipline. *Young Children,* Part 1, **40** (2), 50–58; Part 2, **40** (3), 47–52.

Honig, A. S. (1993, Fall). Toilet learning. *Day Care and Early Education.*

Honig, A. S. (1995). Singing with infants and toddlers. *Young Children,* **50** (5), 72–78.

Honig, A. S. (1996). *Behavior guidance for infants and toddlers.* Little Rock, AR: Southern Early Childhood Association.

Honig, A. S. (1997). Infant temperament and personality: What do we need to know? *Montessori Life,* **9** (3), 18–21.

Honig, A. S. and Brophy, H. E. (1996). *Talking with your baby: Family as the first school.* Syracuse, NY: Syracuse University Press.

Honig, A. S. and Morin, C. (2000). When should programs for teen parents and babies begin? *Journal of Primary Prevention,* **21** (1).

Honig, A. S. and Wittmer, D. S. (1990). Infants, toddlers and socialization. In J. R. Lally (Ed.,), *A caregiver's guide to social emotional growth and socialization* (pp. 62–80). Sacramento, CA: California State Department of Education.

Kinney, J. Haapala, D. and Booth, C. (1991). *Keeping families together: The Homebuilders model.* Hawthorne, NY: Aldine De Gruyter.

Lickona, T. (1983). *Raising good children: From birth through the teenage years.* New York: Bantam Books.

Rofes, E. (Ed.) (1982). *The kids' book of divorce.* New York: Vintage.

Shure, M. B. (1994). *Raising a thinking child: Help your young child to resolve everyday conflicts and get along with others.* New York: Henry Holt.

Shure, M. and Spivack, G. (1978). *Problem-solving techniques in child-rearing.* San Francisco, CA: Jossey Bass.

Swan, R. W. and Stavros, H. (1973A). Child-rearing practices associated with the development of cognitive skills of children in a low socio-economic area. *Early Child Development and Care,* **2**, 23–38.

Welsh, R. (1976). Violence, permissiveness and the overpunished child. *Journal of Pediatric Psychology,* **1**, 68–71.

Winnicott, D. W. (1987). *Babies and their mothers.* Reading, MA: Addison-Wesley.

---

*Keynote address presented at the Child and Family Development Conference, Charlotte, North Carolina, March, 2000.

From *Early Child Development and Care,* 2000, Vol. 163, pp. 79-106. © 2000 by Carfax Publishing Ltd.

Generation XXL

Childhood obesity now threatens one in three kids with long-term health problems, and the crisis is growing.

BY GEOFFREY COWLEY

HAPPY JACK HOVIS was just a month old when he came to live with his aunt Terry Hunter in Charlotte, N.C. She remembers feeding the new baby one evening, then bathing him and settling him into his crib for the night. "He lay in bed and just smiled and smiled and smiled," she says fondly. "I told him, 'You are one Happy Jack!'" As he grew, the bright-eyed boy rarely fussed about his food. He loved fried chicken and green beans cooked in fatback, and he *really* loved eating at McDonald's. By the age of 4, he was so rotund that his pediatrician referred him to a heart specialist and, later, to a hospital-based weight clinic. Happy Jack is now 6, and following a program that combines regular exercise with smaller servings of lighter foods. The regimen is working—he has maintained roughly the same weight for 10 months, two inches taller. But at 118 pounds, he still weighs nearly twice what is normal for his age and height. For this child, slimming down isn't an aesthetic issue. His health—even his life—may depend on it.

Children's impulses haven't changed much in recent decades. But social forces—from the demise of home cooking to the rise of fast food and video technology—have converged to make them heavier. Snack and soda companies are spending hundreds of millions a year to promote empty calories, while schools cut back on physical education and outdoor play is supplanted by Nintendo and the Internet. The consequences are getting serious. By the government's estimate, some 6

million American children are now fat enough to endanger their health. An additional 5 million are on the threshold, and the problem is growing more extreme even as it becomes more widespread. "The children we see today are 30 percent heavier than the ones who were referred to us in 1990," says Dr. Naomi Neufeld, a pediatric endocrinologist in Los Angeles.

Obese kids suffer both physically and emotionally throughout childhood, and those who remain heavy as adolescents tend to stay that way into adulthood. The resulting illnesses—diabetes, heart disease, high blood pressure, several cancers—now claim an estimated half-million American lives each year, while costing us $100 billion in medical expenses and lost productivity. U.S. Agriculture Secretary Dan Glickman predicts that obesity will soon rival smoking as a cause of preventable death, and some health experts are calling for national action to combat it. Meanwhile, the challenge for children, and their parents, is to swim against the current.

Until recently, childhood obesity was so rare that no one tracked it closely. Body-mass index (BMI), the height-to-weight ratio used to measure adult heft, seemed irrelevant to people whose bodies are still growing. But that mind-set is changing. In a gesture aimed at parents and pediatricians, federal health officials recently published new growth charts that extend the BMI system to children. Unlike the adult charts, which classify anyone with a BMI of 25 or higher as "overweight" and any-

one with a BMI of 30 or more as "obese," the childhood charts (following page) use population norms from the 1960s to determine healthy weight ranges for kids 2 to 20. According to the new charts, a typical 7-year-old girl stands 4 feet 1 inch tall and weighs 50 pounds, giving her a BMI of 15. By the age of 17, she stands 5 feet 4 and weighs 125 pounds, for a BMI of 21. To spare parents undue alarm over baby fat or the normal weight gain that precedes growth spurts, the new charts use a broad definition of healthy weight. To be "at risk" of becoming too heavy, a child must fall above what was the 85th percentile during the 1960s (145 pounds for that 5-foot-4 inch girl). Only after hitting what was the 95th percentile (170 pounds for the same girl) does one become "overweight."

EVEN BY THESE LENIENT standards, the proportion of kids who are overweight jumped from 5 percent in 1964 to nearly 13 percent in 1994, the most recent year on record. If the trend has continued—and many experts believe it has *accelerated*—one child in three is now either overweight or at risk of becoming so. No race or class has been spared, and many youngsters are already suffering health consequences. Dr. Nancy Krebs, a pediatrician at the University of Colorado, notes that overweight children are now showing up with such problems as fatty liver, a precursor to cirrhosis, and obstructive sleep apnea, a condition in which the excess flesh around the throat blocks the airway,

Bigger Meals, Bigger Kids

It's hard for children to stay lean when portions keep growing. A look at what Americans are eating, and how it's changing the shape of our bodies:

A traditional McDonald's burger with a 16-ounce Coke and a small order of fries carries 627 calories and 19 grams of fat

Upgrade to a Big Xtra! with cheese, and 'super size' the drink and fries. Now your lunch packs 1,805 calories and 84 grams of fat.

Unsafe at any age: The percentage of American kids who are overweight has more than doubled since the 1960s.

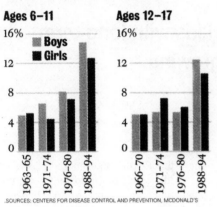

SOURCES: CENTERS FOR DISEASE CONTROL AND PREVENTION, MCDONALD'S

1991

1998

Girth of a nation: In 1991, only four states had obesity rates over 14 percent. By 1998, 37 had hit that threshold.

Is your child overweight? To find out, calculate the child's BMI, and plot it by age on one of the two graphs below:

$$\boxed{} \div \boxed{} \div \boxed{} \times 703 = \boxed{}$$

Child's weight in pounds | Height in inches | Height in inches again | Child's BMI

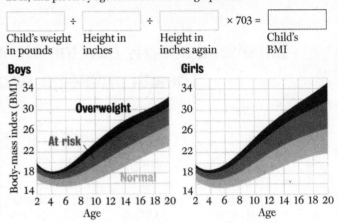

causing loud snoring, fitful sleep and a chronic lack of oxygen that can damage the heart and lungs.

Even type 2 diabetes—known traditionally as "adult-onset" diabetes—is turning up in overweight kids. "Ten years ago I would have told you that type 2 diabetes doesn't occur until after 40," says Dr. Robin Goland of New York's Columbia-Presbyterian Hospital. "Now 30 percent of our pediatric patients are type 2." Unlike type 1 disease, in which the pancreas fails to produce the insulin needed to transport sugar from the bloodstream into cells, type 2 diabetes occurs when a person's cells grow resistant to insulin, causing sugar to build up in the blood. Unless it's carefully managed, this obesity-related condition can damage blood vessels within a decade, setting the stage for kidney failure and blindness as well as amputations, heart attacks and strokes. And because children are not routinely screened for type 2 disease, Goland worries that many cases are going undiagnosed. "You can have this condition without knowing it," she says.

Even if they don't develop diabetes, chronically overweight kids may become prime candidates for heart attacks and strokes. In a recent survey of preschoolers at New York City Head Start Centers, Dr. Christine Williams of Columbia University found that overweight kids as young as

3 and 4 showed signs of elevated blood pressure and cholesterol. "There's a lag between the development of obesity and the chronic diseases associated with it," says Dr. William Dietz of the Centers for Disease Control and Prevention. "We're in that trough right now. Very soon we'll see the rate of cardiovascular disease among teenagers rising."

How does a child end up in this predicament? Genes are clearly part of the story. Nine-year-old Emily Hoffman of Humble, Texas, was born weighing nearly 11 pounds. And though she was raised in ways her pediatricians approved of, everything she ate seemed to turn into fat. By 7 she weighed 180 pounds. But even in kids who are prone to obesity, lifestyle is what triggers it. Felice Ramirez weighed 200 pounds when she started eighth grade in Victoria, Texas, three years ago. And though she has since lost 25, she is constantly nudged in the wrong direction. "My friends go to McDonald's and Sonic and Casa Olé and they just eat and eat," she says. "And when they're not eating, they go to the mall." She has a P.E. class at school, but sitting on the bleachers counts as participation. And though the school cafeteria tries to offer healthy fare, the lines are so long, and the lunch period so short, that kids are often forced to dine on

packaged snacks from the vending machines.

THESE ARE COMMON temptations. Many schools now feature not only soda and snack machines but on-site outlets for fastfood chains. At the same time, recess and physical education are vanishing from the schools' standard curriculum. Virginia is now the only state that still mandates recess as a daily routine—the Atlanta school system recently *banned* it in the hope of raising academic performance—and fewer than half of the nation's schools offer P.E. Not surprisingly, the proportion of high-school kids in daily gym classes fell from 42 percent to 29 percent during the '90s.

No one expects these trends to reverse any time soon. Cynics predict that we'll get serious about childhood obesity about 20 years from now, when today's youngsters are hobbled by arteriosclerosis and endstage renal disease. But nutrition experts are so worried that some now advocate cigarette-style taxes on snack foods and soft drinks. Writing in the current American Journal of Public Health, activist Michael Jacobson and Yale psychologist Kelly Brownell note that a national one-cent tax on soda pop could generate $1.5 billion a year to promote healthful alternatives. (The soft-drink industry is understandably opposed.) Meanwhile, researchers are studying the effects of positive incentives to eat better. In one recent experiment, a team at the University of Minnesota found that when high-school cafeterias offered 50 percent discounts on carrot sticks and fresh fruit, sales increased two- to fourfold.

Protecting our kids may ultimately require such initiatives, but we don't have to wait for the world to change. Dr. Thomas Robinson, a Stanford pediatrician, has shown that simply limiting TV time can help immunize them against obesity. In a study involving 192 third and fourth graders, he found that those who held their screen time to one hour a day were measurably leaner after nine months than those who watched the tube at will.

Setting limits is important, but parents can often accomplish more by setting an example. When Kate Harned of Winter Springs, Fla., was an overweight 8-year-old, her mom's advice about diet and exercise served only to anger her. But when her mother joined Weight Watchers and dropped 55 pounds, her message started to resonate. Kate joined the program herself last year, at 14, and has since come down by six pants sizes. Celeste Santizo has a similar story. When she hit 116 pounds during the second grade this year, her family joined a Los Angeles-based program called KidShape. Besides cutting Celeste's TV time and persuading her to take up handball and tae kwon do, the KidShape counselors got her mother, Martha Santizo, to think differently about the family's routines—and her own. Martha started serving meals on salad-size plates to control portion sizes, and offering water instead of fruit juice when her kids got thirsty. She also bought a tape called "Sweatin' to the Oldies" and slimmed down herself. Eight weeks later, Celeste has lost four pounds and gained a new outlook on life. "She's friendlier," her mom observes. "She has more energy, and I think she's a much happier person." If warding off disease weren't reason enough to get active, that alone would make the case.

With DANIEL PEDERSEN *in Atlanta,* PAT WINGERT *in Washington,* TARA WEINGARTEN *in Los Angeles,* ANDREA COOPER *in Charlotte,* ANNE BELLI GESALMAN *in Houston and* LAURA GATLAND *in Chicago*

From *Newsweek*, July 3, 2000, pp. 40-44. © 2000 by Newsweek, Inc. All rights reserved. Reprinted by permission.

FOCUS ON
Your Family

Kids Who Don't Fit In

**Researchers say that good social skills are critical to success and happiness.
How can parents help children who are left out? BY PAT WINGERT**

THE FIRST SIGN OF A PROBLEM WAS 3-year-old William's refusal to hold hands with other children. As he moved through preschool, he made friends but didn't keep them. By first grade, he was isolated and lonely. The other kids, his mother admits, "thought he was weird." William (not his real name) was painfully aware there was a problem. "He'd ask me, 'Why don't the kids like me?'" his mother recalls. Third grade was a crisis; William was falling apart. "His teacher pulled us in and said, 'He's always crying at school and walking around the periphery of the playground. You should have him tested'."

You should have him tested. That advice is echoed in classrooms around the country as more and more teachers and parents understand the importance of developing good social skills. Researchers now know that success in life—personal happiness, too—depends to a great degree on an individual's "emotional intelligence," the ability to function well in a group and to form meaningful relationships. "Children who are generally disliked, who are aggressive and disruptive, who are unable to sustain close relationships with other children and who cannot establish a place for themselves in the

peer culture are seriously at risk," says psychologist Willard Hartup of the University of Minnesota. That's why kids like William, who run into trouble early, are getting the help they need at an age when the right therapy can really make a difference.

Sometimes the problem is just awkwardness; in other cases, there can be real neurological deficits. In William's case, test results revealed that he was suffering from attention deficit disorder and an inability to read social cues. "He didn't know where his personal space ended and someone else's space began," his mother says. "He couldn't read facial expressions. Sometimes he was nonresponsive when people were talking directly to him. He talked at people, and didn't laugh at the right time."

For three years William attended weekly group therapy, where he would play with other kids with similar problems while the therapist gently prompted and corrected his interactions. He also met with a psychologist for one-on-one help. Now in eighth grade, he continues with individual therapy. He's still "not Mr. Popularity," his mom says, but "he has friends."

Experts agree that the earlier the intervention, the more effective the therapy. But evaluating very young children can be tricky. Many psychologists believe children develop social competence at different rates—just as some children are slow to walk or talk. "On the one hand it's encouraging that more children are getting help early on, " says Jan Wintrol, director of the Ivymount School in suburban Maryland, which diagnoses social, emotional and behavioral problems. "On the other hand, I get concerned about an overemphasis: we think we have to have therapy for everything."

So how does a parent know whether to worry about a kid who's always alone on the playground? The experts advise parents to watch, compare, consult with teachers and, in the end, trust their instincts.

The first hint of trouble often shows up when children are preverbal, between 12 and 24 months, says psychiatrist Stanley Greenspan, author of "The Growth of the Mind." At this stage, children typically "learn to use gestures to get their needs met and express their emotions." Most toddlers learn this automatically. Kids who don't master this skill may also fail to develop in other ways. Parents might begin to notice

The Edge of Kindness

A veteran kindergarten teacher on what she's learned

VIVIAN PALEY NEVER MISSES the opportunity to tell the tale of Teddy. She was visiting a London preschool when some kids from a nearby school for the severely disabled came to visit. Teddy was pushed into the classroom in a wheelchair, his head protected by a padded helmet, his limbs twitching. Paley watched in wonder as the small children incorporated Teddy—who had trouble speaking more than a word at a time—into their play. To Paley, 70, a longtime Chicago kindergarten teacher and the winner of a MacArthur Fellowship for her writing about children, that moment inspired an insightful new book, "The Kindness of Children." In an interview with NEWSWEEK's Pat Wingert, Paley talked about how adults can nurture empathy.

WINGERT: Do you think children are always ready to be kind?
PALEY: Yes, even when they're in a snit. You may have to wait a little and not push. But out of the side of their eye they may see someone, maybe even the child they were fighting with, with a trembling lip, and their eyes filling, and something says to them: "Stop. Do something nice now. This has gone too far." I believe children are always on the edge of committing an act of kindness, always ready to go in that direction.

By sharing stories of kindness, can we inspire children?
When children hear a story about kindness, they are very moved. From our earliest school years, we know all we need to know about hurt feelings and how to help someone salvage hurt feelings.

When does the earliest kindness appear in children?
Even very young children are moved when they see a baby or a friend crying, and they'll go pull their teacher to help. No one has taught this. No one has said to these 18-month-olds, "If you see any human being struggling or suffering, call me right away."

Do you think young children are naturally more accepting than older children or adults?
Absolutely. I've never seen a young child be anything other than very interested in what other children look like, do, say, how they behave—they're fascinated. They have a tremendous, almost scientific interest in each other.

Is that why you've become such an advocate of diversity?
When children with problems come into a regular classroom, there are more opportunities for children and teachers to show kindness. Acting out kindness makes us realize what we're capable of. It feels good to be in power, but it feels terrific to see yourself as the giver of kindness.

You say play helps create a "new life for a wandering soul." What do you mean?
The lonely child only lacks a role to play because play is the language of children. Play is a story. We don't hear the story when kids are in the sandbox, but we could almost write the story from the noises we hear coming out of it. Play was a brilliant invention of whoever created mankind.

You say loneliness is the major struggle when children first enter school. Does that experience foster empathy?
Every child knows loneliness. But because I have been lonely, do I recognize the plight of others who are lonely? That's more subtle, and that's where the artistry comes in, where the modelling comes in. I can't imagine a greater source of satisfaction for a teacher.

How do you help children who don't know how to play?
If I saw a child running through the block like a whirlwind and knocking everything down, I would ask the child to sit with me and watch others who find it easy to play well with others. The class then becomes a kind of laboratory where you can point out what works.

How does the kindness of children inspire us as adults?
It gives me joy as a teacher to be a witness to these things. It gives me the strength to deal with that other side of life, when people are wounded and disencouraged.

that their child isn't interacting the way other children do or that playmates avoid their child. Marshall Duke and Steve Nowicki Jr., psychology professors at Emory University and authors of "Helping the Child Who Doesn't Fit In," call this condition "dyssemia." The abilities to interpret and use nonverbal cues "are the building blocks of social skills," Nowicki says.

Tests can reveal that a child is unable to read facial expressions, body language or tone of voice. Other children can't get their bodies and faces to express the right emotions. And some children can do neither. Some stand much too close to people, or touch them inappropriately. They may talk way too loud—or so softly they can't be heard. They may laugh or cry or get angry at the wrong times, or seem to be talking at people rather than conversing with them. "These are the kind of rules that you only notice when they get broken," Duke says.

Some of these kids may have a brain processing problem that makes it difficult for them to sequence or put their thoughts into action. Others may have a speech disability or a form of autism or developmental problems. Some problems may be aggravated by learning disabilities or attention deficit disorder. Others simply haven't had enough experience interacting with people. Children with depressed, alcoholic or drug-using parents can exhibit the same problems, as can youngsters who are not getting enough one-on-one attention from busy parents or overworked child-care providers. Duke and Nowicki's studies indicate that about 10 percent of children have some form of dyssemia. If those estimates are right, that would be equal to double the number of children who have been diagnosed with attention deficit disorder.

TO FIND THE RIGHT KIND OF HELP, parents can start by asking teachers, the school psychologist or an educational counselor. Some kids join "social skill groups" like William's with other children and a trained therapist acting almost as a coach. Others seek help through family or one-on-one counseling. Some therapists act primarily as consultants, observing a kid's behavior at home and in school and then advising teachers and parents.

Children struggle with these problems at all ages. Maryland pediatrician Sharon Goldman says she has one new patient who's a senior in high school. "She's never gone on a date," Goldman says. "She's never hung out at the mall with friends. She's so exquisitely afraid of how others will view her that she has no friends. She needs to learn to do these things before she goes off to college by herself."

It's never too late to get that help; some therapists who specialize in social skills work only with adults, and others even consult with corporations that are having difficulties with employees. But children benefit the most. Intervention can help kids with mild to moderate social problems have a normal social life. Those with more severe problems may always be a little stiff or quirky in their social exchanges, but with help they have a much better chance of being able to relate to others. As William's mom says, "This stuff doesn't just disappear. But he's going up the ladder. He's going in the right direction." And his future looks a lot less lonely.

From *Newsweek*, March 22, 1999, pp. 76-79. © 1999 by Newsweek, Inc. All rights reserved. Reprinted by permission.

Are Boys the Weaker Sex?

Science says yes. But society is trying to deal with male handicaps

BY ANNA MULRINE

Sandy Descourouez worries about her sons. The eldest, 18-year-old Greg, was never the chatty type, but he became positively withdrawn following his parents' nasty divorce a decade ago. Last year, Greg's problems erupted into the open: He was arrested for stealing a golf cart and caught smoking marijuana. David, 13—loving, messy, and disorganized—struggles with borderline grades and attention deficit disorder. Sandy's baby, 2 1/2-year-old Luke, is a one-boy demolition derby. But his reckless energy isn't her main cause of concern. While the toddler strings together sound effects with reasonably good results, he rarely utters a word.

Sandy initially took Greg's silence for male reserve—that is, until she happened on his journal. The teenager's diary roiled with frustration and pain. Perhaps to positive effect: Greg wrote a letter to his absent father and reached out for help. "I don't know how to talk about these things," he wrote, "and I know you don't either, so maybe we can help each other."

Boys earn 70 percent of the D's and F's doled out by teachers.

Sandy's "boys will be boys" sighs gave way to bewilderment—and fear. The Aurora, Ill., real-estate broker realized that all three sons had problems very distinct from those she had encountered in her daughter, a champion speller; problems that needed attention.

The travails of the Descourouez family mirror America's struggle with its sons. "We are experiencing a crisis of the boy next door," says William Pollack, a clinical psychologist at Harvard University and author of *Real Boys*. Across the country, boys have never been in more trouble: They earn 70 percent of the D's and F's that teachers dole out. They make up two thirds of students labeled "learning disabled." They are the culprits in a whopping 9 of 10 alcohol and drug violations and the suspected perpetrators in 4 out of 5 crimes that end up in juvenile court. They account for 80 percent of high school dropouts and attention deficit disorder diagnoses. And they are less likely to go to college than ever before. By 2007, universities are projected to enroll 9.2 million women to 6.9 million men.

Truth to power. That's not what America expects from its boys. "Maybe because men enjoy so much power and prestige in society, there is a tendency to see boys as shoo-ins for success," says child psychologist Michael Thompson, co-author of *Raising Cain*. "So people see in boys signs of strength where there are none, and they ignore all of the evidence that they are in trouble."

But that evidence is getting tougher than ever to overlook. Today, scientists are discovering very real biological differences that can make boys more impulsive, more vulnerable to benign neglect, less efficient classroom learners—in sum, the weaker sex. "The notion of male vulnerability is so novel, but the biological facts support it," says Sebastian Kraemer, a child psychiatrist in London and author of a recent *British Medical Journal* article on male fragility. "We're only just now beginning to understand the underlying weakness of men, for so many centuries almost universally projected onto women."

What's more, social pressure often compounds biological vulnerability. "Boys today are growing up with tremendous expectations but without adequate emotional fuel or the tools they need to succeed in school or sustain deep relationships," says Eli Newberger, a pediatrician at Boston Children's Hospital and author of *The Men They Will Become*. Girls now outnumber boys in student government, honor societies, school newspapers, and debating clubs. A recent study found girls ahead of boys in almost every measure of well-being: Girls feel closer to their families, have higher aspirations, and even boast better assertiveness skills. "I regularly see girls who are both valedictorian and captain of the soccer team, but I almost never see that in boys," says Leonard Sax, a family physician and psychologist in Poolesville, Md.

Schools are taking note, too—and they are beginning to act. Early childhood specialists, concerned with ever accelerating curriculum demands, are advocating delayed entrance of boys into kindergarten, to give them time to catch up with girls developmentally. Other districts are experimenting with single-sex classrooms within coed schools, in the hopes that all-boy classes will allow boys to improve standardized test scores in reading and writing, much the way girls have narrowed the gap in math and science. (Currently, the average 11th-grade boy writes with the proficiency of the average eighth-grade girl.) In response to charges of the "feminization" of the classroom—including, critics argue, female teachers with too little tolerance for the physicality of boys—schools are beginning to re-examine their attitudes toward male activity levels and even revamp disciplinary techniques.

Boys make up two thirds of learning-disabled students.

The measures aren't without skeptics. "Isn't it ironic that it's only been in the last two decades that we've really considered making schools equitable for girls," says David Sadker, an American University professor and pioneer in research on girls' treatment in the classroom. "And now people are already saying, 'Whoa, too much time on girls. Let's get back to boys.'"

Pole position. Yet the latest research not only documents boys' unexpected vulnerabilities but indicates that they can be traced back to the womb. While more boys than girls are conceived (the speculation is that sperm carrying the male's Y chromosomes swim faster than those carrying the larger X), this biological pole position doesn't last long, says Kraemer. Perhaps to offset the speed advantage, when mothers experience stress, male embryos are more likely to perish. The male fetus is at greater risk of peril from almost all obstetric complications, including brain damage, cerebral palsy, and premature birth. By the time a baby boy enters the world, he is trailing the average girl, developmentally, by six weeks.

Male newborns are also more emotionally demonstrative than females—a fact that has been shown experimentally despite the cultural stereotype to the contrary. When asked to rate photos for expressiveness, adults who had not been told the children's sex were far more likely to dub boys "more intensely expressive" than girls. And when researchers intentionally misidentified the boys as girls, adults gave the

boys presumed to be girls the highest expressiveness marks. In other words, their actual perceptions trumped the stereotypes.

What's particularly interesting, says Thompson, is that while there is evidence that boys may feel more stress in emotional situations, they routinely show less. When placed within earshot of a crying baby, boys have higher increases in heart rate and sweatier palms than girls. But their behavior belies their biological reaction: Their typical response is to turn off the speaker broadcasting the crying.

Judy Chu, a researcher at Harvard University, has also noted how boys' behavior often masks emotional inclinations. "Boys are a lot more attuned and a lot more sensitive than people give them credit for," she says. Chu spent two years having conversations with a group of boys in a preschool classroom outside Boston. At age 4, the boys candidly discussed their feelings about subjects that ranged from sharing toys to hurt feelings. "They were insightful in ways I hadn't expected—so articulate and attentive," says Chu. Over time, however, as the expectations of parents, teachers, and peers compounded, the boys' behavior changed. "They became inattentive, indirect, and inarticulate," says Chu, "and self-conscious about what other boys thought." Chu recalls one child who was friends with a preschool group of kids who had dubbed themselves "the mean team." "I'm friends with all of the girls," he told Chu. "But if Bill [the unofficial leader of the team] finds that out, he'll fire me from the team." As the result of these observations, Chu firmly believes that boys lose their voice, much as girls do in adolescence, and begin to camouflage feelings and behaviors that might put them in conflict with other boys.

Girls **outnumber** boys in student councils and debate clubs.

Their friendships also begin to change. "We associate girls with the sharing of secrets, the emotional intimacy, and boys with the sports and activity-oriented friendships," says Niobe Way, a professor of psychology at New York University. "But what's interesting is that these very tough boys talk about wanting friends to share their secrets with, to confide in."

She recalls Malcolm, great in sports, admired by the other boys. One day, Malcolm learned that one of his closest friends had been talking about him and began to cry. "The conventional wisdom is that gossip and arguments with friends don't affect boys or that they'll just 'fight it out,' then let it roll off their backs," says Way. But that's often a misconception. In Malcolm's case, he announced that he was giving up on his friends ("They won't keep your secrets, and they'll stab you in the back")—an attitude he maintained throughout high school.

When boys get emotional, parents and other adults often encourage them to tone it down. "People come to me time and time again saying, 'My son, he's so sensitive,'" says Thompson. "What they don't realize is that it's not the exception. It's the norm." And so, parents react differently to upset daughters and sons. "The actions can be as subtle as asking a girl what's wrong when she's crying but patting a boy on the head and saying, 'You're OK; now get back out there.'" The result can be emotional isolation that starts in boyhood and plagues men in middle age, often with emotional, and even physical, consequences. "Every now and then I catch myself saying things to my sons that I wouldn't say to my daughter—like 'Be tough, don't cry,'" worries Descourouez. "Now I'm trying not to say anything to them that I wouldn't say to my daughter. They can decide what they want to cry about."

Action figures. But despite the evidence of boys' sensitivity, not all of the old stereotypes are unfounded. As much as day care provider Marcy Shrage encourages sensitivity in her boys, she has noticed how they crave action. At her home in Lawrenceville, N.J., she cares for five boys under the age of 4. She piles them all into her minivan and takes them on drives. She'll stop for senior citizens in crosswalks to model good behavior and take them on long walks through the woods. But, the karate black belt admits, the boys do get most excited when she teaches them martial-arts moves. And though she doesn't allow toy weapons in the house, "There are plenty of days when they'll bite their sandwiches into the shape of guns and start firing away at each other."

It is the unexpected combination of physical aggressiveness and emotional vulnerability that now fascinates scientists at the University of Pennsylvania's Brain Behavior Laboratory, who are looking for explanations in the neurons. According to center director Ruben Gur, they have found some intriguing differences in brain structure—anatomical disparities that make it harder for boys to process information and even read faces but easier for them to excel at gross motor skills and visualize objects in three dimensions.

Women's brains are, on average, 11 percent smaller than men's, says Gur. And while there appears to be a subtle correlation between brain volume and IQ, he adds, there is no difference in the IQs of males and females. "So we have to ask how women manage to have the same IQ in a proportionally smaller brain." The answer is that female brains are not simply a smaller version of male brains. From a strictly evolutionary standpoint, the female brain is a bit more finely developed, says Gur. Brains are composed of gray matter (where information processing is done), white matter (long fibers covered in fat that, much like rubber-coated wire, transmit electrical impulses from brain to body), and spinal fluid (which acts as a buffer from the skull). The most recent research shows that males have less gray matter and more white matter than do females. And the right and left hemispheres of the brain are linked by a bundle of nerves that helps the two sides of the brain communicate. In women, this bundle—the corpus callosum—is thicker. It's the difference, researchers explain, between a narrow path in the woods and a two-lane highway.

As a result, says Gur, female brains tend to be more facile when it comes to verbal skills. This may explain why girls utter their first words earlier, string together complete sentences first, and generally surpass boys in tests that involve verbal fluency. "The female brain is an easier brain to teach," says Michael Gurian, a family therapist and author of *Boys and Girls Learn Differently*. "It's harder for the male brain to learn." It may also explain why, when Sandy Descourouez subscribed to a "developmental milestones" E-mail update from a babyfood site, she learned her son Luke was, like many boys, a "late talker."

Males do have more white matter, however—with longer, more complex nerve networks from their brains to the tips of their toes—allowing boys like Luke to excel at gross motor skills. And their greater volume of spinal fluid, says Gur, also means that male brains are built to sustain blows. "Thank goodness for that," says Descourouez, recalling Luke's penchant for spinning in circles near the fireplace.

Reptilian feelings? There appear to be brain-related differences in male and female emotions as well. The latest research suggests that the emotional brain is "more primitive" in men. Women make use of an emotional processing center adjacent to the speech areas of the brain, which makes it easier for them to link emotions to speech. The female brain is also "architecturally finer—a later arrival in evolution," says Gur. Men make use of an older limbic system "present in more primitive creatures," often known as the reptilian brain. Which means that male emotion is often more closely linked with action.

These are just the sort of details that the "Raising Sons" seminar participants at the Parenting Center in Fort Worth are gathering to learn. Moms and dads circle their chairs and share their fears, trying to come to some sort of agreement on what constitutes "normal" boy behavior: Why is their son struggling in school? Why won't he listen? Is he too sensitive? Too taken with guns and violent video games?

Boys are the culprits in 9 of 10 alcohol and drug violations.

Pam Young debates with fellow "Raising Sons" classmate Brian Rice about her sons' penchant for wrestling. "They seem to know what drives me crazy," she says, conceding that it's also their way of bonding with dad. Rice, by contrast, worries that *his* son doesn't wrestle enough.

Another parent wonders aloud where his son's high spiritedness ends and brattiness begins. "I'm curious about the back talk," he inquires. "I want my son to be an independent thinker, but I also want him to have respect." Young leans in, nodding in agreement. "Yes," she says. "My son is very independent, then very dependent for approval."

In class, parents learn about the selective "pruning" of brain cells that scientists believe can lead to impulsivity—and that is thought to occur more rigorously in adolescent boys than girls. "It would explain why my son acts like a windshield wiper sometimes," says Young. "He's on, then he's off. He gets it, then he doesn't."

Later, a facilitator asks, "What's the only emotion that it's OK for boys to have?" The class pauses for a moment, then answers virtually in unison: "anger." Maybe that's why we have so many angry

boys, the facilitator suggests. And so the parents learn how to teach their sons to match words with feelings, to build a vocabulary for the emotions that they often have trouble expressing.

Boys are **twice** as likely as girls to be held back a grade in school.

Let's get physical. The teachers at Thomas Edison Elementary School in St. Joseph, Mo., have begun to put some of the brain science to the test. Three years ago, when third-grade teacher Denise Young asked the boys in her class a question, she would get frustrated if they didn't respond, and simply move on. Today, she gives them at least 60 seconds to "process" the question. "They need more time to stop, switch gears, and respond," says Young. "But they didn't have it, and I think that's why a lot of boys have gotten into trouble in the past." She also gives them "stress balls" to squeeze while they're reading or working out a problem. "It seems to help them engage when they're also doing something physical," she says.

For more information

- **Real Boys Workbook** by William Pollack. Outlines "Some Do's and Don'ts With Boys." Also specific tips for talking to sensitive sons.
- **Speaking of Boys** by Michael Thompson. *Raising Cain* coauthor answers "the most asked questions about raising sons," delving into topics such as male puberty and underage drinking.
- **The Men They Will Become** by Eli Newberger. A thoughtful look at the emotional tug-of-war within boys.
- **Boys and Girls Learn Differently!** by Michael Gurian. The latest on boys' and girls' thinking styles.

On a typical day, her children stand by their desks as they complete work sheets and work on projects. That's because there is now a greater understanding, says principal Debbie Murphy, of the activity level and physicality of their school's boys. "There was a child who just couldn't sit still in music class, and we decided, well, if it's not going to bother anyone, it's fine if he stands at the back of the room."

Murphy also tried something new during her disciplinary chats with the boys. "I will not make the children talk when they're angry, for starters. Boys, in particular, just have trouble verbalizing when they're upset." Once they've cooled down, Murphy takes them for a stroll. "I find boys have an easier time talking if they're walking, too—it seems to tap into something in their brains," she says. In three years, Edison Elementary has watched its test scores skyrocket from what Murphy calls "ghetto statistics" to among the top 10 percent in the state. Incidents of in-school suspension have decreased from 300 to 22 this year.

The controversial drugging of boys also appears related to fundamental temperamental differences. Family physician Sax became alarmed when, increasingly, he was asked to prescribe Ritalin to otherwise healthy boys who simply couldn't sit still through long lessons. But the fact that boys are prescribed medicines and still fail at twice the rate of girls has given him pause. One of his patients, Andrew Yost, was a bright 8-year-old but uninspired by school and constantly getting into spats with his teachers. Sax suspected ADD and suggested Andrew's family consult with a child psychiatrist from the National Institutes of Health. The specialist confirmed the diagnosis and prescribed Ritalin.

When Sax encountered Andrew again several years later, he had indeed shown dramatic improvement. But it was not the result of the drugs. The difference, according to Andrew's parents, was that they had enrolled him in an all-boys school. "The teachers just seem to understand boy behaviors," says his father, David. "We tried so much before that, but now, I think he's where he should be." Andrew no longer takes any medications and, he adds, "I don't worry as much about what girls think."

By 2007, girls may outnumber boys in college nearly 3 to 2.

Other school districts are experimenting with voluntary single-sex classrooms within coed schools. "Parents are showing up in droves to sign up for the classes," says Anthony Basanese, middle school principal in Pellston, Mich. This fall, fully half of the sixth-grade class will be enrolled in single-sex classes, meeting throughout the day for coed lunch periods and extracurricular activities. "Parents like it because they see their kids doing better in school."

While American University's Sadker worries about the declining presence of male teachers—"down from 20 percent when I was a boy to 15 percent of all elementary school teachers now"—he is also wary of single-sex education. "Why aren't we fixing coed classes instead of running away from them? If we want a democracy that lives and works together, don't we also want one that learns together?"

Too much too soon. But many boys may need a substantial boost in schooling, say Sax and other specialists advocating a later start in kindergarten for boys. "The early curriculum is more accelerated than ever before," says Sax. "Boys are expected to do too much too soon—their brains aren't ready for it." The result, he adds, is too often a lifelong struggle with school. "They begin their school careers in 'the dumb group.' They're frustrated with their lack of ability, they start disliking school, and they begin to avoid it. We're seeing that more than ever now."

The extra year before kindergarten would allow boys to catch up. "Not all girls are precocious, and not all boys are delayed," says Sax. "But I've come to the conclusion that later enrollment would solve 80 percent of the problems we see with boys and school today."

Descourouez is considering holding Luke back from kindergarten. "His speech isn't up to speed," she worries, "and I don't want school to be a miserable experience for him." School is no pleasure for her son David, but she's determined to nurture the tenderness she sees in him. "He designs computer screens that say, 'I love you.' I can't remember the last time Greg said that to me." And she vows not to disregard the silence of her sons. "When they can't find the words for their emotions, I try to help them," she says. As they find the words, she hopes they will break the old patterns—and become husbands and fathers who talk.

From *U.S. News & World Report*, July 30, 2001, pp. 40-47. © 2001 by U.S. News & World Report, L.P. Reprinted by permission.

Effects of
*M*altreatment
and Ways To Promote Children's Resiliency

Barbara Lowenthal

Each year, about four million American children are exposed to traumatic events (Schwartz & Perry, 1994) such as physical, sexual, and emotional abuse; neglect; accidents; severe injuries; and natural disasters. Children may develop posttraumatic stress disorder as a result, leaving them vulnerable to phobias, conduct and behavioral difficulties, anxiety disorders, depression, and other neuropsychiatric disorders. This article will focus on the effects of maltreatment, including abuse and neglect, on young children. The author will discuss possible neurological, psychological, and cognitive consequences, as well as interventions that can promote resiliency in children. As concerned professionals, we need to advocate both for methods of preventing abuse and neglect, and for interventions that will assist maltreated children.

Neurological Effects of Abuse and Neglect

Recent research provides information about the neurology and development of the brain during the first years of life. At birth, the brain is the most immature organ in the human body; it will continue to develop as a result of both genetics and environmental experiences, which can have both positive or negative effects (Terr, 1991). Different areas of the brain are responsible for specific functions (Terr, 1991). The frontal lobe is responsible for abstract thought. Systems in the limbic area regulate affect, emotion, and the attachment process. Other systems in the brain stem regulate the heart rate, blood pressure, and states of arousal (Tauwer, 1989).

> As concerned professionals, we need to advocate both for methods of preventing abuse and neglect, and for interventions that will assist maltreated children.

The brain houses millions of nerve cells or neurons, which are connected to each other by synapses. These synapses, or pathways, compose the "wiring" of the brain (Neuberger, 1997), and allow the various regions of the brain to communicate with each other. Brain development after birth consists of a continuous process of wiring the connections among neurons. While new synapses form, those that are not used will be "pruned." A child's brain will develop 1,000 trillion synapses during the first year of life. By age 10, however, the pruning process occurs more frequently than does the formation of new synapses (Nash, 1997). At that point, the child has about 500 trillion synapses, a figure that remains somewhat constant through adulthood.

A young child's neurodevelopment can be disrupted in two ways: through a lack of sensory experiences, which are necessary for the brain's optimal development (Stermer, 1997), and through abnormally active neurons, caused by such negative experiences as maltreatment and neglect (Perry, 1993). Negative environmental events can result in the malfunctioning of those regions of the brain responsible for the regulation of affect, empathy, and emotions. Continual abuse and neglect also can disrupt infants' attachment process with their caregivers, and, consequently, lead children to mistrust their environments (Nash, 1997).

Humans' so-called fight-or-flight response to stress, which prepares individuals to defend themselves against perceived dangers, may actually make the brain malfunction. Under the stress of the fight-or-flight response, the body exhibits a faster heart rate as well as increased production of a steroid hormone called cortisol. High levels of cortisol can kill brain cells and reduce the number of synapses. Studies of adults who experienced continuous abuse as children indicate that the prolonged stress of maltreatment results in a shrinkage of those regions of the brain responsible for memory, learning, and the regulation of affect and emotional expression (Neuberger, 1997). Other studies show that the brains of maltreated children can be 20 to 30 percent smaller than those of their nonmaltreated peers (Perry, 1993).

Maltreated youngsters' brains tend to be attuned to danger. At the slightest threat, these children will track anxiously any signs of further abusive attacks. Such early experiences of stress form templates in the brain in which the fear responses become fixed; thus, their brains become organized purely for survival. The resulting state of constant alert may help them avoid further maltreatment, but it also degrades their development. These youngsters are at great risk for emotional, behavior, learning, and physical difficulties (Herman, 1992; Terr, 1990). Other potential long-term effects include fewer opportunities for comfort, support, and nurturance.

Other ways that abused children cope with fears are "freezing" and dissociative responses. Because physical flight often is not possible for very young children, they freeze when they have no control over threatening events. The freezing response allows a child time to process and evaluate the stressor. Some caretakers, however, often interpret a freezing response as noncompliance to their instructions, which, if frustration arises, may open the door to further mistreatment. The brain's organization may be further altered if the additional maltreatment lasts long enough. Eventually, youngsters feel anxious and frustrated all the time, even when experiences are nonthreatening. As a result, children may be irritable, hypervigilant, hyperactive, or aggressive; they also might be prone to throwing tantrums and showing a regression in their development (James, 1994).

Dissociation, another common response to maltreatment, occurs when individuals separate their painful experience from conscious awareness. It protects maltreated children against the overwhelming emotions and thoughts connected to their traumatic experiences. When carried to an extreme, however, this response can result in amnesia and hallucinations (Herman, 1992; Terr, 1991). Children also may exhibit personality and self-identity disorders.

Psychological Effects of Abuse and Neglect

The psychological effects of abuse and neglect may include the disregulation of affect, the avoidance of intimacy, provocative behaviors, and disturbances in the attachment process.

> Studies of adults who experienced continuous abuse as children indicate that the prolonged stress of maltreatment results in a shrinkage of those regions of the brain responsible for memory, learning, and the regulation of affect and emotional expression.

Disregulation of Affect. Maltreated children often have difficulty in regulating affect and emotions. They may have intrusive and intensely emotional memories of their maltreatment, which they attempt to control by avoiding displays of their feelings. Sometimes, the only way to identify their emotions is through physiological responses, such as increased heart rates and perspiration. Although these children appear capable of describing other people's feelings, they cannot describe their own.

Avoidance of Intimacy. Survivors of child abuse and neglect tend to avoid intimate relationships, because they believe that getting close to someone else increases their vulnerability and lack of control (James, 1994). Intimacy, in fact, represents a threat, rather than nurturance and love. To avoid intimacy, children may withdraw, avoid eye contact, be hyperactive, or exhibit inappropriate behaviors.

Provocative Behaviors. If maltreated children are unable to find relief through numbing their feelings, they may instead act provocatively and aggressively. They may inflict harm on others, commit self-mutilation or even suicide, and otherwise behave in antisocial ways. Apparently, the underlying purpose behind these provocative and emotional acts is to produce the numbing responses that can lessen their extreme anxieties.

Disturbances in the Attachment Process. Attachment is the bond that young children form with their primary caregivers—usually, their parents (Hanson & Lynch, 1995). Early relationships help shape the development of the child's personality and social-emotional adjustment (Thurman & Widerstrom, 1990). The attachment process is important, as it affects the child's ability to cope with stress, regulate emotions, benefit from social supports, and form nurturing and loving relationships. Maltreated children's attachment processes are disrupted, however (Barnett, 1997). Usually, a caregiver and infant form close, secure emotional bonds, as evident by infants' demonstrably strong preferences for their primary caregivers, and by the enjoyment and comfort that they derive from that closeness. Parents show their attachment in their desire to nurture, comfort, and protect their babies, and by acting uneasy and sad when separated. Because the attachment process promotes a sense of security, trust, and self-esteem, it also furthers the infants' desire to explore and learn from their environments. While secure attachments help children in all areas of development, they are essential in establishing self-identity and self-worth (Moroz, 1993).

Abuse and neglect can impede the attachment process and diminish children's feelings of security and trust in their caregivers. Maltreated children may feel unworthy or unloved, and they may view the world as a dangerous place. When caregivers are neglectful, uncaring, or abusive, children become more vulnerable to stressors, and will have difficulty forming intimate and positive relationships. The children often become angry and resentful toward their caregivers, a feeling that may transfer to other relationships in their lives (Zeanah, 1993).

Effects on Cognition and Learning. Child abuse may adversely affect children's ability to learn. On average, abused, maltreated, or neglected children score lower on cognitive measures and demonstrate poorer school achievement compared to their non-abused peers of similar socioeconomic backgrounds (Barnett, 1997; Vondra, Barnett, & Cicchetti, 1990). Children with uncaring parents or caregivers will learn to view themselves as unworthy, unlovable, and incompetent in school-related and cognitive tasks. Abuse often leads to a loss of self-esteem and a lack of motivation to achieve at school.

Even at a very early age, maltreated children have difficulty adapting to their child care and preschool environments. Abused toddlers respond more negatively, in contrast with non-abused peers, to their mirror images, and they make fewer positive statements about themselves (Vondra, Allen, & Cicchetti, 1990). A study by Erickson, Stroufe, and Pianta (1989) found that physically abused preschoolers were more angry and noncompliant, compared to their non-abused classmates of similar socioeconomic backgrounds. The maltreated children also were more impulsive and disorganized, and were less successful on pre-academic tasks. They lacked the necessary social and work skills for age-appropriate adjustment in their preschool and kindergarten classes. Almost half of the physically abused youngsters were referred for special education or retention by the end of their kindergarten year. Similarly, emotionally abused young children displayed more disruptive, noncompliant behavior and a lack of persistence in their schoolwork, compared to their non-abused peers.

The behavior of the sexually abused children studied by Erickson, Stroufe, and Pianta (1989) was characterized by extreme anxiety, inattentiveness, and difficulty in following directions. Their social behaviors ranged from withdrawal to extreme aggression; consequently, they often were rejected by their classmates. These children commonly depended much more than their peers did on adults, appearing to have a strong need for their teachers' affection and approval. Their dependent behaviors seemed to reflect their roles as victims at home.

Neglected children, compared to children suffering from other forms of abuse, appeared to have the most severe problems, based on a number of investigations (Eckenrode, Laird, & Doris, 1993; Mash & Wolfe, 1991). They were the least successful on cognitive tasks in kindergarten; they were more anxious, inattentive, apathetic; and they had more difficulty concentrating on pre-academic work. Socially, they exhibited inappropriate behaviors and were not accepted by their peers. These youngsters rarely displayed positive affect, humor, or joy. A majority of these neglected children were retained or referred for special education (because of possible learning disabilities and/or social-emotional difficulties) at the end of kindergarten. The lack of stimulation at home might have been an important factor contributing to their poor performances. A lack of opportunities to learn social and pre-academic skills becomes obvious at school.

> On average, abused, maltreated, or neglected children score lower on cognitive measures and demonstrate poorer school achievement compared to their non-abused peers of similar socioeconomic backgrounds.

All types of maltreated children, as they get older, demonstrate more cognitive deficits and are considered more at-risk for school failure and to drop out than their non-maltreated peers (Kurtz, Gaudin, Wodarski, & Howing, 1993; Reyome, 1993). Teachers rated the abused children as being more overactive, inattentive, and impulsive than their non-abused classmates. They appeared less motivated to achieve at school and had difficulty learning. All types of maltreated children behave similarly, because forms of abuse often overlap. In other words, children may suffer from more than one type of abuse, such as a combination of emotional, sexual, and physical maltreatment.

Two studies compared the characteristics of physically abused, sexually abused, and neglected school-age children (Eckenrode, Laird, & Doris, 1993; Kurtz, Gaudin, Wodarski, & Howing, 1993). The physically abused students had significant school problems. Their performance was poor in all academic subjects, especially so in mathematics and language skills. They appeared to be underachievers and were more likely to be retained than their nonmaltreated classmates. As adolescents, they were more likely to drop out of school. Both teachers and parents reported that these children had significantly more behavioral problems than their non-abused peers.

Neglect was associated with the poorest academic achievement among the groups of maltreated students. Teachers reported that these pupils were performing below grade level, and that their rate of school absenteeism was nearly five times that of the comparison group of non-neglected students. Neglect appears to have a greater long-term impact on academic performance than other forms of abuse. The neglected children's adaptive functioning ability, however, was within normal limits. Perhaps these children learned the survival skills out of necessity, because of the lack of care in their homes. Sexually abused children, on the other hand, were similar to nonabused youngsters in terms of academic achievement and in the number of discipline problems. They did not differ significantly in any area of academic performance. Although sexual abuse has negative social-emotional consequences, its effects on academic achievement were not evident in these studies. No matter what type of abuse, however, school personnel must intervene—to help prevent further maltreatment, and to assist these children with their learning problems.

Interventions To Prevent Maltreatment and Promote Resiliency

Abused and neglected children are at high risk for psychological, neurological, and cognitive impairments. Children already may have developed problems by the time they are identified as being maltreated. Consequently, we need to pay greater attention to measures that promote resiliency, including home visits, and to the presence of alternate caregivers, social support interventions, and therapeutic programs.

Availability of Alternate Caregivers. Alternate caregivers must step in when children have been abused by their parents or other primary caregivers. These caregivers may be grandparents, other relatives, foster or adoptive parents, and teachers. Alternate caregivers can provide abused or neglected children with the safety, dedication, and nurturance they need to recover from their traumas.

Therapeutic caregiving can help prevent either the fight-or-flight response or dissociation from becoming "fixed" in children's brains. Thus, children can develop a sense of trust, and remain open to positive learning and emotional experiences. Therapeutic caregiving requires, among other attributes, the ability to acknowledge the child's pain; the ability to recognize that some anti-social behaviors are reflections of painful experiences; an understanding of the child's need to process and integrate these experiences; a willingness to be a part of a treatment team; and a strong belief that caregivers' actions will help the youngster, even if the benefits are not immediately apparent. Caregivers must help these children develop positive self-images (Moroz, 1993). Children need warmth, nurturance, empathy, stability, and a sense of belonging in order to promote their resiliency.

Social Support Interventions. Social support can "include the emotional, physical, informational, instrumental and material aid provided by others to maintain health and well-being, promote adoptions of life events and foster development in an adaptive manner" (Dunst, Trivette, & Deal, 1988, p. 28). Informal support may be provided by family members, friends, and neighbors, as well as by religious organizations and peer support groups. Formal support systems include home visiting programs, parenting classes, and mental health services.

Informal Support Systems. Some of the parents or primary caregivers who abuse their children have suffered from their own maltreatment as children. Poverty and unemployment may increase the likelihood of abuse. Informal support from families, friends, and community members, in the form of providing child care, respite care, counsel during a job search, transportation, or financial aid, for example, can greatly help. Taking advantage of such informal support can help dysfunctional families to end the cycle of abuse and to function more positively (Barnett, 1997).

> All types of maltreated children, as they get older, demonstrate more cognitive deficits and are considered more at-risk for school failure and to drop out than their non-maltreated peers.

Formal Support Systems. Formal community support systems, such as family therapy, are available (Daro, 1993; Manly, Cicchetti, & Barnett, 1994). Such services may supply basic needs, such as food, clothing, and shelter. The programs that teach basic parenting skills are particularly helpful. Such programs also help reduce family stress and pathology (Barnett, Manley, & Cicchetti, 1993).

Intervention Programs for Child Victims. Intervention services, including child care and preschool classes that specialize in the treatment of neglected and abused young children, are increasingly available. Many challenges must be overcome when assisting maltreated children, who may have a combination of language, cognitive, and social-emotional delays (Barnett, 1997). A National Clinical Evaluation study examined the outcomes of 19 separate projects (Daro, 1993) that trained teachers to use therapeutic techniques with maltreated young children, ages 18 months to 8 years. About 70 percent of the abused children demonstrated improvements in their adaptive, cognitive, and social-emotional skills.

Culp, Little, Lefts, & Lawrence (1991) described therapeutic projects that provided services such as play therapy, speech and language therapy, occupational and physical therapies, and home visits. The curriculum was designed to foster children's positive relationships with adults and peers, to increase their abilities to regulate emotions, and to improve self-esteem. Court-mandated services for the

maltreating parents consisted of comprehensive group and individual therapy, and home visits by professionals. Positive outcomes were documented for both the maltreated children and their parents. The results of these studies indicate that abused children and their caretakers require individualized treatments for special problems. The duration of treatment also had an effect on the outcomes. Maltreating parents who were in therapy for 18 months made more improvements in their interactions with the children than did parents who were in treatment for shorter periods of time (Culp, Little, Letts, & Lawrence, 1991). Home visits appeared to help parents manage their stress levels, which, in turn, helped to head off further maltreatment. Other preventive measures consisted of mental health services, which enabled some parents to relieve emotional problems.

Conclusion

Abuse and neglect have many possible negative neurological, psychological, and cognitive effects on young children. More research on childhood traumas and on therapeutic techniques that assist the child victims is needed, and should be advocated by concerned professionals, families, and citizens.

References

Barnett, D. (1997). The effects of early intervention on maltreating parents and their children. In M. J. Guralnick (Ed.), *The effectiveness of early intervention* (pp. 147–170). Baltimore: Brookes.

Barnett, D., Manley, J. T., & Cicchetti, D. (1993). Defining child maltreatment: The interface between policy and research. In D. Cicchetti & S. Toth (Eds.), *Child abuse, child development, and social policy* (pp. 7–73). Norwood, NJ: Ablex.

Barnett, D., Vondra, J. I., & Shonk, S. (1996). Relations among self perceptions, motivation, and school functioning of low income maltreated and non-maltreated children. *Child Abuse and Neglect, 20,* 397–410.

Culp, R. E., Little, V., Letts, D., & Lawrence, H. (1991). Maltreated children's self-concept. Effects of a comprehensive treatment program. *American Journal of Orthopsychiatry, 61,* 114–121.

Daro, D. (1993). Child maltreatment research: Implications for program design. In D. Cicchetti & S. Toth (Eds.),

Child abuse, child development, and social policy (pp. 331–367). Norwood, NJ: Ablex.

Dunst, C., Trivette, C., & Deal, A. (1988). *Enabling and empowering families.* Cambridge, MA: Brookline Books.

Eckenrode, J., Laird, M., & Doris, J. (1993). School performance and disciplinary problems among abused and neglected children. *Developmental Psychology, 29,* 53–62.

Erickson, M. F., Stroufe, L. A., & Pianta, R. (1989). The effects of maltreatment on the development of young children. In D. Cicchetti & V. Carlson (Eds.), *Child maltreatment: Theory and research on the causes and consequences of child abuse and neglect* (pp. 647–684). New York: Cambridge University Press.

Hanson, M. J., & Lynch, E. W. (1995). *Early intervention: Implementing child and family services for infants and toddlers who are at-risk or disabled.* Austin, TX: Pro-Ed.

Herman, J. (1992). *Trauma and recovery.* New York: Basic Books.

James, B. (1994). *Handbook for treatment of attachment-trauma problems in children.* New York: Lexington Books.

Kurtz, P.D., Gaudin, J. M., Wodarski, J. S., & Howing, P. T. (1993). Maltreatment and the school-aged child: School performance consequences. *Child Abuse and Neglect, 17,* 581–589.

Mash, E. J., & Wolfe, D. A. (1991). Methodological issues in research in child abuse. *Criminal Justice and Behavior, 18,* 8–29.

Moroz, K. J. (1993). *Supporting adoptive families with special needs children—A handbook for mental health professionals.* Waterbury, VT: The Vermont Adoptions Project, U.S. Department of Health and Human Services Grant #90–CO–0484.

Nash, J. J. (1997, February 3). Fertile minds. *Time,* 48–56.

Neuberger, J. J. (1997). Brain development research: Wonderful window of opportunity to build public support for early childhood education. *Young Children, 52,* 4–9.

Perry, B. D. (1993). Medicine and psychotherapy: Neurodevelopment and neurophysiology of trauma. *The Advisor, 6,* 13–20.

Reyome, N. D. (1993). A comparison of the school performance of sexually abused, neglected, and non-maltreated children. *Child Study Journal, 23,* 17–38.

Schwartz, E. D., & Perry, B. D. (1994). The post-traumatic response in children and adolescents. *Psychiatric Clinics of North America, 17,* 311–326.

Stermer, J. (1997, July 31). Home visits give kids a chance. *Chicago Tribune, 16.*

Tauwer, C. L. (1989). Critical periods of brain development. *Infants and Young Children, 1,* VII–VIII.

Terr, L. (1990). *Too scared to cry: Psychic trauma in childhood.* New York: Harper and Row.

Terr, L. C. (1991). Childhood traumas: An outline and overview. *American Journal of Psychiatry, 148,* 10–20.

Thurman, S. K., & Widerstrom, A. H. (1990). *Infants and young children with special needs.* Baltimore: Brookes.

Vondra, J. I., Barnett, D., & Cicchetti, D. (1990). Self concept, motivation, and competence among preschoolers from maltreating and comparison families. *Child Abuse and Neglect, 14,* 525–540.

Zeanah, C. H., Jr. (1993). *Handbook of infant mental health.* New York: Guilford Press.

Barbara Lowenthal is Professor, Department of Special Education, Northeastern Illinois University, Chicago, Illinois.

From *Childhood Education,* Summer 1999, pp. 204-209. © 1999 by the Association for Childhood Education International, 17904 Georgia Avenue, Suite 215, Olney, MD 20832. Reprinted by permission.

UNIT 5

Development During Adolescence and Young Adulthood

Unit Selections

Key Points to Consider

- What are alpha, beta and gamma personality types? How are they identified?

- What factors account for the behavior of teenagers who take guns to school and murder their classmates?

- How have adolescents changed as a result of terrorism on America's shores?

- Are modern chemicals feminizing human biology?

- Why is jealousy just as necessary as love? What purpose does it serve? When is jealousy overdone?

- What factors are involved in keeping divorces friendly? Why should they be?

- Is the aging baby-boom generation good for American's economy?

 **Links: www.dushkin.com/online/**
These sites are annotated in the World Wide Web pages.

Adolescence: Change and Continuity
http://www.personal.psu.edu/nxd10/adolesce.htm

AMA—Adolescent Health On-Line
http://www.ama-assn.org/ama/pub/category/1947.html

American Academy of Child and Adolescent Psychiatry
http://www.aacap.org/web/aacap/

Ask NOAH About: Mental Health
http://www.noah-health.org/english/illness/mentalhealth/mental.html

The term "adolescence" was coined in 1904 by G. Stanley Hall, one of the world's first psychologists. He saw adolescence as a discrete stage of life bridging the gap between sexual maturity (puberty) and socioemotional and cognitive maturity. At the beginning of the twentieth century, it was typical for young men to begin working in middle childhood (there were no child labor laws), and for young women to become wives and mothers as soon as they were fertile and/or spoken for. At the turn of the twenty-first century, the beginning of adolescence is marked by the desire to be independent of parental control. The end of adolescence, which once coincided with the age of legal maturity (usually 16 or 18, depending on local laws), has now been extended upwards. Although legal maturity is now 18 (voting, enlisting in the armed services, owning property, marrying without permission), the social norm is to consider persons in their late teens as adolescents, not adults. The years between 18 and 21 are often problematic for youth tethered between adult and not-adult status. They can be married, with children, living in homes of their own, running their own businesses, yet not be able to drive their cars in certain places or at certain times. They can go to college and participate in social activities, but they cannot legally drink. Often the twenty-first birthday is viewed as a rite of passage into adulthood in the United States because it signals the legal right to buy and drink alcoholic beverages. "Maturity" is usually reserved for those who have achieved full economic as well as socioemotional independence as adults.

The articles "Meet the Gamma Girls" and "Generation 9-11" both describe contemporary adolescent behaviors: the first portrays young adolescents, the second older adolescents. Susannah Meadows describes alpha, beta, and gamma types of early adolescent female personalities and some of the explanations for their behavior choices. Barbara Kantrowitz and Keith Naughton paint a more serious picture of older youth who are redefining their identities, their career aspirations, and their patriotism after September 11, 2001.

"Why the Young Kill" addresses the tragic trend for angry adolescents to use weapons to express themselves. It looks at several possible explanations for this aberrant behavior. Male sex hormones, stress hormones, emotional reactivity, a genetic predisposition to an antisocial personality, a difficult temperament at birth, hyperactivity, and the abuse of drugs and/or alcohol are biological possibilities. Environmental answers include a culture that glorifies violence and revenge, the availability of murder weapons, bullying, bad parenting, gang membership, and low self-worth and self-esteem. The article quotes several experts on adolescent violence. The author concludes that youth who kill have a particular biological makeup that is imposed on a particular environment. Neither nature nor nurture is a sufficient answer in and of itself.

As adolescence has been extended, so too has young adulthood. One hundred years ago, life expectancy did not extend too far beyond menopause for women and retirement for men. Young adulthood began when adolescents finished puberty. Parents of teenagers were middle-aged, between 35 and 55. Later marriages and delayed childbearing have redefined the line between young adulthood and middle age. Many people today consider themselves young adults well into their forties.

Erik Erikson, the personality theorist, marked the passage from adolescence to young adulthood by a change in the nuclear conflicts of two life stages: identity versus role confusion and intimacy versus isolation. Adolescents struggle to answer the question, "Who am I?" Young adults struggle to find a place within the existing social order where they can feel intimacy rather than isolation. In the 1960s, Erikson wrote that females resolve both their conflicts of identity and intimacy by living vicariously through their husbands. This is unacceptable to most females today.

The first article about young adulthood addresses the effect of environmental chemicals on traditionally defined male and female behaviors. Leonard Sax argues that many modern chemicals mimic the action of estrogen, the female sex hormone, on human cells. Males may be experiencing feminization due to exposure to these substances. Females are also undergoing noticeable physiological changes. Psychic changes in females include higher graduation rates with accompanying sequels: more status and power.

Despite its title, "The Happy Divorce" actually has useful advice about making marriages work in the new millennium. However, when divorce is inevitable, it can be made more peaceful with some of the suggestions offered in this selection. Nora Underwood addresses the issue of lawyer selection, recommending collaborative law practice. She also speaks about gay breakups and how they can be resolved with less emotional trauma.

The last article in the young adulthood section presents good news for Generation X'ers and Generation Y'ers. When the baby boom generation retires, America should experience a job boom. Daniel Eisenberg gives predictions for hot and cold jobs in the near future. He also discusses the desirability of creative job changes and reeducation or retraining for the coming boom market.

Meet the GAMMA Girls

They're not mean. They like their parents. They're smart, confident and think popularity is overrated. What makes these teens tick.

BY SUSANNAH MEADOWS

W HO CALLED SAME SEATS?

It's lunchtime at Valhalla High School in El Cajon, Calif., and the students have sorted into cliques. The Mexican-American kids occupy two picnic tables on the south lawn, not far from the stoners. The Chaldeans (Christian Iraqi-Americans) have staked out the student center and the punks/Goths line the hallways. Out on the wide east lawn, the prettiest place on campus, are the popular kids, each grade swarming around its own tree. One popular girl—let's call her Wendi—is as close as you can get to being a Barbie doll while still breathing. According to the clique cartography, she's a sophomore. Boys come and go, putting their arms around her just to say hello, and a chasm between her snug top and her denim skirt beckons back. Would it be hard not to be popular? "If I was cut off from all that? If you made me homely looking? And gave me three friends? And made me study all the time? I'd probably shoot myself," she says.

JENNIFER TESCHLER 'What on earth do we have to complain about? Everyone has at least one little thing, but compared to the rest of the world we are doing pretty dandy.'

And then there's Jennifer Teschler, sophomore. Tall and athletic, with a smile that renews itself every time she speaks, the 15-year-old is comfortable in her skin, if not crazy about all the freckles. Independent of any clique, she and her relatively unfabulous girlfriends hang at an unassuming swatch of real estate near the pool. On their way to the corner of grass where the "funny, smart" folks of the croquet club sit, Jen bypasses Wendi and the other long blondes, oblivious to their glow. "Popularity is a funny thing," she reflects later. "The people who consider themselves 'popular' seem mostly unlikable and shallow to me, yet somehow the way they act defines them as 'popular.' Pop-

ular, that is, among themselves. There are a few 'popular' people that I actually like and are depthful enough that I am friends with them, but mainly they seem like snots."

Jennifer Teschler is evidence that a teenage girl in 2002 can be emotionally healthy, socially secure, independent-minded and just plain nice. Her temperament is, to some extent, a matter of luck. But new forces at school and at home allow girls like Jen to thrive. Thanks to a rich new array of girl sports and other activities, Jen is coming into her own in high school, defined by what she does, rather than by her popularity rating. A surge in ethnic-minority students at Valhalla—their numbers have shot up in the district from less than 25 percent a decade ago to more than 35 percent today—has redrawn the lunchtime map, making the once dominant cool white kids just one of many city-states on campus, and giving Jen and others like her more social options. Jen's sense of herself is nurtured by supportive, ever-present parents. And her values are bolstered by open discussion at church and a strong faith.

EMILY WALDRON 'I've always been really close to my family. That's helped me not really want to get away from the house all the time.'

Yet you'd never know such a species existed, given the current media flurry over two best-selling books about teenage "mean girls." In "Queen Bees & Wannabes" (No. 35 on Amazon last week), Rosalind Wiseman argues that if your child is snubbed by one of the popular girls, she may become a victim for good. Rachel Simmons's "Odd Girl Out: The Hidden Culture of Aggression in Girls," currently No. 7 on The New York Times list, calls bullying among girls an epidemic. Not that parents weren't already nervous enough after the last wave of troubled-girl books led by 1994's "Reviving Ophelia." Like those "studies," these new ones capitalize on parental dread, portraying school, especially junior high, as littered with beaten-down and backstabbed girls (next story). "These books go way beyond what we have data on," says William Damon of the Stanford Center for Adolescence. "They're playing to stereotypes."

What the books don't take into account are gamma girls—kids who may not be "popular," but aren't losers either. Wiseman defines "cool," cutthroat girls as Queen Bees; they'd sooner boot someone from their clique than allow their omnipotence to be threatened. Then there are Wannabes, who will do whatever it takes to get in good with the Queen Bee. In a recent story in The Washington Post, Laura Sessions Stepp called the Queen Bees and Wannabes "alphas" and "betas," respectively—but also identified a third breed of resilient girls, the "gammas." They don't long to be invited to parties—they're too busy writing an opinion column in the school paper or surfing and horseback riding. "It's a terrific time to be a young woman," says Dr. Alvin Rosenfeld, author of books on children and parenting. "They can choose to be what they want to be."

REYNA COOKE 'In order to fit in I would have to wear certain clothes, have a certain girlie attitude, go to parties, smoke pot and drink beer. It's kind of degrading.'

To check out today's teen scene myself, I returned for a week to Valhalla High, where I graduated 11 years ago. For the most part, I found that girls weren't any meaner or more desperate than when I attended the 2,200-student public school—in fact I found original, confident teenagers all over the place. At Valhalla, it's no longer so clear who's in and who's out, largely because an explosion in extracurricular activities has dramatically expanded the menu of cool. The prosperous '90s and Title IX, which banned sex discrimination in school sports, brought dozens of new offerings, as they did nationwide. (The number of high-school girls playing sports has ballooned from 300,000 in 1972 to 2.5 million today.) At VHS, there are twice as many girl teams as there were a decade ago.

In my day, there was only one guarantee of coolness: cheerleading, or "cheer," as it was called then. As freshmen, my friends and I gazed at the varsity cheerleaders as if they were movie stars. We knew all their names and dreamed of achieving some of that orange polyester pleated-skirt glamour for ourselves. Today, Jen Teschler competes on one of the school's four girls' water-polo teams, the varsity swim team and the new varsity girls' golf team. She's also a peer facilitator (teaching tolerance in the classroom) and the news editor for the school paper, the Saga. Reyna Cooke, another Gamma who is 15 and a freshman, placed fifth in the state in girls' wrestling five months after taking up the sport. If she can collect more competitors, she'll found a girls' team at Valhalla.

A gamma's parents can be found not only cheering from the sidelines, but out on the field, closer to the action. "Parents today are much more deeply sincere about wanting to put enormous effort into raising good kids," says Rosenfeld. Jen barely

catches her breath after a swim race before she talks excitedly about her Friday-evening plans: dinner out with her dad. Freshman Emily Waldron's dad has coached her soccer team since she was 5 just so they could have that time together. A teacher at Valhalla, he gives his 15-year-old a lift to and from school, and three days a week they work out together at the gym before school.

Church is one more layer of protection for both Jen and Reyna, who often spend Sunday nights at youth group talking about Bible passages and "joys or concerns." Jen says her ideas about waiting to have sex until she's married come from her parents and from church. Youth group is also an extra social life. The evening begins with a game, sometimes Joshball—"My friend Josh made it up," says Reyna. She considers her church friends more reliable than others. "They're more on the good side than the druggie side," she says. "They know how to goof off."

Jen is self-possessed enough that she doesn't even need to try to look cool. At her swim meet, she pads around the deck in her blue one-piece and orange rubber hat with nothing to hide. Other girls wrap their bodies in blue parkas that reach down to their shins. Jen circulates between the warm-up pool and, naturally, her dad, who's cheering from the pool deck. She finishes last in the 200 IM (butterfly, backstroke, breast stroke and freestyle), swimming alone in the pool for her last half-lap. By the time she reaches the wall the cheering has died. You expect this to be humiliating. "Oh no," she says, her face in full blush from the race. "I know I suck at the 200 IM! I admit it freely!" By now her tomato-red toenail polish is almost all chipped off.

Ironically, a gamma's independence is often born when she's picked on in grade school or junior high. There's no doubt about it: girls can be mean. When Jen was in fourth grade, she wore orthodontic headgear to school and read books during lunch. Some girls stole her lunchbox and forced her to be the monkey in the middle. "I was such a nerd!" she says cheerfully. Emily decided to change her social life back in junior high while on a field trip to an amusement park. Everyone in her 11-girl clique was grabbing partners—"I want to be with you!" they cried—except not her. Incredulous that her friends would turn on her, she chose to make a break. Emily never enjoyed feeling as if she had to wear the right clothes or to do her hair, anyway. "I look at my group I used to be friends with, and they're all exactly the same," she says. "High school was a fresh start." Adored by her teachers, she works hard in school and is devoted to soccer. Though she's unusually mature, her aura is pure kid.

The popular kids grow up a little faster. When I ask Wendi, who's 16, about sex, she says, "You mean how everybody has sex all the time?" Yeah, I guess that's what I mean. When I was a student here, sex was basically limited to those with boyfriends or girlfriends. Since then, the national rate of kids 15 to 17 having sex has actually dropped from 54.1 percent to 48.4 percent in 1997. But the news is not as encouraging as it sounds. One explanation for the dip may be the rise of oral sex, which, according to an article that never ran in the school paper after district-office censorship, is viewed by students as a casual alternative to intercourse. The trend has even changed the bases: First base is still pecking and holding hands, Jen tells me. Second

Is She an Alpha, Beta or Gamma Girl?

Most high-school girls can be identified as one of three types—characters as instantly recognizable in Hollywood as they are in the lunchroom. Which table did you sit at?

Alpha Girl

Kirsten Dunst, the ultimate alpha (on celluloid, at least), who somehow manages to be both bitchy and nice.

KINDRED SPIRIT:
BRITNEY, BEYONCE, JENNIFER ANNISTON

IDOLIZES:
GWYNETH PALTROW

HEARTTHROB:
JOSH HARTNETT

AFTER-SCHOOL SNACK:
BAGEL

ON HER FEET:
FLIP-FLOPS

FAVE TV SHOW:
'DAWSON'S CREEK'

FAVE MOVIE:
'LEGALLY BLONDE'

WHO THEY DATE:
STUDENT-BODY PREZ

TECH SAVVY:
TWO-WAY

AFTER-SCHOOL ACTIVITY:
CHEERLEADING

IN THE JEANS;
BOOT CUT

IN HER DISCMAN:
ASHANTI

DREAM COLLEGE:
PRINCETON

MAKEUP ESSENTIAL:
PRESSED POWDER

POST-PROM DESTINATION:
BEACH

READS:
VOGUE

Beta Girl

Beta. The 'b' is for 'b list.' Like Jennifer Love Hewitt, this ever-aspiring girl just wants us to love her.

KINDRED SPIRIT:
JESSICA SIMPSON, TORI SPELLING, MELISSA JOAN HART

IDOLIZES:
MARIAH CAREY

HEARTTHROB:
FREDDIE PRINZE JR.

AFTER-SCHOOL SNACK;
DIET PILLS

ON HER FEET;
WEDGE HEELS

FAVE TV SHOW:
'CHARMED'

FAVE MOVIE:
'CRUEL INTENTIONS'

WHO THEY DATE:
CAPT. OF THE FOOTBALL TEAM

TECH SAVVY:
CELL PHONES

AFTER-SCHOOL ACTIVITY:
DANCE TEAM

IN THE JEANS:
SLIM FIT

IN HER DISCMAN:
ALICIA KEYS

DREAM COLLEGE:
UCLA

MAKEUP ESSENTIAL:
FALSE EYELASHES

POST-PROM DESTINATION:
MOTEL

READS:
COSMO

Gamma Girl

She's pretty. She's funny. She's obsessed with Shakespeare. Julia Stiles is a star, just slightly off-kilter.

KINDRED SPIRIT:
KELLY OSBOURNE, JENNIFER GARNER, SERENA WILLIAMS

IDOLIZES:
GWEN STEFANI

HEARTTHROB:
TOBEY MAGUIRE

AFTER-SCHOOL SNACK:
PIZZA

ON HER FEET:
PUMAS

FAVE TV SHOW:
'BUFFY'

FAVE MOVIE:
'GHOST WORLD'

WHO THEY DATE:
CLASS SMARTASS

TECH SAVVY:
LAND LINES

AFTER-SCHOOL ACTIVITY:
SPORTS

IN THE JEANS:
FLARE

IN HER DISCMAN:
ANI DIFRANCO

DREAM COLLEGE:
BROWN

MAKEUP ESSENTIAL:
LIP GLOSS

POST-PROM DESTINATION:
BOWLING ALLEY

READS:
JANE

base is making out. Third is now oral sex. Home plate hasn't changed. Valhalla kids, especially among the populars, Wendi says, are all too in sync with rising rates of drug and alcohol use among teens across the country. In 1997, one in five 8th-grade girls had smoked marijuana, twice as many as five years before. And girls are keeping up with boys' alcohol consumption for the first time: 38 percent of 12- to 17-year-olds have imbibed. When I ask a class of 14- and 15-year-old freshmen what drugs they've

been around, hands fly up. Pot, ecstasy, crystal methamphetamine, crack, cocaine, acid, mushrooms, PCP, Theraflu, Vicodin, steroids, Ritalin (snorted) and heroin, they say. But heroin, they assure me, is rarer than the others. Not until my junior year did I see alcohol, pot and crystal meth.

Blessed with confidence and self-knowledge, gammas are equipped to shrug off the social pressure to experiment. Drug use is more of a joke than a temptation. Out on her back porch,

Jen talks about her decision to avoid premarital sex. She says she was shocked when her dad recently told her that while he thought waiting was best, it was her own choice, and that she should be sure to be safe. "I was like, whoa!" Her friends tell her she's never going to make it to marriage. "And that just kind of makes me more determined," she says. For now, Jen will gladly stick to comparing notes with her friends on the hottest, nicest and smartest guys. In class, she talks casually with a cute boy who's growing his blond locks out (in an attempt, no doubt, to add some edge to his sweet face). One senses that he surfs and he's not unaware of what the beach does for his good looks. I mention to her that I saw her talking to this guy in class. "Yeah, he's cute, but he's whole-sophomore-class cute." As in, probably too much competition.

TOGETHERNESS: On a Saturday afternoon Jen and her stepmom make sandwiches after a morning of horseback riding

Jen's already dealing with enough competition: when she's a senior the practically straight-A student will be among the largest pool of qualified college applicants ever. Valhalla kids are forced to start getting serious about college as freshmen. Jen's already aiming for a rigorous veterinary school (UC Davis)—and feeling the pressure. As close as she is to her dad, he is also a major catalyst for academic anxiety. A high-school chemistry teacher, he's pressing her to raise her B in honors chemistry. But thinking about her future is also empowering. "I'm a little scared, a little unprepared and a lot excited," says Jen of college. With the number of AP courses quadrupled since I was there, Valhalla graduates are now much better equipped to compete. "These are the best of times," says principal Larry Martinson, who's been at VHS since it opened in 1974. "The opportunities are far greater, the resources are more."

Without being a geek about it, Jen is a leader in the classroom. In her Spanish class, she's the first to raise her hand and offer a translation for "I already knew Pablo when I met Mauricio." Jen is quiet in her next period, algebra II, but everyone keeps his or her mouth shut: Mrs. Wilson, with her patent-leather pumps and Tom Selleck posters on the wall, runs a tight ship. A wiry little class clown circles Jen's desk and passes her gumdrops, but she denies that he likes her.

It's still adolescence, after all, and girls still have to contend with the likes of Wendi. As part of a crowd proud of being "cute and bratty," she boasts of their image. Which is? "Most of us are, like, blonde. When we walk into a room we let people know that we're there. We always have to look so cute. We match. We wear cool stuff? Like skirts and capris? We all have cute cars?" she says, which has made this week particularly harrowing. Her car, a midnight blue pickup, is in the shop, so she's been driving her mom's periwinkle minivan to school. "Everybody's like 'Oh my God'," she says. Yesterday she opted to be dropped off by her mom to avoid the ridicule.

Jen has more perspective—and that's her greatest strength. Indeed, her understanding of herself extends to the occasional insecurities that all of us, including the most popular girls, have felt. "Sometimes I'm convinced confidence is ungraspable," she says. "Other times I seem to have an unending supply. But nearly always there is a little part of me saying 'You're not good enough, you don't fit.' Thank God it is a little part, easily stifled and easily covered up." Jen says the common advice for teens—just be yourself and you'll be fine—is inadequate. "What adults seem to forget," she writes in an e-mail, "is that we are still trying to figure out exactly who 'ourselves' are and what on earth we are doing." That may be, but the 5-foot-8 swimmer, golfer, surfer, blusher, smiler is well on her way.

With MARY CARMICHAEL in New York

Selling Advice—As Well as Anxiety

The 'queen bee' best sellers are stories, not science

BY BARBARA KANTROWITZ

POOR ERIN, ONE MINUTE, SHE'S on top of the world, the most popular girl in eighth grade, and then—bam!—in the blink of an IM, she's an outcast, a total reject, the target of a vicious gossip campaign instigated by her former "friends," the girls who used to jockey just to be near her in the cafeteria. Erin's crime? She was a Queen Bee, manipulating the nuances of preteen social status until her elaborate network of allies and enemies untimately turned on her. Erin's three-year reign of terror made the other girls really, *really* angry. "We wanted her to see what it was like not to have anybody there," said one. The next few months weren't pretty. Erin's grades plummeted, she was shunned at graduation and she even thought about suicide. Her

devastated mom dragged her to a shrink, where Erin finally began to mend her mean ways.

This middle-school morality tale is just one of many scary stories in Rachel Simmons's new best seller, "Odd Girl Out: The Hidden Culture of Aggression in Girls," Simmons's book and another recent best seller by Rosalind Wiseman, "Queen Bees and Wannabes," seem to have struck a particularly sensitive nerve among parents. On their current book tours, both authors have emerged as *über*-experts on mean girls, a topic The Washington Post dubbed the "Teenage Crisis of the Moment." They've appeared on "Oprah" and the morning shows and have been packing in anxious audiences all over the country. (At one panel

Helping Girls Get Wise

Although the recent popular books about girls are based on anecdotes, not scientific research, they do include some useful advice, guidelines and tips. Here are ways author Rosalind Wiseman says parents can help their daughter:

1 ACKNOWLEDGE BULLIES: Don't be in denial about the possibility that your daughter could be a bully. Parental silence will reinforce this behavior.

2 DON'T IGNORE VICTIMS: Believe your daughter when she says that she's a victim of bullying. Girls can do horrible things to each other, and the lessons they learn in early adolescence can set them up for worse experiences in the future. Inspire your daughter by standing up to bullies in your own life.

3 KNOW HOW TO INTERVENE: Whether your daughter is a bully or a victim, avoid your natural desire to intervene by talking to the other parents. After about the age of 10, girls need to be handling these issues on their own. Parents should be championing them behind the scenes, not trying to make it all better.' Parents of bullies should help their daughters develop more emphathetic ways of dealing with people. Victims need to learn to stand up for themselves. The goal in both cases is to help girls negotiate difficult social situations. That's a skill they'll need for the rest of their lives.

4 AVOID GOSSIP: Never gossip about other children. You may think your daughter isn't listening to you, but she is. When you say mean or negative things about other girls, she picks up on it. You are a role model for bad behavior.

5 DON'T LIVE THROUGH HER: Check your own emotional baggage. How important was status to you when you were growing up, and how important is it to you now? Are you working out your own issues through your daughter?

6 ACCEPT THE GOOD AND THE BAD: You do not have to like your children all the time. You will always love them, but there will be times when you don't like their actions. The parent-child relationship is like any other interaction; there are ups and downs.

7 BE A ROLE MODEL: Remember that you have a great deal of influence and power over your daughter. She's watching everything you do. Use your power wisely.

8 TALK ABOUT SEX: Use everyday events, such as viewing a provocative TV show, to bring up talks about sexuality.

9 DOWNPLAY BODY IMAGE: Praise her for her accomplishments, not just for how she looks.

10 CHANNEL STRESS: Help her find healthy ways of handling stress with exercise or activities like art that nurture creative self-expression.

SOURCES: ROSALIND WISEMAN; GIRLS, INC.

discussion featuring both authors, nearly 600 mothers and daughters jammed a community center in suburban Washington.)

All of which might suggest that there's been some fundamental shift in the landscape of the prepubescent female psyche, an epidemic, perhaps, of evil among the bare-midriff set. But even the authors say Girl World in 2002 isn't all that different from the same planet in 1972, when today's mothers were buying *their* first training bras. For both girls and boys, early adolescence is a bubbling cauldron of hormone-laden emotion that can explode, at any moment, into full-blown hostilities. The difference, the authors say, is that boys are most likely to express their anger physically, by shoving someone's face into a toilet or pushing him up against a locker, while girls generally lash out with more subtle but no less effective weapons: the push and pull of ever-shifting friendships. "Our culture," Simmons writes, "refuses girls access to open conflict, and it forces their aggression into nonphysical, indirect and covert forms. Girls use backbiting, exclusion, rumors, name-calling, and manipulation to inflict physical pain on targeted victims."

Ouch! Until recently, these authors contend, no one talked about the ugly parts of Girl World. But a wave of school shootings focussed new attention on bullying by boys, which begat a slew of best-selling books in the late 1990s about boys and how to tame them. It was inevitable, perhaps, that the attention of public—and the publishing world—would eventually shift to girls. In addition to Simmons's and Wiseman's books, other recent titles include Phyllis Chesler's "Woman's Inhumanity to Woman," Emily White's "Fast Girls: Teenage Tribes and the Myth of the Slut" and Sharon Lamb's "The Secret Lives of Girls."

The two most successful entries in this apparently ever-expanding new genre rely largely on anecdotal evidence rather than new social science to prove their point. Wiseman's books, a distillation of the lessons learned in her violence-prevention classes, is a useful, how-to manual for parents with step-by-step instructions for what to do in the trickiest situations. Simmons's thought-provoking book, which she began while a Rhodes scholar, probes the emotional underpinnings of girls' aggression. Her interviews with dozens of 10- to 14-year-old girls and adult women have prompted many readers to pour out their hearts to her—and that was pretty much her goal. I really wanted to write this book so girls would know they're not alone," says Simmons, who confesses to having been both a victim and a bully while growing up in Maryland.

Boys are more likely to express anger physically, the authors say, while girls use gossip, rumors and name-calling

But while readers gobble up these books, social-science researchers are more cautious. The idea of ascribing certain behaviors to an entire gender doesn't really hold up under scrutiny, they say. No one disputes that girls can indeed be nasty, vicious and backbiting—but so can boys. And while it may be true that boys are more likely to express their anger through physical means, girls are not violence-free. In fact, there's been a disturbing increase in violence by girls. Girls now account for 27 percent of all arrests (compared with about 22 percent just a decade ago).

Scientists say gender is simply one component in determining how a person turns out and these books may put too much emphasis on it. Just as important as gender, researchers say, are such factors as sexual orientation, religion, social class, ethnicity and even the type of community where a youngster lives. All of those factors play out within the context of the child's place in a particular family, and the youngster's innate personality traits.

In fact, many scientists think that girls these days may be *less* likely to engage in the kind of mean behaviour described in these books. In the middle-school years, girls (and boys) are looking for ways to define themselves. "I think girls today have a lot more options than they used to," says Cynthia Garcia Coll, director of the department of human development at Brown University, "They can be involved in gymnastics and sports and all these other things." As girls' choices expand, being part of one particular group is less important.

But both the authors and the experts on adolescents do agree that teenagers still want to feel emotionally close to their parents—even when they slam the door and say they just want to be alone. The best advice during times of stress: Listen to your daughter's problems, respect her feelings and be patient. Inside every angst-ridden teenager, there's a grown-up just waiting to emerge.

With PAT WINGERT in Washington

From *Newsweek*, June 3, 2002, pp. 44-51. © 2002 by Newsweek, Inc. All rights reserved. Reprinted by permission.

WHY THE YOUNG KILL

Are certain young brains predisposed to violence? Maybe—but how these kids are raised can either save them or push them over the brink. The biological roots of violence.

BY SHARON BEGLEY

THE TEMPTATION, OF COURSE, IS TO SEIZE on one cause, one single explanation for Littleton, and West Paducah, and Jonesboro and all the other towns that have acquired iconic status the way "Dallas" or "Munich" did for earlier generations. Surely the cause is having access to guns. Or being a victim of abuse at the hands of parents or peers. Or being immersed in a culture that glorifies violence and revenge. But there isn't one cause. And while that makes stemming the tide of youth violence a lot harder, it also makes it less of an unfathomable mystery. Science has a new understanding of the roots of violence that promises to explain why not every child with access to guns becomes an Eric Harris or a Dylan Klebold, and why not *every* child who feels ostracized, or who embraces the Goth esthetic, goes on a murderous rampage. The bottom line: you need a particular environment imposed on a particular biology to turn a child into a killer.

It should be said right off that attempts to trace violence to biology have long been tainted by racism, eugenics and plain old poor science. The turbulence of the 1960s led some physicians to advocate psychosurgery to "treat those people with low violence thresholds," as one 1967 letter to a medical journal put it. In other words, lobotomize the civil-rights and antiwar protesters. And if crimes are disproportionately committed by some ethnic groups, then finding genes or other traits common to that group risks tarring millions of innocent people. At the other end of the political spectrum, many conservatives view biological theories of violence as the mother of all insanity defenses, with biology not merely an explanation but an excuse. The conclusions emerging from interdisciplinary research in neuroscience and psychology, however, are not so simple-minded as to argue that violence is in the genes, or murder in the folds of the brain's frontal lobes. Instead, the pic-

ture is more nuanced, based as it is on the discovery that experience rewires the brain. The dawning realization of the constant back-and-forth between nature and nurture has resurrected the search for the biological roots of violence.

Early experiences seem to be especially powerful: a child's brain is more malleable than that of an adult. The dark side of the zero-to-3 movement, which emphasizes the huge potential for learning during this period, is that the young brain also is extra vulnerable to hurt in the first years of life. A child who suffers repeated "hits" of stress—abuse, neglect, terror—experiences physical changes in his brain, finds Dr. Bruce Perry of Baylor College of Medicine. The incessant flood of stress chemicals tends to reset the brain's system of fight-or-flight hormones, putting them on hair-trigger alert. The result is the kid who shows impulsive aggression, the kid who pops the classmate who disses him. For the outcast, hostile confrontations—not necessarily an elbow to the stomach at recess, but merely kids vacating en masse when he sits down in the cafeteria—can increase the level of stress hormones in his brain. And that can have dangerous consequences. "The early environment programs the nervous system to make an individual more or less reactive to stress," says biologist Michael Meaney of McGill University. "If parental care is inadequate or unsupportive, the [brain] may decide that the world stinks—and it better be ready to meet the challenge." This, then, is how having an abusive parent raises the risk of youth violence: it can change a child's brain. Forever after, influences like the mean-spiritedness that schools condone or the humiliation that's standard fare in adolescence pummel the mind of the child whose brain has been made excruciatingly vulnerable to them.

In other children, constant exposure to pain and violence can make their brain's system of stress hormones unresponsive, like a keypad that has been pushed so often it just stops working. These are the kids with antisocial personalities. They typically have low heart rates and impaired emotional sensitivity. Their signature is a lack of empathy, and their sensitivity to the world around them is practically nonexistent. Often they abuse animals: Kip Kinkel, the 15-year-old who killed his parents and shot 24 schoolmates last May, had a history of this; Luke Woodham, who killed three schoolmates and wounded seven at his high school in Pearl, Miss., in 1997, had previously beaten his dog with a club, wrapped it in a bag and set it on fire. These are also the adolescents who do not respond to punishment: nothing hurts. Their ability to feel, to react, has died, and so has their conscience. Hostile, impulsive aggressors usually feel sorry afterward. Antisocial aggressors don't feel at all. Paradoxically, though, they often have a keen sense of injustices aimed at themselves.

Inept parenting encompasses more than outright abuse, however. Parents who are withdrawn and remote, neglectful and passive, are at risk of shaping a child who (absent a compensating source of love and attention) shuts down emotionally. It's important to be clear about this: inadequate parenting short of Dickensian neglect generally has little ill effect on most children. But to a vulnerable baby, the result of neglect can be tragic. Perry finds that neglect impairs the development of the brain's cortex, which controls feelings of belonging and attachment. "When there are experiences in early life that result in an underdeveloped capacity [to form relationships]," says Perry, "kids have a hard time empathizing with people. They tend to be relatively passive and perceive themselves to be stomped on by the outside world."

RISK FACTORS

Having any of the following risk factors doubles a boy's chance of becoming a murderer:

- **Coming from a family with a history of criminal violence**
- **Being abused**
- **Belonging to a gang**
- **Abusing drugs or alcohol**

Having any of these risk factors, in addition to the above, triples the risk of becoming a killer:

- **Using a weapon**
- **Having been arrested**
- **Having a neurological problem that impairs thinking or feeling**
- **Having had problems at school**

These neglected kids are the ones who desperately seek a script, an ideology that fits their sense of being humiliated and ostracized. Today's pop culture offers all too many dangerous ones, from the music of Rammstein to the game of Doom. Historically, most of those scripts have featured males. That may explain, at least in part, why the murderers are Andrews and Dylans rather than Ashleys and Kaitlins, suggests Deborah Prothrow-Smith of the Harvard School of Public Health. "But girls are now 25 percent of the adolescents arrested for violent crime," she notes. "This follows the media portrayal of girl superheroes beating people up," from Power Rangers to Xena. Another reason that the schoolyard murderers are boys is that girls tend to internalize ostracism and shame rather than turning it into anger. And just as girls could be the next wave of killers, so could even younger children. "Increasingly, we're seeing the high-risk population for lethal violence as being the 10- to 14-year-olds," says Richard Lieberman, a school psychologist in Los Angeles. "Developmentally, their concept of death is still magical. They still think it's temporary, like little Kenny in 'South Park'." Of course, there are loads of empty, emotionally unattached girls and boys. The large majority won't become violent. "But if they're in a violent environment," says Perry, "they're more likely to."

There seems to be a genetic component to the vulnerability that can turn into antisocial-personality disorder. It is only a tiny bend in the twig, but depending on how the child grows up, the bend will be exaggerated or straightened out. Such aspects of temperament as "irritability, impulsivity, hyperactivity and a low sensitivity to emotions in others are all biologically based," says psychologist James Garbarino of Cornell University, author of the upcoming book "Lost Boys: Why Our Sons Turn Violent and How We Can Save Them." A baby who is unreactive to hugs and smiles can be left to go her natural, antisocial way if frustrated parents become exasperated, withdrawn, neglectful or enraged. Or that child can be pushed back toward the land of the feeling by parents who never give up trying to engage and stimulate and form a loving bond with her. The different responses of parents produce different brains, and thus behaviors. "Behavior is the result of a dialogue between your brain and your experiences," concludes Debra Niehoff, author of the recent book "The Biology of Violence." "Although people are born with some biological givens, the brain has many blank pages. From the first moments of childhood the brain acts as a historian, recording our experiences in the language of neurochemistry."

There are some out-and-out brain pathologies that lead to violence. Lesions of the frontal lobe can induce apathy and distort both judgment and emotion. In the brain scans he has done in his Fairfield, Calif., clinic of 50 murderers, psychiatrist Daniel Amen finds several shared patterns. The structure called the cingulate gyrus, curving through the center of the brain, is hyperactive in murderers. The CG acts like the brain's transmission, shifting from one thought to another. When it is impaired, people get stuck on one thought. Also, the prefrontal cortex, which seems to act as the brain's supervisor, is sluggish in the 50 murderers. "If you have violent thoughts that you're stuck on and no supervisor, that's a prescription for trouble," says Amen, author of "Change Your Brain/ Change Your Life." The sort of damage he finds can result from head trauma as well as exposure to toxic substances like alcohol during gestation.

Children who kill are not, with very few exceptions, amoral. But their morality is aberrant. "I killed because people like me are mistreated every day," said pudgy, bespectacled Luke Woodham, who murdered three students. "My whole life I felt outcasted, alone." So do a lot of adolescents. The difference is that at least some of the recent school killers felt emotionally or physically abandoned by those who should love them. Andrew Golden, who was 11 when he and Mitchell Johnson, 13, went on their killing spree in Jonesboro, Ark., was raised mainly by his grandparents while his parents worked. Mitchell mourned the loss of his father to divorce.

Unless they have another source of unconditional love, such boys fail to develop, or lose, the neural circuits that control the capacity to feel and to form healthy relationships. That makes them hypersensitive to perceived injustice. A sense of injustice is often accompanied by a feeling of abject powerlessness. An adult can often see his way to restoring a sense of self-worth, says psychiatrist James Gilligan of Harvard Medical School, through success in work

or love. A child usually lacks the emotional skills to do that. As one killer told Garbarino's colleague, "I'd rather be wanted for murder than not wanted at all."

THAT THE LITTLETON MASSACRE ENDED in suicide may not be a coincidence. As Michael Carneal was wrestled to the ground after killing three fellow students in Paducah in 1997, he cried out, "Kill me now!" Kip Kinkel pleaded with the schoolmates who stopped him, "Shoot me!" With suicide "you get immortality," says Michael Flynn of John Jay College of Criminal Justice. "That is a great feeling of power for an adolescent who has no sense that he matters."

The good news is that understanding the roots of violence offers clues on how to prevent it. The bad news is that ever more children are exposed to the influences that, in the already vulnerable, can produce a bent toward murder. Juvenile homicide is twice as common today as it was in the

mid-1980s. It isn't the brains kids are born with that has changed in half a generation; what has changed is the ubiquity of violence, the easy access to guns and the glorification of revenge in real life and in entertainment. To deny the role of these influences is like denying that air pollution triggers childhood asthma. Yes, to develop asthma a child needs a specific, biological vulnerability. But as long as some children have this respiratory vulnerability—and some always will— then allowing pollution to fill our air will make some children wheeze, and cough, and die. And as long as some children have a neurological vulnerability—and some always will—then turning a blind eye to bad parenting, bullying and the gun culture will make other children seethe, and withdraw, and kill.

With ADAM ROGERS, PAT WINGERT *and* THOMAS HAYDEN

From *Newsweek*, May 3, 1999, pp. 32-35. © 1999 by Newsweek, Inc. All rights reserved. Reprinted by permission.

Generation 9-11

The kids who grew up with peace and prosperity are facing their defining moment

By Barbara Kantrowitz and Keith Naughton

I T WAS A SLEEPY, GRAY AFTERNOON— a challenge to any professor. And for the first few minutes of class last week, University of Michigan sociologist David Schoem had some trouble rousing the 18 freshmen in his seminar on "Democracy and Diversity." One student slurped yogurt while another stretched his arms wide and yawned. A few others casually took notes. But the lassitude ended abruptly when Schoem switched the discussion to America's war on terrorism. For the rest of the hour, the students argued passionately and articulately about foreign policy, racism and media coverage. Then, New Yorker Georgina Levitt offered one view that stopped the debate cold. "September 11 has changed us more than we realize," she said. "This just isn't going to go away."

At Michigan and campuses all around the country, the generation that once had it all—peace, prosperity, even the dot-com dream of retiring at 30—faces its defining moment. College students are supposed to be finding their place in the world, not just a profession but also an intellec-

tual framework for learning and understanding the rest of their lives. After the terrorist attacks, that goal seems more urgent and yet more elusive than ever. In the first week, they prayed together, lit candles and mourned. Now they're packing teach-ins and classes on international relations, the Mideast, Islamic studies, even Arabic. Where they once dreamed of earning huge bonuses on Wall Street, they're now thinking of working for the government, maybe joining the FBI or the CIA. They're energized, anxious, eager for any information that will help them understand—and still a little bit in shock.

**REASON TO BELIEVE
Epstein reached out to
students of many
faiths, all struggling to
understand their
changing world.**

It's too soon to tell whether 2001 will be more like 1941, when campuses and the country were united,

or 1966, the beginning of a historic rift. So far, there have been only scattered signs of a nascent antiwar movement; at Michigan and other campuses, students' views are in sync with the rest of the country's. In the Newsweek Poll conducted last week, 83 percent of young Americans said they approved of President George W. Bush's job performance and 85 percent favored the current military action. These figures are consistent across all age groups. But students also understand that the future is increasingly unpredictable and that long-held beliefs and assumptions will be severely tested in the next few years. "Our generation, as long as we've had an identity, was known as the generation that had it easy," says Greg Epstein, 24, a graduate student in Judaic studies at Michigan. "We had no crisis, no Vietnam, no Martin Luther King, no JFK. We've got it now. When we have kids and grandkids, we'll tell them that we lived through the roaring '90s, when all we cared about was the No. 1 movie or how many copies an album sold. This is where it changes."

After September 11, even the school the cops attended felt out of date

Turning John Jay Into Terrorism U

BY PEG TYRE

WHEN COLLEGE RECRUITMENT fairs resumed following September 11, Alan Weidenfeld, an admissions counselor for John Jay College of Criminal Justice in New York City, found that his information table wasn't attracting the usual handful of prospective students. Instead, it was drawing a crowd. "Students who might have looked at chemistry or biology at another college three months ago are checking our forensic-science program," says Weidenfeld, who estimates inquiries have tripled. Those prospective students, Weidenfeld says, are influenced by patriotism, but they're also thinking about their futures. "Many of them want to know, 'Will John Jay prepare me for the FBI, Secret Service and INS?'"

Professors and administrators at John Jay say the answer to that question is a resounding yes. Founded in 1964, John Jay is the only liberal-arts college in the nation devoted to criminal justice. Once of the 20 City University of New York campuses, John Jay has a reputation as a solid, if uninspiring, academic steppingstone for the uniformed professions. But its campus is also home to some unsung innovators in behavioral science, organized crime an forensics. In the days following September 11, those staffers, along with professors from other parts of the sprawling CUNY system, began to plan a terrorism institute on the campus of John Jay. "It's a new day in criminal-justice education," says college president Gerald Lynch.

The college already offers classes in risk assessment, cybercrime and terrorist cults to its 11,500 students, but next year it hopes to ramp up the toxicology lab and inaugurate nearly three dozen new courses—from analyzing biological assaults to the literature and art of terrorism.

Some ongoing classes have already undergone a mid-semester transformation. Before the attacks, students taking security design discussed threats to Manhattan landmarks. Following September 11, says student Peter Linken, "we needed to have an entirely new discussion on how to prevent the unexpected." At John Jay, that discussion is hardly academic. The school counts a staggering 110 current and former students killed in the World Trade Center. Those losses, says president Lynch, fuel their determination to better equip the crimefighters of the future.

VOLUNTEERS
September 11 has changed the curriculum at Michigan and elsewhere

What will they make of their moment? It's always tricky to generalize about a generation, but before September 11, American college students were remarkably insular. Careers were their major concern both during the high-tech boom (how to cash in) and after (how to get a job). According to the annual survey of college freshmen conducted by UCLA's Higher Education Research Institute, only 28.1 percent of last year's freshman class reported following politics, compared with a high of 60.3 percent in 1966. Nationwide, campus activism has been low key through the 1990s. That was true even at Michigan, the birthplace of SDS and a hotbed of antiwar protest during Vietnam. Alan Haber, a 65-year-old peace protester and fixture on the Ann Arbor campus since his own student days in the 1960s, says

that before September 11, there was no central issue that ignited everyone, just a lot of what he describes as "little projects": protests against sweatshops or nuclear weapons. He thinks that may change as these campus activists begin questioning the U.S. military efforts. "This situation," he says, "bangs on the head and opens a heart."

68% of young adults believe the terror attacks have made people their age more serious about their work and studies

Despite their perceived apathy and political inexperience, this generation may be uniquely qualified to understand the current battle. "I think they realize more than the adults that this is a clash of cultures," says University of Pennsylvania president Judith Rodin, "something we haven't seen in a thousand years." While their parents' high-school history lessons concentrated

almost exclusively on Western Europe, they've learned about Chinese dynasties, African art, even Islam. They are more likely than their parents to have dated a person from another culture or race, and to have friends from many economic and ethnic backgrounds. Their campuses as well are demographically very different from those of a generation ago. "It's gone from a more elite institution to more of a microcosm of the population," says David Ward, president of the American Council on Education, a national association of colleges and universities.

A DAY IN THE LIFE
After the attacks, Gagnon, editor in chief of The Michigan Daily, sent four reporters and two photographers to NY

Others argue that this spirit of tolerance can have a downside, particularly now. When author David Brooks, who wrote a widely discussed Atlantic Monthly article on

At UCLA, a national emergency means more opportunities to teach

Islam, Arabic and Afghanistan 101

BY DONNA FOOTE

THE EMERGENCY MANAGEMENT TEAM at UCLA normally convenes to deal with earthquakes. But at 10 a.m. on September 11 it met to handle an entirely different emergency. Though the campus of 60,000 people appeared to be in no physical danger after the East Coast attacks, the team of top administrators declared a "policy crisis" requiring a rapid response. "We agreed that it was important to connect the event with what we do here every day—which is teach and learn," recalls Brian Copenhaver, provost of UCLA's College of Letters and Science. Within the week an e-mail titled "Urgent Call to action" had gone out to all 3,200 faculty members, seeking volunteers to design and teach a series of one-unit, pass/fail seminars related to the events of September 11—without pay.

By the time the fall quarter began two weeks later, UCLA had some up with 50 (yes, 50) new courses taught by some of the marquee names on campus. Chancellor Albert Carnasale signed on to teach "National Security in the 21st Century." Copenhaver offered a course exploring the sue of terror in Machiavelli's "The Prince." Allan Tobin, director of the UCLA Brain Research Institute, teamed up with his wife, English professor Janet Hadda, to look at the neurobiological effects of terror on creativity.

Instead of hitting the streets with anti-war demonstrations, undergrads are hitting the books. Demand for courses in Arabic and Iranian studies is way up, and the series of 50 seminars, called "Perspectives on September 11," is almost completely full. that may be because the weekly, one-hour classes are part academic inquiry, part group therapy. Unlike most courses at UCLA, where

enrollment is large and professors are distant, the new seminars are limited to 15 students to encourage discussion. Like many students, political-science major Grant Rabenn reacted to the September attacks was fear. "In most classes there is hardly any interaction," Rabenn says. "Here you just go and let out what's inside you."

Jordan Richmond, a music major, is enrolled in three September 11 seminars. On the first day of history professor Vinay Lal's analytic class on terrorism, Richmond recalled finding a Web site by 10:30 a.m. on September 11 that had already posted a WTC obit—noting both the date of the towers' completion and the date of their destruction. Seeing that cybertombstone, "I almost cried," he says. "The event was already contextualized. that blew my mind." The seminars, believes Richmond, have sent him on a journey to learn what he should have already known.

rampant pre-professionalism at Princeton last year, returned there after September 11, he found a surging interest in global affairs and issues of right and wrong—but also a frustration with the moral relativism of much of the curriculum (see this week's Web Exclusive at Newsweek.MSNBC.com). One student told him that he had been taught how to deconstruct and dissect, but never to construct and decide.

Michigan, one of the country's premier universities with more than 38,000 graduate and undergraduate students, has spawned campus groups reflecting virtually every corner of the globe and every world view, from the conservative Young Americans for Freedom to groups that still cling to dreams of a socialist utopia. There are also substantial numbers of Jewish, Arab and Muslim students who have made the politics of the Mideast a personal cause. But on the morning of September 11, senior Geoff Gagnon, editor of The Michigan Daily, the campus newspaper, thought an issue much closer

to home would be sparking angry debate that day. An athlete had been accused of sexual assault—a major story on a Big Ten campus—and Gagnon had been at the paper until well past 3 in the morning nailing down details. He was still groggy when his roommate burst in to tell him that NPR was reporting a "big plane crash in New York." Gagnon rushed from his apartment to the Daily newsroom, where he and his staff gathered around the TV. Soon, classes were canceled for the first time since the 1975 blizzard. "We just watched this thing unfold like everyone else," he says, "except we had to figure out what it meant for the 40,000 people here."

GIVE PEACE A CHANCE Charlotte Greenough chose Michigan for its diversity and was impressed by how so many students drew together in a crisis

Virtually everyone Gagnon spoke to knew someone who might be missing. One of the news editors worried about her mother and stepfather, who worked near the World Trade Center. A reporter who grew up near Pittsburgh was alarmed when she heard about the crash of Flight 93 in rural Pennsylvania. After the first plane hit, they heard an active Michigan alumnus, Jim Gartenberg, interviewed on ABC. Trapped on the 86th floor of the North Tower, he was on the air live, describing the scene just before he was killed in the collapse. Gagnon quickly sent four reporters and two photographers to New York. "We wanted things we weren't going to get from the AP," he says. One of the reporters, David Enders, talked to Gartenberg's pregnant widow, Jill. She said that on Saturday three weeks earlier, her husband woke up exhilarated because it was the start of the college-football season. "He lived for Michigan football," she told Enders.

That first night, nearly 15,000 students gathered for an impromptu

After decades of disrespect and worse, ROTC has become cool again

'They Know I'm About Something'

By Allison Samuels

Growing up in a poor Los Angeles neighborhood that still shows scars from the 1992 riots, David Ramirez watched friends wind up in juvie, or worse, after getting involved in theft and other small-time crimes. He knew he was headed in the same direction if he didn't get a plan.

So in the ninth grade, David enrolled in the Army Reserve Officers' Training Corps program at Inglewood High School. Though he thought the olive uniforms were dorky, David liked the sense of purpose he'd seen in others who enrolled. "The more free time you got, the more you're bound to end up in some type of trouble," says David, now 17. "Plus, I didn't want to be home that

much. In ROTC, everyone's family." He likens his school's ROTC to a secret fraternity. "When I walk in my neighborhood now, the gang guys see me in my uniform and they leave me alone. They know I'm about something."

Dare we say it? ROTC is cool again. Started in 1916 when the United States was faced with world war, ROTC fell out of favor after Vietnam. But it found renewed popularity thanks to gulf-war patriotism and the skyrocketing costs of higher education (ROTC gives scholarships of up to $35,000 a year in exchange for a four- to eight-year commitment to the military). Today it has 200,000 students nationwide, an its ranks have increased considerably since September 11.

For many inner-city kids like David Ramirez, ROTC is sorely needed. The students at his school, divided evenly

among blacks and Hispanics, suffer more than their share of poverty and low self-esteem. "These kids are living very tough lives, and September 11 didn't change that a bit," says Sgt. 1/c Luis A. Melendez, who has headed the Inglewood program since 1994. Usually only a handful sign up each semester, but after September 11 the ranks at Inglewood swelled to 350. "Many of them know that the military was their best option, one way or the other, for any chance out of her," says Melendez.

An average to below-average student before ROTC, David now boasts a 3.5 GPA. He is second in command for the school's ROTC squad and plans to attend West Point next fall with the sponsorship of Rep. Maxine Waters. "I want to show people that someone from this community could get there and make it," he says.

candlelight vigil on the Diag, the main campus crossroads. Some in the huge crowd had spent much of the day anxious for news of relatives or friends. Charlotte Greenough, an 18-year-old freshman from Manhattan whose family lives a few blocks from the World Trade Center, had waited five hours to hear that her parents were safe. She was so frustrated by the constant busy signals that she threw a cordless phone across the room and broke it. "I've never been so scared in my life," she says. Greenough, a committed pacifist, chose Michigan because of its diversity. "You can learn about other people, take any sort of class or go to any religious service or any concert," she says. "I knew that whatever direction I decided to go in, whatever happened, I would be able to follow that up and define myself." When classes resumed on Sept. 12, Greenough was impressed by how students on the huge campus reached out to each other. "People came up to me constantly," she says, "gave me hugs and were so nice to me."

In the first few days after the attacks, everyone seemed to be look-

ing for ways to give and receive comfort. The bell tower played the national anthem. The Rock, a boulder along fraternity row that's often painted in school colors or bright neon hues, was adorned for weeks with American flags and "God Bless America." On Wednesday, junior Joanna Tropp-Bluestone's experimental-art instructor handed his class two huge wooden boards and asked the students to create a mural. Tropp-Bluestone, whose father died of heart disease when she was 10, knew exactly what she wanted to paint in her corner: a hollow red heart. "The only way you get through something like that is with love," she says.

Michigan's president, Lee Bollinger, had been in New York for a meeting on Sept. 11 and managed to get one of the last cars available from Hertz on 57th Street for the 10-hour drive home on Wednesday. As he drove, he was on his cell phone with the football coach, Lloyd Carr, debating whether Saturday's game against Western Michigan University should go on. Carr argued for the game, but Bollinger wasn't con-

vinced. As he sped across New Jersey, Pennsylvania and Ohio, he called colleagues for advice, including Peter McPherson, president of the university's archrival, Michigan State. Finally, as he neared Ann Arbor, Bollinger made his decision. The cavernous Michigan Stadium would be silent on Sept. 15. "It became clear to all of us," Bollinger says, "that the magnitude of this was so great that a few days would not separate ordinary life from this event. People would need to regain ordinary life over a longer period of time."

Young people say careers in medicine (48%), the military (46%) and science and tech (44%) will be more popular now

Over the next week, walk-in traffic doubled at the campus psychological-counseling center. Everyone was feeling vulnerable, says Jim Etzkorn, the clinical director. Many students were worried about being drafted if war erupted. There were also more intense cases of homesickness, especially among freshmen. On Sept. 19, 800 people jammed a panel discussion of the attacks by historians and political scientists who specialize in the Mideast. Even the most uninvolved students understood that they could no longer ignore what was happening on the other side of the world. The Daily was running foreign news on its front page almost every day, and many professors, encouraged by the administration, incorporated discussions of the events into classes on a wide range of subjects.

STAR SPANGLED
Areej El-Jawahir, a Muslim originally from Iraq, opposes bin Laden and supports bombing Afghanistan

For Michigan's Arab and Muslim students, the weeks after the attack brought unexpected terror. On September 11, Areej El-Jawahri, an 18-year-old freshman whose family moved here from Iraq four years ago, was still trying to check on friends in New York when she started receiving threatening e-mail. One said: "We will f--- you bastards for doing this." Later that week, when El-Jawahri mentioned the e-mails in her political-science class, two non-Muslim girls she didn't know well came up and hugged her, and they've since become good friends. "I love this country," she says. "I love the freedom." She supports the bombing of Afghanistan and says that the United States is "defending the Islamic religion from the disgrace of bin Laden." Brenda Abdelall, 20, a political-science and Islamic-studies major from Ann Arbor who is president of the Arab Students Association, said she received a death threat within two hours of the attack. Abdelall, pictured on NEWSWEEK's cover, was afraid to leave her apartment, and her mother

came and got her. Abdelall called the police soon afterward, but the e-mail couldn't be traced. "Walking around, I did feel people were looking at me," she says. She and a friend put together a campus wide teach-in on hate crimes that was attended by 500 people. "Only through education and knowledge can we defeat intolerance on campus," she says.

When he heard about the attacks, Aiman Fouad Mackie, a 21-year-old graduate student in public policy, had just one thought: "Please God, don't let it be Arabs." Since then, he says, many of his Arab friends have received death threats. Mackie is president of Michigan's Lebanese Student Association and he says many members do not show up for meetings now because they're afraid to walk around at night. But, he says, there have been encouraging changes as well. Instead of shouting at each other, pro-Palestinian and pro-Israeli groups are speaking in a more civilized way. Mackie always wanted to work for the government, but now he is even more sure that he'd like to represent the United States overseas, maybe in the Mideast. "The most positive thing coming out of this," he says, "is that Americans will have a better understanding of Islam and Arabs."

PLAYIN' IN THE BAND
Drum major Karen England has to comfort bandmates after an emotional patriotic halftime performance

Foreign students at Michigan and elsewhere have also felt the pressure of extra scrutiny. The university has 4,000 foreign students, the majority in graduate school. So far, officials say, only one is known to have withdrawn because of concerns about safety. However, proposals to tighten immigration and student-visa standards could affect Michigan in the future.

Many students say that something resembling normal life started returning to campus on Sept. 22, when the Wolverines finally met Western Michigan for the postponed match up. In a somber, patriotic tribute, the band formed an American eagle on the field while they played "America the Beautiful." They unfurled a giant flag on the 50-yard line. As she stood saluting, drum major Karen England was stunned by the crowd's reaction. Normally, Michigan football fans clog the aisles at halftime, racing for the concession stands and the restrooms. Instead, the crowd stood as one and sang. After they exited the field to a simple military drum tap, England had to comfort her sobbing bandmates. "I don't think anybody in the band realized the effect this would have," she says. "We were performing for something really important, our country. That week, we had a purpose." (Michigan won, 38–21.)

WE ARE FAMILY
Almost everyone at the Kappa Alpha Theta sorority house feels vulnerable on a campus where safety was taken for granted

Over the next few weeks, the flags that had sprung up over campus began to come down, but the wave of patriotism that swept the campus remains strong. No one felt the change more than the university's Navy ROTC students. Their captain, Dennis Hopkins, was a student at Michigan in the mid-1970s, when ROTC students "got rocks and bottles thrown at you," he says. But his students say that their non-ROTC classmates now view them with a mix of awe and curiosity. Jessica Ryu, a 21-year-old battalion commander from North Carolina, recalls a physical-fitness run across a bridge on campus with 23 other ROTC students—all wearing fatigues. "People stopped on the bridge and started clapping," she says. "Before, we were yelled at for being in the way." Ryu says it bothers her that "it took so many people to die to make others proud to be an American. I felt that from day one."

In late September, as Michigan was struggling with new realities, Bollinger was trying to figure out his own future. He was offered the presidency of Columbia University, and he and his wife, Jean, an artist and a Columbia graduate, spent long hours weighing the pros and cons of the new job. "It was extremely agonizing," he says. But September 11 actually helped tip the scales in favor of Columbia, where he'll take over next summer and where he hopes to do his part to help rebuild New York.

Two months after the attacks, many Michigan students say they're still trying to get back to "normal"—whatever that means now. At the Tau Epsilon Phi fraternity last week, headless Barbies decorated the entrance. The smell of stale beer from a Halloween party lingered in the air. But as they sat under a poster of a vo-

luptuous model, the frat boys seemed remarkably sober. Ben Weinbaum, a 19-year-old sophomore from San Diego, says many of his friends felt guilty going out and having fun. But he doesn't. "Life moves on," he says, "but moving on doesn't mean forgetting. We think about it every day." Joel Winston, a 20-year-old junior majoring in political science, says that although he'd been thinking about working for the government before September 11, he's now more sure than ever of his goal. He wants to help in a way he never imagined before. Even with a shaky economy, he says, "the government is always looking for bright people to do America's work."

Down the street, at the Kappa Alpha Theta sorority, an Arab and a Jew talked about their very different attempts to pick up their lives. The Arab, Rema Mounayer, a 20-year-old junior, was still feeling hurt after another sorority sister told her that her mother had directed her not to sit next to any Arabs on planes. She cried for days. "The fact that it happened in my own sorority killed

me," she says. Lately, she's been thinking of moving out of the sorority even though everyone in her house seems to be on her side. "I can't live in a place where I feel ashamed of who I am," she says. Mounayer says she always understood that in a diverse community like Michigan, there would be people who didn't agree with her, but she never expected to feel like an outsider.

Another sorority sister, Lee Raskin, a 20-year-old from New York's Long Island, is still mourning for her mother's best friend, a lawyer at Cantor Fitzgerald. As she chokes back tears, she says she now calls home many times a day and phones her mother at work "just to check in." When she sees a plane flying low, she worries. At the same time, she's learned to appreciate the moment. "I want to do everything now and not put anything on hold," she says. High on her list: time with her family and a trip to Australia. There's still a whole world to explore.

With JULIE HALPERT *in Ann Arbor and* PAT WINGERT *in Washington*

From *Newsweek*, November 12, 2001, pp. 6-56. © 2001 by Newsweek, Inc. All rights reserved. Reprinted by permission.

THE FEMINIZATION OF AMERICAN CULTURE

How Modern Chemicals May Be Changing Human Biology

Leonard Sax, M.D.

In ancient times—by which I mean, before 1950—most scholars agreed that women were, as a rule, not quite equal to men. Women were charming but mildly defective. Many (male) writers viewed women as perpetual teenagers, stuck in an awkward place between childhood and adulthood. German philosopher Arthur Schopenhauer, for example, wrote that women are "childish, silly and short-sighted, really nothing more than overgrown children, all their life long. Women are a kind of intermediate stage between the child and the man."[1]

Psychologists in that bygone era devoted considerable time and energy to the question of why women couldn't outgrow their childish ways. The Freudians said it was because they were trapped in the pre-Oedipal stage, tortured by penis envy. Followers of Abraham Maslow claimed that women were fearful of self-actualization. Jungians insisted that women were born with a deficiency of imprinted archetypes.

A mature adult nowadays is someone who is comfortable talking about her inner conflicts, someone who values personal relationships above abstract goals, someone who isn't afraid to cry. In other words: a mature adult is a woman.

Back then, of course, almost all the psychologists were men.

Things are different now. Male psychologists today are so rare that Ilene Philipson—author of *On the Shoulders of Women: The Feminization of Psychotherapy*—speaks of "the vanishing male therapist" as a species soon to be extinct.[2] As the gender of the modal psychotherapist has changed from male to female, the standard of mental health has changed along with it. Today, Dr. Philipson observes, the badge of emotional maturity is no longer the ability to control or sublimate your feelings but rather the ability to *express* them. A mature adult nowadays is someone who is comfortable talking about her inner conflicts, someone who values personal relationships above abstract goals, someone who isn't afraid to cry. In other words: a mature adult is a woman.

It is now the men who are thought to be stuck halfway between childhood and adulthood, incapable of articulating their inner selves. Whereas psychologists fifty years ago amused themselves by cataloging women's (supposed) deficiencies, psychologists today devote themselves to demonstrating "the natural superiority of women."[3] Psychologists report that women are better able to understand nonverbal communication and are more expressive of emotion.[4] Quantitative personality inventories reveal that the average woman is more trusting, nurturing, and outgoing than the average man.[5] The average eighth-grade girl has a command of language and writing skills equal to that of the average eleventh-grade boy.[6]

As the influence of the new psychology permeates our culture, women have understandably begun to wonder whether men are really, well, human. "What if these women are right?" wonders one writer in an article for *Marie Claire*, a national woman's magazine. "What if it's true that some men don't possess, or at least can't express, nuanced emotions?"[7] More than a few contemporary psychologists have come to regard the male of our species as a coarsened, more violent edition of the normal, female, human. Not surprisingly, they have begun to question whether having a man in the house is desirable or even safe.

Eleven years ago, scholar Sara Ruddick expressed her concern about "the extent and variety of the psychological, sexual, and physical battery suffered by women and children of all classes and social groups… at the hands of fathers, their mothers' male lovers, or male relatives. If putative fathers are absent or perpetually disappearing and actual fathers are controlling or abusive, *who needs a father*? What mother would want to live with one or wish one on her children?"[8] Nancy Polikoff, former counsel to the Women's Legal Defense Fund, said that "it is no tragedy, either on a national scale or in an individual family, for children to be raised without fathers."[9]

The feminization of psychology manifests itself in myriad ways. Consider child discipline. Seventy years ago, doctors agreed that the best way to discipline your child was to punish the little criminal. ("Spare the rod, spoil the child.") Today, spanking is considered child abuse.[10] You're supposed to *talk* with your kid. Spanking sends all the wrong messages, we are told, and may have stupendously horrible consequences. Psychoanalyst Alice Miller confidently informed us, in her book *For Your Own Good*, that Adolf Hitler's evil can be traced to the spankings his father inflicted on him in childhood.[11]

THE NEW MEN'S MAGAZINES

It isn't only psychology that has undergone a process of feminization over the past fifty years, and it isn't only women whose attitudes have changed. Take a stroll to your neighborhood bookstore or newsstand. You'll find magazines such as *Men's Health, MH-18, Men's Fitness, Gear*, and others devoted to men's pursuit of a better body, a better self-image. None of them existed fifteen years ago. The paid circulation of *Men's Health* has risen from 250,000 to more than 1.5 million in less than ten years.[12] Many of the articles in these magazines are reminiscent of those to be found in women's magazines such as *Glamour, Mademoiselle*, and *Cosmopolitan*: "The Ten Secrets of Better Sex," "The New Diet Pills—Can They Work For You?" or "Bigger Biceps in Five Minutes a Day." (The women's magazine equivalent might be something like "slimmer thighs in five minutes a day.")

Today, the best qualification for leadership may be the ability to listen. The feminine way of seeing the world and its problems is, arguably, becoming the mainstream way.

Men didn't use to care so much about their appearance. Psychiatrists Harrison Pope and Katharine Phillips report that in American culture today, "Men of all ages, in unprecedented numbers, are preoccupied with the appearance of their bodies."[13] They document that "men's dissatisfaction with body appearance has nearly tripled in less than thirty years—from 15 percent in 1972, to 34 percent in 1985, to 43 percent in 1997."[14] Cosmetic plastic surgery, once marketed exclusively to women, has found a rapidly growing male clientele. The number of men undergoing liposuction, for instance, quadrupled between 1990 and 2000.[15]

THE FEMINIZATION OF ENTERTAINMENT AND POLITICS

This process of femininization manifests itself, though somewhat differently, when you turn on the TV or watch a movie. Throughout the mid-twentieth century, leading men were, as a rule, infallible: think of Clark Gable in *Gone With the Wind*, Cary Grant in *North by Northwest*, or Fred McMurray in *My Three Sons*. But no longer. In family comedy, the father figure has metamorphosed from the all-knowing, all-wise Robert Young of *Father Knows Best* to the occasional bumbling of Bill Cosby and the consistent stupidity of Homer Simpson. Commercially successful movies now often feature women who are physically aggressive, who dominate or at least upstage the men. This description applies to movies as diverse as *Charlie's Angels* and *Crouching Tiger, Hidden Dragon*. In today's cinema, to paraphrase Garrison Keillor, all the leading women are strong and all the leading men are good-looking.

A transformation of comparable magnitude seems to be under way in the political arena. Military command used to be considered the best qualification for leadership—as it was with Ulysses Grant, Theodore Roosevelt, Charles de Gaulle, and Dwight Eisenhower, to name only a few. Today, the best qualification for leadership may be the ability to listen. The feminine way of seeing the world and its problems is, arguably, becoming the mainstream way.

In 1992, Bill Clinton ran against George Bush *père* for the presidency. Clinton was an acknowledged draft evader. Bush, the incumbent, was a World War II hero who had just led the United States to military success in Operation Desert Storm. Clinton won. In 1996, Clinton was challenged by Bob Dole, another decorated World War II veteran. Once again, the man who had evaded military service defeated the combat veteran. In 2000, Gov. George W. Bush and Sen. John McCain competed for the Republican presidential nomination. McCain was a genuine war hero whose courageous actions as a prisoner of war in Vietnam had won him well-deserved honors and praise. Bush, on the other hand, was alleged to have used family influence to obtain a position in the Texas National Guard, in order to avoid service in Vietnam. Once again, the man who had never experienced combat defeated the military veteran. Moral of the story: It's all very well to be a war hero, but in our modern, feminized society, being a war hero won't get you elected president. Conversely, being a draft dodger isn't as bad as it used to be.

A number of authors have recognized the increasing feminization of American society. With few exceptions, most of those acknowledging this process have welcomed it.[16] As Elinor Lenz and Barbara Myerhoff wrote in their 1985 book *The Feminization of America*, "The feminizing influence is moving [American society] away from many archaic ways of thinking and behaving, toward the promise of a saner and more humanistic future…. Feminine culture, with its commitment to creating and protecting life, is our best and brightest hope for overcoming the destructive, life-threatening forces of the nuclear age."[17]

The question is, what's causing this shift? Some might argue that the changes I've described are simply a matter of better education, progressive laws, and two generations of consciousness-raising.

I think we can all agree on one point: there have been fundamental changes in American culture over the past fifty years, changes that indicate a shift from a male-dominated culture to a feminine or at least an androgynous society. The question is, what's causing this shift? Some might argue that the changes I've described are simply a matter of better education, progressive laws, and two generations of consciousness-raising: an evolution from a patriarchal Dark Ages to a unisex, or feminine, Enlightenment. I'm willing to consider that hypothesis. But before we accept that conclusion, we should ask whether there are any other possibilities.

FEMINIZED WILDLIFE

We have to make a big jump now, a journey that will begin at the Columbia River in Washington, near the Oregon border. James Nagler, assistant professor of zoology at the University of Idaho, recently noticed something funny about the salmon he observed in the Columbia. Almost all of them were—or appeared to be—female. But when he caught a few and analyzed their DNA, he found that many of the "female" fish actually were male: their chromosomes were XY instead of XX.[18]

Many of these chemicals, it turns out, mimic the action of female sex hormones called estrogens.

Nagler's findings echo a recent report from England, where government scientists have found some pretty bizarre fish. In two polluted rivers, half the fish are female,

and the other half are… something else. Not female but not male either. The English scientists call these bizarre fish "intersex": their gonads are not quite ovaries, not quite testicles, but some weird thing in between, making neither eggs nor sperm. In both rivers, the intersex fish are found downstream of sites where treated sewage is discharged into the river. Upstream from the sewer effluent, the incidence of intersex is dramatically lower. The relationship between the concentration of sewer effluent and the incidence of intersex is so close that "the proportion of intersex fish in any sample of fish could perhaps be predicted, using a linear equation, from the average concentration of effluent constituents in the river."[19]

It's something in the water. Something in the water is causing feminization of male fish.

And it's not just fish. In Lake Apopka, in central Florida, Dr. Louis Guillette and his associates have found male alligators with abnormally small penises; in the blood of these alligators, female hormone levels are abnormally high and male hormone levels abnormally low.[20] Male Florida panthers have become infertile; the levels of male sex hormones in their blood are much lower (and the levels of female hormones higher) than those found in panthers in less-polluted environments.[21]

What's going on?

Our modern society generates a number of chemicals that never existed before about fifty years ago. Many of these chemicals, it turns out, mimic the action of female sex hormones called estrogens. Plastics—including a plasticizer called phthalate, used in making flexible plastic for bottles of Coke, Pepsi, Sprite, Evian water, and so forth—are known to have estrogenic effects.[22] Many commonly used pesticides have estrogenlike actions on human cells.[23] Estrogenic chemicals ooze out of the synthetic lacquer that lines the inside of soup cans.[24] These chemicals and others find their way into sewage and enter the rivers and lakes. Hence the effects on fish, alligators, and other wildlife.

EFFECTS ON HUMANS?

Modern chemicals may have a feminizing effect on wildlife. That's certainly cause for concern in its own right. But is there any evidence that a similar process of feminization is occurring in humans?

Answer: there may be. Just like the Florida panther, human males are experiencing a rapid decline in fertility and sperm count. The sperm count of the average American or European man has declined continuously over the past four decades, to the point where today it is less than 50 percent of what it was forty years ago.[25] This downward trend is seen only in industrialized regions of North America and western Europe. Lower sperm counts are being reported in urban Denmark but not in rural Finland, for example.[26] Of course, that's precisely the pattern

145

one would expect, if the lower sperm counts are an effect of "modern" materials such as plastic water bottles.

Male infertility, one result of that lower count, is now the single most common cause of infertility in our species.[27] The rate of infertility itself has quadrupled in the past forty years, from 4 percent in 1965 to 10 percent in 1982 to at least 16 percent today.[28]

WHAT ABOUT GIRLS?

So far we've talked mainly about the effect of environmental estrogens on males. What about girls and women? What physiological effects might excess environmental estrogens have on them? Giving estrogens to young girls would, in theory, trigger the onset of puberty at an earlier than expected age. In fact, in the past few years doctors have noticed that girls *are* beginning puberty earlier than ever before. Just as the environmental-estrogen hypothesis would predict, this phenomenon is seen only in girls, not in boys. Dr. Marcia Herman-Giddens, studying over seventeen thousand American girls, found that this trend to earlier puberty is widespread. "Girls across the United States are developing pubertal characteristics at younger ages than currently used norms," she concluded.[29]

Rather than labeling all these pubescent eight-year-olds as "abnormal," Dr. Paul Kaplowitz and his associates recently recommended that the earliest age for "normal" onset of puberty simply be redefined as age seven in Caucasian girls and age six in African-American girls.[30] Dr. Kaplowitz is trying, valiantly, to define this problem out of existence. If you insist that normal puberty begins at age six or age seven, then all these eight-year-old girls with well-filled bras suddenly become "normal."

But saying so doesn't make it so. Last year, doctors in Puerto Rico reported that most young girls with premature breast development have toxic levels of phthalates in their blood; those phthalates appear to have seeped out of plastic food and beverage containers. The authors noted that Puerto Rico is a warm island. Plastic containers that become warm are more likely to ooze phthalate molecules into the food or beverages they contain.[31] These authors, led by Dr. Ivelisse Colón, reported their findings in *Environmental Health Perspectives*, the official journal of the National Institute of Environmental Health Sciences (a branch of the National Institutes of Health). On the cover of the issue in which the report appeared, the editors chose to feature the picture of a young woman drinking water from a plastic bottle.

Premature puberty in girls has become so widespread that it has begun to attract the attention of major media. This topic made the cover of *Time* magazine on October 30, 2000. Unfortunately, few of these high-profile articles show any understanding of the possible role of environmental estrogens. The *Time* article barely mentioned the *Environmental Health Perspectives* study, nor did it link the phenomenon of early puberty in girls with declining sperm counts, intersex fish, or tiny penises in alligators. Instead, it featured a picture of a short boy staring at a taller girl's breasts.

What effect might extra estrogen have on adult women? Many scientists have expressed concern that exposure to excessive environmental estrogens may lead to breast cancer. The rate of breast cancer has risen dramatically over the past fifty years. Today, one in every nine American women can expect to develop breast cancer at some point in her life. But this increase is seen only in industrialized countries,[32] where plastics and other products of modern chemistry are widely used. Women born in Third World countries are at substantially lower risk. When they move from a Third World country to the United States, their risk soon increases to that seen in other women living here, clearly demonstrating that the increased risk is an environmental, not a genetic, factor.[33]

CONNECTION?

At this point, you may feel that you've been reading two completely disconnected essays: one about the feminization of American culture, and the second about the effects of environmental estrogens. Could there be any connection between the two?

If human physiology and endocrinology are being affected by environmental estrogens then there is no reason in principle why human psychology and sexuaity should be exempt.

There may be. If human physiology and endocrinology are being affected by environmental estrogens—as suggested by lower sperm counts, increasing infertility, earlier onset of puberty in girls, and rising rates of breast cancer—then there is no reason in principle why human psychology and sexuality should be exempt. If we accept the possibility that environmental estrogens are affecting human physiology and endocrinology, then we must also consider the possibility that the feminization of American culture may, conceivably, reflect the influence of environmental estrogens.

The phenomena we have considered show a remarkable synchrony. Many of the cultural trends discussed in the first half of the article began to take shape in the 1950s and '60s, just as plastics and other modern chemicals began to be widely introduced into American life. There are, of course, many difficulties in attempting to measure any correlation between an endocrine variable—such as a decline in sperm counts—and a cultural variable, such as cultural feminization. One of many problems is that no single quantitative variable accurately and reliably measures the degree to which a culture is becoming feminized. However, we can get some feeling for the synchrony of the cultural process with the endocrine process by considering the correlation of the decline in sperm counts with the decline in male college enrollment.

We've already mentioned how sperm counts have declined steadily and continuously in industrialized areas of North America and western Europe since about 1950. Let's use that decline as our endocrine variable. As the cultural variable, let's look at college graduation rates. Since 1950, the proportion of men among college graduates has been steadily declining. In 1950, 70 percent of college graduates were men; today, that number is about 43 percent and falling. Judy Mohraz, president of Goucher College, warned not long ago that if present trends continue, "the last man to graduate from college will receive his baccalaureate in the year 2067.... Daughters not only have leveled the playing field in most college classrooms, but they are exceeding their brothers in school success across the board."[34]

Plot these two phenomena on the same graph. Use no statistical tricks, no manipulation of the data—simply use best-fit trend lines, plotted on linear coordinates—and the two lines practically coincide. The graph of declining sperm density perfectly parallels the decline in male college graduation rates.

Of course, the correlation between these phenomena—one endocrine, one cultural—doesn't prove that they must derive from the same underlying source. But such a strong correlation certainly provides some evidence that the endocrine phenomenon of declining sperm counts may derive from the same source as the cultural phenomenon of declining male college enrollment (as a percentage of total enrollment).

If this hypothesis is ultimately shown to be at least partly correct, it would not be the first time that items of daily household life contributed to the transformation of a mighty civilization.

THE DECLINE AND FALL OF THE MALE AMERICAN EMPIRE?

I have suggested that the feminization of American culture and endocrine phenomena such as declining sperm counts are both manifestations of the effects of environmental estrogens. To the best of my knowledge, no other author has yet made such a suggestion. If this hypothesis is ultimately shown to be at least partly correct, it would not be the first time that items of daily household life con-

tributed to the transformation of a mighty civilization. A number of scientists, most notably toxicologist Jerome Nriagu, have suggested that one factor leading to the decline and fall of the Roman Empire was the lead glaze popular among the Roman aristocracy after about A.D. 100.[35] Bowls and dishes were glazed with lead, which was also widely used in household plumbing. (Our word *plumbing* comes from the Latin *plumbum*, which means lead.) The neurological symptoms of lead toxicity—mania, difficulty concentrating, and mood swings—were not recognized as manifestations of poisoning. No Roman scientist conducted the necessary controlled experiment: a comparison of families that used lead-glazed pottery with families that did not. The scientific worldview necessary for such an experiment did not exist at the time. It is thought-provoking to consider that something as insignificant as pottery glazing may have brought down the Roman Empire.

Could anything of comparable magnitude be happening right now, in our own culture? Testing the hypothesis I have proposed will be difficult. It is probably not possible to randomize humans to a "modern, plasticized" environment versus a "primitive, no-plastics, no-cans, no-pesticide" environment—and even it were possible, it would not be ethical to do so. (It should be noted, however, that one careful study has already been published demonstrating that men who consumed only organic produce had higher sperm counts than men eating regular, pesticide-treated produce.[36]) Measures of the degree to which a culture is "feminized" would be controversial, and only seldom would such measures be objectively quantifiable.

Nevertheless, the world around us is changing in ways that have never occurred in the history of our species. It is possible that some of these changes in our culture may reflect the influence of environmental estrogens, an influence whose effects are subtle and incremental. To the extent that human dignity means being in control of one's destiny, we should explore the possibility that our minds and bodies are being affected by environmental estrogens in ways that we do not, as yet, fully understand.

NOTES

1. "Dass sie selbst kindisch, läppisch und kurzsichtig, mit einem Worte: zeitlebens grosse Kinder sind—eine Art Mittelstufe zwischen dem Kinde und dem Manne." Arthur Schopenhauer, *Parerga und Paralipomena*, §364 (1851).

2. Ilene Philipson, *On the Shoulders of Women: The Feminization of Psychotherapy* (New York: Guilford Press, 1993), 145.

3. *The Natural Superiority of Women* is of course the title of one of Ashley Montagu's most famous books, initially published in 1953. Montagu issued a final revised edition in 1998, in which he eagerly documented the published research that supported what had been mere conjecture forty years before.

4. Judith Hall, *Nonverbal Sex Differences: Accuracy of Communication and Expressive Style* (Baltimore: Johns Hopkins Univ. Press, 1990). See also: Ann Kring and Albert Gordon, "Sex Differences in Emotion: Expression, Experience, and Physiology," *Journal of Personality and Social Psychology* 74 (1998): 686–703.

5. Alan Feingold, "Gender Differences in Personality: a Meta-Analysis," *Psychological Bulletin* 116, no. 3 (1994): 429–556.

6. U.S. Department of Education, *Educational Equity for Girls and Women* (Washington: U.S. Government Printing Office, 2000), 4. The report can be read online at nces.ed.gov/spider/webspider/2000030.html.

7. Marilyn Berlin Snell, "Wisdom of the Ages," *Marie Claire*, September 1999, 123.

8. Ruddick 1990, cited in Philipson, *On the Shoulders of Women*, 142–43. Emphasis added.

9. Quoted in Cathy Young, *Ceasefire!* (New York: Free Press, 1999), 60.

10. According to both the American Academy of Pediatrics and the American Academy of Family Physicians, there is no situation in which spanking is appropriate. Spanking is always child abuse. You can read the AAFP's statement at www.aafp.org/afp/990315ap/1577.html and the AAP's position at www.aap.org/advocacy/archives/aprspr2.html.

11. Alice Miller, *For Your Own Good: Hidden Cruelty in Child-Rearing and the Roots of Violence* (Noonday Press, 1990).

12. Harrison Pope, Katharine Phillips, and Roberto Olivardia, *The Adonis Complex: The Secret Crisis of Male Body Obsession* (New York: Free Press, 2000), 56.

13. Pope, Phillips, and Olivardia, *The Adonis Complex*, xiii.

14. Pope, Phillips, and Olivardia, *The Adonis Complex*, 27.

15. Pope, Phillips, and Olivardia, *The Adonis Complex*, 31.

16. One notable exception is Rich Zubaty's misogynistic diatribe, *Surviving the Feminization of America* (Tinley Park, Ill.: Panther Press, 1993).

17. Elinor Lenz and Barbara Myerhoff, *The Feminization of America: How Women's Values Are Changing Our Public and Private Lives* (New York: St. Martin's Press, 1985), 2.

18. James Nagler et al., "High Incidence of a Male-Specific Genetic Marker in Phenotypic Female Chinook Salmon From the Columbia River," *Environmental Health Perspectives* 109 (2001): 67–69.

19. Susan Jobling et al., "Widespread Sexual Disruption in Wild Fish," *Environmental Science and Technology* 32, no. 17 (1998): 2498–2506.

20. Louis Guillette et al., "Developmental Abnormalities of the Gonad and Abnormal Sex Hormone Concentrations in Juvenile Alligators from Contaminated and Control Lakes in Florida," *Environmental Health Perspectives* 102 (1994): 680–88.

21. C.F. Facemire et al., "Reproductive Impairment in the Florida Panther," *Environmental Health Perspectives* 103, supplement 4 (1995): 79–86.

22. Susan Jobling et al., "A Variety of Environmentally Persistent Chemicals, Including Some Phthalate Plasticizers, Are Weakly Estrogenic," *Environmental Health Perspectives* 103 (1995): 582–87.

23. Ana Soto, Kerrie Chung, and Carlos Sonnenschein, "The Pesticides Endosulfan, Toxaphene, and Dieldrin Have Estrogenic Effects on Human Estrogen-Sensitive Cells," *Environmental Health Perspectives* 102, no. 4 (1994): 380–83.

24. José Brotons et al., "Xenoestrogens Released From Lacquer Coatings in Food Cans," *Environmental Health Perspectives* 103, no. 6 (1995): 608–12.

25. Shanna Swan, Eric Elkin, and Laura Fenster, "The Question of Declining Sperm Density Revisited: Analysis of 101 Studies Published 1934–1996," *Environmental Health Perspectives* 108 (2000): 961–66.

26. Tina Jensen et al., "Semen Quality Among Danish and Finnish Men Attempting to Conceive," *European Journal of Endocrinology* 142 (2000): 47–52.

27. D. Stewart Irvine, "Epidemiology and Aetiology of Male Infertility," *Human Reproduction* 13 (1998): 33–44.

28. Schmidt, Münster, and Helm (*British Journal of Obstetrics and Gynaecology* 102 (December 1995): 978–84, found that 26.2 percent of couples attempting to have a child have experienced infertility. Most authorities regard this figure as too high, however. The rule of thumb currently popular among infertility specialists is "one couple in six" (i.e., a rate of 16.6 percent).

29. Marcia Herman-Giddens et al., "Secondary Sexual Characteristics and Menses in Young Girls Seen in Office Practice," *Pediatrics* 99, no. 4 (1997): 505–12.

30. Paul Kaplowitz et al., "Re-examination of the Age Limit for Defining When Puberty Is Precocious in Girls in the United States: Implications for Evaluation and Treatment," *Pediatrics* 104, no. 4 (1999): 936–41.

31. Ivelisse Colón et al., "Identification of Phthalate Esters in the Serum of Young Puerto Rican Girls with Premature Breast Development," *Environmental Health Perspectives* 108, no. 9 (2000): 895–900.

32. Pisani, Parkin, and Feraly, "Estimates of the Worldwide Mortality From Eighteen Major Cancers in 1985," *International Journal of Cancer* 55, no. 6 (1993): 891–903.

33. J.L. Standford et al., "Breast Cancer Incidence in Asian Migrants to the United States and Their Descendants," *Epidemiology* 6, no. 2 (1995): 181–83.

34. Judy Mohraz, "Missing Men on Campus," *Washington Post*, 16 January 2000.

35. See Jerome Nriagu's book, *Lead and Lead Poisoning in Antiquity* (Baltimore: Johns Hopkins University Press, 1983). See also Lionel and Diane Needleman, "Lead Poisoning and the Decline of the Roman Aristocracy," *Classical Views* 4, no. 1 (1985): 63–94.

36. T.K. Jensen et al., "Semen Quality Among Members of Organic Food Associations in Zealand, Denmark," *Lancet* 347 (1996): 1844.

Leonard Sax, M.D., Ph.D., is a physician and psychologist practicing in Montgomery County, Maryland.

From *The World & I*, October 2001, pp. 263-275. © 2001 by The World & I, a publication of The Washington Times Corporation. Reprinted by permission.

THE HAPPY DIVORCE

HOW TO BREAK UP AND MAKE UP

BY NORA UNDERWOOD

For a decade, Tom Cruise and Nicole Kidman were Hollywood's patron saints of marriage. When not giving relentless interviews about how they were each other's best friend, they were swinging their two children between them on sunny afternoon walks, posing in couture or snuggling at film openings. Whatever it really was, the marriage seemed like something out of a fairy tale. When it ended—suddenly, to the rest of the world—there were predictions about how ugly the divorce proceedings were going to be. Reportedly there was nastiness behind the scenes, but in public the Hollywood couple seemed to do divorce as perfectly as they'd done marriage. In a few hours one day last November, together at a final meeting with their lawyers, they hammered out how their considerable assets would be split and how custody of the children would be arranged. They even parted ways with an embrace. "We are great friends," Cruise said of Kidman in an interview with *People* magazine shortly after their divorce was negotiated. "She is someone who I love and always will."

> ## "If there are children or a business, friendly divorce is the way to go. But that means having to grit your teeth a little."

In a perfect world, we'd all live happily ever after with the people to whom we had pledged ourselves. Short of that, we'd divorce as (apparently) amicably as Kidman and Cruise did. In reality, 36 per cent of Canadian marriages are expected to end in divorce, a number that has remained relatively stable for decades; the average duration of a marriage that ends, according to Statistics Canada, is just under 14 years. (The oft-cited statistic of almost one in two marriages failing is in fact American—the figure is 43 per cent.) According to Diana Shepherd, editor of Toronto-based *Divorce Magazine*, most North American couples manage to divorce in a civilized way;

only 10 per cent are the nasty, bitter feuds that are the stuff of tabloids and made-for-TV movies. "If there are children or a business involved, a friendly divorce is the only way to go," says Shepherd. "And sometimes friendly means having to grit your teeth a little bit and get on with it, let it go." Until recently there has been little recourse for couples who wanted to avoid the notoriously adversarial legal process for divorce. But a growing number of people are seeking out mediators to help broker a peaceful legal ending, or taking part in divorce ceremonies and rituals to help bring about emotional resolution. In addition, a kinder, gentler legal practice known as collaborative law, which started in the United States during the early 1990s, has moved north and is starting to spread through parts of Canada.

This evolution has been precipitated by a number of factors, not the least being the children of divorce. A growing body of research points decisively to the fact that kids have a much harder time adjusting to new family dynamics when their parents are bickering or engaged in full-scale war. "We did a video of children talking about the impact of divorce," says Rhonda Freeman, director of Families in Transition for the Family Service Association of Toronto. "A nine-year-old in the film said, with a very quizzical look on her face, 'If parents choose to live apart, why do they need to keep fighting?'" There is also strong evidence, Freeman says, that the kids who do best are the ones who feel free to have positive relationships with both parents—particularly parents who have moved on in their own lives. "And that includes ending the conflict," adds Freeman. "Because while you're involved in the conflict, you just don't have the emotional energy or time to devote to your children."

Martin and Deborah (unless full names are given, people cited have been given pseudonyms on request) met when they were 12, got married eight years later, started a retail business together, and raised two children. But 10 years ago, after two decades of marriage, each became involved with someone else. For the sake of the kids (now grown and away from home), as much as for their own, the Ontario couple decided to continue cohabiting—they have never divorced. "I think it's possible that people can go in different directions sometimes without losing the love for the person," explains Martin, who still lives with Deborah and the man Deborah fell in love with a decade ago. "The fact that it hasn't worked out exactly right doesn't mean you should lose sight of what brought you together in the first place."

There are usually other casualties when a long-term relationship breaks up, but Martin and Deborah have managed to maintain positive connections with each other's families as well as with all their friends. And while the community has never fully adjusted to the couple's decision to continue living together, it was best for the kids. "For them it was better than living separately," says Deborah. "They found it difficult to explain to their friends, but their friends all grew to really care about us and all of the weird stuff that people thought was going on was forgotten. Our daughter told us she's really proud of us."

While Martin knew rationally the new arrangement was for the best, it still took him about five years to feel completely comfortable with it emotionally. "But I was lucky that her partner was a person I found to be a very good man, who understood how it would be difficult for me for the love of my life to be with a different person." Martin, meanwhile, has had relationships; one girlfriend even joined the family for a while, but there was friction with Deborah over parenting issues. Overall, says Martin, the struggle was worth it. "Continuity is really important," adds Martin, who still runs a business with Deborah. "For me, a journey through life is far more interesting if you don't force dislocations into it that aren't necessary."

Calgary couple Kate and Tom had been married for 18 of their 20 years together. They had two children, now 17 and 14, and lived happily for a number of years. After a while, though, Kate started to feel lonely in the marriage—that Tom "wasn't there emotionally"—though she concedes she also played a role in the marriage's demise. Finally, just before Christmas two years ago, she asked him to move out.

Despite the grief and anger they both felt as they were separating, Kate and Tom discussed how they needed to manage the situation for the children's sake. "We've worked really hard at being civilized," says Kate, now 47 (Tom is 55). "We never, ever say anything bad about each other because of the kids and because it doesn't pay." The children spend more time with their mother, but Kate makes sure Tom knows everything that's going on at school and at her home. She even suspects the time may come when she and her ex-husband will be good friends. "We were together a very long time," she says, "and I don't think you stop loving someone."

The couple were clear from the beginning that an acrimonious parting wouldn't benefit anyone. "I don't think

you can move on and build a life and have any fun if you're putting energy into being mean or being difficult—or even being right," Kate adds. "It just doesn't pay. Living and loving takes enough energy. Living and hating is just a huge waste of time."

Children may be one of the strongest incentives for divorcing couples to be civil to—or even friends with—each other. But there are other potent factors, among them the very real differences between how this and previous generations view divorce. "Many of the people who are getting divorced today were in fact children of parental divorce, so it does, in a sense, become normalized in a culture," says Robert Glossop, co-executive director of the Ottawa-based Vanier Institute of the Family. "One might speculate that having had the experience of divorce, they do understand how difficult or traumatic it can be. We may be maturing a little bit as a society that recognizes that relationships are fragile, vulnerable and do break up, and that we need to minimize the effects of divorce on children."

Glossop also speculates that because people tend to get married later than they used to, they might approach divorce more maturely. Until recently, there were few options to help people who weren't able to get along in marriage to make a proper go of divorce. But in recent years, more and more couples—and lawyers—are dropping their weapons and abandoning the court system. Divorce mediation is becoming increasingly prevalent, and a growing number of family lawyers are opting out of litigation.

Talking to a collaborative lawyer is like speaking to someone who has just seen the light. For many of the divorce and family lawyers who switch over to collaborative law, there's a profound sense of relief. Years of dealing with angry couples and displaced children take their toll. Traditional divorce, says Brampton, Ont.-based lawyer Victoria Smith, "is so expensive, it takes so long and the outcomes are so unpredictable." A collaborative divorce typically costs between $5,000 and $10,000, while a divorce that ends up in court could cost as much as $70,000. Ultimately, she adds, the things people really care about often aren't dealt with. "Most people who go into family law do it because they want to help," says Smith. "I was really having a sense that we lawyers are often making things worse. Our training is to get the biggest piece of the pie for our client, and in family matters that doesn't work. Relationships were damaged. We often made them worse."

Morrie Sacks's passionate desire to practise family law stemmed from the lingering effects of his own parents' divorce during the 1950s. But he often felt frustrated by the way the system worked. "In the adversarial model, you're waging war and there's this whole idea of victors and losers—the wife looking for maximums and the husband trying to part with minimums," says the Vancouver

THE GAY BREAKUP: NOT SO GAY

Financial strain, intimacy and communication problems, loss of love, parenting differences— many of the issues that may ultimately divide a heterosexual union are identical to those that can split a same-sex relationship. But gay couples must grapple with additional challenges, both in their relationships and in the event of separation. Canadian figure skater Brian Orser famously illustrated one of those challenges in 1998 when his former partner, Craig Leask, brought a palimony suit against him. Orser tried, unsuccessfully, to have the court record of the case sealed, fearing that his career could be harmed once his sexual preference became public knowledge.

In fact, the issue of how "out" a same-sex couple is even when the partners are together can be an added source of stress. "I don't know of very many couples where both people are in the same place at the same time about how public they are about the relationship," says Lori, a health-care worker in her late 30s who, with her partner, social-services employee Lynn, has a two-year-old child (biological mother Lori became pregnant through artificial insemination). The Calgary couple has also experienced the lack of recourse a non-biological parent has to a child once the relationship with the biological parent is over. Lynn has a 13-year-old from a prior union, and had attempted to get legal guardianship of the child when he was five, a few years after she and the biological mother had broken up. But she was denied. Finally, when he turned 12, she tried again and won. Lynn has guardianship status with her child with Lori, but notes that it has less legal heft than adoption.

There are other unique parenting issues to resolve, according to Calgary mediator Lorri Yasenik. A lesbian couple, for example, may have allowed for some access between their child and the sperm donor. "Now we have to organize how it will look if they reorganize themselves into new couples—four mother figures and a donor who may come in and out of the picture," she explains.

Neither has there been, until recently, any precedent regarding spousal support and asset-splitting. But in 1999, in a case known as M versus H, the Supreme Court of Canada ruled it as unfair that a Toronto lesbian had no rights to sue a former partner for support. The following year, Ottawa passed Bill C-23, which ruled that same-sex couples were entitled to the same federally legislated benefits, obligations and status as heterosexual common-law couples.

As Toronto gay rights lawyer Douglas Elliott notes, each province protects the rights of same-sex couples to different extents, but at least now there is a constitutional imperative for support. Still, he adds, because there isn't as reliable a legal framework for same-sex couples, "It does create greater uncertainty and that can create a more contentious approach than would occur in a heterosexual situation." In addition, he says, AIDS may be a complicating factor because if one partner is disabled, the other may have a lifetime obligation to him.

Elliott strongly encourages same-sex couples to draw up prenuptial agreements. But that advice flies in the face of human nature, gay or straight. "I think it's pretty typical of all couples, regardless of their sexuality, to enter into a relationship in a very trusting manner and assume everything will be fine," says Lynn. "So there's not a lot of, 'Let's sit down and draw up a lot of forms—let's go see a lawyer'"

Nora Underwood

lawyer. "In the collaborative model, the shift is to interest-based negotiation, how can problems be resolved. A win-win solution is the goal." Sacks found out about collaborative law two years ago from a client. "This was a gift from God as far as I was concerned," he adds. "We talk about a paradigm shift but that hardly does it justice. It's more like a quantum leap."

How it works—and it only works for people who are looking for a peaceable resolution, not for those hiding assets or out for revenge—is that each person hires a collaborative lawyer and all four proceed through the divorce as a team. Typically, collaborative lawyers also have like-minded child specialists, financial advisers and business valuators on call to help deal with particularly troublesome aspects. Going to court is not an option. "The belief is that people can make their own decisions," explains Smith. "You're still acting as that person's lawyer, but in addition you're acting as a facilitator, providing people with the support they need to make those decisions, making sure they have an opportunity to go beneath the positions they bring in the door and think about what's important in the long term."

John and his wife separated last summer after almost 10 years of marriage. The 36-year-old construction supervisor living in Brampton loves her but found they had little in common apart from their three children. "I could've stayed for the kids," says John. "But between the time I was 12 and 24, my parents went through that. They shot daggers at each other, and I hated it with a passion so I was not going to put my kids through that." Despite how angry his wife was with him—he had an affair before he and his wife separated—she wanted to mediate a settlement together. The couple's primary objective was to remain friends with each other. "It hurt, but the fact that we could sit at a table—and yes, there were tears shed—was a very positive experience," says John. "It was four people, all friends, trying to find solutions and coming up with suggestions."

In the end, according to Calgary mediator Janis Magnuson, that is really what most people prefer. "People want their marriage to end decently," says Magnuson, who runs a business called Constructive Divorce. "They don't want it to cost an arm and a leg and they don't want to hate each other. This process allows people to end relationships respectfully, effectively and efficiently."

A handful of couples are even turning to divorce ceremonies, rituals that signal the end of a relationship and the beginning of a new life apart. Such a ritual has existed in Judaism for millenniums: traditionally, a husband gives a *get* (the Hebrew word for the divorce document) to his wife to free her to remarry; now, in liberal congregations, either spouse can initiate a *get*. Phil Penningroth and his wife of 25 years, Barbara, whom he divorced in 1997, drew on that and other ceremonies for *A Healing Divorce*, their 2001 book about how to symbolically seal a divorce. "I don't think any relationship ends without a lot of strong feelings," says Phil, who lives in Longmont, Colo. "We did not want to let our conflicts carry us away into acrimony and bitterness and estrangement. There were a lot of good things in our relationship and we wanted to do our best to preserve those things, even as we decided to divorce."

In their ceremony, attended by friends, the Penningroths played a video tribute to the marriage, spoke of forgiveness and regrets and of the gratitude they felt for the relationship they'd had. "Marriages, funerals, bar mitzvahs—there are scads and scads of different rituals,"

he says. "The symbols involved in a ritual speak far more powerfully than the words in a divorce decree." Adds Penningroth: "When my father got divorced in the mid-1950s, as far as he was concerned it was just a fight. How can anyone be against something that creates harmony and peace, especially when there are children involved?"

But like any healthy marriage, a good divorce requires commitment and a lot of hard work. "It's still a relationship," says *Divorce* editor Shepherd. "Your marriage is ending but your relationship isn't ending if you have children. It needs to change but it's not over." The payoffs are big for divorced couples who have struggled through the anger and grief and made peace with each other. Judy Moody's first husband was her childhood sweetheart. She married him at 18, after she got pregnant, and within a couple of years they had a second child. But after about five years, the marriage fell apart, and Moody left. They struggled through a few years of arguing and bitterness, and even tried to reconcile once, but ultimately decided to build a post-marital friendship.

Around her Christmas table seven years ago were Moody and her children, her first husband, his wife, Moody's second husband, her in-laws and her former in-laws. "I was never so happy in my whole life because my whole family was there," recalls Moody, who lives in Sutton, Ont. Over the years since their divorce—Moody is now 56—she and her ex-husband have been through a lot together, including the death of their son, Andrew, in 1996. "Bill comes over and we sit and we talk about Andrew and what could have been and what was, and we cry and we laugh and we have a bond. He's the only person I can sit and talk to like that." To Moody and to others who have worked at having a good divorce, the relationship is a natural. "I have a history with him that I don't have with anyone else," says Moody. "When I see him, it's like seeing the best, oldest friend in the world, and I love him with all my heart."

From *Maclean's* January 21, 2002, pp. 25-29. © 2002 by Maclean Hunter Ltd. Reprinted by permission.

THE COMING JOB BOOM

The help-wanted ads may look thin—but thanks to aging baby boomers, that's about to change

By DANIEL EISENBERG

AT A TIME WHEN THE JOB MARKET still seems bleak, the outlook for Alex and Cindi Ignatovsky, both 33, could not be much brighter. After trying out a number of different careers, the Aptos, Calif., couple have recently discovered their true callings. Alex, who had been a paralegal and had also done a brief stint as an insurance salesman, has just started working as a juvenile-probation officer, helping kids wend their way through the crowded criminal-justice system. Cindi, who previously was an editor and a graphic designer, is now busy finishing up an intensive, multiyear program to become an acupuncturist. In her view, as she puts it, "there's as much opportunity as I make of it."

She's right, about both her and her husband's prospects—but not just because they're passionate and adept at what they do. They have also, as it turns out, each chosen fields—in his case, law enforcement and social services, in hers, health care—that are feeling the first ef-

fects of the coming job boom. That's right. Even as thousands of Americans are still getting pink slips, powerful help is on the way. And it has more to do with demographics than economics. The oldest members of the huge baby-boom generation are now 56, and as they start retiring, job candidates with the right skills will be in hot demand. As Mitch Potter of human-resources consultant William M. Mercer says, "The dotcom bubble created a false talent crunch. The real one is coming."

In certain industries, especially those in which burnout and early retirement are common and demand for services is rising, the crunch has already arrived. As the population ages, hospitals can't find enough nurses or medical technicians. Drugstores are competing to hire pharmacists, bidding some beginners' salaries above $75,000. School districts and universities will need 2.2 million more teachers over the next decade, not to mention administrators and librarians, and are already avidly recruiting.

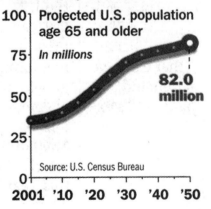

GRAY WAVE Many boomers are retiring, and their numbers will shoot up after 2010

Projected U.S. population age 65 and older

In millions

82.0 million

Source: U.S. Census Bureau

2001 '10 '20 '30 '40 '50

Homeowners can't get their calls returned by skilled contractors, electricians or plumbers. Corporations are scooping up accountants and engineers. For job seekers who have the right skills or are willing to learn them, there are real opportunities in government, construction and technology.

THE HOT JOBS

Some occupations with the largest projected growth, 2000-2010
(*Change in number of jobs*)

Teachers (K-12)	+711,000
Computer-Software Engineers	+664,000
Registered Nurses	+561,000
Truck Drivers	+561,000
Computer-Support Specialists	+490,000
Accountants and Auditors	+181,000
Marketing and Sales Managers	+168,000
Auto Mechanics	+151,000
Health Therapists	+145,000
Police and Sheriff's Officers	+141,000
Social Workers	+141,000
Engineers	+138,000
Lawyers	+123,000
Electricians	+120,000
Recreation and Fitness Workers	+118,000
Sales Representatives	+118,000

THE COLD JOBS

Some occupations with the largest projected losses, or smallest growth, 2000-2010

Farmers and Ranchers	-328,000
Phone-Switchboard Operators	-60,000
Bank Tellers	-59,000
Insurance-Claims Clerks	-58,000
Word Processors/Typists	-57,000
Sewing-Machine Operators	-51,000
Butchers	-13,000
Meter Readers	-13,000
Parts Salespeople	-12,000
Procurement Clerks	-9,000
Movie Projectionists	-3,000
Proofreaders	-2,000
Loggers	-2,000
Funeral Directors	+1,000
Insurance Underwriters	+2,000
Travel Agents	+4,000

Source: Bureau of Labor Statistics

To millions of laid-off workers still pounding the pavement, of course, this might seem like wishful thinking. While the economy grew a whopping 5.8% in the first quarter of 2002, the job market usually lags by at least a few months. To land a job, record numbers of workers are taking pay cuts or switching industries, according to outplacement firm Challenger, Gray & Christmas; many others are starting their own small businesses. But as hard as it may be to believe, it should not be too long before employees are in the driver's seat. A wave of retirements whose full effect is only starting to be felt will soon ripple through the entire economy. And the savviest workers and employers are already preparing for it.

Though the average retirement age is creeping up—and a growing share of Americans, by choice or necessity, are planning to work at least part time well past 65—demographers say there still will not be enough qualified members of the next generation to pick up the slack. So with 76 million baby boomers heading toward retirement over the next three decades and only 46 million Gen Xers waiting in the wings, corporate America is facing a potentially mammoth talent crunch. Certainly, labor-saving technology and immigration may help fill the breach. Still, by 2010 there may be a shortage of 4 million to 6 million workers.

CINDI IGNATOVSKY

After stints as an editor and a graphic designer, the Aptos, Calif., resident, 33, is training for a career in acupuncture

Not enough Americans are trained for these jobs. They lack everything from computer literacy and leadership to critical thinking and communication skills. The recent slump, though, may be helping narrow the skills gap in a surprising way. Although generous social-welfare systems in industrialized countries such as Germany and Britain make it easy for the laid off to wait around for a factory to reopen, Americans tend to take the initiative during a downturn, getting educated or trained for a better job and in the process adding to the country's stock of human capital. Applications to graduate programs in everything from law and business to education and engineering are up from last year by 30%–100%. That approach should pay off. Although 1.9 million Americans with a high school diploma or less got the ax from September 2000 to October 2001—a time when the economy was slumping—1.2 million people with college or vocational degrees were hired, according to the Employment Policy Foundation.

ANN CALLAHAN

A flight attendant for most of the last 30 years, Callahan, 53, is now a nurse in the neonatal clinic at Baptist General Hospital in Kendall, Fla.

It isn't just the younger generation that's going back to school, either. Bruce LeBel, 59, a veteran aircraft mechanic who lost his job after Sept. 11, is learning how to service the computer networks that help run more and more factories and power plants. Many of his former colleagues "are afraid to try anything different. They want to stay with a dead horse," he says. "But the only thing that can save me is having a skill that's in demand." To help other job hunters follow LeBel's example, here's a guide to the best job opportunities today—and tomorrow.

A HEALTHY PROGNOSIS

If lately you have had to wait to fill a prescription or get your doctor on the phone, you know why no industry holds more promise than health care.

• **CAREGIVERS** Nurses and pharmacists aren't the only ones being snapped up by hospitals. All across the country, sonogram operators, who make a median salary of $42,000, and radiology techni-

Firms Brace For a Worker Shortage

Last spring, when Daimler Chrysler offered early retirement to thousands of older autoworkers, it got more than it bargained for. So many people accepted the deal that the company faced a potential shortage of critical skills at its plants and had to withdraw some offers. With half the auto industry's work force eligible to retire in the next five years, Ford and GM took Chrysler's lead and scaled back their early-retirement programs.

In the wake of the past year's downsizing, and with the economy growing again, it won't be too long before the rest of corporate America follows the automakers in slamming their personnel policies into reverse. The smartest firms are already changing the way they recruit. Instead of filling positions as they open up, companies are developing a "constant pipeline of qualified candidates," says Kathy McGirr, senior vice president of talent acquisition and development at Fidelity Investments. With the help of software start-up Hire.com, Fidelity has developed a pool of 17,000 internal candidates for promotion or transfer, plus more than 100,000 outside prospects.

Much as colleges do with alumni, some companies, including Agilent Technologies, are nurturing ties with former employees and hiring them back as needed. Other firms are urging older workers to stay around longer. Ohio cosmetics maker Bonne Bell has created a separate factory floor with its own parking, bathroom and exercise room for 100 employees 55 and older.

IBM Canada and Monsanto have pioneered the use of on-call retirees. More than 600 ex-workers take part in Monsanto's Retiree Resource Corps, which encourages them—former managers, tax lawyers and secretaries—to return to plug temporary staffing gaps for as much as 1,000 hours a year (the maximum allowed without jeopardizing retirement benefits). In the process, they pass on their vast institutional memory.

As the talent wars heat up again, and a growing number of workers opt to be independent contractors or to job hop at will, managers will also have to work harder than ever to retain people and develop all of them—not just standouts—to their fullest potential. Rather than dampening the rush toward free agency, many observers believe the recent ax wielding will only encourage it. "It's not that everybody is dying to be a free agent," says Bruce Tulgan, author of *Winning the Talent Wars* (W.W. Norton & Co.). "It's that people are realizing they have no choice." And companies will soon have no choice but to accept that their best workers are holding most of the cards.

—By Daniel Eisenberg. With reporting by Joseph R. Szczesny/Detroit

cians are being hired. The people who help patients get back on their feet are also hot properties. Over the next decade, according to the Bureau of Labor Statistics, there will be 255,000 openings for all manner of therapists, including physical and respiratory therapists and speech pathologists.

• **DRUGMAKERS** Firms that dream up wonder drugs are in one of the few industries that have continued to hire in droves. Swiss-based Novartis AG, which has embarked on a major expansion in the U.S., hired more than 1,800 workers last year and plans to keep hiring at a brisk pace. That includes everyone from marketing and manufacturing staff to people in finance, human resources and, of course, research science. This array of jobs pays anywhere from $30,000 to $300,000 a year. Likewise,

Abbott Laboratories hopes to fill 5,000 new positions this year, including posts for sales reps who can drive product launches.

• **GENE HUNTERS** The much hyped biotech industry is finally starting to deliver on its promise, with more small companies shifting from basic research to drug development. That means more jobs, from lab work to medical writing, are in the pipeline as well. Genentech, based in South San Francisco, Calif., is increasing its head count each year by 297, or about 6% annually, hiring everyone from Ph.D.s to community-college grads who can work in manufacturing. Just in the budding field of bioinformatics, in which specialists can make more than $100,000 a year using computers to plow through reams of genetic data, there will be an estimated 20,000 unfilled jobs by 2005.

Chemists are also being wooed across industries.

UNCLE SAM WANTS YOU

Long before Sept. 11 ushered in a new era of respect for government, Washington was poised to enjoy an unlikely job boom. Almost half the Federal Government's 1.8 million workers will be eligible to retire within five years. From the Food and Drug Administration (FDA) and Park Service to the Commerce, Energy and State departments, agencies are bracing for a brain drain, especially at the managerial level. And these aren't your classic paper-pushing jobs—although many of those, as at the busy Social Security Administration, are also going begging.

- **LAW ENFORCEMENT** Organizations—from the FBI and the CIA to the Coast Guard and the Defense, Justice and State departments—are revving up their recruiting efforts, looking for everyone from computer programmers, budding young diplomats and spooks to lawyers and linguists. The Immigration and Naturalization Service wants to hire thousands of new border-patrol guards and immigration inspectors to process and keep better track of new arrivals to the country; these positions require just a high school diploma and, with overtime, can pay around $40,000 in the first year.

- **BIG THINKERS** To help assess the growing tide of innovations that washes across its desks, the Patent and Trademark Office is desperate to find more qualified engineers and intellectual-property lawyers. Other high-end specialists are needed, such as drug reviewers at the FDA; accountants and statisticians at the Labor and Treasury departments, the Internal Revenue Service and the Securities and Exchange Commission; and trade experts at Commerce.

GET YOUR HANDS DIRTY

In the dotcom mania of the '90s, it was easy to forget that skilled tradespeople can make good money.

- **CONSTRUCTION** A recent industry study showed that at least one-third of St. Louis' 80,000 construction workers are expected to retire in the next five years—a microcosm of the situation nationwide; the industry needs to attract 240,000 new workers each year, from project managers to iron workers, just to compensate for the exodus. The top tradespeople in their fields, such as plumbers, electricians, carpenters, bricklayers, roofers and painters, can make upward of $100,000 a year.

- **MANUFACTURING** Even in this beleaguered sector, in which many firms have made huge layoffs, companies are having a hard time finding the right people. More than 80% of firms say they face a shortage of qualified machinists, craft workers and technicians, according to a recent survey by the National Association of Manufacturers. That

deficit is likely to widen. Although manufacturing will not grow much overall during the next decade, a rapidly aging work force will create more than 2 million job openings—with many positions paying more than $50,000—for welders, tool- and diemakers, line managers and others.

- **TECHNICIANS** As machines keep getting more complex, with tiny microprocessors governing their every move, finding enough people to repair and maintain them is becoming harder. Heating and air-conditioning technicians are in high demand. Nationwide there are about 60,000 vacancies for car mechanics, who can earn anywhere from $30,000 to $100,000.

ENGINEERING THE FUTURE

Despite the layoffs from busted dotcoms, jobs will be abundant in other areas of technology. Computer storage, enterprise software and semiconductors are still growth areas. Analysts expect corporate information-technology spending to stabilize this year and rebound in 2003.

BRUCE LEBEL

Laid off after 9/11, the 59-year-old aircraft mechanic from Belleflower, Calif., has learned to service computer networks that help run many factories

- **ENGINEERS** Over the past 15 years, the number of students graduating with a bachelor's degree in engineering dropped 50%, to 12,400. Companies like Texas Instruments are hiring electrical engineers for product-design, sales and marketing departments. Other engineers—software, mechanical, aerospace, civil and structural—are also hot properties.

- **COMPUTER MONITORS** Computer-related jobs will be among the fastest growing in the next decade. Leading the way will be those key employees who help large companies maintain their daunting tangles of technology, from system analysts and support specialists to database administrators.

THE DESK SET

Thousands of investment bankers, consultants and lawyers have become casualties of the latest round of corporate downsizing. But the long-range picture looks better. As baby boomers scale back their time at the office to concentrate on other activities, from golf to philanthropy, corporate America will be desperate to find qualified managers and executives as well as support staff, from administrative assistants to paralegals.

- **FINANCE AND ACCOUNTING** H&R Block has been busy hiring 1,200 financial advisers and marketing staff members as it broadens its tax-preparing business. Financial-services firms continue to look for financial planners and asset managers. Despite their role at Enron and in other corporate scandals this year, accounting and auditing are especially attractive fields, expected to grow nearly 20% in the next decade.

SANDY AND DAVE JENDAL

Since losing their corporate jobs, both wife and husband, who live in Aurora, Ill., have started small businesses, hers in house painting and his in Web services

- **ENERGY** The oil, gas and utility sector is bringing on finance and marketing graduates to help navigate deregulation. Companies such as TXU, Exxon Mobil and Koch Industries are still hiring. A graying work force means the industry also needs to find a new generation of petroleum engineers, geologists and geophysicists.

TO KEEP PACE IN TODAY'S FAST-MOVING economy, job hunters must be, above all, flexible. Steve Reyna, 28, who four years ago went to work at TDIndustries, a Dallas-based mechanical contractor that specializes in air-conditioning and plumbing projects for high-tech companies, knows this better than most. After training as a sheet-metal technician, Reyna moved on to work in the so-called clean rooms of semiconductor companies, learning a little welding and plumbing along the way. Just one of more than 1,300 employees at TDIndustries who are rigorously cross-trained, Reyna is now ready to work "wherever they need me." If the number crunchers turn out to be right, that could soon mean just about everywhere.

—With reporting by Cathy Booth Thomas/Dallas, Unmesh Kher/New York, Sean Scully/Los Angeles, Maggie Sieger and Leslie Whitaker/Chicago, Daniel Terdiman/San Francisco, with other bureaus

From *Time*, May 6, 2002, pp. 40-44. © 2002 by Time, Inc. Magazine Company. Reprinted by permission.

UNIT 6

Development During Middle and Late Adulthood

Unit Selections

Key Points to Consider

- Should middle-aged men replace their declining testosterone with supplements?

- What options exist for women with menopausal discomforts? How safe is HRT?

- Does 16 million Americans having diabetes constitute an epidemic? Why is it so common?

- What hard truths should workers know to keep their jobs in America?

- How does the new unretirement work? Why is it being so highly praised?

- Can new imaging technology diagnose early signs of brain deterioration before dementing conditions do much damage? How close are scientists to understanding, treating, and/or preventing Alzheimer's disease?

- What new insights have come from the study of the Mankato nuns?

- What are the differences between end-of-life care options, such as hospitals, nursing homes, hospice facilities, and in-home hospice care?

 **Links: www.dushkin.com/online/**
These sites are annotated in the World Wide Web pages.

The Alzheimer Page
http://www.biostat.wustl.edu/ALZHEIMER/

American Psychological Association's Division 20, Adult Development and Aging
http://www.aging.ufl.edu/apadiv20/apadiv20.htm

Grief Net
http://rivendell.org

National Aging Information Center (NAIC)
http://www.aoa.dhhs.gov/naic/

Rose.Net's "For Seniors Only"
http://www.rose.net/seniors.htm

Joseph Campbell, a twentieth-century sage, said that the privilege of a lifetime is being who you are. This ego-confidence often arrives during middle and late adulthood, even as physical-confidence declines. There is a gradual slowing of the rate of mitosis of cells of all the organ systems with age. This gradual slowing of mitosis translates into a slowed rate of repair of cells of all organs. By the 40s, signs of aging can be seen in skin, skeleton, vision, hearing, smell, taste, balance, coordination, heart, blood vessels, lungs, liver, kidneys, digestive tract, immune response, endocrine functioning, and ability to reproduce. To some extent, moderate use of any body part (as opposed to disuse or misuse) helps it retain its strength, stamina, and repairability. However, by middle and late adulthood, persons become increasingly aware of the aging effects of their organ systems on their total physical fitness. A loss of height occurs as spinal disks and connective tissues diminish and settle. Demineralization, especially loss of calcium, causes weakening of bones. Muscles atrophy, and the slowing of cardiovascular and respiratory responses creates a loss of stamina for exercise. All of this may seem cruel, but it occurs very gradually and need not adversely affect a person's enjoyment of life.

Healthful aging, at least in part, seems to be genetically preprogrammed. The females of many species, including humans, outlive the males. The sex hormones of females may protect them from some early aging effects. Males, in particular, experience earlier declines in their cardiovascular system. Diet and exercise can ward off many of the deleterious effects of aging. A reduction in saturated fat (low density lipid) intake coupled with regular aerobic exercise contributes to less bone demineralization, less plaque in the arteries, stronger muscles (including heart and lung muscles), and a general increase in stamina and vitality. An adequate intake of complex carbohydrates, fibrous foods, fresh fruits, fresh vegetables, unsaturated fats (high density lipids), and water also enhances good health.

Cognitive abilities do not appreciably decline with age in healthy adults. Research suggests that the speed with which the brain carries out problems involving abstract (fluid) reasoning may slow, but not cease. Complex problems may simply require more time to solve with age. On the other hand, research suggests that the memory banks of older people may have more crystallized (accumulated and stored) knowledge and more insight. Creativity also frequently spurts after age 50. One's ken (range of knowledge) and practical skills (common sense) grow with age and experience. Older human beings also become expert at the cognitive tasks they frequently do. Many cultures celebrate these abilities as the "wisdom of age."

The first article about middle adulthood speaks to the question of "Man Power." Are older men wiser? Do they make more sense and therefore merit their positions of leadership? Jim Thornton discusses his own experience with supplementation of testosterone, the male hormone. He concludes that the high testosterone levels of younger men may contribute to their impulsivity and aggressiveness and hurt their occupational achievement. Lower levels have their own benefits for older men.

The second article about middle adulthood speaks to the flip side of "Man Power" by "Sorting Through the Confusion Over Estrogen." While hormone replacement therapy (HRT) can reduce the hot flashes and night sweats that traumatize some midlife women, it is not the wonder drug it was once thought to be. Jane Brody discusses the new negative findings published in early 2002.

The third article discusses the explosion of new cases of diabetes in the United States. Sixteen million Americans have been diagnosed, and many more undiscovered cases probably exist. Diabetes does have a genetic basis. However, it is more likely that the gene for type-2 diabetes, the most common form of the disease, will be expressed when a person is overweight and gets relatively little physical exercise. This article tells how diabetes affects the body and describes some of the treatments used to control it.

The fourth adulthood selection outlines "12 Things You Must Know to Survive and Thrive in America." Ellis Cose's article is described as a roster of hard truths for a new age. They may be hard, but they are also valuable truths that everyone needs to know to succeed.

Erik Erikson suggested that the most important psychological conflict of late adulthood is achieving a sense of ego integrity. This is fostered by self-respect, self-esteem, love of others, and a sense that one's life has order and meaning. The articles in the subsection on late adulthood reflect Erikson's concern with experiencing ego integrity rather than despair.

"The New Unretirement" describes the art of making a second career an avenue toward self-fulfillment and ego integrity. Marc Freedman describes several role models for unretirement: seniors who have left jobs and allowed the change in their lives to be a prelude to growth and personal enrichment. They define themselves by what they can offer to the future. While they have pride in their pasts and what they accomplished, they now look to how far they can go by mentoring the young for tomorrow's challenges.

"The Disappearing Mind" describes the loss of memory that accompanies Alzheimer's and related diseases. It also explains how new imaging technology can diagnose dementing conditions much earlier than ever before. New treatments may be able to stop the dementia, and/or prevent it from ever occurring in the future.

The third article discusses the longitudinal study of Mankato nuns that has helped unlock many of the secrets of Alzheimer's disease. The Human Genome Project revealed where some genetic precursors are located. The nuns have now shed light on environmental triggers, and on lifestyles that protect the brain from mental deterioration. Cardiovascular disease and lack of folic acid are triggers. Cognitive exercises and positive emotions seem to help ward off mental deterioration.

The last article describes choices for end-of-life care. The hospice philosophy is explained. Advance directives, the costs of care, and survival tips for caregivers are also considered.

MAN POWER

ONE GUTSY GUY CHECKS OUT THE NEW **TESTOSTERONE GEL** AND FINDS THAT MASCULINITY IS FAR MORE THAN SKIN DEEP

BY JIM THORTON

THE PHARMACIST HANDS ME A SMALL BOX CONTAINING 30 foil pouches that resemble those miniature ketchup packets at a fast-food joint. In exchange for this one-month supply of AndroGel, the new easy-to-use testosterone supplement, I fork over $170—an expense I'm positive my insurance company won't cover.

The pharmacist tells me to rub the goo on my shoulder every day, preferably in the morning. "Don't accidentally get any on your wife," he adds, explaining this could "virilize" her—give her facial hair, deepening voice, and whatnot. "Make sure to wash your hands after applying it. And it's probably a good idea to wear a T-shirt during sex."

I tell him my first stop won't be the bedroom but the golf course, where I've challenged my prescribing urologist and former college buddy, Jay Hollander, to a round of match play at a club near his home in Detroit. The pharmacist chortles and says, "In that case, put some on right away and get your Big Bertha out!" I know he's joking, but part of me hopes there's a kernel of truth here. Since AndroGel hit the market last June, the media has been awash in hoopla about this latest magical elixir and its alleged fountain-of-youth effects on everything from sex drive to muscle mass.

Testosterone replacement isn't new, but earlier delivery systems had major drawbacks. Pills, for example, were linked to liver toxicity and are no longer recommended for use in men. Intramuscular injections require large needles and can be quite painful. Testosterone patches cause skin irritation in many men, and because they're so large—about a four-inch-by-four-inch square—it's hard to keep it private at the gym.

AndroGel is invisible and as easy to apply as lotion. Its main drawback is cost—as much as $180 per month versus $9 to $20 for injections. It's intended for men whose bodies fail to make enough natural testosterone, but we heard similar blather about Viagra, and now there's a whole subculture of nonimpotent users, from swingers to escorts, who reportedly pop the pills like sexual vitamins.

Might not AndroGel turn a hormone-normal guy into a turbocharged super male?

The experts say no. I say, let me find out for myself.

A half-hour after leaving the pharmacy, Jay and I stand on the first tee, surveying the fairway. Jay plays golf every other day; I play every other year. Still, I have a confidence bordering on cockiness that I'll win. My shoulder, after all, is well-anointed with man juice, which even now is leaching from my skin into my bloodstream, where it will join forces with the no-doubt whopping quantities my testicles—the body's testosterone factory—are already making.

'Will the gel turn me into a turbocharged super male?'

I almost feel sorry for Jay, who has only his pathetic endogenous testosterone to aid him in our match. Two hours earlier, he ran me through a battery of tests (see "Before You Go for the Goo…") to make sure there were no reasons, other than general foolhardiness, for me not to attempt this trial. My blood samples have been sent to the lab and will take a week or so to analyze. Still, both of us are confident this will be a formality. I'm in good shape. I've been swimming competitively since high school. In one month, I'll be competing in the U.S. Masters Swimming national championships in Baltimore. My physical exam and medical history both look fine. As the good doctor dictated into his recorder, "James Thornton is in excellent health, and his review of systems is entirely unremarkable."

As a lifelong hypochondriac, I'm thrilled by the word "unremarkable." And over the next few hours, I proceed to win the golf match by a comfortable four holes. In the rush of triumph, the high of victory, I can almost feel the testosterone surging through me.

Testosterone. Say it slowly and the syllables emanate sexual muscularity like a fine-tuned Italian race car.

BEFORE YOU GO FOR THE GOO...

Think you're a candidate for hormone replacement? Symptoms of low testosterone include erectile difficulty, reduced libido, fatigue, osteoporosis, breast enlargement, small testicles, infertility, reduced musculature, the loss of facial or body hair, and a lowered sense of well-being. According to Alvin Matsumoto, M.D., a professor of medicine at the University of Washington School of Medicine, you may need to undergo the following tests before taking testosterone supplements:

BLOOD TEST If your symptoms suggest low testosterone levels, most physicians will follow with a relatively inexpensive "total testosterone" test. If this comes back low or borderline, you may be asked to undergo more sophisticated tests for the "free" form of testosterone. Ideally, all such testing should be done in the morning when testosterone levels are highest. If the results point to hypogonadism, your doctor may want to repeat the tests. Testosterone levels often fluctuate, and changes can be triggered by everything from diet to stress. One low score doesn't mean you have a problem. (Men concerned with infertility may want to undergo a sperm count.)

ANALYSIS OF OTHER HORMONE LEVELS Your doctor may attempt to determine if your low testosterone problem is primary (the testicles aren't functioning normally) or secondary (the testicles aren't getting the right signals). Depending on what's happening, it may be possible to correct the problem without supplements.

PROSTATE EXAM Testosterone's chemical descendant, called DHT, fuels the growth of both healthy and cancerous prostate tissue. Because of this, men with known or suspected prostate cancer should probably not receive supplements. Ditto for men suffering from breast cancer. Even if you're cancer-free, you should have your PSA levels monitored if you use a supplement, since older men commonly have BPH (benign prostatic hyperplasia).

BLOOD COUNT AND LIPID PROFILE The phrase "red-blooded male" has a basis in fact. Testosterone, it turns out, increases the percentage of red blood cells in a man's bloodstream. If your hematocrit is high, supplemental testosterone can overly "thicken" your blood. There's also a slight chance that it can lower your "good" HDL cholesterol levels. Men with heart, kidney, or liver disease should be closely monitored if they receive testosterone. —J.T.

When sufficient quantities circulate in the blood of men, it turbocharges libido, sprouts beards, beefs up muscles, hardens bones, and inclines our minds toward the kind of rambunctious competitiveness that is both the signature blessing and occasional curse of masculinity.

Men start producing testosterone when we're still in the womb—as early as the twelfth week of pregnancy. But the real tsunami comes in adolescence. Testosterone circulates from the testicles to the blood, turning on the genes that make us men. By the time we turn 30, testosterone levels begin to decline at the rate of about 1 percent a year, though most men still produce enough for a healthy libido and healthy erections (that said, it's definitely more a hormone of desire than performance). The "normal" range for testosterone is quite broad—somewhere between 240 to 1,000 nanograms of the stuff per deciliter of blood. Trying to boost your level within the normal range can backfire.

"The key point to realize is that the human body balances," says Harvard researcher Richard Spark, M.D., author of Sexual Health for Men (Perseus, 2000). "When you give a normal man testosterone supplements, it just causes him to shut down his own internal production. Over time, his testicles will start to shrink."

Fortunately, this shrinkage is reversible once you stop taking supplements. There are other risks—from prostate problems to breast development to overly thickened blood—that make testosterone supplements ill-advised for men with normal levels, though the risk-to-benefit calculus shifts dramatically when your testosterone levels dip below normal. And by age 70, an estimated 10–25 percent of men have testosterone levels low enough to affect their sex drive and other aspects of mood and body physiology.

"When people hear 'low testosterone' they usually think about impaired sex drive, but that's really just the tip of the iceberg," says Ronald Swerdloff, M.D., chief of the division of endocrinology at Harbor-UCLA Medical Center. "Hypogonadism [low testosterone] can cause osteoporosis and decreased muscle strength in men, leaving them susceptible to falls and fractures. It can lead to abdominal obesity, low energy, and depressed mood and possibly even affect their thinking ability. With replacement therapy, these men often can enjoy a truly improved quality of life."

Multicenter studies presented by Swerdloff and his colleague, Christina Wang, M.D., at the Endocrine Society's annual meeting last June found that testosterone, whether administered by a patch or gel, did indeed improve sexual function, mood, muscle strength and mass, and body fat in hypogonadal men. Yet, according to the society, less than 200,000 of the four to five million American men who suffer hypogonadism are currently being treated for it. AndroGel may change that. Men may soon be slapping on testosterone like after-shave lotion. And based on the information I received from my urologist, I'm horrified to say this might include men like me.

It's a week later, and I'm staring in disbelief at my test results, which Jay's secretary has just faxed to my home in Pittsburgh. I skip over the few items that are normal and zero in on the many that aren't. Bottom line: My red blood cells, hemoglobin, and hematocrit (a measure of your blood's oxygen-carrying capacity) are all low—the telltale signature of anemia. Even worse, my pretreatment "free" testosterone (a form that isn't bound to other molecules and is readily available for use) is frighteningly close to the absolute bottom of the normal range.

"If it falls any farther," I tell my wife, Debbie, "you'd better start thinking about changing your sexual orientation."

Even to me, this forced levity rings with false bravado. I read on: lousy total cholesterol, sky-high "bad" LDL cholesterol, elevated chloride and BUN levels (whatever these might be). With intimations of mortality rattling my brain, I do what no hypochondriac should ever do: go on the Internet to learn about my conditions. I'll fast-forward through the details and simply say that of the dozens of explanations for my infirmities, the only ones that offer me any hope for survival are aspirin and alcohol abuse.

For much of my adult life, I've capped off each day with three or four beers, followed by a chaser of three or four aspirins. Doctors have long understood that hardcore alcoholic men frequently see their testosterone levels sink as a result of wretched nutrition and hormonal changes. But even worse for my system (though not necessarily my testosterone levels) is the aspirin. On one obscure Web site, I find the following: "In men and postmenopausal women, anemia is usually due to gastrointestinal blood loss associated with ulcers or the use of aspirin or [other] nonsteroidal anti-inflammatory medications [like ibuprofen]."

I decide on the spot to stop drinking and throw away my jumbo bottles of generic aspirin and ibuprofen. I also resolve to keep anointing myself with testosterone. I begin, as well, to fill out the paperwork to get reimbursed by my insurance company for the AndroGel. Disheartening as it is to admit, it looks like I have a legitimate need for it. I also try to console myself. Some experts say that diminishing testosterone may not be such a bad thing.

"I think you can make the case that some young men have too much testosterone and only when they get a little older do they become reasonable," says Stanley Korenman, M.D., a reproductive endocrinologist at UCLA School of Medicine. "Throughout history, the world has been run by older men. Young men make better soldiers because they're stronger, more aggressive, and more impulsive. Older men are wiser, they make more sense, and they are the ones who go into positions of leadership."

Georgia State psychology professor James Dabbs, Ph.D., says his research supports the idea that high testosterone hurts occupational achievement. Unemployed men, he found, have higher average testosterone levels than blue-collar workers, who in turn have higher average levels than white-collar workers. Waning testosterone may also make men better husbands and fathers. "It's very clear in birds," says Dabbs, "that the testosterone levels of the males drop dramatically once they start nesting." A study presented at the Endocrine Society's meeting last summer showed a similar drop in men following the birth of a child. Lowering testosterone with age, Dabbs speculates, may help predispose men to the gentler activities of parenthood. Bottom line: Men may need high testosterone to get a mate—and lower testosterone to keep her.

As much as I love my wife, I still want high testosterone levels. The supplements clearly work in hypogonadal men. But what about borderline cases like me? Will we enjoy at least a subtle variation of these benefits? It's this hope for rejuvenation that keeps me slathering on the AndroGel every morning for the next three weeks.

It's Sunday, August 20, the final day of the four-day U.S. Masters Swimming national championships. My legs and deltoids screaming with lactic acid, I surge forward the final dozen agonizing strokes to the wall and hit the automatic timing pad hard. The scoreboard flashes the finishing times for all eight swimmers in this one-of-many heats of the men's 100-meter freestyle. I'm too tired to look up to see how poorly I've swum this race, which, in my mind, is swimming's marquee event. Some 1,380 swimmers have traveled to Baltimore to test themselves against the nation's best age-group swimmers. Participants range in age from 19 to 91 and include at least nine former Olympians. The competition is brutal. Seventy-seven new national records and 51 new world age-group marks have been set over the first three days.

Medals are awarded to the top ten competitors in each event in each age group. Riddled as I am with iron-poor blood and pathetic natural testosterone production, I have no delusions of grandeur. If I finish in the top 15 of men 45—49, it will be a miracle of the Lazarus variety. Earlier I asked officials to add a third gender category to the competition: pink-blooded guys like me who, in the spirit of fairness, really should be swimming against the more muscular women. The officials declined my request.

When the starter's horn signaled the start of my heat, I leapt off the blocks, already exhausted. For several hours before the race, a photographer shot endless pictures of me flexing my eel-like muscles, pictures meant to illustrate the considerable power conferred upon me by AndroGel.

Truth be known, after four weeks of religious self-anointment, I'd noticed no changes whatsoever, be they physical, emotional, sexual, or cognitive. The fact that the photographer could make me appear even a tad muscular is testimony less to the AndroGel than to his genius. Unfortunately, all that flexing also left my muscles tight and fatigued, precisely the opposite state I had hoped for.

An hour after the race is over, the final results are posted. It's like the *Twilight Zone*—by some mad fluke,

I've finished seventh in my age group! What's more, my time is only a second or so off my best college performance 30 years ago.

When I pick up my medal, I keep all thoughts of AndroGel to myself. The last thing I want now is to attract the attention of urine-testers.

A couple of days after my return home, I smear my shoulder with the final dose of AndroGel and head to a local lab for retesting. My beer-and-aspirin sobriety has now stretched out for three weeks, and I'm anxious to learn if my body's begun slouching its way back toward good health. The nurse siphons off four tubes of my blood. Perhaps I'm deluding myself, but it looks a wee bit darker than last time.

A week later when the fax comes in, I'm guardedly overjoyed: The hemoglobin has clawed its way into the thick of the normal range, and red blood cells and hematocrit appear to be following fast. My testosterone has also climbed, though the change is modest. Before, I stood on the precipice of abnormality; with a little help from AndroGel, I've taken one baby step closer to the middle of the "low normal" quadrant.

When I reinterview the experts about why the AndroGel had little effect on me, they echo their earlier sentiments: Low-normal is still normal. Momentarily, I toy with asking my doctor to renew the prescription at a higher dose. But just as quickly, I dismiss this notion. I have never felt any symptoms associated with low testosterone, so I'm not sure what I'm hoping to improve. Of course, if I lose my next golf match, I just may call my pharmacist.

Jim Thornton won a National Magazine Award for health writing in 1998.

Reprinted with permission from _AARP Modern Maturity,_ January/February 2001, pp. 47-48, 50, 70. © 2001 by the American Association of Retired Persons.

Sorting Through the Confusion Over Estrogen

By JANE E. BRODY

Susan McGee of Bethesda, Md., and Jane Quinn of Brooklyn were not planning to take hormones at menopause. But after many months of sleep disrupted nightly by drenching sweats and changes of bedclothes, they gave in.

Ms. McGee said she became so sleep deprived that she could hardly do her job and feared falling asleep while driving. Ms. Quinn found it increasingly difficult to concentrate on her work, became uncharacteristically irritable and began to think she was losing her mind. The hormones quickly restored their sleep and their sanity.

> **Susan McGee of Bethesda, Md., found relief from symptoms like sleeplessness by taking hormones at menopause. Now she is concerned about findings of new studies.**

These two are among millions of American women near, at or beyond menopause who are asking why so much remains unknown about a drug that has been on the market for 60 years, and what they should make of new findings that are surprising and disappointing proponents of hormone replacement therapy, or H.R.T.

Estrogen—sold today in myriad forms with and without a companion hormone progesterone—was originally marketed to counter the annoying and sometimes disruptive symptoms of menopause.

But in the decades since its initial approval by the Food and Drug Administration in 1942, estrogen had acquired a reputation as an antidote to many of the illnesses and afflictions of aging. Scores of observational and case studies supported this

view, and rug makers and their advertising agencies embraced it with enthusiasm. By 2000, the therapy had become a $2.75 billion business.

The benefits of temporary use of estrogen to weather disruptive menopausal symptoms have not been challenged. Nor is there concern about vaginal applications of estrogen to counter the atrophy that can destroy the joy of lovemaking.

Rather, the focus is on how long a woman can safely stay on hormone replacement that is taken orally or by skin patch and what effects, good or bad, the long-term therapy may have on her health.

Most of the data on the presumed benefits of hormone replacement come from observational studies of women who chose to take it or not. Although in analyzing their findings, researchers tried to account for differences between these groups of women, there is always a chance that factors not considered could have influenced the results, especially since women who choose to use hormones tend to have healthier habits over all and are likely to be followed more closely by their physicians.

To establish facts required a large clinical trial in which women were randomly assigned to take hormones or a look-alike placebo, with neither the women nor their doctors knowing who was on what regimen until the study was completed. Major new findings from such clinical trials have seriously challenged estrogen's image as a preventive of chronic disease, raising doubts about the benefits of lifelong hormone replacement.

First, the Heart and Estrogen/Progestin Replacement Study, known as HERS, found that the hormone combination did not prevent heart attacks and cardiac deaths in women who already had heart disease. Initially, in fact, women who took the combination actually had slightly more heart problems than women given dummy pills.

In July, the Women's Health Initiative, or W.H.I., abruptly ended a study of the same drug combination, marketed as Prempro, in younger and initially healthy postmenopausal women. This well-designed clinical trial found small but statistically significant increases in health risks—including breast cancer, heart attacks, strokes, and blood clots—that outweighed the benefits, a lower risk of hip fractures and colon cancer.

Estrogen "is not a drug to be used for prevention," Dr. Bruce Ettinger says.

"W.H.I. changed the way we think about estrogen; this is not a drug to be used for prevention," said Dr. Bruce Ettinger, a longtime researcher on hormone replacement at the Kaiser Permanente Medical Care Program in Oakland, Calif. "Giving the drug to a lot of healthy women is not the right thing to do."

He and others suggest that women taking it to relieve severe menopausal symptoms should use the lowest possible dose and taper off as soon as possible.

These findings are of grave concern to the more than 40 million women in the United States at menopause or beyond it and 20 million others who will reach it in the next decade.

Hormone replacement therapy has soared in popularity in recent decades after observational studies reported that it might greatly reduce the risk of heart disease and osteoporosis and might even protect against Alzheimer's disease and the mental decline associated with aging.

When added to the widely held belief that estrogen could prevent wrinkles, preserve sexual vigor and maintain a youthful distribution of body fat, the claims made the therapy hard to resist for women willing to take a pill every day or apply a skin patch every week.

Now, as the more precise studies being producing data, claims for estrogen are being scaled back to the only two approved indications for treatment: preservation of bone density and the original reason for marketing this hormone, to relieve the hot flashes, night sweats and vaginal dryness and atrophy that disturb about half of American women to varying degrees when ovarian function slows to a near halt.

These, in fact, are the only benefits manufacturers are permitted to claim in advertising their estrogen products.

If these findings concerned only the therapy's benefits, the 20 million women already on hormone replacement and the 1.4 million who reach menopause each year would face a relatively simple choice. But the recent findings that the therapy may bring risks vastly complicate things for women who must now decide whether these risks outweigh benefits already known and those yet to be established.

The pioneering Women's Health Initiative was not begun until 1993, amid rising concern about the relative lack of studies of women's health problems and pressure from Dr. Bernadine Healy, who was then the director of the National Institutes of Health. Today many women wonder why this kind of research did not take place much earlier.

"These studies are incredibly expensive," noted Dr. Wulf Utian, executive director of the North American Menopause Society. "The government-sponsored W.H.I. study cost $600

million so far. Why would drug companies go to such an expense when their products were already on the market and being widely used for reasons not even listed on the label?"

Dr. Isaac Schiff, director of obstetrics and gynecology at the Massachusetts General Hospital in Boston, said, "Drug companies would not underwrite studies that might find something wrong with their products." Wyeth-Ayerst Laboratories financed the HERS study because it hoped to be able to advertise its drug Prempro as a preventive and treatment for heart disease.

To be sure, the studies completed to date are not the final word on the risks and benefits of hormone replacement. Nor can they be used to determine which, if any, kind or combination of hormones may tip the balance in favor of benefits over risks and for which women.

The American College of Obstetricians and Gynecologists noted those limits in a long advisory to doctors and specified that the Women's Health Initiative findings applied only to the Prempro formulation. But it added, "Caution is warranted for different preparations, and their safety should not be assumed in the absence of conclusive data."

A number of prominent experts have issued similar warnings.

After HERS findings were announced for women with heart disease, for example, two physicians wrote that doctors should tell women about new doubts over the therapy's benefits and evidence of its risks. The message—from Dr. Sailey E. McNagny, a former principal health initiative investigator now working in Wellesley, Mass., and Dr. Nanette K. Wenger, a cardiologist at Emory's medical school—appeared in a letter to The New England Journal of Medicine.

"We've learned a lesson the hard way," Dr. McNagny said. "Until a medication is studied long term, it should not be prescribed long term for healthy women."

But not every expert, and certainly not every physician, is willing to abandon hormone replacement based on the new studies. "Clinical trials are not the end of the story," said Dr. Roger Lobo, professor of obstetrics and gynecology at Columbia-Presbyterian Medical Center in New York. "There are still big gaps in our knowledge as to which regimens are safer than others. We need to look at all the available data and not discount the observational studies. Women are different, the regimens are different and the times are different."

"We have to get away from the silver bullet mentality," says Dr. Wulf Utian.

Even the new studies have their weaknesses. For example, the best-designed new studies involved only one or two forms of hormone replacement, either conjugated equine estrogens alone or a combination of these estrogens and a synthetic progesterone (progestin). Some experts believe that other formulations may yield different results, but they have yet to be tested in large randomized clinical trials, and until they are there is no way to know.

But Dr. Ettinger and some other experts say further studies will be hard to do. Given the hazards found, new studies are unlikely to be approved by review committees. Getting women to enroll and agree to be randomly assigned to take either a hormone or a placebo for many years may also be hard. So women and their physicians are left to review the best available evidence about the various alternatives.

Factored into a woman's decision should be her ability to tolerate menopause, her personal and family health risks and her willingness to adopt other established protective measures like diet and exercise.

As Dr. Utian put it, "We're not paying enough attention to talking about healthy living as a treatment for menopause." He added, "We have to get away from the silver bullet mentality. What's good for one woman is not necessarily good for another."

Possible Risks

HEART DISEASE It is the leading killer of American women, and physicians had many good reasons for assuming that estrogen would help protect against it.

Women develop heart disease 10 to 15 years later than men do, and a woman's risk of heart disease does not start rising until after menopause.

Estrogen is known to maintain elasticity of arterial walls, improve blood flow, raise H.D.L. (the good cholesterol) and lower L.D.L. (the bad), reduce levels of the clotting factor fibrinogen and raise levels of clot inhibitors, all of which should help to keep the heart and its blood vessels healthy.

In addition, several long-term observational studies involving tens of thousands of women found that those taking hormone replacement experienced a reduction of as much as 50 percent in their risk of developing heart disease.

Most convincing were the results of the Nurses' Health Study, an observational study involving 121,700 female nurses presumed to be reasonably uniform in health consciousness, who have been followed since 1976. Among the 42,000 who reached menopause, those who chose to take hormones experienced by 40 percent fewer "major coronary events," including heart attacks and sudden cardiac death.

But HERS, a clinical trial conducted among 2,763 postmenopausal women (average age 67) who already had heart disease, found that the hormone combination did nothing to prevent future attacks, In fact, for the first year or two, women receiving the hormones had more heart attacks than those on a placebo. For a few years after that, those taking the hormones did better, but the benefit did not last, and after seven years the study showed no overall protection from the drugs.

Perhaps for these older women it was too late for estrogen to be protective. Perhaps it helps only those whose hearts and blood vessels are initially healthy. the Women's Health Initiative study of 27,000 women, nearly all of them healthy at the start, tested this hypothesis using either estrogen alone or the hormone combination marketed as Prempro.

The part of the study involving 16,000 women randomly assigned to take Prempro or a placebo was abruptly halted in July when those on the hormone combination were found to suffer more breast cancers, heart attacks, strokes and blood clots than women on the placebo.

The arm of the health initiative study involving estrogen alone is continuing among 11,000 participants who have had hysterectomies and thus do not need progestin to protect the uterus. For now, the researchers cannot say whether estrogen taken alone prevents heart disease.

As Dr. McNagny put it, "The apparent cardioprotection reported in observational and case-control studies may not be caused by H.R.T., but may instead be a result of fundamental differences between women who choose to take H.R.T. and those who do not."

STROKE Findings on stroke prevention have been contradictory, tempering an initial enthusiasm for estrogen's ability to protect the brain against clots.

Although, for example a large study of retirees in 1991 showed a 70 percent reduction in the risk of stroke among women who were using estrogen (compared with those who never did), the Nurses' Health Study found no decrease in strokes among hormone users, and the best designed study—the Women's Health Initiative—showed a small hormone-related increase in strokes.

Again, the presumed protection seen in some observational studies may be related to the kind of woman who chooses hormones rather than the hormones themselves.

BLOOD CLOTS Hormone therapy can increase a woman's risk of developing clots deep in her leg veins and life-threatening clots that lodge in the lungs. Data from the health initiative indicated that if 10,000 women took Prempro for a year, 18 more would develop blood clots than would have occurred if none took it. This risk appears to be highest in the first year of hormone use and declines greatly thereafter.

Nonetheless, researchers recommend that certain women at increased risk of developing clots should think twice about taking estrogen. They include women who are obese, who smoke, who have high blood pressure or a history of blood clots, as well as those who must remain relatively immobile for a prolonged period. Each of these factors also increased the risk of clots.

CANCER After a study more than a decade ago showed that taking estrogen alone after menopause increased by 14-fold the risk of developing cancer of the uterine lining, the endometrium, women who had not had a hysterectomy were advised to take a natural or synthetic progesterone with estrogen.

But this protective measure, which had never been tested for long-term safety, may have had a more dire adverse effect than the one it prevented.

Based on the Women's Health Initiative, among 10,000 women taking the estrogen-progestin product Prempro for one year, 8 additional cases of invasive breast cancer would be expected to occur, with the risk increasing slightly with each year of use. It was mainly this finding that led to the abrupt halt in the study.

Hormone Therapy: Risks and Benefits

New findings on one form of hormone replacement therapy have challenged the theory that the treatment can protect postmenopausal women from many of the ills of aging. One study, the Women's Health Initiative, found that some health risks actually increased slightly among women using the therapy, a combination of the hormones estrogen and progestin. The study involved women aged 50 to 79.

A MIXED PICTURE Women taking the therapy had more of some illnesses than those who did not. With other ailments, the therapy appeared to be protective. Researchers analyzed the data to calculate excess risk and benefits.

Examples: For every 238 women who received the therapy for about five years, 1 contracted breast cancer attributed to the hormones. But for every 48 women treated for five years, 1 escaped a fracture she would otherwise have had.

RISKS	BENEFITS
Breast Cancer **1 in 238** women diagnosed.	**Preventing any type of fracture** **1 in 48** women got this benefit.
Heart attack **1 in 237** women had one, either fatal or nonfatal.	**Preventing hip fractures** **1 in 403**
Any stroke **1 in 225** women had one.	**Preventing colorectal cancer** 1 in 336
Nonfatal stroke **1 in 265** women had one.	**Other benefits** Estrogen is the most effective remedy for symptoms of menopause itself, like hot flashes and vaginal dryness.
Blood clot in lung **1 in 227** women had one.	
Any blood clot **1 in 105** women had one.	

LOWER RISKS IN SHORT-TERM THERAPY

Treatments for one year.

RISK	WOMEN IN STUDY WHO EXPERIENCED IT
Heart attack	**1 in 1,429**
Nonfatal stroke	1,428
Any stroke	1,250
Breast cancer	1,250
Blood clot in lung	1,250
Any blood clot	556

PREVENTION OF:	WOMEN WHO GOT BENEFIT
All fractures	**1 in 227**
Colorectal cancer	1,667
Hip fractures	2,000

Sources: Journal of the American Medical Association; Dr. George F. Sawaya, University of California, San Francisco

Estrogen has long been known to promote the growth of breast cancer, a fact that has prompted the use of estrogen-blocking drugs like tamoxifen to prevent this disease in high-risk women. But there are several indication that progesterone, which causes breast cells to proliferate, may play an even greater role in fostering breast cancer.

A large study published two years ago in The Journal of the National Cancer Institute indicated that progesterone greatly increased the breast cancer risk associated with estrogen alone. For each five years of hormone therapy, continuous use of a combined product like Prempro increased the risk of breast cancer by 24 percent, whereas those taking estrogen alone had only a 9 percent increase in risk. When the two hormones were used sequentially, the risk was even greater than it was with continuous use.

In a review published last year in The Journal of Midwifery & Women's Health, Mary Ellen Rousseau, a nurse-midwife in Hamden, Conn., concluded that these "results showed strong evidence that adding progestins to replacement regimens substantially increased the small increase in the risk of breast cancer" associate with estrogen alone.

She continued, "If the main purpose for adding progestins is to protect the endometrium from cancer, then this study may well tip the balance because the adverse effect on the breast may outweight the beneficial effects on the endometrium."

Overall, hormone replacement studies have found that the risk of breast cancer increases by 2.3 percent for each year of hormone use, but that after 10 years of therapy there is about a 30 percent to 40 percent increase in breast cancer cases.

Since most studies involved Prempro or a similar drug, it is not known whether a comparable risk would accompany other hormone products. After five years, the arm of the health initiative that involves estrogen alone has not yet found an increase in breast cancer risk. That study is continuing.

But there is something of a silver lining: women who develop breast cancer while on hormone replacement have higher survival rates than nonusers, even though the hormones make breast tissue denser and mamographic detection of tiny cancers more difficult. Also, once hormone use is stopped, the risk declines to that of nonusers.

For ovarian cancer, the data are limited and the results mixed. Women who took birth control pills, with similar hormones, are less likely than nonusers to develop ovarian cancer, probably because the hormones suppress ovulation. But postmenopausal women do not ovulate and among them, a study of more than 200,000 women found that those who took estrogen replacement for 10 or more years staring in the 1970's or early 1980's (when doses were much higher than they are today) were 2.2 times as likely to die of ovarian cancer as nonusers. This risk gradually declined when hormones were discontinued.

A nationwide Swedish study found an elevated risk of ovarian cancer among hormone replacement users, especially when the therapy involved sequential use of estrogen and progestin for 10 or more years.

OTHER HEALTH RISKS Several studies have found that hormone replacement increases a woman's risk of gallbladder disease. In HERS, the women assigned to take Prempro had a 38 percent increase in the need for gallbladder surgery. Those who stayed on the hormones for three more years were nearly 50 percent more likely to need the surgery. In another finding from HERS, daily hormone use was associated with a worsening of urinary incontinence.

Possible Benefits

OSTEOPOROSIS By their early 30's women start to lose more bone than their bodies replace, but the rate of bone loss accelerates greatly at menopause. The only health claim manufacturers can make about hormone replacement is that it prevents the loss of bone that occurs when women stop producing premenopausal levels of estrogen. Estrogen can also increase bone density in women who have suffered some bone loss. Thus, estrogen replacement can reduce the risk of osteoporosis and, it has been assumed, the fractures that accompany this density loss.

But to achieve maximum protection, hormone therapy should be started within five years of menopause and may need to be continued indefinitely. The longer after menopause that therapy is delayed, the more bone is likely to be lost and the less effective the hormones are in stabilizing bones. In older women who did not have osteoporosis and were receiving the hormones, the HERS results indicated no reduction in incidence of fracture after four years, and similarly, no reduction in height loss from vertebral bone loss.

While any duration of hormone therapy can delay the risk of osteoporosis and fractures, once estrogen is stopped, considerable bone loss can occur rapidly. In addition, there appears to be a limit to how much bone mineral can be increased with hormone replacement. A randomized clinical trial of 495 women found last spring that beyond three years of therapy no further gains were seen in bone density.

The F.D.A. lets manufacturers say that hormone therapy prevents osteoporosis, but they cannot claim it is an effective treatment. Although hormone therapy can increase bone density at any age, the hormones' effectiveness appears to diminish when started later in life.

Experts like Dr. Ettinger, now wary of long-term hormone therapy, say bones can be protected in other ways, including the drug raloxifene (or Evista), which prevents bone loss and breast cancer and may protect the heart.

BRAIN The possibility that estrogen benefits the aging brain is biologically plausible. The brain is loaded with receptors for estrogen, strongly suggesting that it is directly or indirectly vital to brain function. Estrogen affects the survival of brain cells, and it influences chemicals that send messages between brain cells, or neurotransmitters.

It also affects the formation of synapses that connect brain neurons and protects against oxygen deprivation. Estrogen increases blood flow, removes cell-damaging compounds called free radicals and increases the dendritic spines needed for nerve cell interactions.

Clinically, higher blood levels of estradiol, the most prominent premenopausal estrogen, are associated with better mental performance, and in women with menopausal symptoms, estrogen has improved verbal memory, vigilance, reasoning and the speed of motor responses. But this could be from estrogen-induced improvements in sleep patterns, rather than the direct effects on the brain.

Observational studies like the Baltimore Longitudinal Study of Aging found a halving of the risk of Alzheimer's disease in women using estrogen, and the large Leisure World study of a retirement community in Southern California found that women who had ever used postmenopausal estrogen were a third less likely to develop Alzheimer's than those who had never taken the therapy. In addition in the Leisure World study, the risk of Alzheimer's dropped sharply as the dosage and duration of estrogen increased.

But even short-term estrogen therapy may be beneficial. In a five-year study of 1,124 elderly women, those who took estrogen for less than one year at the time of menopause were half as likely to develop Alzheimer's, suggesting that neurons may be especially susceptible to damage at the onset of menopause.

Still lacking, however, is proof from randomized clinical trials that estrogen can delay Alzheimer's or improve mental performance in women in the early stages of this disease. Well-designed studies have produced conflicting results.

OTHER BENEFITS Estrogen may help to prevent Parkinson's disease. In a study of 72 women who developed Parkinson's disease from 1976 to 1995, researchers at the Mayo Clinic found that those whose ovaries were surgically removed before menopause faced a threefold increased risk of developing this disease, but the risk was reduced by 50 percent in women who took estrogen after menopause.

A study of monkeys published in The Journal of Neuroscience revealed that estrogen deprivation led to the death of brain cells that produce dopamine, the neurotransmitter in short supply in Parkinson's patients. In 10 days of having their ovaries removed, the monkeys lost major dopamine-producing neurons.

Of estrogen, Dr. Isaac Schiff says, "For hot flashes, there's nothing better."

Estrogen may also protect against colon cancer. An American Cancer Society study in which more than 400,000 women were followed for seven years found that the longer a woman took estrogen, the less likely she was to die of colon cancer. Whereas those who took estrogen for up to one year had a 19 percent reduction in deaths from colon cancer, those on estrogen for 11 or more years were 46 percent less likely than non-users to die of colon cancer, even if they had stopped taking the hormone. But current users of the hormone had a lower risk of dying of this cancer than those who took estrogen and then stopped.

Although this was an observational study and thus subject to bias, the randomized Women's Health Initiative study also noted nearly a 40 percent lower risk of colorectal cancer among users of the hormone combination Prempro.

But the most certain benefits of estrogen replacement involve relief of menopausal symptoms, especially hot flashes and night sweats, as well as vaginal and mucous membrane dryness. Estrogen also helps to preserve a more youthful distribution of body fat, keeping more in women's hips and thighs than around their waists. By preserving skin moisture, estrogen can also delay the appearance of wrinkles.

"Quality of life is very, very important," said Dr. Schiff of Massachusetts General. "From a heart and breast cancer point of view, the drug should be outlawed. But for hot flashes, there's nothing better." But for vaginal dryness, which can radically alter a woman's ability to enjoy sex, and for recurrent urinary tract infections, vaginal application of estrogen works well without incurring the risks associated with swallowing a pill every day.

Some women choose to stay on hormone replacement because they say it makes them feel better. But, Dr. Ettinger said: "Clinical trials are not supporting this. I think it's a strong placebo effect. When we switched women to half the estrogen dose and progestin once every six months, overall they said they felt better."

From the *New York Times*, September 3, 2002, pp. F1, F6. © 2002 by The New York Times Company. Reprinted by permission.

An American Epidemic
Diabetes

The silent killer: Scientific research shows a 'persistent explosion' of cases
—especially among those in their prime

BY JERRY ADLER AND CLAUDIA KALB

SOMETHING TERRIBLE WAS HAPPENING to Yolanda Benitez's eyes. They were being poisoned; the fragile capillaries of the retina attacked from within and were leaking blood. The first symptoms were red lines, appearing vertically across her field of vision; the lines multiplied and merged into a haze that shut out light entirely. "Her blood vessels inside her eye were popping," says her daughter, Jannette Roman, a Chicago college student. Benitez, who was in her late 40s when the problem began four years ago, was a cleaning woman, but she's had to stop working. After five surgeries, she has regained vision in one eye, but the other is completely useless. A few weeks ago, awakening one night in a hotel bedroom, she walked into a door, setting off a paroxysm of pain and nausea that hasn't let up yet. And what caused this catastrophe was nothing as exotic as pesticides or emerging viruses. What was poisoning Benitez was sugar.

Heredity
Genes help determine whether you'll get diabetes. **In many families, multiple generations are struck.** But heredity is not destiny— especially if you **eat well and exercise.**

Benitez is a representative victim of what many public-health experts believe will be the next great lifestyle-disease epidemic to afflict the United States: diabetes.

(Technically, type-2 diabetes, which accounts for 90 to 95 percent of all cases.) At five feet one and 140 pounds, Benitez is overweight; 85 percent of all diabetes sufferers are overweight or obese. She was born and reared in Mexico; Hispanics and blacks are more likely to contract diabetes than Caucasians. As the American population becomes increasingly nonwhite and obese, the disease is rapidly spreading. A study by doctors from the Centers for Disease Control and Prevention startled people last week with the finding that the prevalence of diagnosed cases of diabetes increased by a third (from 4.9 to 6.5 percent) between 1990 and 1998. But demographics explain only part of this "persistent explosion" of cases, says Dr. Frank Vinicor, director of the CDC's diabetes division; even among Caucasians— even those of normal weight—the rates are on the rise. The actual number is almost surely higher, since many cases go undiagnosed for years.

But the most alarming statistic in the CDC study was the breakdown of cases by age. For people in their 40s, the incidence of diabetes increased 40 percent over the eight years; for people in their 30s, it went up nearly 70 percent. "It's becoming a disease of the young," says Dr. Arthur Rubenstein, a leading endocrinologist and dean of the Mount Sinai School of Medicine in New York. In that light, Roman is an even more significant example. She is only 18, and she has type-2 diabetes, too.

In fact, until recently the disease Roman and her mother have was known as adult-onset diabetes, because it usually

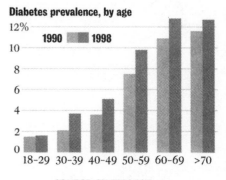

Diabetes prevalence, by age

1990 ■ 1998

(bar chart with percentage axis from 0 to 12% and age groups: 18-29, 30-39, 40-49, 50-59, 60-69, >70)

SOURCE: CENTERS FOR DISEASE CONTROL AND PREVENTION

struck people middle-aged or older. The other kind was "juvenile" diabetes, now called type 1, which is an entirely different disease altogether. But in America, getting fat is no longer a prerogative of adults, and diabetes, which is strongly linked to obesity, is spreading down the age ladder. The rise in type-2 disease among teenagers is "extraordinarily worrying," says Rubenstein, because diabetes can take decades to reveal its most appalling effects—including ulcerating sores, blindness, kidney failure, strokes and heart disease. "If people become diabetic at age 10 or 15 or 20," he says, "you can predict that when they are 30 or 40, they could have terrible complications." You can also predict that they are going to need a lot of expensive health care; on average, medical-care spending for diabetics runs $10,000 to $12,000 annually—three to four times higher than on healthy people, every year for life. A number of promising new drugs and therapies may make diabetes easier to live with, but it will be a medical miracle if they end up saving money.

We're Living Dangerously ...

Too many calories and too little exercise are the key risk factors for type-2 diabetes. Some 90 percent of people with type-2 diabetes are overweight.

PHYSICAL INACTIVITY

Between a quarter and a third of U.S. adults report no physical activity. Many others get very little.

INACTIVITY, U.S. MEDIAN

Men	26.0%
Women	30.8
Total	27.8

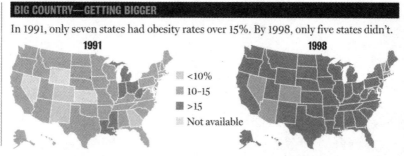

BIG COUNTRY—GETTING BIGGER

In 1991, only seven states had obesity rates over 15%. By 1998, only five states didn't.

1991   1998

- <10%
- 10-15
- >15
- Not available

OBESITY RATE

The percentage of Americans who are considered obese, or roughly 30 pounds overweight, has soared:

PERCENT OF U.S. ADULTS WHO ARE OBESE

1991	12%
1998	18

... And Paying a High Price

During the '90s, the prevalence of type-2 diabetes increased by 33% overall, and by 70% among people in their 30s. Diabetes now affects 16 million Americans.

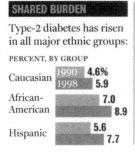

SHARED BURDEN

Type-2 diabetes has risen in all major ethnic groups:

PERCENT, BY GROUP

Caucasian	1990	4.6%
	1998	5.9
African-American		7.0
		8.9
Hispanic		5.6
		7.7

A GROWING EPIDEMIC

Nine states had diabetes rates over 6% in 1991. By 1998, 22 states crossed that line.

1991   1998

- <4%
- 4-6
- >6
- Not available

A GROWING BILL

The direct cost of treating diabetes is $44 billion per year. The total outlay, including indirect costs, is $98 billion.

RELATED COSTS, IN BILLIONS

Diabetes	$98
All Cancers	107

KEN SCHILES

SOURCES: CDC, NIH, BRFSS

REX RYSTEDT, SCIENCE PHOTO LIBRARY—PHOTO RESEARCHERS (INSET)

Age

It usually strikes after 40, but new data shows **a dramatic rise among people in their 30s.** Children are now being diagnosed with type 2 as well, sounding alarms about the nation's long-term health—and **making the term 'adult-onset diabetes' obsolete.**

Diabetes is a disorder of the very engine of life, a subtle calamity at the molecular level. Its hallmark is a failure to metabolize glucose, the ubiquitous sugar molecule carried by the bloodstream to fuel every part of the body. Deprived of their prime energy supply, muscle and nerve cells slow their function, which is why early diabetes may manifest itself as lethargy and irritability. That was the experience of Maria DelMundo, 46, a Rochester, Minn., mother who weighed around 190 (she's 5 feet 2) when she stopped by her doctor's office for a checkup in 1991. "I just wasn't feeling good—tired and out of sorts," she recalls;

in effect, she was undernourished even while eating her fill of the "buttery icing and whipped cream, French pastries and Häagen-Dazs" she loves.

At the same time, glucose accumulates in the patient's blood, and can reach concentrations two to three times normal and even higher. The excess is eventually excreted by the kidneys, which require copious quantities of water as a dilutant. That's how Keith Wein, 42, a mechanical engineer from Irvine, Calif., caught his diabetes—or, rather, his wife, Michelle, did. "I thought something was wrong when all of a sudden he started drinking water nonstop," says Michelle, a nutritionist. "He would come home from the grocery store with six or eight bottles of Crystal Geyser"—and spend a corresponding amount of time going back and forth to the bathroom. But these are subtle signs easy to overlook or deny. Steven Mallinson, a strapping six-foot, 190-pound hiker and cyclist, discovered he had diabetes at the age of 25 when he enrolled as a paid participant in a research study of a new drug, unrelated to insulin. The drug company took one look at his blood and urine samples and kicked him off the study, telling him to call his doctor *immediately*. "That's one of the problems," says Dr. Richard Hellman of the American Association of Clinical Endocrinologists. "A lot of people are

walking around with either diabetes or a predecessor [condition] and they're not even aware of it. The symptoms are not specific, and they tend to come late."

Race

African-Americans, Hispanics and American Indians— who have the highest rates of type 2 in the world—are at greater risk than Caucasians. Still, no one is immune: **the prevalence of the disease has increased across all racial groups** over the last decade.

Researchers are still investigating all the ways in which high blood-sugar levels do damage. One obvious effect is on the arteries, especially in the eyes, kidneys and extremities; sugar seems to both weaken the capillary walls and clog the small vessels. Hemorrhages destroy the retina; impaired circulation leads to ulcers in the legs and feet for which amputation may be the only cure. The risk of heart disease doubles

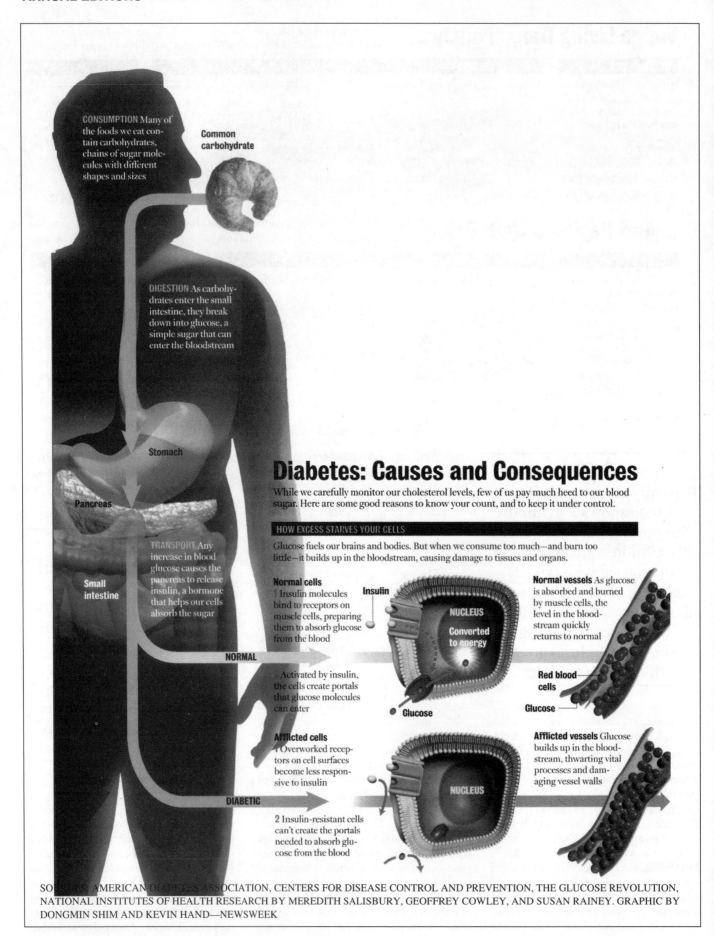

CONSUMPTION Many of the foods we eat contain carbohydrates, chains of sugar molecules with different shapes and sizes

Common carbohydrate

DIGESTION As carbohydrates enter the small intestine, they break down into glucose, a simple sugar that can enter the bloodstream

Stomach

Pancreas

Small intestine

TRANSPORT Any increase in blood glucose causes the pancreas to release insulin, a hormone that helps our cells absorb the sugar

Diabetes: Causes and Consequences

While we carefully monitor our cholesterol levels, few of us pay much heed to our blood sugar. Here are some good reasons to know your count, and to keep it under control.

HOW EXCESS STARVES YOUR CELLS

Glucose fuels our brains and bodies. But when we consume too much—and burn too little—it builds up in the bloodstream, causing damage to tissues and organs.

Normal cells
1 Insulin molecules bind to receptors on muscle cells, preparing them to absorb glucose from the blood

Insulin

NUCLEUS
Converted to energy

NORMAL

Activated by insulin, the cells create portals that glucose molecules can enter

Glucose

Normal vessels As glucose is absorbed and burned by muscle cells, the level in the bloodstream quickly returns to normal

Red blood cells

Glucose

Afflicted cells
1 Overworked receptors on cell surfaces become less responsive to insulin

DIABETIC

2 Insulin-resistant cells can't create the portals needed to absorb glucose from the blood

NUCLEUS

Afflicted vessels Glucose builds up in the bloodstream, thwarting vital processes and damaging vessel walls

SOURCES: AMERICAN DIABETES ASSOCIATION, CENTERS FOR DISEASE CONTROL AND PREVENTION, THE GLUCOSE REVOLUTION, NATIONAL INSTITUTES OF HEALTH RESEARCH BY MEREDITH SALISBURY, GEOFFREY COWLEY, AND SUSAN RAINEY. GRAPHIC BY DONGMIN SHIM AND KEVIN HAND—NEWSWEEK

TREATMENTS

When diet and exercise don't keep diabetes in check, drugs or insulin can help. There are several classes of medications:

Stimulators Drugs like Glucotrol prompt pancreatic cells to make more insulin

Sensitizers Glucophage and related treatments help make cells more responsive to whatever insulin is present in the body

Carb blockers Precose and Glyset help regulate blood-sugar levels by slowing the breakdown of carbohydrates in the digestive tract

EFFECTS

Uncontrolled diabetes can trigger a startling array of serious medical problems.

Eyes Diabetes is the leading cause of new cases of blindness in people 20 to 74

Kidneys Nearly half of new cases of end-stage kidney disease stem from diabetes

Heart Diabetics suffer two to four times the usual rate of cardiovascular disease

Genitals Eight percent of diabetic men suffer from impotence

Nerves Most diabetics suffer nerve damage, and many end up requiring leg amputations

KIM KULISH–SABA

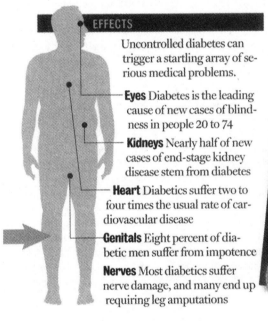

What to Eat

Foods with higher glycemic indices push glucose more rapidly into the bloodstream, taxing the insulin response.

FOOD	GLYCEMIC INDEX
Grapefruit half	25
Grapefruit juice	48
Nonfat yogurt, artificial sweetener	14
Nonfat yogurt, with sugar	33
Tomato soup	38
Green pea soup	66
Ravioli, meat-filled	39
Macaroni and cheese, packaged	64
Brown rice	55
Instant white rice	87
Pumpernickel bread	51
French baguette	95

for men; for women it goes up fourfold. Yet the misperception of diabetes as a relatively benign condition persists. "The word is not yet out about how serious it is," says Anne Daly of the American Diabetes Association. "There's no diabetes that's not bad. It's all serious."

Glucose metabolism is regulated by the hormone insulin, which is produced by the pancreas gland, a fist-size clump of tissue behind the stomach. In normal people, the pancreas secretes insulin in response to a rise in blood sugar, which happens after a meal. The relatively uncommon type-1 diabetes is marked by a straightforward shortage of insulin, which typically shows up around puberty. Researchers consider this an autoimmune disease, possibly brought on by a viral infection. And the treatment is straightforward in concept, if not always in practice: you supply the missing insulin, if necessary by injecting it before meals. Although the name "juvenile" diabetes has stuck, it's a disease you have for life; luckily, though, there's no evidence that its incidence is on the rise in the United States.

Type 2 is an altogether more complicated disease, a spiraling derangement in a network of positive and negative feedback loops linking the pancreas, liver (which stores and releases glucose), muscles, nerves, fat cells and brain (the only organ capable of deciding *not* to open a pint of rum-raisin ice cream). Perversely, the muscle cells refuse to absorb glucose from the blood, a phenomenon called insulin resistance. At least in the early stages of the disease, type-2 diabetics usually have normal insulin production. In fact, they may have above-normal insulin, as their pancreas produces more and more of it in a futile attempt to keep up with the rise in blood sugar. Over time, though, people may need more insulin than their pancreas can supply, and these patients, too, often become dependent on injecting themselves with insulin.

What could cause such a devastating misreading of biochemical messages? Inevitably, genetics seems to play a role. Just

Helping to Break **Bad Habits**

Present danger: Why so many people ignore doctor's orders and put their lives at risk.

BY ROBIN S. GOLAND, M.D

IT SOUNDS SIMPLE. WITH PROPER ATTENtion to blood sugar and diet, a person with diabetes can go a long way toward staying healthy. But it's not simple. Many people with diabetes risk illness and even death by leaving their disease untreated. The vast majority of people who are referred to the diabetes center where I work have excellent access to health care and good doctors. Yet their diabetes is out of control.

A 58-year-old executive came to my office several years ago, referred for what his primary-care doctor called "noncompliance with his diabetes regimen." The patient was at least 20 pounds overweight, he did not follow his diet and he rarely checked his blood sugar, saying he didn't understand how and when to do it. His wife nagged him so often about his health that he called her the "chief of the diabetes police force." He came to my office unwillingly and feeling sheepish, the way people do when they intend to go to the gym but never get around to it.

Ignoring diabetes may seem as irresponsible as smoking cigarettes or driving drunk. But in many ways it's more understandable. For one thing, the disease moves so slowly that people with diabetes often feel perfectly fine. About one third of those with type-2 diabetes—more than 5 million people—don't even know they have it.

For those who know or suspect they have diabetes, denial can be a powerful obstacle to treatment. Because diabetes has genetic roots, many people at risk have already watched a relative go blind or lose a leg. Not knowing that treatments have improved dramatically over the past decade, these people assume, wrongly, that such complications are inevitable. Patients have asked me, "What's the point of giving up the food I love if I'm going to go blind anyway?"

Then there's the intimidating prospect of a lifetime of vigilance. To properly care for their disease, people with diabetes may have to check their glucose between sets of tennis. Or excuse themselves from a business meeting to eat a snack. Taking care of diabetes "is not for an hour, it's not for a week, it's not just for Wednesdays," a patient once told me. "Diabetes never takes a vacation." The relentlessness of the regimen creates in many a sense of isolation and fatigue. When no one else in the restaurant needs to worry about health when the food is slow to arrive, staying motivated to care for the disease gets harder and harder.

To make matters worse, people with diabetes get insufficient support from the U.S. health-care system. Diabetes centers around the country are closing because

many insurers do not reimburse for preventive treatment. And many doctors, with their growing caseloads, don't have time to give people with diabetes the attention they need. Too often they tell patients to lose weight or get more exercise without ensuring that real lifestyle changes are taking place.

People with diabetes need more than preprinted menus and one-time lessons in finger pricks. They need long-term, individualized educational and nutritional counseling. Not only do people with diabetes need to learn the difference between an English muffin and a bagel; they need to learn about various glucose meters and medications—and then get comfortable using them. And then there's the matter of long-term maintenance. Some people manage diabetes well on their own. But others need ongoing attention and an understanding ear when they fall off the wagon. There's good news, though. In the three years since he visited our center, that 58-year-old executive has brought his blood-sugar level down to normal. He's stopped gaining weight and has no complications from diabetes. Now he's telling his friends and family that while treating diabetes is no fun, it's doable in an active, healthy life—and it's better than the consequences of ignoring it.

---

last week a team at the Whitehead Center for Genome Research identified a variant form of a gene on human chromosome 1 that appears to increase the risk of type-2 disease by about 25 percent—although it's carried by as much as 85 percent of the population, so having it doesn't seem to be cause for any special alarm. Certain population groups are especially prone to diabetes; among the Pima Indians of the Southwestern United States half of all adults suffer from it. Living in a harsh climate where food is naturally scarce during much of the year, they may have inherited a so-called thrifty gene that lowers metabolism in times of famine, at the price of increased susceptibility to diabetes. But it took the United States, land of the 40-ounce soda, to elevate that susceptibility to

a crisis; the closely related tribe of Pimas in Mexico who farm and eat a traditional diet don't have nearly the same rate of diabetes. The correlation between type-2 diabetes and obesity is overwhelming: 13.5 percent of obese patients in the CDC survey had the disease, compared with 3.5 percent of those of normal weight. "As people get fatter, the risk of diabetes goes up dramatically," says Vinicor of the CDC. The exact nature of the relationship is extraordinarily complex and poorly understood, but the simplest way to think about it may be that for unknown reasons, the same things that make you fat also put you at risk for diabetes—lack of exercise and a high-calorie diet.

The very complexity of the glucose-insulin cycle, though, affords numerous

opportunities to intervene with therapies. The obvious therapy, of course, is insulin. For years the only available form was harvested from cows or pigs, but now human insulin is being manufactured directly by recombinant DNA techniques. And not just insulin—drug companies are coming out with *new and improved insulin*, engineered with molecular changes to make it last longer in the body or be absorbed more easily into cells. Until recently, insulin had to be injected under the skin as often as five to seven times a day, in a complex calculus of food intake, energy output and dosage designed to keep blood sugar from going either too high or too low. Howard Mitchell of Bangor, Maine, 46, who weighs 280 pounds and is a type-2 diabetic, wears an insulin pump like a beeper,

Are You at Risk?

Because type-2 diabetes causes no symptoms at first, it often goes unmanaged for too long. Some possible warning signs:

- **Frequent urination**
- **Constant thirst or hunger**
- **Blurred vision**
- **Numb or tingling extremities**
- **Frequent skin infections**
- **Slow healing of cuts and bruises**

Getting Tested

When people have symptoms, or clear risk factors, physicians use two basic tests to diagnose type-2 diabetes

- **Fasting test:** Blood glucose should be below 110mg/dl after an overnight fast
- **Oral tolerance test:** Blood glucose should not be higher than 140mg/dl two hours after the patient swigs a cup of glucose-laden fluid

which he can program to deliver a measured dosage whenever he needs it. Now, he says, "my life is no different than anyone else's." An implantable version may be available soon; someday a completely self-contained unit may be able to measure blood glucose directly and deliver insulin automatically.

Other drugs, such as the sulfonylureas, which have been around since the 1950s, stimulate production and release of insulin by the pancreas; many type-2 diabetics take some form of these. But newer drugs, some introduced within the last year or two, offer far more possibilities for control. Glucophage is one; it controls blood sugar directly by promoting glucose storage in the liver. A class of drugs called TZDs make muscle and fat cells more sensitive to insulin, combating type-2 disease right at the source. And there are drugs that work in the gut to inhibit starch digestion, slowing the process enough to flatten the glucose "spike." "All these are new developments since 1995," says John Buse, director of the diabetes center at the University of North Carolina at Chapel Hill. "There's 255 different combinations of drugs, insulin, exercise and diet modification; I probably use 245 of them in my practice."

But there's another surefire way to control blood sugar and lessen the complications of diabetes; it calls for eating a healthy diet in the first place. A recurring theme in the conversations of diabetics is the foods they had to give up. Maria Mendoza, a college janitor in Los Angeles, cut down from "six or seven tortillas a day" to two after she was diagnosed with type-2 diabetes in 1985, and gave up "tacos, sweets, chocolates and *pan dulce* [sweet bread]." "I can't eat what I want, and that makes me sad," she says. "At times, I feel so deprived I want to cry." But increasingly, doctors have come to believe that an absolute ban on refined sugar is too restrictive. With conscientious monitoring of their blood sugar, regular exercise and the right attitude, many diabetics can now allow themselves an occasional sweet. Provided, of course, it is part of the same low-fat, high-fiber, low-calorie diet that researchers recommend for just about every other major problem in American public health. Sophisticated patients don't just stick to a diet: they monitor what they eat obsessively, and plot it against blood-sugar levels that they measure themselves (with a blood-glucose meter and a drop of blood from a finger) as often as five times a day. "My goal is to keep my glucose level under 150," says Michael Negrin, a 41-year-old New York businessman. (The number refers to milligrams of glucose per deciliter of blood.) "Yesterday I woke up and it was 179. I took my medicine and ate breakfast, and it went down to 122. After lunch, a corned-beef sandwich, I went up to 156. I worked out in the evening, and I was down to 58."

Evidence is also accumulating that the lack of exercise contributes to diabetes. Dr. Alan Shuldiner of the University of Maryland has been studying Amish families in Pennsylvania, who have about half the rate of diabetes found in the general Caucasian population—even though their diet is no healthier and the adults are just as likely to be fat. What sets them apart is that they don't have cars; when they're not riding a buggy, they're on scooters or roller skates, and (without telephones) they spend a lot of time going back and forth just to chat. And, says Shuldiner, with the absence of television, "you never see obese Amish children. Never."

It's a tough prescription, and the doctor hasn't been born yet who could get Americans to live like the Amish—even with those great pretzels and shoofly pie. But somewhere between the contemporary lifestyle and the 18th-century one there has to be a happy medium that can let us enjoy our food and comforts—and avoid the coming scourge of poisoning by sugar.

With KAREN SPRINGEN *in Chicago*, ANA FIGUEROA *in Los Angeles*, JOHN LAUERMAN *in Boston*, JOAN FELICE RAYMOND *in Cleveland and* ERIKA CHECK, HEATHER WON TESORIERO *and* SUSAN RAINEY *in New York*

From *Newsweek*, September 4, 2000, pp. 40-47. © 2000 by Newsweek, Inc. All rights reserved. Reprinted by permission.

12 Things You Must Know to Survive And Thrive in America

Excerpt: Black men face a new America, one in which there are no limits to their dreams—at least for some. A roster of hard truths for the new age.

BY ELLIS COSE

THOSE OF US WITH FOREBEARS BRANDED by history hold in our hearts an awful truth: to be born black and male in America is to be put into shackles and then challenged to escape. But that is not our only truth, or even the one most relevant. For in this age of new possibilities, we are learning that the shackles forged in slavery are far from indestructible, that they will yield, even break, provided that we attack them shrewdly.

Today's America is not our grandfathers' or even our fathers' America. We are no longer forced to hide our ambition while masking our bitterness with a grin. We don't face, as did our forefathers, a society committed to relentlessly humiliating us, to forcing us to play the role of inferiors in every civilized sphere. This doesn't mean that we are on the verge of achieving the all-encompassing revolution, of reaching that lofty state of exalted consciousness that sweeps all inequities away. What it does mean is that we have a certain social and cultural leeway; that, in a way our forefathers could only dream about, we are free to define our place in the world.

That freedom is nowhere near absolute. But today's obstacles are not nearly as daunting as those faced by our ancestors. It's the difference between stepping into the ring with both hands lashed behind your back and stepping in with one hand swinging free.

Still, if the one hand is all you have, you must use it twice as well as your opponent uses his. And because you have so much less room for error, you must fight strategically, understanding when to retreat and when to go all out and how to deflect the blows that inevitably will come your way. You must under-

stand, in short, how to compete in this new arena, where the rules are neither what they seem nor quite what they used to be. So what I have set out below is a list of things that may help us in our competition. Call them new world rules, or keys to survival, or Cose's commandments; or, better yet, call them hard truths of this new age—an age of both unlimited potential and soul-crushing inequality.

1. **Play the race card carefully, and at your own peril**. As Johnnie Cochran cleverly demonstrated when he saved O. J. Simpson's hide, there is a time when playing the race card makes perfectly good sense. In November 2000, researchers at the University of Michigan published a study showing that white mock jurors were especially likely to find blacks guilty in seemingly racially neutral situations. But when an explicit racial context was provided, when an assailant's offense was provoked by a perceived racial insult, whites were no longer so likely to see blacks as more guilty; they treated black and white defendants more or less equally. The lesson seems to be that there is some value in certain circumstances in reminding people about the reality of racism; for when they are reminded of racism (which is different from being accused of it), they make a greater attempt to be fair. Life, however, usually is not conducted under controlled experimental conditions. And as the Simpson trial demonstrated, Americans see racially charged incidents very differently. We (meaning blacks) have been so battered by and sensitized to racism that we sometimes see it where

it doesn't exist. Whites have such an emotional investment in denying that they are racists that they often refuse to acknowledge racism when it is perfectly obvious to us. Other racial groups, depending on their experiences and sensitivities, also view racially tinged incidents through an ethnocentric lens. Given such psychologically complex phenomena as racial guilt and racial pain, you are not likely to find much empathy or understanding when you bring racial complaints to whites. The best you can generally hope for is an awkward silence accompanied by the suspicion that you are crying wolf. This is not to say that you should grin and bear bad treatment, but that you are generally better off finding a less charged terrain than that of racial grievance on which to fight the battle.

2. **Complain all you like about the raw deal you have gotten in life, but don't expect those complaints to get you anywhere**. America likes winners, not whiners. And one of the encouraging developments of this new, more enlightened age is that America even, at times, embraces winners who are black. There is a certain strong incentive to do so, since the very existence of black winners can be made into a rather fantastical argument that discrimination no longer hinders black advancement. Whiners, on the other hand, simply remind too many Americans of history they would prefer to forget, and of unpleasant current realities they would prefer not to face. Thankfully, we have moved past the time when whites collectively spent much time hating us; these days they mostly just don't care. Did that boss (teacher, classmate, administrator, stranger) call you stupid because of your color, or despite it? Were you assumed to be a ballplayer instead of a scholar simply because you're black? Was your rival promoted ahead of you because he's white? Was your intellect (ability, judgment) questioned in an instance where your white colleague's would not have been? You can drive yourself crazy trying to figure it out and also end up wasting a lot of energy that could be best directed elsewhere. An editor in Chicago, where I began my writing career, gave me a valuable piece of advice. "If you're going to be a writer," he said, "you'd better develop a thick skin." Much the same could be said about just being a black man in America. If you are going to survive with your sanity and emotional health intact, you're going to have to learn not to sweat much of the routine stuff that makes being a black man difficult. If you can engage life with a certain amount of humor, or at least with a sense of charity, you'll not only be happier but a lot less likely to need blood-pressure medication.

3. **Expect to do better than the world expects of you; expect to live in a bigger world than the one you see**. One of the most unfortunate realities of growing up as a black male in America is that we are constantly told to lower our sights; we are constantly nudged, unless we are very lucky and privileged, in the direction of mediocrity. Our dreams, we are told in effect, cannot be as large as other folks' dreams; our universe, we are led to believe, will be smaller than that of our nonblack peers. Franklin Raines, head of the Fannie Mae Corporation, speaks of

his early exposure to a life beyond inner-city Seattle as "a period of time when my world grew bigger," when his sophistication and exposure increased. What Raines really is describing is the natural progression of knowledge and the optimal progression of life. When Arthur Ashe wrote that his "potential is more than can be expressed within the bounds of my race or ethnic identity," he was speaking for all of us. When Maurice Ashley, America's first black grandmaster of chess, talks of a "rope of destiny pulling me along," he is talking of something we all should feel. For those of us who are accustomed to hearing, "You will never amount to much," dreams may be all that give us the strength to go on. And as we dream big dreams, we also must prepare ourselves to pursue them, instead of contenting ourselves with fantasies of a wonderful existence that will be forever beyond our reach.

4. **Don't expect support for your dreams from those who have not accomplished very much in their lives**. The natural reaction of many people (especially those who believe they share your background) is to feel threatened or intimidated or simply to be dismissive if you are trying to do things they have not done themselves. As a very young man and a "junior leader" in my neighborhood Boys Club, I was invited to a dinner at which multimillionaire W. Clement Stone spoke. After delivering a stirring talk detailing his personal journey of success, Stone handed out an inspirational book (whose title I can no longer recall), which I took with me to bed that evening. Don't share your dreams with failures, warned the book, which went on to explain that people who had not done much in their own lives would be incapable of seeing the potential in yours. While that is certainly not true in all cases, it is true much too often. The book's observation helped me to understand why some people I knew seemed more interested in telling me what I could never accomplish than in helping me achieve what I could. It also helped me understand why I owed it to myself to tune out the voices around me telling me to lower my sights.

5. **If someone is bringing out your most self-destructive tendencies, acknowledge that that person is not a friend.** No one should, willy-nilly, toss away friendship. People who will care for you, who will support and watch out for you, are a precious part of a full and blessed life. But people who claim to be friends are not always friends in fact—as Mike Gibson, an ex-prisoner who is now a Morehouse student, ultimately learned. His time behind bars taught Gibson to "surround myself with people who want to see me do good." On the streets he learned that when things got tough, the very buddies who had encouraged him to break the law were nowhere to be found: "When I was in the cell, I was there by myself... I always found myself alone." It's easy to be seduced by those who offer idiotic opinions disguised as guidance. It's even easier to find people who attach themselves to you for their own selfish reasons, or who will say they have your back when, in reality, they're only looking out for themselves. It's sometimes a bit harder to let them go,

177

which sometimes is what you must do in the interest of your own survival.

Too many of us are trying to cope alone, when we would be much better off if we would just reach out for help.

6. **Don't be too proud to ask for help, particularly from those who are wiser and older**. While working on a previous book, "Color-Blind," I interviewed mathematician Philip Uri Triesman, who has had astounding success teaching advanced mathematics to black students who previously had not done very well. Unlike Chinese-American students who typically studied in groups, blacks, he had discovered, tended to study alone. For blacks, the solitary study ritual seemed to be a matter of pride, reflecting their need to prove that they could get by without help, that they were not inferior to whites. By getting them, in effect, to emulate some of what the Chinese-Americans were doing, Triesman spurred the black students to unprecedented levels of accomplishment. Too often (and not only in math), we feel we have to face our problems alone. We are uncomfortable admitting our pain, our inexperience, our incompetence; and, as a result, we sometimes ignore resources we usefully could tap. Whether in schools, in the streets or in corporate suites, too many of us are trying to cope alone when we would be much better off if we reached out for help.

7. **Recognize that being true to yourself is not the same as being true to a stupid stereotype**. A few years ago when I visited Xavier University, a historically black college in New Orleans, I was moved by a student who proudly proclaimed the university to be a school full of nerds. At a time when many black men and boys are trying their best to act like mack-daddies and bad-ass muthas, Xavier (which sends more blacks to medical schools than any other university) is saying that it has another image in mind: blackness really has nothing to do with projecting a manufactured, crude street persona. Xavier celebrates accomplishment instead of denigrating it, and it makes no apologies for doing so. We desperately need to promote archetypes other than rappers, thugs and ballplayers of what it is possible and desirable for us to be—if for no other reason than that so few of us can find success on such limited terrain.

8. **Don't let the glitter blind you**. Almost invariably when I have spoken to people who had made their living selling drugs, they talk a lot like "Frank," who said, "I didn't want to be the only dude on the streets with busted-up shoes, old clothes." They talk of the money, the women, the cars, the gold chains— the glamour, the glitter of the dealer's life. Only later do most acknowledge that the money, for most dealers, is not all that

good, and that even when it is, it generally doesn't last very long—partly because the lifestyle so often leads to either prison or an early grave. Maybe you don't care about that. Nonetheless, I urge you to realize that you have a better chance (provided you prepare for it) of getting a big job at a major corporation than of making big money for a long time on the streets—and the benefits and security are a hell of a lot better.

9. **Don't expect competence and hard work alone to get you the recognition or rewards you deserve**. For all our skepticism about the so-called system, it sometimes seems that people of color are the only ones alive who truly believe in the meritocracy. We work hard, pour all our energy into our jobs and then are stunned and shattered when our hard work is not rewarded. Why, we ask, is our ability not being recognized? Why is our hard work being overlooked? Why can't they see our talent? The answers are as varied as the possible circumstances, but the general rule is that any organization (government, private business, educational or other) is essentially a social body that rewards those fully engaged in the game. To the extent we try to hold ourselves above that process, we end up losing.

It is never too late to accomplish something in life. But lost ground can be very hard to make up.

10. **You must seize the time, for it is already later than you think**. When working on "The Rage of a Privileged Class," a book I published in 1994, I was touched by a confession from Basil Paterson, lawyer, high-ranking Democratic National Committee official and former deputy mayor of New York. "It's too late for me to get rich because I spent too much time preparing for what I've got... Most of us are 10 years behind what we should have been. We didn't get credentials until we were older than other folks," he said. Paterson was talking of a particular generation, one hobbled by a much more blatant, more virulent form of discrimination than exists for the most part today; but the essence of what he said is still true—at least for those without well-to-do parents or fancy educations. Daniel Rose, founder of the Harlem Educational Activities Fund, tells his young disciples: "Your chief competitor started yesterday. And you are already a day behind." While it is never too late to accomplish something in life, lost ground is hard to make up, and it only gets harder the longer one waits, as competition becomes even stiffer and opportunities dry up.

11. **Even if you have to fake it, show some faith in yourself**. Confidence, lightly worn, can be contagious, and you might even manage to fool yourself into letting go of your doubts. "A lot of our kids don't believe in themselves because they've been told by so many people that they ain't worth s—t.

I was labeled the bad kid, so I know how that feels," says Chicago youth worker J. W. Hughes. "Go to any high school with black males and tell them they are smart enough to go to any university in the world. Many of them will say, 'Not me.' I know that because [I was] one of them," says Zachary Donald, a member of the Omega Boys Club, a San Francisco-based non-profit dedicated to rescuing young souls from the street. So much energy has been expended undermining our confidence, picking apart our faith in ourselves, that we sometimes forget faith does not depend on the beliefs of others or on demonstrating a list of accomplishments. "Faith is the substance of things hoped for, the evidence of things not seen," says the Bible (Hebrews 11:1). And there is so much that we have not yet seen, so much waiting to be revealed when it comes to our potential on this planet. But the first step is to believe that we can go where others say we can't.

12. **Don't force innocent others to bear the price of your pain**. Sister Simone Ponnet, executive director of Abraham House (a New York Roman Catholic organization that works with prisoners and their families), spoke feelingly of ex-convicts and prisoners who lamented growing up fatherless, or with abusive fathers, and then ended up treating their own children no better. Even some of us who haven't been locked down at times feel so much pain, so much anger that we feel justified in taking out our frustrations on everyone around us. Threatened in so many realms, unable to control the forces enveloping us, we sometimes try too hard to exert control in the few areas we think we can: sometimes over women, sometimes over children and sometimes over random souls unlucky enough to get in our way. Before giving in to the temptation to turn loved ones into targets, we should remind ourselves that those who love us are the best hope we have to regain whatever humanity we have lost; that they, in other words, are our salvation.

ALL THAT I HAVE SAID ABOVE FOCUSES on the personal, on what we, as individuals, can do to improve the quality of our lives. This is not to say that I believe the only problems we have in America are individual ones. Nothing could be farther from the truth. Huge and systemic problems remain that prevent America from being the best country that it can be. We continue, as a country, to leave our young people uneducated and, often, illiterate. We continue to stress incarceration where we should be stressing human reclamation. We continue to confound the dream of true equality by rejecting the investments in remediation and infrastructure needed to achieve it. We continue to permit society to label young black men as undesirable, as troublemakers, and we throw up our hands in exasperation when the self-fulfilling prophecy becomes fact. I could go on, but those are subjects for another day.

Here I am purposely less concerned with the systemic than with the personal, with some things you might want to consider as you figure out how to live your life. And, as such, I would like to end on a hopeful note, by restating what I sincerely believe to be true: there is more leeway than there has ever been in history for you to become whatever you would be; for you to accomplish whatever you dream; for you to escape the prisons of stereotypes and caricatures that our forefathers could not avoid.

We are entitled to our big dreams, just as we deserve an America that is as welcoming to us as it is to a white kid from Cuba, Croatia or Ireland. We deserve, in other words, the fairness we have always been promised, and the opportunity to compete free of the burdens we have always carried, burdens economic, emotional and historical, burdens that still stand in the way of our receiving our due and of America achieving a true meritocracy.

Adapted from "The Envy of the World," by Ellis Cose. To be published by Washington Square Press. Copyright © 2002 by Ellis Cose.

From *Newsweek*, January 28, 2002, pp. 52-55. © 2002 by Newsweek, Inc. All rights reserved. Reprinted by permission.

The New
Unretirement

The fine art of making a second career your life's work

BY MARC FREEDMAN

MARV WELT WAS TEACHING A GROUP of inner-city kids how to fish at Whitaker Pond in Portland, Oregon, when two of them suddenly took off running.

Bewildered, Welt looked around for the cause of their fright—and saw two cows that had come down to the water for a drink. "They had never seen a cow before," Welt recalls with a smile, "and they didn't know how a cow would act."

It wasn't the first time Welt had to explain the bovine temperament, nor will it likely be the last. For the past seven years, he has spent almost every day with kids from the 16 Portland schools that participate in the Help Our Salmon program, an environmental education program he founded after retiring from his job as a management consultant. "When I retired I thought to myself, What can I do? I'm not going to sit around all day, so I might as well get out and do something. I love the outdoors and I love to fish, and I wanted to share that with the kids."

Welt is not alone. In fact, he's part of a growing movement of retired professionals who are transforming what it means to grow older in America. Not content to embrace the "golden years" notion of leisure, recreation, and disengagement, the 75-year-old Welt and others like him are looking for something different in later life. Liberated from the career ambitions and monetary pressures of midlife employment, they are embracing opportunities that promise greater meaning, stimulation, and

the chance to make a difference in others' lives.

"The New Face of Retirement," a national survey of Americans, ages 50 to 75, conducted in late 1999 by Peter D. Hart Research Associates, shows clearly that if earlier work fed the body, men and women in their later years are now looking for ways to better serve the soul. The survey found that only 28 percent of Americans in this age group view retirement in the old terms—as a time to take it easy and focus on recreation. Instead, 65 percent want to stay active, to take on new challenges, and to begin a new chapter in life.

And while the Baby Boomers could infuse civic organizations with vast numbers of volunteers in the coming years, the current generation of older Americans is doing the heavy lifting: serving as role models for this new kind of retirement and, in some cases, inventing the institutions needed to enable succeeding generations to play a more vital role in our communities.

Bill Schwartz is one of the new role models for unretirement. He laughs in recalling the time a few years ago when he was stopped on the streets of San Mateo, California, by one of his former patients. "You used to be Dr. Schwartz, didn't you?" she blurted.

The 69-year-old internist, seven years retired from private practice, is pleased to report that he remains Dr. Schwartz today, although the venue for practicing medicine has shifted to

the Samaritan House Clinic, the free health center that Schwartz founded nearly a decade ago to provide indigent families with medical care.

In 1988, Samaritan House, a community organization dedicated to helping the poor and homeless, was looking for a few volunteer doctors to provide free medical care to its clients in the evening. Schwartz answered the call. Soon he was examining patients once a week in Samaritan House's office.

As demand for the doctor's services grew, Schwartz began opening the clinic six times a month, then twice a week until he simply retired from his private practice to start a full-time operation that now serves more than 5,000 patients a year, relying principally on the volunteer services of 40 doctors and a slew of dentists, pharmacists, and others. Today the clinic has become such a vital part of San Mateo that Schwartz and his associates regularly get calls from doctors in their 50s and 60s who want to help out.

Schwartz's labor of love was not part of his retirement plan. He had hoped to travel and paint, maybe even play a little golf. But he has found in his work with Samaritan House a sense of accomplishment missing in his earlier years. "In private practice, I used to get 15, 20 minutes, tops, with a new patient. Here, we can take two hours." The result, he says, is the kind of trust that can lead to better, and more holistic, care.

He tells the story of a man who showed up at Samaritan House complaining of neck and back pain. Instead of dispensing muscle relaxants and rushing off to the next patient, the clinic doctors were able to take the time to learn the root cause of his ailment. The man had neck pain, he eventually confessed, because he was living in his car. The Samaritan House team was able to offer a prescription with longer-term promise: They found him shelter through their parent organization.

The ability to provide that kind of holistic care has been a source of enormous fulfillment, say Schwartz and his colleagues. According to Bill Schwartz, the doctors of Samaritan House "are having more fun than we have any right to."

After spending more than three decades working for the Philadelphia water department, Harold Allen retired in his late 50s with a full pension. But he soon realized that he wasn't exactly cut out for a life of leisure.

He quickly returned to work, where he spent the next three years helping prepare prison inmates for jobs once they returned to society. While rewarding, the job also left him discouraged. One of the men he was counseling failed a drug test just before his scheduled release. "I realized he didn't want to get out of prison," Allen says. "Here's a guy who had no family—prison inmates were the closest thing to a family for him."

The experience left Allen thinking about the children of these men, and the need to reach young people before they were too far along a path to prison. So when he learned about the Experience Corps, he unretired for a second time to work as a mentor at Taylor Elementary School, in the tough North Philadelphia neighborhood known as "the badlands."

The Experience Corps—a national program mobilizing older Americans on behalf of children and schools—operates in 18 cities across the country. Volunteers like Allen dedicate 15 hours a week or more to mentoring children, getting more parents involved in schools, and helping build support for public education.

For the half-dozen children Allen mentors one-on-one each week, he is a combination grandparent, teacher, confidant, and cheerleader, helping them build faith in themselves while guiding them through the often treacherous terrain of growing up poor in the inner city.

"I was drawn to Experience Corps by the possibility of being able to effect some kind of positive change," says Allen, who is now convinced that the mentors get as much out of the program as they give. He describes his close-knit teammates in Experience Corps as being like a second family, but says the biggest bonus is so much unreserved appreciation from the kids. "When you arrive, they run to you," he says. "It just blows you away."

For most of her 51 years, Mary Vallely has lived within a ten-mile radius of her childhood home on Chicago's North Side. But in June 1997, Vallely took a bold step out of her comfortable Midwestern life to join the fastest growing group in the Peace Corps: older volunteers. That year, she and her husband, Gus Wilhelmy, 65, quit their jobs and traveled to Nizhny Novgorod, Russia's third-largest city.

For Vallely, it was the fulfillment of a long-deferred dream. As a young undergraduate in the 1960s, she had written the Peace Corps for information, but learned that she needed to be a college graduate to apply. After graduating, she got married and the opportunity slipped away. But the dream never completely died. "We had the sense that life had been good to us and we needed to give back to the world," she says. "Plus, I saw it as an opportunity for me to review my life from another perspective."

Once in the program, Vallely and Wilhelmy were given the task of helping put Nizhny Novgorod's fledgling nonprofit organizations on more solid footing. Organizations would secure funding, start operating, and promptly run out of money because they weren't managing their resources well. A main problem was unrealistic expectations. In a typical example, one man, a veteran, wanted to open a chain of 100 stores that would sell food at greatly discounted

rates. Vallely and Wilhelmy convinced him to start with a single store and then build from there.

The couple also designed a one-year, four-level program that taught sustainability skills to key people in nonprofit organizations—and learned how to work in close partnership themselves. "He was the creative genius," Vallely says, "and I was the one who could put structure to it." Despite the frequent challenges with language and cultural differences, Vallely and Wilhelmy also helped raise $600,000 in direct funding and in-kind contributions to nonprofits during their time in Russia.

After their return, Vallely eased back into a paid work environment, and the couple are spending more time with their children and grandchildren, having achieved new clarity about those things that are most important in life.

Says Vallely: "I got out of Peace Corps what I always thought I'd get—a new perspective. I'm now much more ready to live a simpler life."

The lure of a simpler, more meaningful life was also the impetus for a major midlife change for Sarah Patterson. A fiftysomething San Francisco attorney with a thriving Social Security disability law practice, Patterson had measured success by a condominium in Pacific Heights and a comfortable existence. But this also led her to more and more management responsibilities and further away from her first love—helping people.

By 1997, Patterson had already started thinking about retiring from her practice. It was about then that she stumbled upon an article in the newsletter of the Jesuit Volunteer Corps (JVC) announcing a new JVC initiative for volunteers 50 and older. The new "Elder Corps" would focus on the JVC's four core values: spirituality, community, simple living, and social justice. "I hated the name, loved the concept," Patterson recalls, adding "I read the article and just knew I was going to do it."

Within a year, Patterson had turned over her law practice to a partner and was at an Oregon beach retreat with 18 other 50-plus volunteers. She ended up in Portland, living with a New England couple in their 70s, a 54-year-old widower from Minnesota, a 60-year-old former Peace Corps volunteer, and a 74-year-old therapist and grandmother of 25—and "trying to figure out how to live on $80 a month."

Her JVC assignment was at the Cascade AIDS Project, where her work ranged from handing out food vouchers and bus passes to becoming an advocate for community concerns. She also became involved in coordinating the agency's legal clinic, locating pro bono attorneys to help the project's clients deal with pressing issues.

The JVC program so changed Patterson's outlook on life that, after her one-year stint, she abandoned the San Francisco rat race and moved north, splitting her time between Portland and Truckee, California. She is now concentrating on photography, showing her work in a number of galleries. As for her legal career, Patterson says she's not entirely ready to "hang up my spurs—but I'm surprised how easy it was to leave daily practice. When I think of daily practice now, I think of meditation."

If you're interested in your own "second career," the following groups offer a range of opportunities: The AARP Volunteer Center,

202-434-3200, volunteer@aarp.org; Big Brothers Big Sisters of America, 215-567-7000, www.bbbsa.org/; Experience Corps, 415-430-0140, www.experiencecorps.org/; Peace Corps, 800-424-8580, www.peacecorps.gov/; Retired and Senior Volunteer Program (RSVP), 202-606-5000, www.cns.gov/senior; SCORE, 800-634-0245, www.score.org/.

Marc Freedman is the author of Prime Time: How Baby Boomers Will Revolutionize Retirement and Transform America (*Public Affairs, 2000*).

From *Modern Maturity*, January/February 2001, pp. 53-61. © 2001 by Modern Maturity AARP.

The Disappearing Mind

By the year 2050, as many as 14 million Americans could be suffering from Alzheimer's disease. Scientists are now using imaging technology to diagnose the condition at its earliest stages—and racing to develop new treatments that can stop it's terrifying progression. Will they succeed?

BY GEOFFREY COWLEY

Do SENIOR MOMENTS SCARE YOU? Eight years ago Nancy Levitt had one that would unsettle anyone. She was in her mid-40s at the time, and watching her father drift into the late stages of Alzheimer's disease (several aunts and uncles had suffered similar fates). Levitt's son was about to graduate from high school, so she called a mail-order company to order fluorescent-light sticks for him and his friends to wear around their necks at a party. When her package arrived in the next day's mail, the receipt and postmark knocked her flat. She had ordered the same gift a few days earlier—and lost all recollection of it. "I just freaked," she says. Suddenly, every forgotten name, misplaced pencil and misspelled word became a prophecy of doom. Was she getting Alzheimer's herself?

When Levitt sought testing at UCLA, researchers gave her the usual cognitive tests—name some simple objects, repeat a list of words—and assured her she was fine. But the occasional lapses continued, so she returned to the same clinic several years later and enrolled in a study aimed at distinguishing early Alzheimer's from run-of-the-mill forgetfulness. This time the researchers didn't just talk to her. They placed her under a scanner and recorded detailed images of her brain, both at work and at rest. Alzheimer's disease has traditionally been diagnosed by exclusion. If you lagged significantly on a memory test—and your troubles couldn't be blamed on strokes, tumors or drug toxicity—you were given a tentative diagnosis and sent on your way. To find out for sure, you had to die and have your brain dissected by a pathologist. Levitt didn't have to do any of that. By looking at the images on his video screen, Dr. Gary Small was able to give her some reassuring news. She didn't have Alzheimer's disease—and the odds were less than 5 percent that she would develop it any time soon. Levitt calls the images "the most wonderful thing I've ever seen."

> ## "Without a good method of early detection, the best Alzheimer's treatment would be worthless."
> —DR. FERENC JOLESZ

Technology is changing all of medicine, but it is positively transforming our understanding of Alzheimer's. Armed with state-of-the-art PET scanners and MRI machines, specialists are learning to spot and track the disease in people who have yet to suffer symptoms. It's one thing to chronicle the brain's disintegration, quite another to stop it, but many experts are predicting success on both fronts. Drugmakers now have two dozen treatments in development. And unlike today's medications, which offer only a brief respite from symptoms, many of the new ones are intended to stall progression of the disease. As Alzheimer's runs its decades-long course, it replaces the brain's exquisite circuitry with mounds of sticky plaque and expanses of dead, twisted neurons. No drug will repair that kind of damage. But if the new treatments work as anticipated, they'll enable us to stop or slow the destruction while our minds are still intact. A decade from now, says Dr. Dennis Selkoe of Harvard Medical School and Boston's Brigham and Women's Hospital, physicians may monitor our brain health as closely as our cholesterol levels—and stave off Alzheimer's with a wave of the prescription pad.

Until we can control this awful illness, early detection may seem a fool's errand. "With diagnostics ahead of therapeutics,

A-BETA FORMATION

Disease stage: APP is a normal protein housed in the outer membranes of brain cells. When APP is snipped by scissorlike enzymes called beta and gamma secretase, a fragment called A-beta is released. If the brain does not clear A-beta, it builds up and causes trouble.

Attack strategy: Secretase inhibitors may stall A-beta production by disabling the scissorlike enzymes. Such drugs are in animal testing.

there's a lot of potential for harm," says University of Pennsylvania ethicist Arthur Caplan. He worries that entrepreneurs will peddle testing without counseling, leaving patients devastated by the findings. He wonders, too, whether employers and insurers will abandon people whose scans show signs of trouble. Advocates counter that early detection can help patients make the most of today's treatments while giving them time to adjust their plans and expectations. With so many people at risk, they say, anything is better than nothing. Some 4 million Americans have Alzheimer's today, but the number could hit 14 million by 2050 as the elderly population expands.

> **"There are a lot of people who could benefit from today's treatments, but they aren't getting help."**
>
> **–DR. GARY SMALL**

The diagnostic revolution began during the 1990s, as researchers learned to monitor neurons with an imaging technique called PET, or positron-emission tomography. Unlike an X-ray or CT imaging, PET records brain activity by homing in on the glucose that fuels it. And as Small's team has discovered, it can spot significant pathology in people who are still functioning normally. Instead of glowing with activity, the middle sections of their brains appear dim and torpid. And because Alzheimer's is progressive, abnormal scans tend to become more so with time. In a study published last fall, UCLA researchers scanned 284 people who had suffered only minor memory problems. The images predicted, with 95 percent accuracy, which people would experience dementia within three and a half years.

PET scanning has yet to transform patient care; few clinics have the machines, and Medicare doesn't cover their use. But scientists are now using the technique to see whether drugs already on the market (such as the anti-inflammatory ibuprofen) can slow the brain's decline. And PET is just one of several potential strategies for tracking preclinical Alzheimer's. San Diego researchers have found that seniors who score inconsistently on different mental tests are at increased risk of dementia—even if their scores are generally high. And in a study published this spring, research-

ers at the Oregon Health Sciences University hit upon three signs of imminent decline in octogenarians. The 108 participants were all healthy at the start of the study, but nearly half were demented six years later. As it turned out, they had entered the study with certain traits in common. They walked more slowly than their peers, requiring nearly two extra seconds for a 30-foot stroll. They lagged slightly on memory tests. And their MRI scans revealed a slight shrinkage of the hippocampus, a small, seahorse-shaped brain structure that is critical to memory processing. The changes were subtle, says Dr. Jeffrey Kaye, the neurologist who directed the study, but they presaged changes that were catastrophic.

Powerful as they are, today's tests show only that the brain is losing steam. The ideal test would reveal the underlying pathology, letting a specialist determine how much healthy tissue has been replaced by the plaques and tangles of Alzheimer's. It's not hard to fashion a molecule that will highlight the wreckage. Unfortunately, it's almost impossible to get such a probe through the ultrafine screen that separates the brain from the bloodstream. If a probe is complex enough to pick out plaques and tangles, chances are it's too large to pass from the bloodstream into the brain. At UCLA and the University of Pittsburgh, researchers have developed probes that are small enough to get through, yet selective enough to provide at least a rough measure of a person's plaque burden. At Brigham and Women's Hospital, meanwhile, radiologist Ferenc Jolesz is trying to open the barrier to bigger, better probes. His technique employs tiny lipid bubbles that gather at the gateway to the brain when injected into the bloodstream. The bubbles burst when zapped with ultrasound, loosening the mesh of that ultrafine screen and allowing the amyloid probe to enter. Lab tests suggest the screen will repair itself within a day, but no one yet knows whether it's safe to leave it open that long.

One way or another, many of us now seem destined to learn we have Alzheimer's disease while we're still of sound mind. The question is whether we'll be able to do anything more constructive than setting our affairs in order and taking a drug like Aricept to ease the early symptoms. Fortunately the possibilities for therapy are changing almost as fast as the diagnostic arts. Experts now think of Alzheimer's not as a sudden calamity but as a decades-long process involving at least a half-dozen steps—each of which

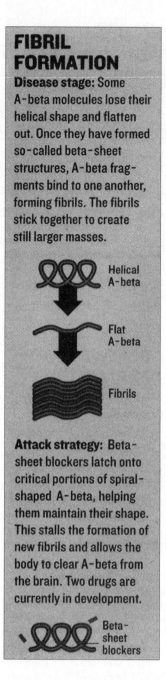

FIBRIL FORMATION

Disease stage: Some A-beta molecules lose their helical shape and flatten out. Once they have formed so-called beta-sheet structures, A-beta fragments bind to one another, forming fibrils. The fibrils stick together to create still larger masses.

Helical A-beta

Flat A-beta

Fibrils

Attack strategy: Beta-sheet blockers latch onto critical portions of spiral-shaped A-beta, helping them maintain their shape. This stalls the formation of new fibrils and allows the body to clear A-beta from the brain. Two drugs are currently in development.

Beta-sheet blockers

provides a target for intervention. Slowing the disease may require four or five drugs rather than one. But as AIDS specialists have shown, the right combination can sometimes turn a killer into a mere menace.

THOUGH EXPERTS STILL QUARREL ABOUT the ultimate cause of Alzheimer's, many agree that the trouble starts with a scrap of junk protein called amyloid beta (A-beta for short). Each of us produces the stuff, and small amounts are harmless. But as A-beta builds up in the brain, it sets off a destructive cascade, replacing healthy tissue with the plaques seen in Alzheimer's suf-

Brain Spotting

For the first time, PET scans can spot plaque in the brains of Alzheimer's patients. The advance will allow for confident early detection of the disease.

PLAQUE BUILDUP Red areas in the brain scan of an Alzheimer's patient show plaque accumulation. The healthy brain shows none.

Alzheimer's brain

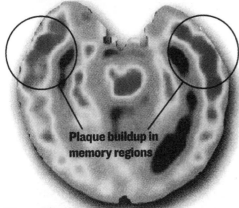

Plaque buildup in memory regions

Normal brain

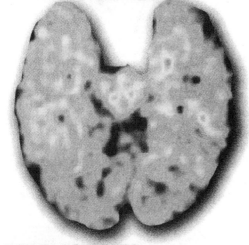

BRAIN ACTIVITY Blue areas in the Alzheimer's patient's memory regions indicate reduced activity caused by the plaque.

Alzheimer's brain   **Normal brain**

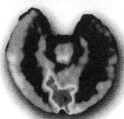   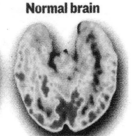

Leading causes of death in the U.S., all ages, 1999

Heart disease	725,192
Malignant tumors	549,838
Vascular disease	167,366
Respiratory disease	124,181
Accidents	97,860
Diabetes	68,399
Pneumonia/flu	63,730
Alzheimer's	**44,536**
Kidney disease	35,525
Blood disease	30,680

Projected cases in the U.S.*

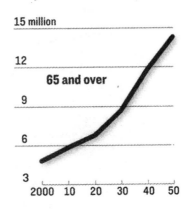

15 million

12

65 and over

9

6

3

2000   10   20   30   40   50

Projected cases by age group*

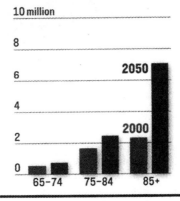

10 million

8

6   2050

4

2   2000

0

65–74   75–84   85+

PLAQUE FORMATION

Disease stage: A-beta fibrils bind with proteins like SAP. The SAP reinforces the fibrils, making them less soluble and harder for the body to clear. Fibrils bind with other fibrils and grow into plaques.

 SAP

A-beta fibril

 A-beta bound to SAP

Attack strategy: Specially designed chemicals bind SAP before it can link to fibrils. This helps prevent fibril accumulation. A few drugs are in early trials.

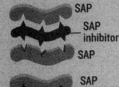 SAP

SAP inhibitor

SAP

SAP bound to inhibitor

SOURCES: GARY W. SMALL, M.D., UCLA;; DENNIS EVANS, M.D.; CDC

ferers. No one knew where this pesky filament came from until 1987, when researchers discovered it was part of a larger molecule they dubbed the amyloid-precursor protein (APP). Thanks to more recent discoveries, they now know exactly how the parent molecule spawns its malevolent offspring.

proteins faster than others, but after seven or eight decades of service, even the healthiest brain carries an amyloid burden. When it reaches a certain threshold, the brain can no longer function. That's why Alzheimer's dementia is so rampant among the elderly. Given enough time, anyone would develop it.

cell development, damaging bone marrow and digestive tissues. A few companies are still pursuing gamma blockers, but beta secretase now looks like a safer target for therapy. More than a half-dozen drugmakers are now working on beta inhibitors. "In the industry," says Dr. Ivan Lieberburg of Elan, "we're hoping that the beta-secretase inhibitors will have as much therapeutic potential as the statins." Those, of course, are the cholesterol-lowering medicines for which 35 million Americans are now candidates.

PLAQUE BUILDUP

Disease stage: As Alzheimer's progresses, more and more healthy brain tissue is displaced by tough, insoluble plaque. In the process, the brain loses the ability to produce acetylcholine, a neuro-transmitter critical to memory and cognition.

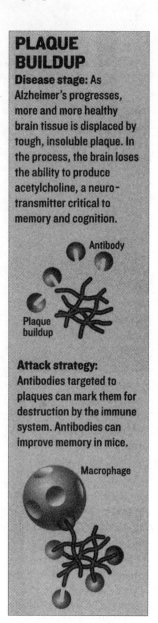

Attack strategy: Antibodies targeted to plaques can mark them for destruction by the immune system. Antibodies can improve memory in mice.

NEURON DEATH

Disease stage: The death of acetylcholine-producing neurons is due partly to a brain chemical called glutamate. Alzheimer's patients have abnormal levels, and their surviving brain cells become insensitive to the normal glutamate bursts that aid in new memory formation.

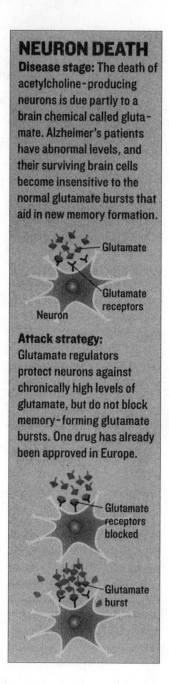

Attack strategy: Glutamate regulators protect neurons against chronically high levels of glutamate, but do not block memory-forming glutamate bursts. One drug has already been approved in Europe.

MENTAL IMPAIRMENT

Disease stage: The dearth of acetylcholine makes it harder for brain cells to exchange signals. Memory and cognition fade as a result.

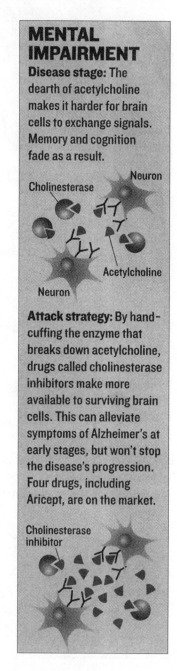

Attack strategy: By hand-cuffing the enzyme that breaks down acetylcholine, drugs called cholinesterase inhibitors make more available to surviving brain cells. This can alleviate symptoms of Alzheimer's at early stages, but won't stop the disease's progression. Four drugs, including Aricept, are on the market.

APP is a normal protein that hangs from a neuron's outer membrane like a worm with its head in an apple. While performing its duties in and around the cell, it gets chopped up by enzymes called secretases, leaving residues that dissolve in the brain's watery recesses. Occasionally, however, a pair of enzymes called beta and gamma secretase cleave APP in just the wrong places, leaving behind an insoluble A-beta fragment. Some people produce these junk

The ideal Alzheimer's remedy would simply slow the production of A-beta—by disabling the enzymes that fabricate it. Elan Corp. was the first drugmaker to try this tack. During the mid-'90s its scientists developed several gamma-secretase blockers and tested them in animals—only to find that they sometimes derailed normal

Secretase inhibitors may be our best hope of warding off Alzheimer's, but they're not the only hope. As scientists learn more about the behavior of A-beta, they're seeing opportunities to disarm it before it causes harm. One thing that makes A-beta fragments dangerous is their tendency to bind with one another to form tough, stringy fibrils, which then stick together to create still larger masses. Three companies are now testing compounds designed to keep A-beta from forming fibrils—and at least two other firms are working to keep fibrils from aggregating to create plaque. All of their experimental drugs have helped reduce amyloid buildup in plaque-prone mice, suggesting they might help people as well. But human studies are just now getting underway.

Suppose for a moment that all these strategies fail, and that amyloid buildup is simply part of the human condition. As Selkoe likes to say, there's more than one way to keep a bathtub from overflowing. If you can't turn down the faucet, you can always try opening the drain. Recognizing that most of the people now threatened by Alzheimer's have already spent their lives under open amyloid faucets, researchers are pursuing several strategies for clearing deposits from the brain. One elegant idea is to mobilize the immune system. Three years ago Elan wowed the world by showing that animals given an anti-amyloid vaccine mounted fierce attacks on their plaques. Vaccinated mice reduced their amyloid burdens by an astounding 96 percent in just three months. The vaccine proved toxic in people, triggering attacks on normal tissue as well as plaque, but the dream isn't dead. Both Elan and Eli Lilly are now developing ready-made antibodies that, if successful, will target amyloid for removal from the brain without triggering broader attacks by the immune system.

Even later interventions may be possible. As a person's amyloid burden rises, so does the concentration of glutamate in the brain. This neurotransmitter helps lock in memories when it's released in short bursts, but it kills neurons when chronically elevated. At least two teams are now betting they can rescue cells surrounded by amyloid, simply by shielding them from glutamate. One possible life jacket is a drug called Memantine, which is already approved in Europe. It covers a receptor that lets glutamate flow freely into neurons, but without blocking the glutamate bursts needed for learning and memory. New York's Forest Laboratories is now launching an American trial of the drug, and hoping for approval by next year.

If even half these treatments fulfill their promise, old age may prove more pleasant than today's projections suggest. For now, the best we can expect is an early warning and perhaps a year or two of symptomatic relief. That may seem a paltry offering, but it's a far cry from nothing. As Small argues in a forthcoming book called "The Memory Bible," people at early stages of Alzheimer's can do a lot to improve their lives, but few of them get the chance. Three out of four are already past the "moderate" stage by the time their conditions are recognized. Some may find solace in ignorance. But the case for vigilance is getting stronger every day.

With ANNE UNDERWOOD and ANDREW MURR

From *Newsweek*, June 24, 2002, pp. 43-50. © 2002 by Newsweek, Inc. All rights reserved. Reprinted by permission.

THE NUN STUDY
ALZHEIMER'S

How one scientist and 678 sisters are helping unlock the secrets of Alzheimer's

By MICHAEL D. LEMONICK and ALICE PARK MANKATO

IT'S THE DAY AFTER EASTER, AND THE first crocus shoots have ventured tentatively above the ground at the convent on Good Counsel Hill. This is Minnesota, however; the temperature is 23°F and the wind chill makes it feel far colder. Yet even though she's wearing only a skirt and sweater, Sister Ada, 91, wants to go outside. She wants to feed the pigs.

But the pigs she and the other nuns once cared for have been gone for 30 years. Sister Ada simply can't keep that straight. In recent years, her brain, like a time machine gone awry, has been wrenching her back and forth between the present and the past, depositing her without warning into the days when she taught primary schoolchildren in Minnesota or to the years when she was a college student in St. Paul. Or to the times when she and the sisters had to feed the pigs several times a day.

Like some 4 million Americans, Sister Ada (not her real name) is suffering from Alzheimer's disease; as the years go by, she'll gradually lose her memory, her personality and finally all cognitive function. But advanced age does not automatically lead to senility. Ada's fellow nun, Sister Rosella, 89, continues to be mentally sharp and totally alert, eagerly anticipating the celebration of her 70th anniversary as a sister without the slightest sign of dementia. In a very real sense, this pair of retired schoolteachers haven't finished their teaching careers. Along with hundreds of other nuns in their order, the School Sisters of Notre Dame, they have joined a long-

term study of Alzheimer's disease that could teach the rest of us how to escape the worst ravages of this heartbreaking illness.

The groundbreaking research they are helping conduct probably won't lead directly to any new drugs, and it's unlikely to uncover a genetic or biochemical cause of Alzheimer's. Doctors know, however, that preventing disease can be a lot easier and cheaper than trying to cure it. It was by studying the differences between people who get sick and people who don't—the branch of medical science known as epidemiology—that doctors discovered the link between smoking and lung cancer, between cholesterol and heart disease, between salt and high blood pressure. Epidemiology also led to the understanding that cooked tomatoes may help protect against prostate cancer, and that fruits and vegetables tend to stave off cancers of all sorts.

Now it's Alzheimer's turn. Precious little is known about this terrible illness, which threatens to strike some 14 million Americans by 2050. Its precise cause is still largely mysterious, and effective treatments are still years away. But epidemiologists are beginning to get a handle on what kinds of people are most seriously ravaged by Alzheimer's—and, conversely, which people tend to escape relatively unscathed.

Much of this knowledge comes from a single, powerful piece of ongoing research: the aptly named Nun Study, of which Sisters Ada and Rosella are part.

Since 1986, University of Kentucky scientist David Snowdon has been studying 678 School Sisters—painstakingly researching their personal and medical histories, testing them for cognitive function and even dissecting their brains after death. Over the years, as he explains in Aging with Grace (Bantam; $24.95), a moving, intensely personal account of his research that arrives in bookstores this week, Snowdon and his colleagues have teased out a series of intriguing—and quite revealing—links between lifestyle and Alzheimer's.

Scientists know that genes can predispose people to Alzheimer's disease. But as described in nearly three dozen scientific papers, Snowdon's study has shown, among other things, that a history of stroke and head trauma can boost your chances of coming down with debilitating symptoms of Alzheimer's later in life; and that a college education and an active intellectual life, on the other hand, may actually protect you from the effects of the disease.

Perhaps the most surprising result of the Nun Study, though, is the discovery that the way we express ourselves in language, even at an early age, can foretell how long we'll live and how vulnerable we'll be to Alzheimer's decades down the line. Indeed, Snowdon's latest finding, scheduled to be announced this week, reinforces that notion. After analyzing short autobiographies of almost 200 nuns, written when they first took holy orders, he found that the sisters who had expressed the most positive emotions in their writing

What Alzheimer's Does to the Brain

Spreading from the bottom to the top

The disease is characterized by the gradual spread of sticky plaques and clumps of tangled fibers that disrupt the delicate organization of nerve cells in the brain. As brain cells stop communicating with one another, they atrophy—causing memory and reasoning to fade

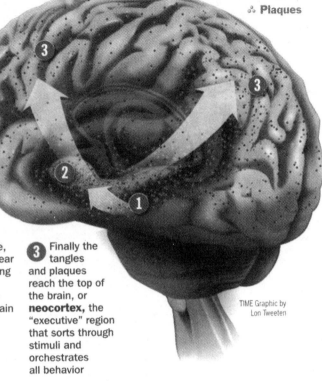

⁂ **Tangles**
⁂ **Plaques**

TIME Graphic by
Lon Tweeten

1 Tangles and plaques first develop in the **entorhinal cortex**, a memory-processing center essential for making new memories and retrieving old ones

2 Over time, they appear higher, invading the **hippocampus**, the part of the brain that forms complex memories of events or objects

3 Finally the tangles and plaques reach the top of the brain, or **neocortex**, the "executive" region that sorts through stimuli and orchestrates all behavior

GRAY MATTERS

A brain ravaged by Alzheimer's, right, shrinks in size and weight as the disease destroys neural tissue. The once tightly packed ruts and grooves on the surface of a healthy cerebral cortex, left, become visibly pitted with gaps and crevices

---

as girls ended up living longest, and that those on the road to Alzheimer's expressed fewer and fewer positive emotions as their mental functions declined.

These findings, like many of Snowdon's earlier conclusions, will undoubtedly spark a lively debate. As laboratory scientists and clinicians are quick to point out, cause and effect are notoriously difficult to tease out of population studies like this one, and exactly what the emotion-Alzheimer's link means has yet to be established. But even hard-nosed lab scientists admit that the Nun Study has helped sharpen the focus of their research. The study has impressed the National Institutes

of Health enough that it has provided $5 million in funding over the past decade and a half. "It is," says Dr. Richard Suzman, director of the National Institute on Aging, "a very innovative, pioneering study."

Snowdon wasn't out to change the world when he first began visiting the convent of the School Sisters of Notre Dame on Good Counsel Hill in Mankato, Minn. He wasn't even planning to study Alzheimer's disease. Snowdon was desperately trying to find a research project that would secure his position at the University of Minnesota. He was a young assistant professor of epidemiology at the time—a field he'd been introduced to as a young boy

who raised chickens to earn money. "I learned a lot about what it takes to stay healthy from taking care of those chickens," he recalls. "That's what epidemiology is all about—the health of the whole flock."

Chicken studies wouldn't cut it with the Minnesota administration though, so Snowdon was interested when a graduate student, an ex-nun, told him about the aging sisters at her former order, living out their retirement in a convent just two hours away. He was already familiar with the advantages of studying religious groups, whose relatively uniform backgrounds mean fewer variations in lifestyle to con-

33.Q

M. Nicholas Kunkel

12.

A Short Sketch of My Life

When I was first told that I saw the light of day on a Tuesday noon, there automatically ran through my mind the old nursery rhyme pretending to predict one's fate by making it depend on the day of the week on which one was born. It goes something like this

"Monday's child is fair of face,

Tuesday's child is full of grace"

Now, I don't want to feign that I had dreamed of being a nun from the age of reason but it at least was a good encouragement and something to strive for as an ideal. I remember little of my baby days and what I do I have had to take on hearsay. From all accounts I was perfectly normal with regard to mischief and, being the first of my fond parents' offspring, might have

A Way with Words

Analyzing autobiographical sketches written by the sisters in their 20s, before they took their vows, Snowdon discovered that the number of ideas they packed into their sentences was a powerful predictor of who would develop Alzheimer's 60 years later

LOW IDEA DENSITY, HIGH RISK	HIGH IDEA DENSITY, LOW RISK
I was born in Eau Claire, Wis., on May 24, 1913, and was baptized in St. James Church. My father, Mr. L. M. Hallacher, was born in the city of Ross, County Cork, Ireland, and is now a sheet-metal worker in Eau Claire.	When I was first told that I saw the light of day on a Tuesday noon, there automatically ran through my mind the old nursery rhyme pretending to predict one's fate by making it depend on the day of the week on which one was born.

found the data. An order of nuns whose economic status, health care and living conditions were especially uniform would be an excellent starting place for an epidemiological study of the aging process. So he went out for a series of visits. Both Snowdon and the sisters had to overcome inhibitions—theirs at becoming research subjects, his from a Roman Catholic school background that made him uncomfortable asking personal questions of a

nun. But they finally agreed that he would quiz them periodically to learn about what factors might be involved in promoting a healthy old age.

At first, the study didn't look as if it would reveal much. For one thing, Snowdon wasn't really sure what aspect of aging to focus on. For another, he had to count on the nuns to recall those aspects of their lives, including the years before entering the order, that had differed—and memory,

even among the mentally competent, is notoriously unreliable. But then, after several months, he stumbled on two olive-green metal file cabinets—the personal records of all the young women who had taken their vows at the Mankato convent. "Everything changed when we discovered the archives," says Snowdon.

Because the records were relatively standardized, Snowdon could extend his study of aging far beyond the few years in late life that such studies traditionally cover. Most precious of all were the auto-biographies written by each sister on her entry into the order. They were full of basic information about where the sisters were born, who their parents and siblings were, and why each one decided to join the order. With these documents, moreover, Snowdon now had an objective measure of the sisters' cognitive abilities while they were still young and in their prime. An epidemiologist could not have designed a better way to evaluate them across time. "For many years," says the National Institute's Suzman, "we had an inadequate sense of how connected late-life health, function and cognition were to early life. But in the past decade, spurred by the Nun Study, there is a growing appreciation for that connectedness."

The first results, compiled after a year of research, confirmed earlier studies suggesting that people with the most education were most independent and competent later in life (most of the sisters were teachers; many had master's degrees). And breaking with academic tradition—but establishing one of his own—Snowdon first presented his conclusions, not through a journal or a conference but directly to the nuns. Recalls Sister Rita Schwalbe, then one of the convent's administrators: "He threw us a thank-you party, and we thought that was it."

Not even close. Snowdon's study attracted the attention of leading Alzheimer's researchers, who explained to him that the elderly women represented an ideal population for studying this mysterious disease. On average, 10% of people over 65 come down with Alzheimer's, a number that rises to 50% by age 85. Given the aging population of the convent, they knew that a significant proportion of the nuns would have the disease.

The most serious drawback to studying the sisters for Alzheimer's is that there's only one sure way to diagnose it: examine the patient's brain after he or she dies. If he were to proceed, Snowdon would need written permission to perform autopsies, not only on the Mankato nuns but also, to get a large enough sample, on members of the order at six other Notre Dame convents as well. "They really had to trust us," he says. "We could have turned out to be Dr. Frankensteins for all they knew."

So one day in 1990, a nervous Snowdon stood in front of the assembled sisters in Mankato, many of whom he'd got to know as friends, and made his pitch. "We sat in our chairs and held our breath," recalls Sis-

ter Rita Schwalbe, who by then had joined Snowdon's research team. "Then one of the sisters piped up, 'He can have my brain, what good is it going to do me when I'm six feet under?' And that broke the ice."

HOW SHARP IS YOUR MEMORY?

Snowdon uses a longer version of the following quiz to pick up signs of memory loss. You can use it to test your own memory. If you are concerned about the results, discuss them with your physician.

VERBAL FLUENCY

How many animals can you name in 60 seconds?

WORD-LIST MEMORY

1. Have a friend read the following 10 words aloud:

    Leg
    Cheese
    Tent
    Motor
    Flower
    Stamp
    Cup
    King
    Forest
    Menu

2. Try to commit them to memory.
3. Go over the list twice more, each time in a different order. How many can you recall on the third try?

DELAYED WORD RECALL TEST

Wait five minutes. Now how many words can you recall?

WORD RECOGNITION

1. Ask your friend to write 20 words on separate index cards—the 10 words from the list above mixed in with ten different words
2. Have your friend show you the cards one at a time
3. How many words can you pick out from the original list?

ADD UP YOUR SCORES. If the total is less than 29, you may have difficulty with short-term memory. Ask your doctor about doing a more thorough exam.

In all, more than 90% of the sisters living in the Mankato convent agreed to donate their brains. After visiting six other convents, Snowdon ended up with a 68% consent rate overall, one of the highest in any tissue-donation study. "I didn't really know what it was going to be about," says Sister Nicolette, an engaging 93-year-old who is the only one of the 16 girls who took their vows in 1925 to both survive and remain mentally intact. "But I thought if science could learn something from this program, then I was glad to be a part of it." In 1991, the first participant, a resident of Good Counsel Hill convent, died, and the Nun Study received its first brain.

Snowdon, who had accepted a position at the University of Kentucky's Sanders-Brown Center on Aging, was working with a team of neurologists and psychologists to devise a battery of tests for assessing the sisters' mental and physical abilities—tests that could later be correlated with the results of brain exams. He joined forces with James Mortimer, an eminent researcher on aging then at the Minneapolis Veterans Administration Medical Center, to study the nuns' youthful autobiographies in more detail, and their relationship led to an interesting discovery: autopsies by other scientists had shown that the physical destruction wrought by Alzheimer's didn't inevitably lead to mental deterioration. The reason, according to one leading theory, was that some folks might have an extra reserve of mental capacity that kept them functioning despite the loss of brain tissue.

So he and Mortimer, along with University of Kansas psychologist Susan Kemper, began analyzing the autobiographies for evidence of such extra capacity. Kemper, an expert on the effects of aging on language usage, had earlier shown that "idea density"—the number of discrete ideas per 10 written words—was a good marker of educational level, vocabulary and general knowledge. Grammatical complexity, meanwhile, was an indicator of how well memory was functioning.

Applying these measures to the sisters' autobiographies, Snowdon and Kemper found to their astonishment that the elderly sisters who showed signs of Alzheimer's had consistently authored essays low in both idea density and grammatical complexity a half-century or more earlier. One of the lowest-scoring samples begins: "My father, Mr. L.M. Hallacher, was born in the city of Ross, County Cork, Ireland, and is now a sheet-metal worker in Eau Claire." By contrast, one of the highest-scoring essays conveys the same type of information but in a dramatically different way: "My father is an all-around man of trades, but his principal occupation is carpentry, which trade he had already begun before his marriage with my mother."

Idea density turns out to be an astonishingly powerful predictor of Alzheimer's disease—at least among the School Sisters of Notre Dame. Snowdon found by reading nuns' early writings, he could predict, with 85% to 90% accuracy, which ones would show the brain damage typical of Alzheimer's disease about 60 years later. "When we first looked at the findings," says Snowdon, "we thought, 'Oh my God, it's in the bag by the time you're in your 20s.'"

But Alzheimer's is not that simple. One especially telling case: Sister Bernadette (not her real name), who had shown no outward signs of Alzheimer's and whose youthful autobiography was rich with ideas and grammatical complexity, turned out at death to be riddled with the plaques and tangles of Alzheimer's (*see diagram*). Says Snowdon: "Lesson No. 1 in my epidemiology training is that there are hardly any diseases where one factor alone, even in infectious disease, will always cause illness."

These results posed a chicken-and-egg problem: Did higher brain capacity protect the sisters from developing the symptoms of dementia, or were those with lackluster biographies already suffering very early signs of some brain abnormality that predisposed them to mental decline later? That question remains unanswered—but follow-up studies, to be published next month in the journal *Psychology and Aging*, suggest that exercising what brain capacity you have offers some protection. While all the sisters show age-related decline in mental function, those who had taught for most of their lives showed more moderate declines than those who had spent most of their lives in service-based tasks. And that, says Kemper, supports the commonsense idea that stimulating the brain with continuous intellectual activity keeps neurons healthy and alive. (Of course, notes Snowdon, these activities are not absolute protectors. For some, a genetic predisposition may override even a lifetime of learning and teaching.)

Another crucial finding from the Nun Study came in 1997, by which time Snowdon had accumulated some 100 brains for analysis. He and neurologist Dr. William Markesbery, director of the Alzheimer's Disease Research Center at the University

of Kentucky, were intrigued by an idea advanced by other researchers that strokes and other brain trauma might contribute to the dementia of Alzheimer's disease. Selecting only the brains of sisters who had earned a bachelor's degree—to eliminate any differences attributable to education—they found that among nuns with physical evidence of Alzheimer's in the brain, those who had evidence of strokes as well almost inevitably showed outward symptoms of dementia. But only half the nuns without strokes were comparably afflicted. Says Suzman, of the National Institute on Aging: "This is one of the first studies to look at the cardiovascular component of Alzheimer's disease."

It's also one of the first to suggest a way to stave off Alzheimer's symptoms. "If your brain is already progressing toward Alzheimer's," says Snowdon, "strokes or head trauma (which can produce similar kinds of brain damage) can put you over the edge." His advice: wear a helmet while biking, motorcycling or playing contact sports; buckle your seat belt; and drive a car with air bags. Meanwhile, keep strokes at bay by keeping your cardiovascular system in shape: avoid tobacco, get regular exercise and eat a balanced, healthy diet.

WHERE ARE THEY NOW?

Nuns, ages 75 to 102, who volunteered to join the Nun Study in 1986	**678**
Nuns who have died	**334**
Brain autopsies that have been performed	**more than 300**
Nuns, ages 84 to 106, who survive	**344**
Nuns who are symptom free	**about 100**

Diet may play a role in Alzheimer's in other ways as well. In 1998 British researchers announced that Alzheimer's victims have low concentrations in their blood of the nutrient folate, also called folic acid. That's an intriguing result, especially in light of other studies showing that folic acid deficiency plays a role in some forms of mental retardation in children and in

cognitive problems in adults. So Snowdon began looking at levels of folic acid, along with 18 other micronutrients (including beta carotene, magnesium, zinc and cholesterol) in blood samples of 30 sisters who had died since the study began.

Sure enough, he found that the sisters with high folate levels showed little evidence of Alzheimer's-type damage in their brain after death. This makes a certain amount of sense; folate tends to counteract the effects of homocysteine, an amino acid produced in the body that has been implicated in cardiovascular disease. Plenty of folate in the blood would thus mean less chance of stroke—and might even protect brain cells from damage by homocysteine in the brain.

Unfortunately, the other micronutrients haven't panned out so well. It makes sense that antioxidants like vitamin E and vitamin C, which soak up cell-damaging "free-radical" molecules in the body, would protect against cell destruction. Although vitamin E looked promising in an earlier study, neither substance had an obvious effect on the Notre Dame sisters. Nor, on the other side of the equation, did mercury or aluminum in the diet, both of which had been implicated in earlier studies as possible triggers for Alzheimer's.

But another hunch turned out to be far more productive. When Snowdon and Kemper first read the sisters' autobiographies in the early 1990s, they noted that the writings differed not just in the density of ideas they contained but also in their emotional content. "At the time," he says, "we saw that idea density was much more related to later cognitive ability. But we also knew that there was something interesting going on with emotions." Studies by other scientists had shown that anger and depression can play a role in heart disease, so the team decided to take another look.

This time they searched for words suggesting positive emotions (such as happiness, love, hope, gratitude and contentment), as well as negative ones (sadness, fear, confusion and shame). Snowdon found that the sisters expressing negative emotions did not live as long as the sisters conveying more positive ones. He has already begun another analysis, comparing the emotional content of the nuns' early autobiographies with the ones they penned in late life, as part of the Nun Study. As mental abilities decline, his preliminary review has found, the expression of positive emotions also drops. While he suspects the whittling away of positive feelings are a consequence of the neurological changes of Alzheimer's, it is still possible that emotional states may play a role in determining cognitive function. To find out, Snowdon will next compare the emotional content of the sisters' writings with their autopsied brains, to see if positive emotions work to keep nerve connections snapping and if negative emotions dampen and eventually extinguish them.

By now, 15 years after he first climbed Good Counsel Hill, Snowdon has identified half a dozen factors that may predict or contribute to Alzheimer's disease. He could sit each sister down right now and tell her what her chances are. But should he? As he has all along, Snowdon will put his dilemma to the sisters themselves: next month he will meet with the Notre Dame leadership to discuss whether to break the news to the high-risk nuns—and how to answer the inevitable questions about what they might do to prevent or slow down the disease.

"So far," he says, "I have a certain comfort level in making some recommendations because there are other good reasons for preventing strokes, for reading, for taking folic acid. If our findings showed something that had no other known benefit besides preventing Alzheimer's, then we would be on much thinner ice." Even so, it's not clear precisely how much folic acid to take, and Snowdon's team is divided on whether to boost the intake of vitamins C and E beyond the normal recommended doses (Markesbery says yes; Snowdon says not until we know more).

These questions will become more urgent as the population bulge of the baby boom generation reaches the Alzheimer's years—and new research is showing that those years may start earlier than anyone had thought. Just two months ago, scientists suggested that many cases of a condition known as mild cognitive impairment, in which patients in their 40s and 50s exhibit memory and recall problems, are very likely the first step on the way to Alzheimer's disease. If so, then it's important to start slowdown strategies as soon as possible. A cure for Alzheimer's is still the ultimate goal, but, says Snowdon, "until there is a magic bullet that can stop the plaques and tangles from growing, we're going to have to take a multipronged approach that will include things like avoiding head injuries and strokes and adding nutritional supplements like folate and antioxidants."

Meanwhile, the Nun Study will continue. Snowdon and his team are attempting to study the sisters' brains before they die, using MRI scans to track how the brain deteriorates with age and how such changes correlate with those in speech, memory and behavior. And to ensure that the sisters' generous gift to science will continue to educate others, Snowdon is trying to have the brain bank and archive records permanently endowed. That way, future generations will continue to benefit from lessons that women like Sisters Ada, Rosella and Nicolette are teaching all of us about how to age with grace and good health.

From *Time*, May 14, 2001, pp. 54-64. © 2001 by Time Inc. Reprinted by permission.

Start the Conversation

The MODERN MATURITY guide to end-of-life care

The Body Speaks

Physically, dying means that "the body's various physiological systems, such as the circulatory, respiratory, and digestive systems, are no longer able to support the demands required to stay alive," says Barney Spivack, M.D., director of Geriatric Medicine for the Stamford (Connecticut) Health System. "When there is no meaningful chance for recovery, the physician should discuss realistic goals of care with the patient and family, which may include letting nature take its course. Lacking that direction," he says, "physicians differ in their perception of when enough is enough. We use our best judgment, taking into account the situation, the information available at the time, consultation with another doctor, or guidance from an ethics committee."

Without instructions from the patient or family, a doctor's obligation to a terminally ill person is to provide life-sustaining treatment. When a decision to "let nature take its course" has been made, the doctor will remove the treatment, based on the patient's needs. Early on, the patient or surrogate may choose to stop interventions such as antibiotics, dialysis, resuscitation, and defibrillation. Caregivers may want to offer food and fluids, but those can cause choking and the pooling of dangerous fluids in the lungs. A dying patient does not desire or need nourishment; without it he or she goes into a deep sleep and dies in days to weeks. A breathing machine would be the last support: It is uncomfortable for the patient, and may be disconnected when the patient or family finds that it is merely prolonging the dying process.

The Best Defense Against Pain

Pain-management activists are fervently trying to reeducate physicians about the importance and safety of making patients comfortable. "In medical school 30 years ago, we worried a lot about creating addicts," says Philadelphia internist Nicholas Scharff. "Now we know that addiction is not a problem: People who are in pain take

pain medication as long as they need it, and then they stop." Spivack says, "We have new formulations and delivery systems, so a dying patient should never have unmet pain needs."

In Search of a Good Death

If we think about death at all, we say that we want to go quickly, in our sleep, or, perhaps, while flyfishing. But in fact only 10 percent of us die suddenly. The more common process is a slow decline with episodes of organ or system failure. Most of us want to die at home; most of us won't. All of us hope to die without pain; many of us will be kept alive, in pain, beyond a time when we would choose to call a halt. Yet very few of us take steps ahead of time to spell out what kind of physical and emotional care we will want at the end.

The new movement to improve the end of life is pioneering ways to make available to each of us a good death—as we each define it. One goal of the movement is to bring death through the cultural process that childbirth has achieved; from an unconscious, solitary act in a cold hospital room to a situation in which one is buffered by pillows, pictures, music, loved ones, and the solaces of home. But as in the childbirth movement, the real goal is choice— here, to have the death you want. Much of death's sting can be averted by planning in advance, knowing the facts, and knowing what options we all have. Here, we have gathered new and relevant information to help us all make a difference for the people we are taking care of, and ultimately, for ourselves.

In 1999, the Joint Commission on Accreditation of Healthcare Organizations issued stern new guidelines about easing pain in both terminal and nonterminal patients. The movement intends to take pain seriously:

to measure and treat it as the fifth vital sign in hospitals, along with blood pressure, pulse, temperature, and respiration.

The best defense against pain, says Spivack, is a combination of education and assertiveness. "Don't be afraid to speak up," he says. "If your doctor isn't listening, talk to the nurses. They see more and usually have a good sense of what's happening." Hospice workers, too, are experts on physical comfort, and a good doctor will respond to a hospice worker's recommendations. "The best situation for pain management," says Scharff, "is at home with a family caregiver being guided by a hospice program."

The downsides to pain medication are, first, that narcotics given to a fragile body may have a double effect: The drug may ease the pain, but it may cause respiratory depression and possibly death. Second, pain medication may induce grogginess or unconsciousness when a patient wants to be alert. "Most people seem to be much more willing to tolerate pain than mental confusion," says senior research scientist M. Powell Lawton, Ph.D., of the Philadelphia Geriatric Center. Dying patients may choose to be alert one day for visitors, and asleep the next to cope with pain. Studies show that when patients control their own pain medication, they use less.

Final Symptoms

Depression This condition is not an inevitable part of dying but can and should be treated. In fact, untreated depression can prevent pain medications from working effectively, and antidepressant medication can help relieve pain. A dying patient should be kept in the best possible emotional state for the final stage of life. A combination of medications and psychotherapy works best to treat depression.

Anorexia In the last few days of life, anorexia—an unwillingness or inability to eat—often sets in. "It has a protective effect, releasing endorphins in the system and contributing to a greater feeling of well-being," says Spivack. "Force-feeding a dying patient could make him uncomfortable and cause choking."

Dehydration Most people want to drink little or nothing in their last days. Again, this is a protective mechanism, triggering a release of helpful endorphins.

Drowsiness and Unarousable Sleep In spite of a coma-like state, says Spivack, "presume that the patient hears everything that is being said in the room."

Agitation and Restlessness, Moaning and Groaning The features of "terminal delirium" occur when the patient's level of consciousness is markedly decreased; there is no significant likelihood that any pain sensation can reach consciousness. Family members and other caregivers may interpret what they see as "the patient is in pain" but as these signs arise at a point very close to death, terminal delirium should be suspected.

Hospice: The Comfort Team

Hospice is really a bundle of services. It organizes a team of people to help patients and their families, most often in the patient's home but also in hospice residences, nursing homes, and hospitals:

• Registered nurses who check medication and the patient's condition, communicate with the patient's doctor, and educate caregivers.
• Medical services by the patient's physician and a hospice's medical director, limited to pain medication and other comfort care.
• Medical supplies and equipment.
• Drugs for pain relief and symptom control.
• Home-care aides for personal care, homemakers for light housekeeping.
• Continuous care in the home as needed on a short-term basis.
• Trained volunteers for support services.
• Physical, occupational, and speech therapists to help patients adapt to new disabilities.
• Temporary hospitalization during a crisis.
• Counselors and social workers who provide emotional and spiritual support to the patient and family.
• Respite care—brief noncrisis hospitalization to provide relief for family caregivers for up to five days.
• Bereavement support for the family, including counseling, referral to support groups, and periodic check-ins during the first year after the death.

Hospice Residences Still rare, but a growing phenomenon. They provide all these services on-site. They're for patients without family caregivers; with frail, elderly spouses; and for families who cannot provide at-home care because of other commitments. At the moment, Medicare covers only hospice services; the patient must pay for room and board. In many states Medicaid also covers hospice services (see How Much Will It Cost?). Keep in mind that not all residences are certified, bonded, or licensed; and not all are covered by Medicare.

Getting In A physician can recommend hospice for a patient who is terminally ill and probably has less than six months to live. The aim of hospice is to help people cope with an illness, not to cure it. All patients entering hospice waive their rights to curative treatments, though only for conditions relating to their terminal illness. "If you break a leg, of course you'll be treated for that," says Karen Woods, executive director of the Hospice Association of America. No one is forced to accept a hospice referral, and patients may leave and opt for curative care at any time. Hospice programs are listed in the Yellow Pages. For more information, see Resources.

The Ultimate Emotional Challenge

A dying person is grieving the loss of control over life, of body image, of normal physical functions, mobility and strength, freedom and independence, security, and the illusion of immortality. He is also grieving the loss of an earthly future, and reorienting himself to an unknowable destiny.

At the same time, an emotionally healthy dying person will be trying to satisfy his survival drive by adapting to this new phase, making the most of life at the moment, calling in loved ones, examining and appreciating his own joys and accomplishments. Not all dying people are depressed; many embrace death easily.

Facing the Fact

Doctors are usually the ones to inform a patient that he or she is dying, and the end-of-life movement is training physicians to bring empathy to that conversation in place of medspeak and time estimates. The more sensitive doctor will first ask how the patient feels things are going. "The patient may say, 'Well, I don't think I'm getting better,' and I would say, 'I think you're right,'" says internist Nicholas Scharff.

At this point, a doctor might ask if the patient wants to hear more now or later, in broad strokes or in detail. Some people will need to first process the emotional blow with tears and anger before learning about the course of their disease in the future.

"Accept and understand whatever reaction the patient has," says Roni Lang, director of the Geriatric Assessment Program for the Stamford (Connecticut) Health System, and a social worker who is a longtime veteran of such conversations. "Don't be too quick with the tissue. That sends a message that it's not okay to be upset. It's okay for the patient to be however she is."

Getting to Acceptance

Some patients keep hoping that they will get better. Denial is one of the mind's miracles, a way to ward off painful realities until consciousness can deal with them. Denial may not be a problem for the dying person, but it can create difficulties for the family. The dying person could be leaving a lot of tough decisions, stress, and confusion behind. The classic stages of grief outlined by Elisabeth Kübler-Ross—denial, anger, bargaining, depression, and acceptance—are often used to describe post-death grieving, but were in fact delineated for the process of accepting impending loss. We now know that these states may not progress in order. "Most people oscillate between anger and sadness, embracing the prospect of death and unrealistic episodes of optimism," says Lang. Still, she says, "don't place demands on them

Survival Kit for Caregivers

A study published in the March 21, 2000, issue of **Annals of Internal Medicine** shows that caregivers of the dying are twice as likely to have depressive symptoms as the dying themselves.

No wonder. Caring for a dying parent, says social worker Roni Lang, "brings a fierce tangle of emotions. That part of us that is a child must grow up." Parallel struggles occur when caring for a spouse, a child, another relative, or a friend. Caregivers may also experience sibling rivalry, income loss, isolation, fatigue, burnout, and resentment.

To deal with these difficult stresses, Lang suggests that caregivers:

- Set limits in advance. How far am I willing to go? What level of care is needed? Who can I get to help? Resist the temptation to let the illness always take center stage, or to be drawn into guilt-inducing conversations with people who think you should be doing more.
- Join a caregiver support group, either disease-related like the Alzheimer's Association or Gilda's Club, or a more general support group like The Well Spouse Foundation. Ask the social services department at your hospital for advice. Telephone support and online chat rooms also exist (see Resources).
- Acknowledge anger and express it constructively by keeping a journal or talking to an understanding friend or family member. Anger is a normal reaction to powerlessness.
- When people offer to help, give them a specific assignment. And then, take time to do what energizes you and make a point of rewarding yourself.
- Remember that people who are critically ill are self-absorbed. If your empathy fails you and you lose patience, make amends and forgive yourself.

to accept their death. This is not a time to proselytize." It is enough for the family to accept the coming loss, and if necessary, introduce the idea of an advance directive and health-care proxy, approaching it as a "just in case" idea. When one member of the family cannot accept death, and insists that doctors do more, says Lang, "that's the worst nightmare. I would call a meeting, hear all views without interrupting, and get the conversation around to what the patient would want. You may need another person to come in, perhaps the doctor, to help 'hear' the voice of the patient."

What Are You Afraid Of?

The most important question for doctors and caregivers to ask a dying person is, What are you afraid of? "Fear aggravates pain," says Lang, "and pain aggravates fear." Fear of pain, says Spivack, is one of the most common problems, and can be dealt with rationally. Many people do not know, for example, that pain in dying is not inevitable. Other typical fears are of being separated from loved ones, from home, from work; fear of being a burden, losing control, being dependent, and leaving things undone. Voicing fear helps lessen it, and pinpointing fear helps a caregiver know how to respond.

How to Be With a Dying Person

Our usual instinct is to avoid everything about death, including the people moving most rapidly toward it. But, Spivack says, "In all my years of working with dying people, I've never heard one say 'I want to die alone.'" Dying people are greatly comforted by company; the benefit far outweighs the awkwardness of the visit. Lang offers these suggestions for visitors:

•Be close. Sit at eye level, and don't be afraid to touch. Let the dying person set the pace for the conversation. Allow for silence. Your presence alone is valuable.

•Don't contradict a patient who says he's going to die. Acceptance is okay. Allow for anger, guilt, and fear, without trying to "fix" it. Just listen and empathize.

•Give the patient as much decision-making power as possible, as long as possible. Allow for talk about unfinished business. Ask: "Who can I contact for you?"

•Encourage happy reminiscences. It's okay to laugh.

•Never pass up the chance to express love or say goodbye. But if you don't get the chance, remember that not everything is worked through. Do the best you can.

Taking Control Now

Sixty years ago, before the invention of dialysis, defibrillators, and ventilators, the failure of vital organs automatically meant death. There were few choices to be made to end suffering, and when there were—the fatal dose of morphine, for example—these decisions were made privately by family and doctors who knew each other well. Since the 1950s, medical technology has been capable of extending lives, but also of prolonging dying. In 1967, an organization called Choice in Dying (now the Partnership for Caring: America's Voices for the Dying; see Resources) designed the first advance directive—a document that allows you to designate under what conditions you would want life-sustaining treatment to be continued or terminated. But the idea did not gain popular understanding until 1976, when the parents of Karen Ann Quinlan won a long legal battle to disconnect her from respiratory support as she lay for months in a vegetative state. Some 75 percent of Americans are in favor of advance directives, although only 30–35 percent actually write them.

Designing the Care You Want

There are two kinds of advance directives, and you may use one or both. A Living Will details what kind of life-sustaining treatment you want or don't want, in the event of an illness when death is imminent. A durable power of attorney for health care appoints someone to be your decision-maker if you can't speak for yourself. This person is also called a surrogate, attorney-in-fact, or health-care proxy. An advance directive such as Five Wishes covers both.

Most experts agree that a Living Will alone is not sufficient. "You don't need to write specific instructions about different kinds of life support, as you don't yet know any of the facts of your situation, and they may change," says Charles Sabatino, assistant director of the American Bar Association's Commission on Legal Problems of the Elderly.

The proxy, Sabatino says, is far more important. "It means someone you trust will find out all the options and make a decision consistent with what you would want." In most states, you may write your own advance directive, though some states require a specific form, available at hospital admitting offices or at the state department of health.

When Should You Draw Up a Directive?

Without an advance directive, a hospital staff is legally bound to do everything to keep you alive as long as possible, until you or a family member decides otherwise. So advance directives are best written before emergency status or a terminal diagnosis. Some people write them at the same time they make a will. The process begins with discussions between you and your family and doctor. If anybody is reluctant to discuss the subject, Sabatino suggests starting the conversation with a story. "Remember what happened to Bob Jones and what his family went through? I want us to be different...." You can use existing tools—a booklet or questionnaire (see Resources)—to keep the conversation moving. Get your doctor's commitment to support your wishes. "If you're asking for something that is against your doctor's conscience" (such as prescribing a lethal dose of pain medication or removing life support at a time he considers premature), Sabatino says, "he may have an obligation to transfer you to another doctor." And make sure the person you name as surrogate agrees to act for you and understands your wishes.

Filing, Storing, Safekeeping...

An estimated 35 percent of advance directives cannot be found when needed.

•Give a copy to your surrogate, your doctor, your hospital, and other family members. Tell them where to find the original in the house—not in a safe deposit box where it might not be found until after death.

Five Wishes

Five Wishes is a questionnaire that guides people in making essential decisions about the care they want at the end of their life. About a million people have filled out the eight-page form in the past two years. This advance directive is legally valid in 34 states and the District of Columbia. (The other 16 require a specific state-mandated form.)

The document was designed by lawyer Jim Towey, founder of Aging With Dignity, a nonprofit organization that advocates for the needs of elders and their caregivers. Towey, who was legal counsel to Mother Teresa, visited her Home for the Dying in Calcutta in the 1980s. He was struck that in that haven in the Third World, "the dying people's hands were held, their pain was managed, and they weren't alone. In the First World, you see a lot of medical technology, but people die in pain, and alone." Towey talked to MODERN MATURITY about his directive and what it means.

What are the five wishes? Who do I want to make care decisions for me when I can't? What kind of medical treatment do I want toward the end? What would help me feel comfortable while I am dying? How do I want people to treat me? What do I want my loved ones to know about me and my feelings after I'm gone?

Why is it so vital to make advance decisions now? Medical technology has extended longevity, which is good, but it can prolong the dying process in ways that are almost cruel. Medical schools are still concentrating on curing, not caring for the dying. We can have a dignified season in our life, or die alone in pain with futile interventions. Most people only discover they have options when checking into the hospital, and often they no longer have the capacity to choose. This leaves the family members with a guessing game and, frequently, guilt.

What's the ideal way to use this document? First you do a little soul searching about what you want. Then discuss it with people you trust, in the livingroom instead of the waiting room—before a crisis. Just say, "I want a choice about how I spend my last days," talk about your choices, and pick someone to be your health-care surrogate.

What makes the Five Wishes directive unique? It's easy to use and understand, not written in the language of doctors or lawyers. It also allows people to discuss comfort dignity, and forgiveness, not just medical concerns. When my father filled it out, he said he wanted his favorite afghan blanket in his bed. It made a huge difference to me that, as he was dying, he had his wishes fulfilled.

For a copy of Five Wishes in English or Spanish, send a $5 check or money order to Aging With Dignity, PO Box 1661, Tallahassee, FL 32302. For more information, visit www.agingwithdignity. org.

• Some people carry a copy in their wallet or glove compartment of their car.

• Be aware that if you have more than one home and you split your time in several regions of the country, you should be registering your wishes with a hospital in each region, and consider naming more than one proxy.

• You may register your Living Will and health-care proxy online at uslivingwillregistry.com (or call 800-548-9455). The free, privately funded confidential service will instantly fax a copy to a hospital when the hospital requests one. It will also remind you to update it: You may want to choose a new surrogate, accommodate medical advances, or change your idea of when "enough is enough." M. Powell Lawton, who is doing a study on how people anticipate the terminal life stages, has discovered that "people adapt relatively well to states of poor health. The idea that life is still worth living continues to readjust itself."

Assisted Suicide: The Reality

While advance directives allow for the termination of life-sustaining treatment, assisted suicide means supplying the patient with a prescription for life-ending medication. A doctor writes the prescription for the medication; the patient takes the fatal dose him- or herself. Physician-assisted suicide is legal only in Oregon (and under consideration in Maine) but only with rigorous preconditions. Of the approximately 30,000 people who died in Oregon in 1999, only 33 received permission to have a lethal dose of medication and only 26 of those actually died of the medication. Surrogates may request an end to life support, but to assist in a suicide puts one at risk for charges of homicide.

Good Care: Can You Afford It?

The ordinary person is only one serious illness away from poverty," says Joanne Lynn, M.D., director of the Arlington, Virginia, Center to Improve Care of the Dying. An ethicist, hospice physician, and health-services researcher, she is one of the founding members of the end-of-life-care movement. "On the whole, hospitalization and the cost of suppressing symptoms is very easy to afford," says Lynn. Medicare and Medicaid will help cover that kind of acute medical care. But what is harder to afford is at-home medication, monitoring, daily help with eating and walking, and all the care that will go on for the rest of the patient's life.

"When people are dying," Lynn says, "an increasing proportion of their overall care does not need to be done by doctors. But when policymakers say the care is nonmedical, then it's second class, it's not important, and nobody will pay for it."

Bottom line, Medicare pays for about 57 percent of the cost of medical care for Medicare beneficiaries.

Another 11 percent is paid by Medicaid, 20 percent by the patient, 10 percent from private insurance, and the rest from other sources, such as charitable organizations.

Medi-what?

This public-plus-private network of funding sources for end-of-life care is complex, and who pays for how much of what is determined by diagnosis, age, site of care, and income. Besides the private health insurance that many of us have from our employers, other sources of funding may enter the picture when patients are terminally ill.

•**Medicare** A federal insurance program that covers health-care services for people 65 and over, some disabled people, and those with end-stage kidney disease. Medicare Part A covers inpatient care in hospitals, nursing homes, hospice, and some home health care. For most people, the Part A premium is free. Part B covers doctor fees, tests, and other outpatient medical services. Although Part B is optional, most people choose to enroll through their local Social Security office and pay the monthly premium ($45.50). Medicare beneficiaries share in the cost of care through deductibles and co-insurance. What Medicare does not cover at all is outpatient medication, long-term nonacute care, and support services.

•**Medicaid** A state and federally funded program that covers health-care services for people with income or assets below certain levels, which vary from state to state.

•**Medigap** Private insurance policies covering the gaps in Medicare, such as deductibles and co-payments, and in some cases additional health-care services, medical supplies, and outpatient prescription drugs.

Many of the services not paid for by Medicare can be covered by private long-term-care insurance. About 50 percent of us over the age of 65 will need long-term care at home or in a nursing home, and this insurance is an extra bit of protection for people with major assets to protect. It pays for skilled nursing care as well as non-health services, such as help with dressing, eating, and bathing. You select a dollar amount of coverage per day (for example, $100 in a nursing home, or $50 for at-home care), and a coverage period (for example, three years— the average nursing-home stay is 2.7 years). Depending on your age and the benefits you choose, the insurance can cost anywhere from around $500 to more than $8,000 a year. People with pre-existing conditions such as Alzheimer's or MS are usually not eligible.

How Much Will It Cost?

Where you get end-of-life care will affect the cost and who pays for it.

•**Hospital** Dying in a hospital costs about $1,000 a day. After a $766 deductible (per benefit period), Medicare reimburses the hospital a fixed rate per day, which varies by region and diagnosis. After the first 60 days in a hospital, a patient will pay a daily deductible ($194) that goes up (to $388) after 90 days. The patient is responsible for all costs for each day beyond 150 days. Medicaid and some private insurance, either through an employer or a Medigap plan, often help cover these costs.

•**Nursing home** About $1,000 a week. Medicare covers up to 100 days of skilled nursing care after a three-day hospitalization, and most medication costs during that time. For days 21–100, your daily co-insurance of $97 is usually covered by private insurance—if you have it. For nursing-home care not covered by Medicare, you must use your private assets, or Medicaid if your assets run out, which happens to approximately one-third of nursing-home residents. Long-term-care insurance may also cover some of the costs.

•**Hospice care** About $100 a day for in-home care. Medicare covers hospice care to patients who have a life expectancy of less than six months. (See Hospice: The Comfort Team.) Such care may be provided at home, in a hospice facility, a hospital, or a nursing-home. Patients may be asked to pay up to $5 for each prescription and a 5 percent co-pay for in-patient respite care, which is a short hospital stay to relieve caregivers. Medicaid covers hospice care in all but six states, even for those without Medicare.

About 60 percent of full-time employees of medium and large firms also have coverage for hospice services, but the benefits vary widely.

•**Home care without hospice services** Medicare Part A pays the full cost of medical home health care for up to 100 visits following a hospital stay of at least three days. Medicare Part B covers home health-care visits beyond those 100 visits or without a hospital stay. To qualify, the patient must be homebound, require skilled nursing care or physical or speech therapy, be under a physician's care, and use services from a Medicare-participating home-health agency. Note that this coverage is for medical care only; hired help for personal nonmedical services, such as that often required by Alzheimer's patients, is not covered by Medicare. It is covered by Medicaid in some states.

A major financial disadvantage of dying at home without hospice is that Medicare does not cover out-patient prescription drugs, even those for pain. Medicaid does cover these drugs, but often with restrictions on their price and quantity. Private insurance can fill the gap to some extent. Long-term-care insurance may cover payments to family caregivers who have to stop work to care for a dying patient, but this type of coverage is very rare.

Resources

MEDICAL CARE

For information about pain relief and symptom management: **Supportive Care of the Dying** (503-215-5053; careofdying.org).

For a comprehensive guide to living with the medical, emotional, and spiritual aspects of dying:

Handbook for Mortals by Joanne Lynn and Joan Harrold, Oxford University Press.

For a 24-hour hotline offering counseling, pain management, downloadable advance directives, and more:

The Partnership for Caring (800-989-9455; www.partnershipforcaring.org).

EMOTIONAL CARE

To find mental-health counselors with an emphasis on lifespan human development and spiritual discussion:
American Counseling Association (800-347-6647; counseling.org).

For disease-related support groups and general resources for caregivers:
Caregiver Survival Resources (caregiver911.com).

For AARP's online caregiver support chatroom, access **America Online** every Wednesday night, 8:30–9:30 EST (keyword: AARP).

Education and advocacy for family caregivers:
National Family Caregivers Association (800-896-3650; nfcacares.org).

For the booklet,
Understanding the Grief Process (D16832, EEO143C), e-mail order with title and numbers to member@aarp.org or send postcard to AARP Fulfillment, 601 E St NW, Washington DC 20049. Please allow two to four weeks for delivery.

To find a volunteer to help with supportive services to the frail and their caregivers:
National Federation of Interfaith Volunteer Caregivers (816-931-5442; nfivc.org).

For information on support to partners of the chronically ill and/or the disabled:
The Well Spouse Foundation (800-838-0879; www.wellspouse.org).

LEGAL HELP

AARP members are entitled to a free half-hour of legal advice with a lawyer from **AARP's Legal Services Network**. (800-424-3410; www.aarp.org/lsn).

For **Planning for Incapacity,** *a guide to advance directives in your state,* send $5 to Legal Counsel for the Elderly, Inc., PO Box 96474, Washington DC 20090-6474. Make out check to LCE Inc.

For a **Caring Conversations** *booklet on advance-directive discussion:*
Midwest Bioethics Center (816-221-1100; midbio.org).

For information on care at the end of life, online discussion groups, conferences:
Last Acts Campaign (800-844-7616; lastacts.org).

HOSPICE

To learn about end-of-life care options and grief issues through videotapes, books, newsletters, and brochures:
Hospice Foundation of America (800-854-3402; hospice-foundation.org).

For information on hospice programs, FAQs, and general facts about hospice:
National Hospice and Palliative Care Organization (800-658-8898; nhpco.org).

For **All About Hospice: A Consumer's Guide** (202-546-4759; www.hospice-america.org).

FINANCIAL HELP

For **Organizing Your Future,** *a simple guide to end-of-life financial decisions,* send $5 to Legal Counsel for the Elderly, Inc., PO Box 96474, Washington DC 20090-6474. Make out check to LCE Inc.

For **Medicare and You 2000** *and a* **2000 Guide to Health Insurance for People With Medicare** (800-MEDICARE [633-4227]; medicare.gov).

To find your State Agency on Aging: **Administration on Aging, U.S. Department of Health and Human Services** (800-677-1116; aoa.dhhs.gov).

GENERAL

For information on end-of-life planning and bereavement: (www.aarp.org/endoflife/).

For health professionals and others who want to start conversations on end-of-life issues in their community:
Discussion Guide: On Our Own Terms: Moyers on Dying, based on the PBS series, airing September 10–13. The guide provides essays, instructions, and contacts. From PBS, www.pbs.org/onourownterms Or send a postcard request to On Our Own Terms Discussion Guide, Thirteen/WNET New York, PO Box 245, Little Falls, NJ 07424-9766.

Funded with a grant from The Robert Wood Johnson Foundation, Princeton, N.J. *Editor* Amy Gross; *Writer* Louise Lague; *Designer* David Herbick

Index

Index

Test Your Knowledge Form

We encourage you to photocopy and use this page as a tool to assess how the articles in *Annual Editions* expand on the information in your textbook. By reflecting on the articles you will gain enhanced text information. You can also access this useful form on a product's book support Web site at *http://www.dushkin.com/online/*.

NAME: _____ DATE: _____

TITLE AND NUMBER OF ARTICLE:
_____

BRIEFLY STATE THE MAIN IDEA OF THIS ARTICLE:

_____

LIST THREE IMPORTANT FACTS THAT THE AUTHOR USES TO SUPPORT THE MAIN IDEA:

_____

WHAT INFORMATION OR IDEAS DISCUSSED IN THIS ARTICLE ARE ALSO DISCUSSED IN YOUR TEXTBOOK OR OTHER READINGS THAT YOU HAVE DONE? LIST THE TEXTBOOK CHAPTERS AND PAGE NUMBERS:

_____

LIST ANY EXAMPLES OF BIAS OR FAULTY REASONING THAT YOU FOUND IN THE ARTICLE:

_____

LIST ANY NEW TERMS/CONCEPTS THAT WERE DISCUSSED IN THE ARTICLE, AND WRITE A SHORT DEFINITION:

We Want Your Advice

ANNUAL EDITIONS revisions depend on two major opinion sources: one is our Advisory Board, listed in the front of this volume, which works with us in scanning the thousands of articles published in the public press each year; the other is you—the person actually using the book. Please help us and the users of the next edition by completing the prepaid article rating form on this page and returning it to us. Thank you for your help!

ANNUAL EDITIONS: Human Development 03/04

ARTICLE RATING FORM

Here is an opportunity for you to have direct input into the next revision of this volume.
We would like you to rate each of the articles listed below, using the following scale:

1. **Excellent: should definitely be retained**
2. **Above average: should probably be retained**
3. **Below average: should probably be deleted**
4. **Poor: should definitely be deleted**

Your ratings will play a vital part in the next revision.
Please mail this prepaid form to us as soon as possible.
Thanks for your help!

RATING	ARTICLE	RATING	ARTICLE
	1. Brave New World		35. The Disappearing Mind
	2. The First Human Cloned Embryo		36. The Nun Study: Alzheimer's
	3. A State of the Art Pregnancy		37. Start the Conversation
	4. Shaped by Life in the Womb		
	5. The Mystery of Fetal Life: Secrets of the Womb		
	6. Four Things You Need to Know About Raising Baby		
	7. The World of the Senses		
	8. Who's Raising Baby?		
	9. Wired for Thought		
	10. Psychosexual Development in Infants and Young Children		
	11. Raising a Moral Child		
	12. Intelligence: The Surprising Truth		
	13. Child Psychologist: Jean Piaget		
	14. Metacognitive Development		
	15. "High Stakes Are for Tomatoes"		
	16. The Future of Computer Technology in K–12 Education		
	17. Choosing to Learn		
	18. The Trauma of Terrorism: Helping Children Cope		
	19. Raising Happy Achieving Children in the New Millennium		
	20. Generation XXL		
	21. Kids Who Don't Fit In		
	22. Are Boys the Weaker Sex?		
	23. Effects of Maltreatment and Ways to Promote Children's Resiliency		
	24. Meet the Gamma Girls		
	25. Why the Young Kill		
	26. Generation 9-11		
	27. The Feminization of American Culture		
	28. The Happy Divorce: How to Break Up and Make Up		
	29. The Coming Job Boom		
	30. Man Power		
	31. Sorting Through the Confusion Over Estrogen		
	32. An American Epidemic: Diabetes		
	33. 12 Things You Must Know to Survive and Thrive in America		
	34. The New Unretirement		

(Continued on next page)

BUSINESS REPLY MAIL
FIRST-CLASS MAIL PERMIT NO. 84 GUILFORD CT

POSTAGE WILL BE PAID BY ADDRESSEE

McGraw-Hill/Dushkin
530 Old Whitfield Street
Guilford, Ct 06437-9989

NO POSTAGE
NECESSARY
IF MAILED
IN THE
UNITED STATES

ABOUT YOU

Name   Date

Are you a teacher? ❑   A student? ❑
Your school's name

Department

Address   City   State   Zip

School telephone #

YOUR COMMENTS ARE IMPORTANT TO US!

Please fill in the following information:
For which course did you use this book?

Did you use a text with this ANNUAL EDITION?   ❑ yes ❑ no
What was the title of the text?

What are your general reactions to the *Annual Editions* concept?

Have you read any pertinent articles recently that you think should be included in the next edition? Explain.

Are there any articles that you feel should be replaced in the next edition? Why?

Are there any World Wide Web sites that you feel should be included in the next edition? Please annotate.

May we contact you for editorial input?   ❑ yes ❑ no
May we quote your comments? ❑ yes ❑ no